GAMES OF PROPERTY

GAMES OF PROPERTY

Law, Race, Gender, and Faulkner's *Go Down, Moses*

THADIOUS M. DAVIS

Duke University Press

Durham and London

2003

© 2003 Duke University Press   All rights reserved
Printed in the United States of America on acid-free paper ⊗
Typeset in Janson by Tseng Information Systems, Inc.
Library of Congress Cataloging-in-Publication Data
appear on the last printed page of this book.

FOR MY FAMILY OF FRIENDS
WHO HAVE BROUGHT ME THIS FAR

CONTENTS

Illustrations   viii

Acknowledgments   x

Introduction: The Game of Genre   1

1   The Game of Challenge   43

2   The Object of Property   77

3   The Game of Boundaries   119

4   The Subject of Property   174

5   Conclusion:
The Game of Compensation   223

Notes   263

Bibliography   309

Index   330

ILLUSTRATIONS

Caroline Barr   6

Early English map of the Mississippi River to New Orleans   13

Engraving used by antislavery societies   17

Mississippi at statehood in 1817   29

Percentage of slaves by county in Mississippi in 1850   32

Chickasaw lands   36

Chickasaw and Choctaw cessions of land in Mississippi   36

1819 map of Mississippi before cessions of Chickasaw and

Choctaw lands   37

1850s advertisements for runaways   63

Sketch showing persons as property   81

1835 advertisement for a group sale   95

Faulkner role-playing as "lord of the manor"   186

Rowan Oak. Faulkner's home in Oxford, Mississippi   187

Faulkner and Andrew Price   188

Andrew Price splitting wood outside his cabin   189

Caroline Barr holding Faulkner's niece, Dean Faulkner   191

Caroline Barr and Faulkner's four-year-old daughter, Jill   192

Faulkner in 1942 when *Go Down, Moses* was published   196

ACKNOWLEDGMENTS

My special thanks to the generous hosts at Camp Armageddon, Stone-ham, Maine: Nell Irvin Painter for listening to my musings about games and for reading early drafts with patience; and Glenn Shafer for talking an uninformed literary person through the basics of game theory and for providing readable materials in that field.

My thanks to those Faulkner scholars who in different but invaluable ways contributed to my work on this project: Linda Wagner-Martin who asked me to write on *Go Down, Moses*, inspired me to think and read cre-atively, and edited the essay I produced with her marvelous intelligence, critical acumen, and easy grace; Joseph Blotner for his kind support over many years; Judith Sensibar, Minrose Gwin, Eric Sundquist, and Joel Williamson for the gift of their thinking about Faulkner; Lee Jenkins, the late George Kent and Erskine Peters, and the early black critics on Faulkner for persevering when no one listened or read; all my Faulkner students for their conversations and challenges; and Emily Dalgarno, the extraordinary teacher who made it all possible by guiding me to Faulk-ner.

My appreciation is boundless for those audiences who over the years have listened to my Faulkner talks and responded with enthusiasm as well as with tough questions. I am especially indebted to M. Thomas Inge, James Miller, Xavier Nichols, the Graduate School and the Univer-sity Center of the City University of New York for invitations to speak on Faulkner there, as well as at Randolph-Macon University, the Cen-ter for Southern Studies at University of South Carolina, the Modern Language Association Annual Convention, and CUNY's "William Faulk-ner in a Franco-American Perspective" Conference; to Doreen Fowler,

Ann J. Abadie, Donald Kartiganer, and the late Evans Harrington for invitations to the Faulkner and Yoknapatawpha conferences at the University of Mississippi. I am pleased to say that the presence of Christine Smith and her son Evan at the Faulkner Centenary brought me into contact with new generations of critical and savvy Faulkner readers.

My deep gratitude to Barton St. Armand for his inspirational gift of a first edition of *Go Down, Moses* at just the moment when I needed a push to continue; to Michael S. Harper for his Callie Barr poem and poetic dispatches; to Nellie Y. McKay and Leslie Sanders for their unfailing generosity of spirit even in the worst of times; to Aishah Rahman, Jean Fagan Yellin, and Frances Smith Foster for their wonderfully uplifting good humor and positive karma; to Cecelia Tichi for being a colleague par excellence; and to my sister Claudia and niece Carita Ribet for providing amazing models of survival whole.

My continued gratitude to my former research assistant, Barbara Le Van, for her efficiency, focus, and grace under the pressure of working with a true Gemini; to Mark L. Barr and Helene Pellett for their assistance with the finishing touches; to Judith Sensibar and Nell Irvin Painter for reading the manuscript in early stages; to Linda K. Kerber for reading a chapter and giving wonderfully astute advice; to Vanderbilt University for providing a one-semester sabbatical and to the Program in African-American Studies at Princeton University for offering a place to write during that sabbatical; and to the Huntington Library for the incomparable gift of an R. Stanton Avery Distinguished Fellowship and the riches of its archives and beauty of its gardens to complete the manuscript. My sincere thanks to Sharon P. Torian, Reynolds Smith, and the Duke University Press readers who moved Moses forward from wandering in the desert.

I gratefully acknowledge the generosity of Dean Faulkner Wells, the Yoknapatawpha Press, for permission to use photographs; the assistance of Jennifer Aronson, curator of Visual Collections, and Jennifer W. Ford, Archives and Special Collections, J. D. Williams Library, University of Mississippi; and Robert W. Hamblin, director of the Center for Faulkner Studies, Southeast Missouri State University, for responding to blind queries and providing photographic prints.

During a fall of unimaginable disaster in New York City, my stouthearted Cheti and faithful Petra almost saw me through. Their loss was made bearable by my colleagues at the Center for Scholars and Writers, New York Public Library.

The control the court sought was the *total* submission of blacks. —A. Leon Higginbotham Jr., *In the Matter of Color: Race and the American Legal Process: The Colonial Period*

In trying to describe the provisional aspect of slave law, I would choose words that revealed its structure as rooted in a concept of . . . black antiwill. I would characterize the treatment of blacks by whites in their law as defining blacks as those who had no will. . . . If "pure will" or total control equals the perfect white person, then, impure will and total lack of control equals the perfect black person. —Patricia J. Williams, *The Alchemy of Race and Rights: Diary of a Law Professor*

Claiming of Rights

Defending a slave charged with stealing a letter from a post office, an enterprising counsel argued that, according to the recent ruling of *Dred Scott v Sandford* (1857), a slave was not a legal person and thus not subject to the law.[1] His slippery argument in *U.S. v Army* (1859) raised to another level of absurdity the issue of persons as property and property in persons, which had challenged the legal system from the colonial period in the seventeenth century through the founding of the nation in the eighteenth and into the middle of the nineteenth centuries, when former "property," such as Sojourner Truth and Frederick Douglass, spoke eloquently as "persons" against chattel slavery. Roger B. Taney, the presiding chief justice of the Supreme Court in the *Dred Scott* case, began that decision by raising the key question of civil rights for slaves: "The question is simply this: Can a negro, whose ancestors were imported into this country, and sold as slaves, become a member of the political community formed and brought into existence by the Constitution of the United States, and as such become entitled to all the rights, and privileges, and immunities, granted by that instrument to the citizen?"[2]

Taney's answer to the question was a stunning blow to all people of African descent in the United States, whether free or slave. He determined that even before the nation's founding, "the negro race" had been "regarded as beings of an inferior order, and altogether unfit to associate with the white race, either in social or political relations; and so far inferior, that they had no rights which the white man was bound to respect, and that the negro might justly and lawfully be reduced to slavery for his benefit. He was bought and sold, and treated as an ordinary article of merchandise and traffic, whenever a profit could be made of it."[3] The decision concluded that the entire race—slave, free, or mulatto—was contained in the same degraded position of exclusion from "civilized Governments and the family of nations" and was "not regarded as a portion of the people or citizens of the Government" formed as the United States.

The denial of all rights of citizenship to black people in the *Dred Scott* decision was quickly interpreted by the defending counsel in the *U.S. v Army* case as the denial of their rights as legal persons. This defense was rejected, however, in a ruling that stated, "It is true that a slave is the property of the master, and his right of property . . . is secured by the Constitution and laws of the United States, and it is equally true that he is not a citizen. . . . Yet, he is a person, and always described as such . . . in the public acts of the United States."[4] The justice writing the decision was the same Roger B. Taney of the *Dred Scott* case, who had, without irony, defined the slave as both person and as property: "The loss which the master sustains in his property . . . is incidental, and necessarily arises from its two fold character, since the slave, as person, may commit offenses which society has a right to punish . . . although the punishment may render the property of the master of little or no value. But this hazard is invariably and inseparably associated with this description of property."[5]

The convoluted legal divide articulated so confidently between rights and nonrights, between person and property, between citizens and "articles of merchandise" is the starting point for this book's meditation on the definition of property and its ongoing implication in conceptualizations of the rights and representations of African Americans. Yet, like both the *Dred Scott v Sandford* and the *U.S. v Army* decisions, these issues do not merely involve people of African descent but seep through the whole fabric of society. Nor do they pertain only to the pre-Emancipation period but rather spill over into this new century in which the nation and the legal system continue to grope through the ideological and juridical residue of persons as property and rights in property concepts—shedding light, in particular, on present-day issues of ownership and rights to the body, as in organ harvesting and transplants, artificial insemination, sperm and egg donations (or sales), as well as on proprietary questions around fetuses, prisoners, and mental patients.

The messy but dynamic entanglements of slavery and law, property and rights, power and domination, race and gender, games and sport, ideologies and philosophies, literature and history, memory and imagination, experiential realities and imaginative projection, social constructions and cultural phenomena have all necessarily informed and engaged my thinking about this subject—so much so that I can state with great confidence that reading Faulkner has not gotten any easier. Since the late 1970s and 1980s when interdisciplinarity and theory, along with black studies, women's studies, and cultural and gender studies produced new Faulkners, all of whom are resistant to closure, the old Faulkner has happily been retired. This multiplicity of Faulkners has created an exciting but challenging set of epistemologies for any Faulkner reader or for a reader of any of the Faulkners. For those readers still concerned with race—its construction, its mutability, its fixity, its ideology, its history, its representation, and all of its ever-moving fluid permeations—this period since the 1980s has been both a watershed and a drought. Like many of them, I am now plunged headlong into rethinking the Faulkner canon.

I have placed Faulkner's *Go Down, Moses* (1942) centrally in this project because of its unrelenting attention to issues of ownership of land and of people, its argumentative discourse on the philosophical bases of ownership, and its focus on legal issues of inheritance, succession, and possession. Because the text extends in time from the 1830s through the 1940s, it takes into account the century in which slave law was codified then vacated, in which questions of property in persons were decided, challenged, hardened, reversed, and dismissed as enslaved persons went from being defined as property without will to being freed persons and "righted" citizens under the U.S. Constitution and its Thirteenth, Fourteenth, and Fifteenth Amendments. *Go Down, Moses* as a fictional text also provides access to powerful representations and narrative constructions with which to grapple with the complexities of racial power and domination in property rights and with legal interpretations over time, yet within a specified region—the South, especially Mississippi—which provides a micro-environment for studying the relationships among property, race, gender, and law.

However, this study is not exclusively focused on Faulkner or *Go Down,*

Moses. While it does offer a late twentieth-, early twenty-first-century reading of this difficult text—one that should prove particularly useful in teaching, bringing, as it does, many silent and overlooked characters fully into discursive expression and interpretation—it moves beyond Faulkner's novel and places it in dialogue with a broad range of issues, concerns, and practices. Law, and in particular critical race theory, along with legal history and social history and some aspects of game theory, all inform this project, as do gender theory and literary theory.

Go Down, Moses may initially seem an odd choice for this project, especially given that *Absalom, Absalom!* (1936) has so often been considered not only William Faulkner's best work but also a historical novel par excellence. Although the designation "best" is obviously subjective, I once shared this evaluation of *Absalom, Absalom!* because there Faulkner focused his attention on the methods that historical consciousness employs in the process of coming to terms with social history and racial identity as part of the private meaning necessary for public understanding of the self with all of its masks set either firmly in place or artfully aside. After that intense and complex novel, in which Faulkner paralleled world events by concentrating on dynasty, power, design, and conflict among blood kin that culminated in the Civil War itself, his subsequent novels seemed much less powerful and compelling. I was not alone in that assessment; Faulkner critics as varied as Joseph Blotner, Cleanth Brooks, Myra Jehlen, Lee Jenkins, and Michael Millgate shared a similar view of his post-*Absalom* work.

Now I am not so certain. I have come to believe that *Go Down, Moses*, which I had previously dismissed as a "baggy monster," ranks among Faulkner's greatest fictional achievements. Perhaps my change of opinion is partly due to years of teaching this troublesome text and attempting to answer the direct and invested questions of students seeking not synthesis but relevance between their contemporary concerns and *Go Down, Moses*. Perhaps I have a different opinion of the novel simply because it speaks to my current interests in race, gender, and law. Whatever convergences of time and temperament may be at play, I now think that in long-range assessments of Faulkner's impressive canon, *Go Down, Moses* will stand prominently in the list of his major works, in part because it takes on knotty ideologies of race and gender that are manifest in the production of white shame in a culture of legalized slavery, in a culture legitimating property in persons. Issues of affect, the subjective and conscious side of emotion, intertwine with issues of race to elevate *Go Down, Moses* to a level commensurate with that typically accorded Faulkner's most acclaimed fiction.

I believe that just as he wrote into *Absalom, Absalom!* much of his otherwise inexpressible grief and guilt after the death of his brother Dean in 1935, Faulkner poured into *Go Down, Moses* his inconsolable grief and shame after the 1940 death of Caroline Barr, the black woman who not only took care of him during his childhood but also remained a constant presence throughout his entire adulthood. His guilt over Dean's accidental death, which occurred in an airplane Faulkner had purchased, could be expressed within the *Absalom* narrative as fratricide, with its symbolic antecedent of brother killing brother being clearly located within Western consciousness in the biblical story to which his title alluded. However, his shame and his recognition of shame as a white southern man at the social treatment of a black servant woman, born in slavery, had no clear antecedents within the expressive discourses available to him. The biblical account of the enslavement of the Israelites in Egypt and Moses' leading them out of bondage, though expressive of the larger issues of slavery, oppression, and freedom and symbolically connected to the condition of black people in the United States, as the spiritual he appropriated for his title portends, did not speak directly to the emotions of shame and culpability. Moreover, the southern cultural narratives of concubinage and miscegenation during the antebellum period did not address the kind of sin against a black woman that Faulkner attempted to express after Caroline Barr died.

Shame and its association with death infuse the text with an emotion more palpable than either grief or loss. Experiences of shame come suddenly and with an element of surprise; in the process, according to Helen Merrell Lynd, they "throw a flooding light on what and who we are and what the world we live in is."[6] Shame thus becomes a defining emotion. In "The Old People," one of the chapters of *Go Down, Moses*, McCaslin Edmonds recognizes its centrality: "And even suffering and grieving is better than nothing; there is only one thing worse than not being alive, and that's shame."[7] An insistent longing to articulate shame across generational and racial lines but within the prevalent expressive discourses of familial generations and race difference marks *Go Down, Moses* as one of Faulkner's major fictional achievements.

For many years, however, I resisted what seemed to be mandatory at-

Caroline Barr, born during slavery, was Faulkner's nursemaid during his childhood and as "Mammy Callie" continued to serve his family until her death in
1940. Courtesy of the Center for Faulkner Studies, The Brodsky Collection,
Southeast Missouri State University.

tention to *Go Down, Moses* for Faulkner scholars who addressed issues of race. My reading of that text was that its overwhelmingly self-conscious sermonizing and cobbling together of disparate parts made it somewhat suspect and clearly problematic. I valued the text precisely because of its instability, permutations, uncertainties, and fissures, basically for its modernist aesthetic and intellectual stance, so none of the claims for unity or coherence ever seemed compelling to me; but beyond that, as a reader with a particular social identity (black, female, southern), I found the representation of blacks, from Tomey's Turl in "Was" to Butch Beauchamp in "Go Down, Moses," reactionary, perhaps most particularly so for the ciphered black women—Tennie, Mannie, Molly, Nat, Fonsiba, Eunice, Tomasina. In fact, even one of Faulkner's most celebrated textual creations seemed to me profoundly retrograde; every time I read "The Old People" and "The Bear," I configured Old Ben, the bear, with a black man's face. In my interactive participation with the narrative and in my interpretation of its deep structure, Old Ben loomed as that mighty abstraction, "The Negro," the trope par excellence of endurance and sufferance. Descriptive, symbolic language and emblematic passages intensified the association and, concomitantly, distanced me as a black reader from the text.[8] Ensconced in the margins, I read against the grain of received critical thinking about both "The Bear" and *Go Down, Moses*.

More recently, I began my own retrospective—a rereading and rethinking of Faulkner's novels—still largely from the margins, a space that has grown increasingly familiar if not comfortable in the past twenty years. *Go Down, Moses* has remained as problematic for me as ever, but with some differences. I understand it as modernist historical fiction, an embodied exploration of a troubled personal time that Faulkner represents as mid-nineteenth and early twentieth century, but I also understand it as a book written more than half a century ago with a social lens contemporaneous with that time. Taking both of these temporal frames into account becomes for me a textual effort to make comprehensible a shifting world by holding a space from which to contemplate, interrogate, and evaluate my own material and experiential world. Space is associated with chance, as Susan Sontag suggested: "Space is black, teeming with possibilities, positions, intersections, passages, detours, U-turns, dead ends, one-way streets."[9] In a sense, *Go Down, Moses* has become for me a space of possibilities and positions.

Considered from the vantage point of space as an opportunity for possibility, both my reading of the text and my relational stance have changed. Importantly, I understand *Go Down, Moses* as a discursive practice participating with other discursive practices—including those as disparate as law, games, and sport—in the broad phenomenon of culture, as well as in structures of power. In fact, as Michel Foucault theorizes about the productivity of power, "power produces; it produces reality; it produces domains of objects and rituals of truth. The individual and the knowledge that may be gained of him [or her] belong to this production."[10] Indeed, I worry less about the visible figure of the bear playing nature as a trope of blackness and more about what happens to the text when I exercise my authority as a reader and locate Tomasina's son Terrel, called Tomey's Turl, at the center of a reading of *Go Down, Moses*.[11] Surely she must be joking, those of you who have contemplated every page of that book must be thinking. Tomey's Turl—surely she can't mean Tomey's Turl, but rather Isaac McCaslin or even Ike's black kinsman, Lucas Beauchamp. And those of you less familiar with *Moses* are probably wondering who or what is Tomey's Turl.

But, yes, I am serious about situating Tomey's Turl, the comic, stereotyped slave who appears as an actor only in the wildly slapstick opening chapter, "Was," at the center of a reading of *Go Down, Moses* at a moment when extended readings of a single text are already suspect. For from that radical repositioning, Tomey's Turl functions to transgress and disrupt the power and authority of whites over both lives and stories. After much struggling with *Go Down, Moses* from the position of my own raced and gendered readerly identity, I have come to appreciate Faulkner's raced and gendered writerly identity, which we, neither of us, can escape. In the process, I have approached Tomey's Turl from the legal perspective of his being a righted and willful black subject resistant to subjugation, domination, and oppression. By situating Tomey's Turl at the center of my thinking about Faulkner's text and as a subject with both a will and rights, I stage not merely an act of resistance but one of liberation from the typical paradigms of power. That liberation stems from challenges critical race theory has posed to "the ways in which race and racial power are constructed and represented in American legal culture and, more generally, in American society as a whole."[12] Positioning Tomey's Turl at the center of this extended meditation on *Go Down, Moses* allows me not only to approach the text with a fresh perspective but also to utilize modes of analysis largely unavailable before the last decades of the twentieth century when poststructuralist and postmodernist work moved away from the process of uncovering interpretations inherent within a text.

In a statement appearing as an epigraph to this book, Patricia J. Williams uses the term "black antiwill" to "characterize the treatment of blacks by whites in their law," that is, the defining of blacks in legal terms as without will: "if 'pure will' or total control equals the perfect white person, then impure will and total lack of control equals the perfect black person."[13] To attribute will to a fictional character who is not merely enslaved but represented as comic is to engage in an oppositional reading of the text and the character. Similarly, to reconceptualize that character as having rights, or as a righted subject, opens a space for reading the text differently and without a partial view of blacks or a compartmentalized vision of humanity. By centering Tomey's Turl as both a trope and a trump, signifying black rights and will, I have also come to a different appreciation for the pleasures and possibilities of the text. As Tzvetan Todorov states in "Reading as Construction": "It is only by subjecting the text to a particular type of reading that we construct an imaginary universe on the basis of the text. The novel does not imitate reality, it creates reality."[14] However, I am not yet convinced that the ideology or the structure of Go Down, Moses or that the cultural work of decentering textual spheres of influence and strongholds of power will displace cultural hegemony and racial supremacy. Yet I know that necessarily inscribed within my attention to Go Down, Moses is my own continued stake in the power of literature and the efficacy of words.

At the same time in my work on Go Down, Moses, I seek to deconstruct power, in particular white racial power, by means of two structures: the structure of game and the structure of law. Both are simultaneously frames and discourses that when linked to race produce specific responses to power. Games, I take to be liberatory and democratic. Law, I take to be constrictive and arbitrary. Both are marked by a narrativity connecting them in my analysis to literary texts in general and to fiction in particular. Games and masculinist sport are interconnected with law and property in representing racialized society in Go Down, Moses. Sport encompasses public and physical activities, including hunting, that have competitive elements, that are "pursued for victory, pleasure, or the demonstration of excellence."[15] In the social state of Faulkner's text, sport and games derive meanings from an effort to duplicate the competition for and control of property within the circumscription of law. Property as a concept is dynamic, yet also codified in law as relations and bundled in legal discourse with political values. A property relation can be defined, for instance, in labor (Locke), as utility (Bentham), or in protection (Marx). Both law and games are forms of social control and discursive bodies of social commentary. Legal boundaries are, however, all arbitrary but also compensatory for players whose moves are regulated by rules displaced or dislodged from the assumptions of law within the social state. These seemingly disparate modes of thinking about the text contribute to an interpretive strategy for reading *Go Down, Moses*— one that allows for the multivocality and density of ideas (compatible and competing ideas) in Faulkner's text. In reading a white, masculinist power dynamics of law and property combined with games and sport in the text, I attend to the condition of enslavement and domination, to the difference of race and of gender, and to the naturalizing of change and instability.[16] The tenuous connections of game, play, and sport to the text come together momentarily in this reading of two competing narratives: a narrative of legality with property and ownership at its core; a narrative of games with masculinist sport and social ritual at its center.

I am not attempting to insert a new metanarrative into the criticism or to uncover a new master narrative within the text, but rather to intervene in already existing determinations of the hermetic, coherent, stable text and expand the reading of *Go Down, Moses* as multiply interpretable. In fact, despite the many readings that justify exclusive claims of its organic unity, *Go Down, Moses* reasserts itself as problematic in terms of conventional definitions of genre. The question of whether *Go Down, Moses* is a novel or a story sequence has been situated at the center of readings of Faulkner's text, in part because of its original title and in part because of its physical properties.[17] The extensive scholarship on Faulkner's revision of short stories to produce the book manuscript has informed both sides of the question.[18] Formalist readings have observed the integrated "wholeness" of the text and, based on considerations of the formal properties of the novel, have identified thematic, symbolic, and structural strategies and clusters that mark the text as a novel. With equal attention to aspects of (short) fiction, however, another group of critics has insisted that the text is finally a sequence of stories, though one cleverly connected in a modernist mode. For the most part, readings of *Go Down, Moses* as a unified novel have superseded those regarding it as separate short stories. At least one extended treatment, Dirk Kuyk's *Threads Cable-strong: William Faulkner's* Go Down, Moses (1983), proceeds from the assumption of plausibility on both sides of the genre question and observes that "*Go Down, Moses* takes us . . . into the unfamiliar and therefore hazardous middle ground between novels and collections of stories."[19] Nonetheless, Kuyk then asks, "How does *Go Down, Moses*, despite its obvious fragmentation, come to seem whole?"—and he allows the answer to control the subsequent reading.[20]

The question of genre for *Go Down, Moses* does not have to be answered in either-or/neither-nor terms. In fact, if claims of unity are dissolved by an attention to the reader as self-authorized to create a reading experience out of engagement with the text, and if claims of fragmentation (that is, story sequence) are suspended by an attention to the configuration of games marking the text as both contest and contested site, then momentarily at least Faulkner's authority over his text becomes bounded and the issue of its genre transgressable. Accordingly, I locate Tomey's Turl, rather than Isaac McCaslin or his ancestor Lucius Quintus Carothers McCaslin, at the center of this project, along with the issue of property and ownership. He is a figure of transgression and hybridity closely linked to the problems inherent in property in persons. Tomey's Turl's hybridity—his status as both black and white, as both within and without familial structures—combines with his willful transgression of cultural constrictions, social domination, and political economy to open a critical space for reading *Go Down, Moses* as a miscegenated text, one whose form and logic resist containment and defy boundaries.

Tomey's Turl's genesis in the narrative is expressed bodily in a game of running that culminates in a game of hide-and-seek; materially in an enactment of property ownership; and textually in a word game that is transcribed in a legal business record. Locating him at the center of my reading of *Go Down, Moses* allows for an interpretation of the text as miscegenated and hybrid—miscegenated in its mixture of materials from the traditions of comic black-faced minstrelsy and tragic southern plantation romance. In using *miscegenated* to describe the text, I also evoke the conventional meaning of the term as race mixing, along with its negative connotations (e.g., polluted, impure, or tainted), which I attach to shame as a feeling pervading the text and intermixing with, but also incarcerating, other emotions and structures within *Go Down, Moses*. Tomey's Turl figuratively grounds the plantation society as a carceral or disciplinary society in which the bodies of enslaved people are produced as controlled entities, sites of both coerced labor and erotic bondage. Within Tomey's Turl's story, Faulkner connects the slave economy and the sexual economy.

His given name is Terrel, pronounced and spelled Turl. That he is most often called Tomey's Terrel seems oddly appropriate because that name retains his social history, positions him both inside and outside of McCaslin domination, and refigures his mother, Tomasina (Tomey), who died giving birth to him. While the name Tomey's Turl carries the possessive and therefore implies ownership, that name merely links mother and son and abstracts from their relationship the presence of the white father who is parent to them both and owns them both. That absence is what must be reinserted into the relational structure in order to read the core discourses of the text. The son's name bears witness to Tomasina and the crime against her, so that the silence forced on the mother gives way to the verbal testimony of the son's name. That name, Tomey's Turl, evokes and memorializes Tomasina, whose own name thus retains both meaning and memory in the text long after her literal death. The naming nevertheless may also be an embedded effort to feminize the black man, to domesticate and tame him into a subjugated (and sexualized) object of property, because the very name Tomey's Turl contains both a gender blending and an obscuring of gender. The male slave's masculinity, then, is a buried and less accessible marker of his identity.

Eric Sundquist has observed the connections between *Go Down, Moses* and *Absalom, Absalom!*, in which Faulkner also addressed both miscegenation and incest, as "the disintegration of the barrier—against an actualization of miscegenation as incest—that Henry's murder of Bon holds in place: as though struggling ever more insistently to unify the fictional domain of Yoknapatawpha, Faulkner crossed the threshold that unites two distinct castes in one family of violated blood in *Go Down, Moses*."[21] Sundquist's reading of the linkages between *Go Down, Moses* and *Absalom, Absalom!* prompts another: that Tomey's Turl can be said to occupy a space similar to that of Charles Bon, the unacknowledged mixed-race son and mysterious presence at the center of *Absalom, Absalom!* That analogous space compounds the weight I attach to the slight narrative figuration of Tomey's Turl. That both Charles and Terrel are

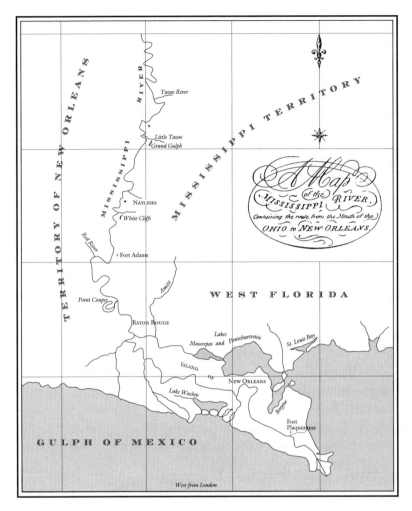

Early English map of the Mississippi River to New Orleans, showing the Mississippi Territory. Reprinted in the nineteenth century with sketches by Charles Alexander Lesueur (1778–1846).

the unacknowledged sons of powerful fathers whose absences worry the text and vex the sons compounds the analogy.

Born in slavery during June of 1833, "*yr stars fell*," Tomey's Turl is the son of Tomasina and the grandson of Eunice.[22] His birth in the year of the great meteor shower, called falling stars, signals his link to notions of divine retribution, God's wrath, the end of the world or the end of slavery, as interpreted by blacks and whites in the South who based their readings of the meteor shower on the Book of Revelation (6:13). Because his enslavement follows from the maternal condition, he is, like his mother and grandmother, the property of Carothers McCaslin, whose given name is Lucius Quintus Carothers McCaslin, but who is also referred to as both "L. Q. C." and "old Carothers." In the 1780s Carothers left Carolina for the Mississippi frontier where he purchased land from a Chickasaw and created a plantation. In 1807 he traveled to New Orleans where he purchased Eunice, who gave birth to a daughter Tomasina in 1810. Tomasina's son, Terrel—Tomey's Turl, as he is called in "Was," the opening chapter of *Go Down, Moses*—is both the son and the grandson of Carothers McCaslin, who violates his own daughter, Tomasina, and fathers her son. Tomey's Turl's textualized origin appears to be a word game analogous to the Sphinx's riddle that Oedipus solves. His lineage is embedded in the "facts" and the ellipses bound and recorded riddle-like in the McCaslin commissary ledgers and "decoded" in the winter of 1883–1884 by another grandson of Carothers McCaslin, Isaac "Ike" McCaslin, a boy of sixteen, who functions as a detective solving a crime puzzle and as a reader creating meaning in a fashion similar to Quentin Compson in *Absalom, Absalom!*

In "The Bear" young Ike McCaslin reads a sequence of entries in the ledgers of his family's plantation. The scene of his reading and the script he reads together form an "evocative power of an action."[23] Turl's birth is signified by the words of the text, and both his father's identity and his father's incestuous rape of his mother are interpreted from the silences and ellipses within the text.

> *Eunice Bought by Father in New Orleans 1807 $650, dolars. Marrid to Thucydus 1809 Drownd in Crick, Cristmas Day 1832.*
>
> . . . .
>
> *June 21th 1833 Drownd herself*
>
> . . . .
>
> *23 Jun 1833 Who in hell ever heard of a niger drownding him self*
>
> . . . .
>
> *Tomasina called Tomy Daughter Thucydus @ Eunice Born 1810 dide in Child bed June 1833 and Burd. Yr stars fell*
>
> . . . .
>
> *Turl Son of Thucydus @ Eunice Tomy born Jun 1833 yr stars fell Fathers will*
>
> ("The Bear," 255–57)

These entries provide *Go Down, Moses* with a dual power: the awe of recognition and acknowledgment, and the force of shame and its linkage to death. More than an exercise in detection, they make tangible how the economic power of ownership precipitates the physical and psychological abuses of chattel, human property—issues that elevate the narrative above farce.

The encoded incest, committed by Carothers in the 1830s and revealed in Ike's reading of the commissary ledgers in the 1880s, has most typically led to an interpretive focus on the white McCaslin men (e.g., their relation to the land and to slavery, their exercise of power or repudiation of it, their subjugation of blacks and women), as a way of reading cultural, familial, or identity formation and disintegration in the text. Minrose Gwin, for instance, rightly sees the ledgers "as the highly claustrophobic space of 'bound blackness' written by white men and functioning as a site of contemplation and exorcism for white men."[24] Rarely has the implied incest resulted in attention to the text as a configuration of Terrel's hybridity or of his position as figure of transgression against the political and sexual economies or the social order dominating the text. The games marking *Go Down, Moses* as contest and contested site also mark Tomey's Turl as the trope, the embodiment, the represented contest and contested site, that necessarily refocuses attention to the text. In refocusing attention on Tomey's Turl and, by means of his story, on the larger narrative, I intervene in the practice of privileging stories of the cultural or racial elite while dismissing or not hearing the stories of those Others whose very existences make possible those majority narratives. As Mary Frances Berry has suggested about the law, "Whose story counts in legal decisions rests heavily on who controls political and economic power, in a process that is circular and progressive. The stories of the powerful are the only ones that count, and the counting further enhances the power of the tellers in the economic and political arena. The exclusion of their stories reflects the historical silencing of African Americans."[25]

In locating a reading of the text apart from an already identified or a possibly identifiable master code, I am refusing to extend the "right" of a master's authority over a slave, over human property, and ultimately over historical and cultural forces as signifiers. A. Leon Higginbotham has recognized "a nexus between the brutal centuries of colonial slavery and the racial polarization and anxieties of today. The poisonous legacy of legalized oppression based upon the matter of color can never be adequately purged from our society if we act as if slave laws never existed."[26] His warning is being heeded, legal historians having begun to take seriously the existence then and implication now of laws regulating slaves as property and slavery as an institution. As a direct result, legal studies of slave laws are filtering into a number of related cultural, literary, and historical discourses.

Slave laws existed to codify a concept of blacks as inadequately human, to reduce blacks to a subcategory of humanity, and thereby to consolidate white authority and power over black lives, black labor, and black economic productivity. Such a consolidation has continued to have consequences throughout the twentieth century and into the twenty-first. In particular, the presumption of inferiority has hampered the progress of blacks in seeking equal access to education, housing, and employment, despite repeated efforts at "remedies." It is no coincidence that inferiority is one of the precepts Higginbotham and Anne F. Jacobs have distilled from the relevant colonial and antebellum Virginia cases and statutes into "the legal and moral foundations of American slavery and early race-relations law": inferiority, property, and powerlessness.[27] Although there may not have existed a uniform set of slave laws over time and in different states, there were laws that undergirded slavery and slave society, assuming the inferiority of slaves, their condition as property, and their powerlessness. Peter Bardaglio has summarized the general consentience *among* those laws: "Every slave state had a slave code. . . . These codes established the property rights of those who owned slaves, spelled out the duties owed by slaves to masters, provided safeguards for the white community against slave-uprisings, and delineated the treatment that masters could exercise over their slaves. Despite their diversity, the codes shared some fundamental assumptions, such as generally defining slaves as personal rather than real property. As 'chattels personal,' slaves could be purchased, sold, leased, used as collateral, inherited, and even freed under certain circumstances."[28]

Property interests in persons were rarely neutralized under law but instead increased the inequities in the treatment and perception of people of African descent. Early American law and political and property concepts were influenced by William Blackstone's *Commentaries on the Laws of England*. Slave laws as regulations of social control and protections for property rights have continued to affect black people in the United States and to provide a cautionary tale for other classes and groups of

Engraving used by antislavery societies to raise the issue of the humanity of enslaved people and to plead for the abolition of slavery.

people lacking power in our society. In their conclusion to "Property First, Humanity Second: The Recognition of the Slave's Human Nature in Virginia's Civil Law," Higginbotham and Barbara K. Kopytoff offer reasons for the necessity in contemporary society to be cognizant of slave laws and consequently to be vigilant about the making and interpretation of law in our own time. By turning a blind eye to those who were enslaved, judges and legislators calculated "that some human beings were not worth protecting against vested interests," and they left as a legacy of their unwillingness to protect the powerless a concern in the present about the will and the ability of those in power, particularly lawyers and judges, "to be fair and just to the powerless of our society."[29] Higginbotham and Kopytoff use their work on slave law in Virginia as the basis for their conclusion: "A legislature and an activist judiciary, primarily concerned with protecting property interests, recognized the human needs, aspirations, and suffering of the most powerless of people in the society, the slaves, only when to do so served the interests of powerful whites like themselves. When such recognition ran contrary to those interests, they withdrew their human sympathies and turned to discussing the importance of property rights, economic hardships to vested interests, and settled rules of law, which they claimed even a court of equity could not overturn" (540).

I am reminded of the precariousness of fairness and justice for the disempowered when feminist legal scholar Robin West comments, "It is not so clear . . . why women's suffering is so pervasively dismissed or trivialized by legal culture."[30] It occurs to me that the history of the legal construction of black women and their treatment historically under law would speak directly to this issue, but even today, despite numerous references to Toni Morrison's *Beloved* and to black women in slavery by feminists, there remains little conception that laws related to black people, and specifically slave law pertaining to black women, could have any bearing on the world of "white" legal jurisprudence and its consequences for women as a class.

Neither the conception of slaves as only property nor the formulation of slaves as completely powerless can be accepted as valid, because both conceptions are legal constructions that subordinate the rights of humanity to the rights of property in order to preserve the social order. These formulations stemmed from economic considerations that depended on the condition of forced enslavement and its juridical interpretations for validity. Acknowledging the existence of slave law includes for me meditating on the questions that assist historical recovery and reconstruction of slavery's social reality, questions that "seek to comprehend the manner in which legal principles were molded and manipulated" in the service of slavery and in maintaining rights of property.[31]

I am asserting in this meditation that Tomey's Turl should not be "unrighted," particularly as he is read in the twenty-first century. "In law, rights are islands of empowerment," Patricia J. Williams observed in "On Being the Object of Property": "To be unrighted is to be disempowered, and the line between rights and no-rights is most often the line between dominators and oppressors."[32] The legal language of rights becomes a reminder of the possibility of imaginary empowerment. While there is no escaping Tomey's Turl's creation as a slave in Faulkner's text, to consider him as a subject denied his legal rights opens the possibility of re-reading Tomey's Turl and contemplating the possible indices of empowerment within his actions, speech, and motivations, and in so doing to begin a fresh dialogue about Faulkner's critique of power in *Go Down, Moses*. "Rights contain images of power," Williams wrote, "and manipulating those images, either visually or linguistically, is central in the making and maintenance of rights. In principle, therefore, the more dizzyingly diverse the images that are propagated, the more empowered we will be in society."[33] Her conception of power residing within rights enabled me to rethink *Go Down, Moses* with Tomey's Turl as a subject struggling to assert the rights denied him by his material condition as property, and also allowed me to conceptualize how images of power are embedded in the specific rights Tomey's Turl seeks to recuperate in the text.

Much of my project, the consideration of Turl as a righted subject and of the issues of property, has been informed by the defining elements and interdisciplinary methodology of critical race theory. Two of the defining elements, in particular, speak to my interests in the Faulkner canon and in issues of race: first, the representation of racism "not as isolated instances of conscious bigoted decisionmaking or prejudiced practice, but as larger, systemic, structural, and cultural, as deeply psychologically and socially ingrained"; and second, the insistence on "recognition of the experiential knowledge of people of color and our communities in analyzing law and society," to which I add literature because of the primary focus of my analysis.[34] Put another way, shared interests unite the practitioners of critical race theory in coming to understand how white hegemony subordinated people of color and how "the rule of law" and "equal protection" under law functioned in tandem with the hierarchical social structure to maintain a system of oppression. What attracted me to this recent development in legal theory was the clearly articulated determination "not merely to understand the vexed bond between law and racial power but to change it."[35] That desire for a responsible intervention in order to foster a stronger, fairer, more just and equitable society for everyone is especially appealing on a humanistic and intellectual level. Critical race theory translates into "outsider jurisprudence," as Mari Matsuda terms it when she describes the necessary uses of social and experiential reality in an historical, revisionist effort "to know history from the bottom": "From the fear and namelessness of the slave, from the broken treaties of the indigenous Americans, the desire to know history from the bottom has forced [critical race] scholars to sources often ignored: journals, poems, oral histories, and stories from their own experiences of life in a hierarchically arranged world."[36] This methodology suggests an affinity with literary analysis, an affinity foregrounded in Matsuda's vision of law as "essentially political" and the work of critical race theory as "the pragmatic use of law as a tool for social change and the aspirational core of law as the human dream of peaceable existence."[37] Both a form of political resistance and a liberatory practice, critical race theory does not elide the ambiguity and contradictions that are so much a part of the treatment of race and racial subjects under law, and so much a part of the creation of literary texts in the modern period.

Thus, for me as a racially defined woman reading reflexively, Faulkner's modernist *Go Down, Moses* can be deconstructed in terms of political action, of the assertion of civil rights, and of resistance to the domination of ideological tyrants. Within Faulkner's text, the historical conditions of western expansion (specifically the settling of the Mississippi frontier) and of chattel slavery (the establishing of legal slavery within Mississippi), I consider inscriptions of a white masculinist consolidation of power in property and pleasure in progeny (without the intermediate stage of sexual intercourse, which is always already over in the construction of this text and which may be read as rape in the case of Carothers McCaslin's sexual aggression against both Eunice and Tomasina). In the struggle for a consolidation of power is the seldom-visible resistance to subjugation and the rarely articulated countermove for empowerment. The historical engagements foreground, then, the social and legal contests for power that motivate positioning Terrel as a righted challenge to domination and as a willful site of resistance to oppression.

Crying in the Wilderness

Faulkner produced the miscegenated text *Go Down, Moses* during the early 1940s and imbricated discursive connections to the legal codes and philosophical theories underpinning property rights and chattel slavery in Mississippi during the first half of the nineteenth century. Resident within the language he chose are tropic and narrative challenges to juridical and patriarchical authority over the lives of human beings who are reduced to property and property rights.

Faulkner reiterates the symbolic importance of the referent "Go Down, Moses," by using it as the title for the overall volume and, significantly, for the very last chapter. And because the spiritual is so closely connected with the experiential reality of black people under slavery, it binds his book to blacks and vexed markers of race. "Go Down, Moses" is not only the title of one of the best-known and most-performed spirituals, but it is also the title that James Weldon Johnson plays off in "Go Down Death—A Funeral Sermon" in *God's Trombones: Seven Negro Sermons in Verse*, published in 1927, two years after his *Book of American Negro Spirituals* appeared with "Go Down, Moses" as the first inclusion.[38] Although its precise authorship is unknown, this spiritual became part of the literature of the antislavery movement and was first printed in 1861 in the *New York Tribune*, when its analogous narrative of a destined delivery from enslavement took on greater immediacy at the onset of the Civil War. Since that time, "Go Down, Moses" has endured in several versions as one of African Americans' favorite spirituals because of its familiar biblical archetype of relief from oppression and its promise of retribution for the sin of enslavement.

"Go Down, Moses" is a song of struggle, of standing up to tyrants and to the tyranny of slavery. Its conjoined message of resistance and retaliation, along with freedom and deliverance, was not lost on black people. It is a message Frederick Douglass, the most famous of the nineteenth-century black abolitionists, came to in his thinking about slavery:

> This struggle may be a moral one, or it may be a physical one, and it may be both moral and physical, but it must be a struggle. Power concedes nothing without a demand. It never did and it never will. Find out just what any people will quietly submit to and you have found out the exact measure of injustice and wrong which will be imposed on them. The limits of the tyrants are prescribed by the endurance of those whom they oppress. In the light of these ideas, Negroes will be hunted at the North, and held and flogged at the South so long as they submit to those devilish outrages, and make no resistance, either moral or physical.[39]

The willingness to stand up to injustice and to struggle for justice and right is the message that Douglass, formerly enslaved himself, understood as crucial to the abolition of slavery.

The core narrative of deliverance stems from Exodus, chapters 3–15. In the biblical account, Moses delivers the Israelites out of bondage in Egypt and leads them to Canaan, the Promised Land. The text evokes a strong affinity with the condition of enslaved blacks and their hope for God's intercession and deliverance. It is no accident, as Richard Newman points out, that the biblical Moses appears so often in the spirituals.[40] The account in Exodus repeats the phrase spoken by God, "Let my people go" (Exodus 5:1), that becomes the dramatic refrain in the spiritual. Its repeated and direct demand for the liberation of the enslaved has caused "Go Down, Moses" to become linked to Nat Turner and the 1831 rebellion he led in Southampton County, Virginia. Whether Turner was author or subject of the spiritual is unproven; nevertheless, the historical reality is that the powerful lyrics of literal freedom from physical enslavement were so apparent that some cautious slaveholders, made anxious by Turner's revolt, refused to allow "Go Down, Moses" to be sung on their plantations.

Importantly, however, freedom as a political message in the spiritual combines with death, despair, and their opposites, life and hope. "Go Down, Moses" is a powerful expression of liberation ideology, according to Cornel West, because it "put forward a political message of freedom and a hope for endurance in the face of death and despair after one arrives at the penultimate promised land of these United States."[41] Spirituals in general and clearly "Go Down, Moses" in particular "challenge any Enlightenment notion of human autonomy," by highlighting what West terms the intrinsic paradox of human freedom: "we must be strong enough to resist the prevailing forms of bondage yet honest enough to acknowledge our weakness in the face of death and disappointment. This honesty about our weakness is itself a supreme form of strength that precludes paralysis and impotence." In effect, West emphasizes that "Go Down, Moses," like all African American spirituals, has the ability to "perplex" or confound "primarily because of this uncanny tension between a profound pagan sense of the tragic and a deep Christian sense of justice."[42]

Within the Exodus story and its historical application to slavery in the United States, human bondage is a shameful act defying conceptions of right and justice, and it is a discourse on the survival of dehumanization and shame. Linda Wagner-Martin has stated, "The integrity of a captive people—subject to inhuman treatment but still believing in salvation—is the keystone image for this novel. When critics [such as Cleanth Brooks] have suggested that 'The McCaslins' would have been a more directive title, they overlook the resonance of both painful—because realistic—expectations and promise which 'Go Down, Moses' as title provides. It suggests Faulkner's undertaking: to write a shameful, and shaming, story, rather than a prideful one."[43] Shame is one of the primary affective legacies circulating through the generations of McCaslins. It is a response to the defamation of a people and of the concepts of justice and right.

Intricately linked to histories of enslavement and deliverance, "Go Down, Moses" also encodes a narrative about legal authority and the trope of justice in its lyrics. Justice overarches conceptions of law and rights. "Law has become located in national cultures," according to George Fletcher, "but justice stands above all culture. It is an Archimedean point beyond history and social practices."[44] The spiritual attests to the power of justice and identifies three levels of authority and sources of laws affecting the lives of human beings. It references the story of enslavement and ownership, so that the subject is property and the message is an injunction against holding property in persons or human beings in slavery. The Lord speaks,

> Go down, Moses
> Way down in Egyptland,
> Tell old Pharaoh
> To let my people go.[45]

His command to Moses evokes the highest authority, a transcendent spiritual and moral authority. Moses, the Lord's servant, is the human agent, moral representative, and divinely appointed leader. Pharaoh, ruler of the land and representative of the state, is both social law maker and moral law breaker. The site of struggle is between these forces of law, symbolic of patriarchal power and rule in sacred and secular realms.

Not to be overlooked in the patriarchal culture presented in the biblical narrative and its transference to the spiritual is the assumed primacy of the Lord, the Father, the Authority, the Law. Faulkner infuses the Law of the Father as represented in the spiritual throughout his text. Law, in its several permutations and conflicting judgments, forms one of the symbolic cores of Faulkner's narrative. "Father's Will," a repetition with a difference—a legal document and a personality trait—signals Faulkner's overt association of law and authority with the father and patriarchy.

The spiritual posits the right of challenging legal authority on the grounds of divine law, justice, and morality. The command of the Lord ("Let my people go; / If not I'll smite your first-born dead"), which Moses executes, carries with it the weight of power, with which God in his wrath shall seek retributive justice and punish the enslavers. The command bears as well the appeal of divine righteousness.

> When Israel was in Egyptland
> Oppressed so hard they could not stand
> No more shall they in bondage toil
> Let them come out with Egypt's spoil.

By means of his grace God will share the benefits of society with the enslaved in a form of distributive justice. The spiritual affirms that human beings are righted subjects for whom freedom, not enslavement, is normative; that there is a righteous and just morality displayed in God's justice and power, goodness and love; and that morality will operate against harsh, unfair legal edicts. Whether it shall prevail is not addressed.

The metaphorical core of the spiritual is submerged in Faulkner's novel, so that, taken as a whole, the spiritual reiterates the conflicting codes within the text. It places in opposition the tropes of an ideal standard and a legal standard for evaluating human actions. It magnifies the inherent contradiction in slavery: people as property. On the one hand, Moses' attempt to lead the Israelites out of Egypt is right action because it promotes an ideal—freedom rather than bondage as the right of human beings—whereas on the other hand, Pharaoh's attempt to maintain the enslavement may be considered appropriate action because it conforms to a civil law and the ethics of custom. Yet enslavement is morally objectionable, undeniably reprehensible. The rightness of the action or the goodness it achieves within the social order is overwhelmed by the harm done to the Israelites and, ultimately, is negated by the divine command, "Let my people go." The intercession of what might be called extralegal intervention, or the trope of divine intervention, directly on behalf of the oppressed establishes the always already possible though immediately repressed in the narrative allusions. Familiarity with the lyrics of the spiritual and the antecedent story in Exodus opens the narrative of law alongside the discourse of bondage and thus makes possible a consideration of conscience and morality in relation to legal and political demands.

The pervasive imposition of a separate and inferior social place on blacks in Mississippi was an accepted condition during the period in which Faulkner began work on the stories that would become *Go Down, Moses*. Subordination colors his attitude toward race and his language regarding blacks, as revealed in his letters to Robert Haas about the formulation of the manuscript. Faulkner announced his "four stories about niggers" and his intention to "build onto [them] . . . write some more."[46] His use of the offensive term *nigger* in a letter to someone not part of the Deep South culture of Mississippi reflects the extent to which *nigger* was naturalized in his discourses and in his ideology. His use of the term suggests "assaultive speech," defined in critical race theory as "words that are used as weapons to ambush, terrorize, wound, humiliate, and degrade."[47] Faulkner's discursive practices, and to an extent their informing ideologies regarding blacks, would become more conflicted during his writing of *Go Down, Moses,* perhaps in part due to the death in January 1940 of Caroline Barr, the black woman who raised him and to whom he dedicates the text.

By 1 May 1941, Faulkner had already given his collection of stories on relations between the races in Mississippi the title *Go Down, Moses,* as well as identified much of the material for inclusion to Haas.[48] That title in its uncontested association with blacks and their history of enslavement and subjugation in the United States immediately signals not only an allusion to race but, significantly, to oppression. Yet, it was not until he expanded the stories "A Point of Law" and "Gold Is Not Always" into "The Fire and the Hearth" and added the fourth section of "The Bear" that Faulkner clarified the dominant vision of the work, a vision of property in persons that helps to prevent it from being just another novel about race relations and to differentiate it from subsequent distinguished novels such as *Night Fire* (1946) by Edward Kimbrough and *The Voice at the Back Door* (1956) by Elizabeth Spencer, both authors being Mississippians who during Faulkner's lifetime attempted to address the issues of racial interaction in their heritage and history.[49]

One disruption of Faulkner's initially "comic" vision of the text is located in the figure of Terrel, Tomey's Turl. Once he has been conceptualized in the fourth part of "The Bear" as the product of incest between a slave owner and his enslaved daughter, he disturbs the subsurface of the text and explodes the boundary of his containment within a conventional narrative of what Faulkner had simply called "relations between the races." Terrel's very presence produces a tension that cannot be resolved or reconciled. Faulkner initially conceived of Tomey's Turl as a grotesquely comic stereotype, a very trifling dark-skinned slave in "Was."[50] By transforming Tomey's Turl into the near-white, enslaved half-brother of his owners, however, Faulkner reconfigures Terrel to signify the hidden exertions of raw, abusive power in slaveholding societies and the economic excesses of property in people. And though Terrel remains enslaved, Faulkner "frees" him from the social controls most apparent in slavery, and this nominal loosening of visible restraints sets the stage for his self-conscious and self-interested action and agency.

Fundamental to my thinking about Tomey's Turl, the mixed-race slave held as property by his blood relatives, is game theory, which maximizes the individual. In considering Tomey's Turl through the lens of game theory, I locate him as a racialized, *individual*, gendered male who would otherwise be erased from view and collapsed into a subordinate and invisible space. When viewed as self-interested, Tomey's Turl becomes an agent, visible and individualized, yet he is also inescapably property and owned, a slave in the fictional narrative. In positioning Tomey's Turl as a lens through which to view the connection between property and narrative or storytelling, I interpret *Go Down, Moses* as a bounded but multivalent space, mirroring enslavement and bondage, in which collisions of ideologies and stories occur. In chapter 1 of this volume I consider Tomey's Turl as a game player, whose invention of games functions to deregulate claims of ownership and whose strategies for autonomy not only have consequences for his white half-brothers and the slaveholding society represented in "Was," but also reverberate both in "Pantaloon in Black," the tonally different (from the rest of the book) narrative representing the central character Rider's confrontation with white resistance to black meaning, and within the sociohistorical culture outside of the text.

This reading of Tomey's Turl and the necessity of his individualizing stances in the face of dehumanizing slavery runs counter to Carol M. Rose's helpful interpretation of how feminist theory and narrative theory intersect in the use of storytelling to neutralize the tendencies of game theory: "That is, we use storytelling to break the spell of individual maximization, even among those more powerful than we; we tell tales to create a community in which cooperation is possible. . . . The narrativity of classical property theory . . . links the storytelling of classical property theory to a kind of moral discourse . . . narrative as an exhortation to the listener to overcome a game-theoretic, self-interested 'nature' and to follow instead the cooperative preference orderings that a property regime require."[51] In my reading, which takes into account race and the dehumanization of racial enslavement, Terrel instead follows a positive strategy of individual maximization and becomes a subject whose very presence is a calculation of how power not only operates but can be subverted in a historically specific, oppressive social order.

That focus on power and its consequences within two interconnected spheres, race and property, leads my attention to legal issues of slavery, ownership, and domination. Race alone did not operate to oppress blacks; instead, "the *interaction* between conceptions of race and property," as Cheryl L. Harris has explained, "played a critical role in establishing and maintaining racial and economic subordination."[52] In chapter 2 I take up aspects of that interaction in the conceptions of property and issues of resistance to and gender in ownership. I look not only at Tomey's Turl's relation to property and its implication in one of *Go Down, Moses*'s best-known chapters, "The Bear," but also at the excesses of masters and their legal claims of absolute control over human property informing U.S. legal culture throughout the nineteenth century. In particular, I juxtapose the legal discourse that attempted to reduce blacks to creatures without will with the recorded acts of resistance and agency by enslaved people, especially women who responded to bodily dominance and physical assault. With this lens, I turn to gender issues involved in the sexual commodification of female slaves and to the abuses of rape and incest as extensions of the denial of will and personhood in making blacks the object of property and extensions of the master's will.

In writing *Go Down, Moses* Faulkner explored the explosive issues surrounding slavery as ownership of people and the literal domination of people as property. His interest is specifically with the southern social order that developed out of a slave economy. Faulkner chose the interfamilial black-white relationships existing over a spectrum of time, from the pre–Civil War period to the World War II era, extending through three generations of whites and four of blacks, as a way of concretizing that social order. Central to those relationships is the concept of property as it relates to human rights and to the rights of the individual. At the end of the 1930s and into the early 1940s, rights was a major discourse in the American South, in the United States, and in Europe as well. With the New Deal as a remedy to the Depression and its revival of the governmental right to property by eminent domain, property rights and powerlessness became central issues in the nation, particularly in the South. At the same time, with the rise of Hitler and Nazism in Germany, abuses of rights set the stage for more dramatic confrontations with America's racial apartheid, which legally deprived blacks of civil rights and legal personhood.

Mississippi, with its inflexible, closed society and vigorous enforcement of Jim Crow, came notoriously to represent the oppression of blacks and the deprivation or denial of the right of citizenship to blacks. As Bertram Wilbur Doyle stated in 1937: "Tradition . . . assigns the Negro his place in the South, law defines it, sentiment supports it, custom and habit continue it, and prejudice maintains it in those instances where it seems to be breaking down." [53] Doyle's conclusion, based on his observation of social ritual in the South, privileges law in the ongoing oppression and subordination of blacks. Mississippi, however, presented an even more rigid manifestation of legalized oppression and intolerance. In a 1939 study of Indianola, Mississippi (called "Cottonville"), Hortense Powdermaker observed that whites believed that blacks were "innately inferior" and "by nature" fit only for servile employment; correspondingly, blacks understood that all aspects of their lives were affected by "the racial situation and the system with which it is interlocked," so that each black person within the community believed "that he must watch his behavior in the company of whites, lest he give offense and suffer for it." [54] Powdermaker concluded that law and custom in Mississippi confirmed the subservient place of blacks, that a system of swift punishment for real and imagined grievances, either under the legal system or according to the racial codes, controlled the lives of blacks and the thinking of whites. Those conditions in the mid-twentieth century had their foundational basis in the legal, economic, and social structures engendered out of the emergence of chattel slavery in Mississippi and the concomitant efforts to define blacks as slaves.

As early as June 1818, in *Harry and Others v Decker and Hopkins* (concerning a petition for freedom), the Supreme Court of Mississippi ruled that "slavery is condemned by reason and the laws of nature." [55] By 1821, however, the court had accepted the legality of slavery in Mississippi, while maintaining that slaves were "reasonable and accountable beings." [56] The ongoing attempts to codify the position of slaves within a democratic society resulted in often contradictory legal decisions. The law, as Margaret Burnham points out, tried "to accommodate slavery's first principle—humankind as property—even while it sought to set in legal stone bourgeois republican notions of equality and human rights.

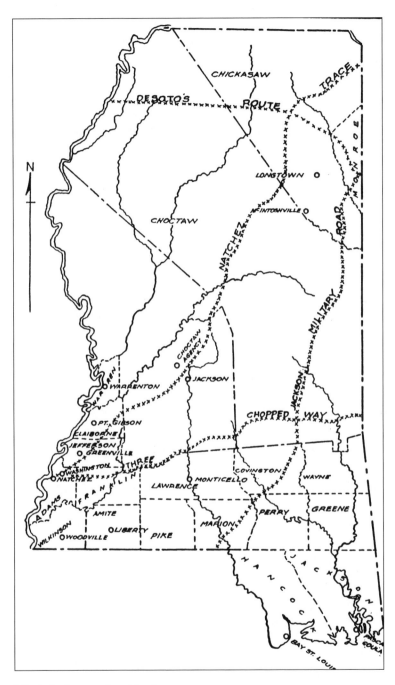

Mississippi at statehood in 1817.

What was required was a system of laws flexible enough to hold the slave to the common code of conduct in certain circumstances while exempting him in others, a system which respected the slaveholding rights to rule their property without altogether yielding the states' right to govern aspects of Black-white slave-master relations."[57] Not surprisingly, the dual response to enslaved people engendered contradictory legal rulings.

The court's decision in *State v Jones*, the case of a white man accused of murdering a slave, not only condemned the murderer to death by hanging on 27 July 1821 but also established the legal rights of the slave in Mississippi. Justice Joshua G. Clark, the first chancellor of the state, wrote the decision:

> Has the slave no rights, because he is deprived of his freedom? He is still a human being, and possesses all those rights, of which he is not deprived by the positive provisions of law, but in vain shall we look for any law passed by the enlightened and philanthropic legislature of this state, giving even to the master, much less to a stranger, power over the life of a slave. Such a statute would be worthy of the age of Draco and Caligula, and would be condemned by the unanimous voice of the people of this state, where, even cruelty to slaves . . . meets with universal reprobation.[58]

The slave, then, a "reasonable and accountable being," was deprived of his freedom, but allowed "all those rights of which he is not deprived by the positive provision of law." Judge Clark's ruling rejected the claim made by the defense that slaves were outside common law, the argument made by Judge John Hall in *State v Boon*, an 1801 North Carolina case. Clark concluded that Hall's opinion had been based on "erroneous principles" of Roman law which denied the slave any rights under the law. Unfortunately, under the "positive provision of law" and despite Judge Clark's attempt to define some measure of rights for those enslaved, slaves were increasingly denied rights, because enslavement by its very nature forced them into a subcategory of human beings and made them vulnerable to legal encroachments on their rights.

The results of such complicated and contradictory thinking about slaves are apparent in the repeated efforts to clarify the person-property split in reference to enslaved people. The most comprehensive of Mississippi's laws pertaining to slaves and slavery, as well as to free blacks, is the compilation of 1857, the last of the antebellum slave codes, which

included ninety-eight subdivisions, all based on the bifurcated premise that "slaves had a dual status as both property and persons in Mississippi, so that while it was the slave-person who was tried before the
court, it was the slave-property that was taken by the state when a capital
verdict was rendered."[59] Slaves were in the language of the Mississippi
Supreme Court in 1859, "artificial persons" who were not subject to common law, which applied to "natural persons" or citizens: "Experience has
proved . . . that masters and slaves cannot be governed by the same laws.
So different in position, in rights, in duties, they cannot be the subjects
of a common system of laws."[60] This distinction between "artificial" and
"natural" persons produced a legal climate in Mississippi for continuing the subhuman and subservient categorization of blacks as property
even as the political climate in the larger nation was beginning to question such categorizations. These legal maneuvers in the 1859 codes were
emboldened by the 1857 *Dred Scott* decision, which codified black inferiority whether slave or free: "The stigma of the deepest degradation was
fixed upon the whole race."[61] That rhetoric and the underlying narrative
supported the legal story that justified enslavement. Slavery then was declared the natural place for blacks separated from whites by "indelible
marks" of inferiority.

By 1860, the year of Lincoln's election and one year after John Brown's
raid on Harper's Ferry, laws controlling slaves in Mississippi included
prohibitions against marriages, contact with free blacks, defense or testimony against whites, learning to read or write, and leaving a plantation
without a pass.[62] These were added to numerous existing communally
sanctioned customs as well as state and local laws, such as the one that
forbade slaves to be freed by the owners' will.[63] While chattel slavery
in Mississippi neither existed technically after the 1 January 1863 Emancipation Proclamation nor existed legally after the Thirteenth Amendment to the Constitution, legislative attempts to deny blacks their freedom continued. The Black Code of 1865, for example, was as intent on
denying rights as earlier slave codes of 1857 had been.[64] The 1865 codes
in Mississippi did grant some rights to blacks, such as the right to sue or
be sued, to testify in state courts, to marry legally, and to own personal
property.[65] Nonetheless, these codes also attempted to restrict the lib-
erties of freed blacks and to deny them justice under the existing legal
system. For example, young black children were subject to "binding out"
as unpaid apprentices, with their former masters being given priority in

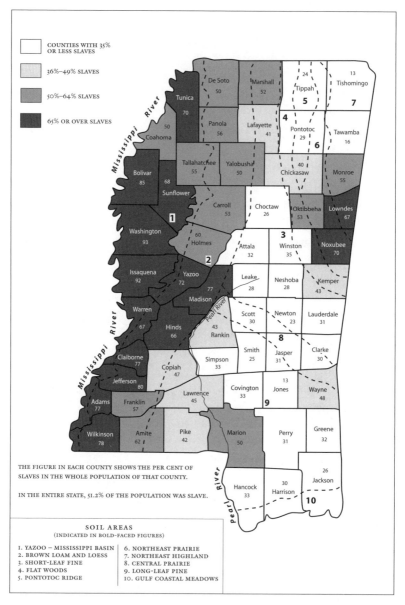

Percentage of slaves by county in Mississippi in 1850. From Charles Sackett Sydnor, *Slavery in Mississippi* (1933).

choosing them for service. Furthermore, any black without a job or home by 1 January 1866 was fined as a vagrant, but the fine could be paid by hiring out, again with the former master receiving preference.[66] In addition, blacks could not bear arms or own guns, could not rent farm land, and could not perform certain forms of work without a license.[67] Even though the vast majority of Mississippi's Black Code was repealed during Reconstruction in 1870, the lasting result was that blacks were kept in a position of inferiority—socially, economically, and legally as well.[68]

Despite Mississippi's ratification of the Fourteenth and Fifteenth Amendments to the U. S. Constitution in 1870, oppressive conditions continued and essentially prepared for a system of "Jim Crow" laws following the Mississippi Constitution of 1890.[69] These laws defined the rights of blacks as different from those of whites, instituting racial codes that continued to stamp blacks as inferior and justified their exclusion from full access to justice and equality. Specifically, after the 1883 United States Supreme Court ruling in *United States v Stanley* that the Civil Rights Act of 1875 was unconstitutional, recreational, educational and public facilities became increasingly segregated by race between the late 1880s and the turn of the century.[70] In 1890 the twenty-fifth anniversary of Appomattox, when 744,749 Mississippians were black and 544,851 were white, the state enacted the 1890 Constitution, which stated in article III, section 5: "All political power is vested in, and derived from, the people; all government of right originates with the people, is founded upon their will only, and is instituted solely for the good of the whole."[71] Nevertheless, the term *people* meant "white" people. Just as in the pre-Emancipation era, blacks were once again relegated to an "artificial" status separate from "people."

The 1890 Constitution's article XII, "Franchise," virtually dismissed blacks from any consideration in "the good of the whole." Known as the "Mississippi Plan," the article introduced prerequisites for voting: proof of having paid taxes for the two-year period preceding an election; residency requirements for the state and district; a uniform poll tax of two dollars; and proof of never having been convicted of certain crimes (e.g., bigamy, perjury, theft, and burglary).[72] Most damaging to blacks because of its pernicious and arbitrary application was the "understanding clause," which required the reading and interpreting of any designated section of the 1890 Constitution.[73] Moreover, section 245 of article XII provided: "Electors in municipal elections shall possess all the qualifications herein prescribed, and such additional qualifications as may be provided by law."[74] This provision opened the way for further local restrictions against prospective black voters.

Upheld by the Mississippi Supreme Court in *Sproule v Fredericks* (1892) and by the United States Supreme Court in *Williams v Mississippi* (1898), two years after the court made the "separate but equal" ruling in *Plessy v Ferguson* (1896), the "Mississippi Plan" not only avoided the Fifteenth Amendment but also effectively disenfranchised blacks and reestablished white supremacy, just as the *Forest Register,* a Mississippi newspaper, had proclaimed in its masthead for years: "A white man in a white man's place. A black man in a black man's place. Each according to the 'eternal fitness' of things."[75] Although Justice John Marshall Harlan had dissented from the Supreme Court's *Plessy v Ferguson* finding by stating, "Our Constitution is colorblind. . . . The arbitrary separation of citizens on the basis of race is a badge of servitude wholly inconsistent with civil freedom and the equality before the law established by the Constitution," his position had little impact in Mississippi or elsewhere in the United States.[76] From the 1890s through the early decades of the twentieth century which Faulkner depicts in *Go Down, Moses,* blacks in the state were legally controlled by a caste position rather than by slavery, and despite the Fourteenth or Fifteenth Amendment, they existed in racial degradation and economic deprivation. (The Mississippi Plan was not amended until 1972 and not repealed until 1975.)

The 1890 Constitution, however, was not the only way blacks were rendered unequal under Mississippi law. In *Dark Journey: Black Mississippians in the Age of Jim Crow,* Neil McMillen found that what was termed "negro law" continued tenets of the antebellum slave code and determined how blacks would be treated under the law. His informant, attorney Sidney Fant Davis, described this informal branch of Mississippi law as "unwritten, learned only through experience and observation, and fully understood . . . by the native born."[77] This inferior positioning of blacks in Mississippi pervades Faulkner's text and produces the disproportionate power and authority of white elites such as his McCaslin family.

Mississippi, in its very specificity, followed the general course of the larger American society in its legal treatment of blacks. In revisiting some twenty years after its initial publication her formulation of black people serving as "the mudsills" of an American white social majority determined to protect by law and the Constitution its "superior economic, political, social, and military power" in *Black Resistance/White Law: A History of Constitutional Racism in America* (1971) Mary Frances Berry stated, "The legal system supports our capitalistic economic system. Because capitalism requires inequality, the only real question is who will be the repositories of the inequality. To date, black people have disproportionally been those repositories."[78] Black people in the South, and in Mississippi in particular, experienced a disproportionate amount of inequitable treatment at the hand of "the law" during the one hundred years following Emancipation.

The legal constructions and contradictions related to black people in Mississippi as persons and property were simultaneously the product of a system of law and the manipulations of a social order. In *Go Down, Moses*, Faulkner examines the strong belief in the right to property as a basic right and constructs his characters, both black and white, around the right to property and the use or abuses of property within a patriarchal society and family and within a slaveholding economy. Because of the very nature of Faulkner's discourse on property, a moral core appears resident within the text in the characters' attitudes toward property and toward the power it signifies. The ideological context pervading Faulkner's novel stems mainly from the existence of chattel slavery (and its legacies) as an alternative to free labor in Mississippi rather than from philosophical treatises on property. It also acknowledges the Chickasaws' vexed relation to land and to slaves in Mississippi. In October 1832 the Chickasaws agreed to cede to the United States government all the land they owned on the east side of the Mississippi River. This treaty, expanding an 1830 treaty that also delimited the Chickasaws' rights to their ancestral lands in Mississippi, provided that "each single tribal member be given an allotment of 640 acres, while families of five members or less would receive 1,280 acres, those of six to ten members would have 1,920 acres, while larger families would be granted 2,680 acres. The owning of one to ten slaves would net a family an additional 320 acres."[79] The involvement of the Chickasaws with slavery, like other Native Americans in the lower South region, complicated Faulkner's conception of ownership and property.

Faulkner employs property and the rights that arise from ownership of private property, such as bequests and inheritance, not only to structure and to underscore black-white relationships and to raise fundamen-

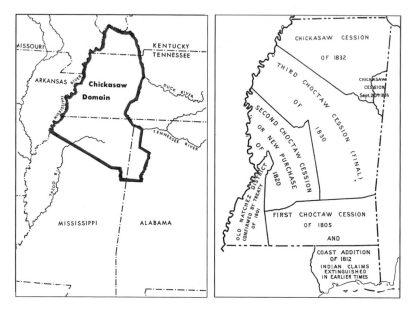

Chickasaw lands ranging from what would later be Kentucky, into Tennessee, Mississippi, and Alabama.

Chickasaw and Choctaw cessions of land in Mississippi. From Charles S. Sydnor and Claude Bennett, *Mississippi History* (1930).

tal questions about the value of the human being, but also to interrogate the law as a field of inquiry and a relation of power.[80] He frames his questions—what does it mean to be a legal subject? what are the responsibilities as well as the rights of the human being?—from the perspective of the white southerner in a specified environment, who possesses, owns, inherits, and holds "property" (and concomitantly power), and whose right to dispose of property as he chooses is protected by law.[81] His questions and his storytelling are gendered male and raced white. Indeed, the construction of the narrative around issues of property and succession almost immediately supplies a masculine gender signature because of the legal and societal displacement of women from centrality to these issues in the nineteenth and early twentieth centuries in Mississippi.

Race, seemingly constructed in the text as black, white, and native, is another matter. In all of its formations and discourses (racial enslavement, racial subordination, racial supremacy, racial entitlements, etc.), race permeates and structures *Go Down, Moses*, particularly around issues of law. At the same time, the perspective dominating the text is natu-

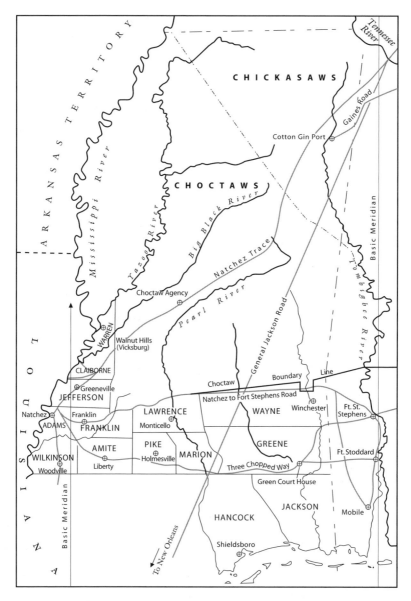

An 1819 map of Mississippi showing the roads and the Chickasaw and Choctaw lands before cessions. From *Mississippi Official and Statical Register* (1908).

ralized as a white racial one. This naturalizing of a white perspective and consciousness is perhaps in keeping with Stephen Ross's explanation of consciousness in *Go Down, Moses* as "the fixed ground from which the reader's experience derives," and not merely "consciousness" in an abstract form, but specifically grounded in Isaac McCaslin's perspective.[82] Ross states: "Ike's consciousness is coextensive with the text's discourse, beginning and ending not with his physical birth or death but with the text itself; Ike lives everywhere within the discourse."[83] A point not to be overlooked in this situating of Ike, however, is that the figure whose bodily existence engenders the discourse and resides within Ike's consciousness is Tomey's Turl. The figure of Tomey's Turl presides over Ike's development, over his construction of his grandfather and his paternal heritage, over his relation to land, property, and succession, and over sexuality and progeny.

According to discursive logic in *Go Down, Moses*, legal, racial, and moral codes are all manifestations of or responses to "property" and its attendant "rights." These codes complicate the social and familial relations within the text, so that they directly affect Tomey's Turl, his mother and grandmother, his children and their progeny, just as much as they do the white McCaslins and Edmondses, who "own" not merely land but people, and people who exist in a familial relation to them. Legal codes, those practices of both custom and statute that constitute the authorities, interact with racial codes, those beliefs and attitudes that regulate interpersonal conduct between whites and blacks, in defining the place of individuals within the society depicted in the novel. Moral codes, those virtues, values, and ideals, often abstract and intuitive, operate in *Go Down, Moses* on a different, often sublimated, level of awareness and authority with regard to infusing human life with meaning. Moral codes intersect with legal and racial codes to define humanity in individual and societal terms. At the point of convergence, the three codes bring together both past and present experience—words, thoughts, and deeds—to create the ideological core informing the text and contributing to its complexity. However, because all three codes also exist in diffusion throughout the text, they function to establish individual priorities within social mandates that inform separate structures and patterns of meaning as well. Legal, racial, and moral codes, then, function separately to demark interpretive strategies, but together they configure a positive capacity within the text to determine and modify thought as well as behavior, and thereby, potentially, to bring about social change, and perhaps justice. Nevertheless, only individual, personal change occurs within *Go Down, Moses*, because the dynamic realignment of values, attitudes, practices, and beliefs necessary for reformation in a static society takes place only as potential within a few isolated experiences, and justice remains elusive.

In this reading of Tomey's Terrel as dynamic, disruptive, and as a central creative force, the static center of the text nonetheless contains Lucius Quintus Carothers McCaslin (old Carothers), who, similar to Thomas Sutpen in *Absalom! Absalom!*, creates a plantation and progeny in the narrative past and dominates the ideological discourses on ownership and property in the narrative present though he has been dead for nearly one hundred years. His name is borrowed from Lucius Quintus Cincinnatus Lamar, the Mississippi lawyer, politician, and justice of the United States Supreme Court, who began his career in 1849 after moving to Faulkner's hometown, Oxford, and who later in his career wrote the Mississippi Act of Secession. This naming may be read as a connection between the discourses of ownership/property and law in the text. Much like Justice Lamar, the fictional L. Q. C. achieves influence and power, but his is primarily over his descendants, two of whom provide the dual lens through which he assumes substance and meaning. The two are his grandsons, the white Isaac McCaslin and the black Lucas Beauchamp. Both are linked by their connection to Tomey's Terrel, the representation of the abuse and the endurance of the plantation system: Lucas is Terrel's son and Isaac is the son of Theophilus McCaslin, one of Terrel's twin half-brothers with whom he lived. Although both Isaac and Lucas are entitled to a bequest from their grandfather on their twenty-first birthday, Ike renounces his patrimony, the McCaslin plantation, whereas Lucas asks for his inheritance, a thousand dollars—money his father refused to accept from old Carothers's will. Both respond to a social script with a scene of shame as the main site of familial and social history. Their actions reflect their different attitudes toward Carothers, as well as their different degrees of removal from the actual experience of Carothers and his relationship to Tomey's Terrel, which is the signal scene of shame in the text.

In chapter 3, I identify the spatial configurations initially demarcated by Terrel in his games of running and seeking and later taken up by his son Lucas (whose survival requires the repression and refusal of the site of memory that involves the shame of his father's birth and enslavement) and his nephew Isaac (who increasingly lives within the site of memory of Terrel and out of shame attempts to act in Terrel's place). I include as well the corresponding implications of these interlocking spaces and the multivalent usages of will as both a legal term related to bequests and a human force linked to power.

In chapter 4, I interrogate the complicated relationship between race and property in *Go Down, Moses* and between slavery and its legacies of valorized ownership and white masculine identity formation for Faulkner in the 1930s and 1940s. A discourse on whiteness as privilege and power is central to reading property claims in *Go Down, Moses* and to recognizing how gender, specifically masculinity, is marked and consolidated out of race and property relations.

"How do people *change* norms to accommodate different property arrangements that might enhance their well-being?" Carol A. Rose asks in *Property and Persuasion*. Her response goes directly to a relevant notion of storytelling's significance: "Here is where narrative matters: stories, allegories, and metaphors can change minds. Through narratives, or so it is said, people can create a kind of narrative community in which the storyteller can suggest the possibility that things could be different and perhaps better (or, alternatively, worse)."[84] In chapter 5, I examine the dual resolution of Tomey's Terrel's story in new configurations of containment (a narrative of black criminality produced by the incarceration and death of Terrel's great-grandson and a narrative of intrafamilial miscegenation marked by the apparition and maternity of his great-granddaughter). I reflect on Faulkner's usages of those narrative resolutions for extratextual purposes, as well as my own version of how rethinking Terrel's story as producing the race-inflected, powerful center of *Go Down, Moses* becomes compensation for readings of Faulkner, and this text in particular, that elide race. This subversive strategy results in a fresh narrative of compensatory action within the processes of both storytelling and analysis. Todorov's view of narrative "as the chronological and sometimes causal linkage of discontinuous units" grounds a reflexive consideration of both the reading of Faulkner's narratives by black scholars invested in studies of race and the changes between the 1970s and the end of the twentieth century that have occurred in discourses on race as a category of analysis.[85] In utilizing Todorov's conception of narrative, I think through the residue of property in persons and proprietary rights narratives within contemporary legal discourses, such as civil rights and reparations.

But to return to the subject of narrative in connection with Rose's question regarding how people change norms, one answer for Tomey's Terrel surely lies in his game playing, his active disruption of the status quo on not one but two plantations, and his alliance across race, gender, and time lines to make his story audible. For his creator, Faulkner, another answer may be apparent in the articulation of a miscegenated story as a compensation for property and the shame originating in its human abuses. For Terrel's nephew Isaac McCaslin, who inherits his story but has the freedom to make it heard, to be fully effective in his moral stance against the legal and racial codes enslaving whites as well as blacks, he must, like Moses in the spiritual, act and lead other whites to follow a higher authority in defiance of unjust laws of ownership and property. To renounce Pharaoh's authority but to leave the Israelites in bondage is not enough. For Ike and for his generation, though they perform rituals of brotherhood and equality in the game of hunting, there is no ameliorating vision accompanied by action to untangle the knotty complexities of property and its problematical impact on white or black individuals. For Ike's kinsman Terrel, whose origin he deciphers and whose fate is inextricably connected to his own, there is no fully articulated version in the text of how his very existence undermines the rigid separation of races and the accepted belief in a racial hierarchy. That is the work of the following chapters.

CHAPTER 1 | The Game of Challenge

Deregulating Race

Tomey's Turl's position in *Go Down, Moses* as represented contest and contested site is crucial to reading the narrative richness as well as the interconnected tropes of games, sport, property, and law. As one of the most self-conscious game players in the text, Tomey's Turl bears closer analysis, even though his position in relation to any of the games is almost undetectable. "A game is a description of strategic interaction that includes the constraints on the actions that the players *can* take and the players' interests, but does not specify the actions that the players *do* take."[1] Locating Turl's subjectivity within the actual and symbolic representations of games allows for a more nuanced access to characterization and to theme within a text so vexed by buffoonery and slapstick humor in its initial chapters that the pre-Emancipation South and enslaved people come across as poorly narrated, offensive jokes.

The narrative strategy and the kinship connections are complex and masked within humor in "Was," the opening chapter of *Go Down, Moses*. Begun as a third-person narrative centered on an old man born in 1867 — "Isaac McCaslin, 'Uncle Ike,' past seventy and nearer eighty than he ever corroborated any more" — "Was" quickly shifts to a story Isaac remembers.[2] He narrates the story told to him many years before by his cousin, McCaslin "Cass" Edmonds. Sixteen years older than Ike, Cass had witnessed as a boy the events in 1859 that led not only to the marriage of Ike's parents, Theophilus "Buck" McCaslin and Sophonsiba

"Sibbey" Beauchamp, but also to the marriage of the enslaved couple, Terrel ("Tomey's Turl"), owned by Buck McCaslin and his twin brother Amodeus ("Buddy"), and Tennie, owned by Sophonsiba and her brother, Hubert. The interconnected narrative of memory, hearing, history, and telling functions both as an origins myth for Ike and as a familial history that introduces Tomey's Turl and his relationship to the McCaslin-Edmonds family. Tomey's Turl is the half-brother to the McCaslin twins, the son of their father, Carothers McCaslin, the founder of the Mississippi McCaslin family. The narrative embodiment of Tomey's Turl as a substantive figure is twofold: within the kinship bonds of the white family that owns him; and within Ike's understanding of his own social history.[3]

In "Was" Tomey's Turl is initially constructed in the ambiguity of relational identity and in the context of an unclarified species of runaway: " 'Damn the fox,' Uncle Buck said. 'Tomey's Turl has broke out again' " (5). However, Tomey's Turl is also constituted as a game player who uses games as a site of resistance to power and, importantly, as a means of deregulating claims of ownership. The dialectic between his social condition (as a slave who has run) and his individual autonomy (as the instigator of a game in which he is a major and decisive player) produces his identity. That identity is thus based on the political economy of slavery and the market value of slaves. He is represented as a rational decision-maker who pursues a defined objective and who strategizes on the basis of his knowledge of how the other players will behave. In Cass's recollection, Turl "went there every time he could slip off, which was about twice a year. He was heading for Mr Hubert Beauchamp's place. . . . Tomey's Turl would go there to hang around Mr Hubert's girl, Tennie, until sombody came and got him" (5). Tomey's Turl is represented in motion, in action, and thus as an agent, even though his agency is constrained by two sets of circumstances: the racist ideology informing the conceptions of "nigger" and enslaved property; and the game strategy of silence that disallows his voicing either the motive or desire in his behavior.

Beginning with Tomey's Turl's running, *Go Down, Moses* deploys games (fox-hunting with dogs, gambling with cards and dice, racing) as constructions both of chance and of strategy that represent the arbitrariness and the boundedness of forms of identity and of economic and social interaction as these forms intersect with the regularity, protection, and compensation of law. "Social interaction appears to reproduce unceasingly an interplay of differing preferences within which individuals run the risk of upsetting society by following their egotistical impulses. Rational understanding of this conflict of interest leads to what game theory terms a game of strategy."[4] Games of strategy are different from games of skill and chance, because they require the player to assume a role, which he conceives and acts out. The assumption of the role of player within the game becomes a form of social empowerment, even though it may conflict with accepted social beliefs or codes. Laws are, like games, manifestations of social practices. "Law represents both a discourse and a process of power. Norms created by and enshrined in law are manifestations of power relations. These norms are coercively applied and justified in part by the perception that they are 'neutral' and 'objective.'"[5]

The legal codes constricting Tomey's Turl to a nonrelational positionality in regard to the McCaslin twins, Theophilus and Amodeus, are those that define a slave as property and as labor, not as human or as brother. Slave law rests on the motivating principle of "undifferentiated communalism," which reduces all slaves to labor under the total social control of masters who own labor.[6] This principle of slave law is not merely a matter of economic exploitation of labor; instead it is an ultimate formulation of dehumanization, of negating the human being and treating that negated "thing" as an abstraction termed "labor." That Tomey's Turl is constructed visually as "that damn white half-McCaslin" (6), positions him on the boundary of race and slave law. While it is possible to read Turl from the social perspective and expressive culture of the white McCaslins and Beauchamps as a representation of disorder and unreason, as Cass Edmonds suggests in his telling of the events to his cousin Ike, Tomey's Turl may also be read as a racialized person who deregulates the power of law and paternity over his movement and his expression. His very existence constitutes a challenge to the claims of integrity in the slaveholding society, and his conscious violation of the rules and controls instituted to maintain the rigid social order is more than insubordination or withholding of labor. It is resistance not only threatening insurrection but also what Ira Berlin terms "direct assault on order itself."[7]

Because the laws of society are suspended in play, sport, and games, and replaced by a new order of rules and regulations, games provide freedom from the normal social order and its dehumanizing boundaries in *Go Down, Moses*. In this context Tomey's Turl attains freedom within the "free space" games represent. Despite the imposition of another formulaic set of boundaries within the duration of a game, games are attractive precisely because of their freedom from the restrictions of society and from the power hierarchy that controls racial interaction. Games clear a neutral space for the reformation of the possibilities of interaction based on the terms and conditions of the game. The game allows for the creation of order within play. Just as Christian Messenger has suggested, "Faulkner did not see play standing outside ordinary or real life; he saw it rising organically from the conditions of everyday life" with the resultant shifts in the very nature of play in Faulkner's texts—"a bursting of restrictive forms in ritual."[8] In Tomey's Turl's case the sadly ordinary condition of enslavement gives rise to his free play in games. He resists confinement within the ideologies of race by reordering his world and reconstituting himself as empowered to act and to be a subject. He intervenes in the legal practice of dehumanization, destabilizes the impact of law, and reclassifies himself against the hegemonic ideology and structure of a slave culture.

Within his game of "runaway," Tomey's Turl assumes subjectivity.[9] He is active, he is intentional, and he is inquiring. He can negotiate the alternative strategizing of his would-be captors, Buck McCaslin and his nephew Cass Edmonds, who are also his opponent game players and convinced that he is beatable in the race to the Beauchamp place, because "nobody had ever known Tomey's Turl to go faster than his natural walk, even riding a mule" (8). No matter his speed, Turl commits the offense that according to plantation codes was the most punishable, because "the runaway slave epitomized alienation from bondage."[10] That alienation then disrupts the social order and eclipses the slave owner's authority. The "comic and romanticized gamesmanship" that Michael Oriard links specifically to Buck and Buddy is not merely their "comic sportiveness culminating in the brilliantly tortured prose of 'The Bear,'" it is also the vehicle for what is invisible to Oriard: the agency of the enslaved Tomey's Turl.[11]

The game Tomey's Turl initiates is variously labeled a run (race), a hunt, a chase, a contest, and a courtship. It can also be defined, however, as a game of challenge and a stratagem for exercising will. It functions within the formal characteristics of play as "a free activity standing quite consciously outside 'ordinary' life" and "proceed[ing] within its own proper boundaries of time and space according to fixed rules and in an orderly manner." [12] As a "stepping out of 'real' life into a temporary sphere of activity with a disposition of its own," Tomey's Turl's game "is 'played out' within certain limits of time and place" and "contains its own course and meaning." [13] In general, his moves challenge the power and authority of whites and subvert their expectations of superiority. In particular, his moves challenge one key aspect of his containment in slavery: his right to sexual expression, which has been excluded from the eccentric world of the McCaslin place. As such, Tomey's Turl's challenge is to the right of his McCaslin owners to restrict his will to court Tennie, deny his desire for a wife, or essentially to enforce his conformity to their refusal of sexuality.

Read from the perspective of Tomey's Turl as a race for full expression of a mature, sexual self within society, the game of runaway is a periodic reminder (played out twice a year) that despite attempts to reduce slaves to children without will, enslavement did not necessarily produce simplistic objects of property. Tomey's Turl's game of challenge, then, takes on the cultural logic and hegemony based on the legal conception of "black antiwill" that would determine his total subjugation in a social, economic, and political order. Master-slave relations, so often based on "a vision of blacks as simple-minded, strong-bodied economic 'actants,' " function unlike market theory which "always takes attention away from the full range of human potential in its pursuit of a divinely willed, rationally inspired, invisibly handed economic actor." [14] In the game of runaway Tomey's Turl becomes a complex thinker, a strategist with a clear objective, and his "athletic energy" to execute his game marks him as physically and sexually mature. [15] By means of his creation and play of the game, Turl defines a black masculinity within a space that otherwise, given the cultural conditions of enslavement, would deny not only his manhood but also his very personhood.

Unlike Buck and, in particular, Buddy, Tomey's Turl is not content to remain in an unattached social condition. He desires and wills. In desiring a mate and in specifying the mate he desires, he separates himself from the undifferentiated middle-aged "boys" at the McCaslin place. Buck and Buddy are, in Daniel Hoffman's view, "superannuated boys," who "turn all of life into games." [16] Buck and Buddy are constructed within the social roles designated as masculine and feminine, but they play off the expectations for gender formation within their society. Buck drinks, wears a tie, farms the land, and socializes outside the confines of his property; Buddy cooks, does not drink, and remains at home in an unconventional domestic space, even though he is the expert poker player. Buck resists courting Sophonsiba Beauchamp because the twins exist within a space where "ladies were so damn seldom thank God that a man could ride for days in a straight line without having to dodge a single one" (*Go Down, Moses*, 7), and within that space they can behave without acknowledging their sexuality or the misogyny implicated in their descriptions of women.

Aversion and avoidance, Buck and Buddy's responses to sexuality, to masculinity, and to women, may also be read as a rebellion against their father, old Carothers, and his aggressive heterosexuality, particularly in his old age. The twins clearly reject completing and living in a monument to their father and his way of life: "as soon as their father was buried [the two brothers] moved out of the tremendously-conceived, the almost barn-like edifice which he had not even completed, into a one-room log cabin which the two of them built themselves and added other rooms to while they lived in it, refusing to allow any slave to touch any timber of it other than the actual raising into place the logs which two men alone could not handle, and domiciled all the slaves in the big house" (250–51). In reconfiguring the space in which they would reside and removing it from the model of the "big house" begun by their father, they resist his influence and vitiate his legacy. They bury the father, but rather than replacing him and his authority in a Freudian move, they dismantle and deny his way of life; however, like model oedipal sons, they also render themselves "dead" to the society they inhabit. In refusing slave labor on their cabin, they bypass direct involvement in the expected, "beneficial" by-products of forced slave labor. They engage in various "mechanisms of separation" to deflect their knowledge of what James Snead terms the "false signification of human beings as commodities."[17]

Although Buck and Buddy do not free their slaves, they reject the conventional nineteenth-century relationship of containment and virtual imprisonment for slaves on the plantation:

> each sundown the brother who superintended the farming would parade the negroes as a first sergeant dismisses a company, and herd them willynilly, man woman and child, without question protest or recourse, into the tremendous abortive edifice scarcely yet out of

embryo, as if even old Carothers McCaslin had paused aghast at the concrete indication of his own vanity's boundless conceiving: he would call his mental roll and herd them in and with a hand-wrought nail as long as a flenching-knife and suspended from a short deer-hide thong attached to the door-jamb for that purpose, he would nail the door of that house which lacked half its windows and had no hinged back door at all, so that presently and for fifty years afterward, when the boy himself was [too] big to hear and remember it, there was in the land a sort of folk-tale: of the countryside all night long full of skulking McCaslin slaves dodging the moonlit roads and the Patrol-riders to visit other plantations, and of the unspoken gentlemen's agreement between the two white men and the two dozen black ones that, after the white man had counted them and driven the home-made nail into the front door at sundown, neither of the white men would go around behind the house and look at the back door, provided that all the negroes were behind the front one when the brother who drove it drew out the nail again at daybreak (251)

Buck and Buddy thus allow the McCaslin slaves to escape, at least temporarily at night, the boundaries delimiting their freedom of movement, and the twins themselves escape from the expected patterns of bonds and control initiated by their father.

Their actions constitute both a game and a ritual in which they deny the necessity of imprisoning blacks and circumvent the expected responsibility of slaveholders to contain slaves. Their repeated nightly activity approaches ritual because they invest that activity and the corresponding behavior of the slaves with symbolic meaning, and by means of that ritual they remove themselves by small degrees from the corruption of both the slave system and their degenerate father. In a space functioning between adult seriousness and child play, the twins have created a game in which they can make fun of the slave system of containment and mock their own roles as slave owners. In deconstructing games, however, it becomes apparent that games also provide a structure within which risk and gains can be calculated. Read from this perspective, Buck and Buddy's treatment of their slaves is calculated to maximize acquiescence to the condition of enslavement and to minimize the risk of those slaves attempting a permanent escape. From the perspective of those enslaved on the McCaslin place, the game of acquiescence to locked and unlocked doors, to morning curfews and night rambles, iterates their hand in negotiating some measure of their existence and gaining a concession for their cooperation. That they can be partners in "the unspoken gentlemen's agreement" places them in a contractual arrangement that would ordinarily be outside their legally enforceable capacity as slaves and property. Their limited and incomplete freedom of movement nonetheless enables them to function, and to be seen to function, as agents troubling the white slaveholding community's established rules of conduct and expectations for slaves.

While the McCaslins' practice is presented humorously in seeming innocence, the letting loose of slaves, according to nineteenth-century accounts, provoked trouble in the neighborhood by causing unrest among those enslaved on other plantations. One planter, exasperated by the antics of a neighbor's slaves and the disturbances they caused on his place and aware that a slave could be put to death for striking a white man, threatened to "swear that the negroes Struck him," although they had not, if their owner did not better control their behavior.[18] The McCaslin twins, in facilitating a form of slave unrest within their larger slaveholding community, remove themselves from active participation in the vigorous containment of slaves and ferment individualism and independence in the practice of slave management.

Perhaps a more significant marker of why Buck and Buddy attempt to distance themselves from the behavioral codes of their father may be interpolated from the same pages of the commissary ledgers that Ike uses to discern old Carothers McCaslin's incestuous sexual domination of his enslaved daughter Tomasina and his fathering of her son, Turl. Ike, the son of Buck and Sophonsiba Beauchamp McCaslin and the grandson of old Carothers, is sole heir to the plantation because his father's twin, Buddy, never married and died childless. Fascinated by the ledgers as representative of his own heritage and inheritance, Ike first reads the record books during the winter of 1883–1884, when he is still a boy of sixteen. The pages combine the economics of ownership and the economics of sexuality in a narrative of the cost and price of enslavement, and they constitute a recognition on the part of the twins of their father's "own vanity's boundless conceiving" (251). In Buck McCaslin's hand is the entry "*Eunice Bought by Father in New Orleans 1807 $650. dolars. Marrid to Thucydus 1809 Drownd in Crick Cristmas Day 1832*" (255). Then the ledgers contain an exchange initiated by Buddy about Buck's entry:

"June 21th 1833 Drownd herself. . . . 23 Jun 1833 Who in hell ever heard of a niger drownding him self. . . . Aug 13ᵗʰ 1833 Drownd herself" (256). Surely the twins have questions about Eunice's death, just as Ike, Buck's son, would have later when he contemplated their entries.

> he leaned above the yellowed page and thought not Why drowned herself, but thinking what he believed his father had thought when he found his brother's first comment: Why did Uncle Buddy think she had drowned herself? finding, beginning to find on the next succeeding page what he knew he would find, only this was still not it because he already knew this:
>
> > *Tomasina called Tomy Daughter of Thucydus @ Eunice*
> > *Born 1810 dide in Child bed June 1833 and Burd. Yr stars fell*
>
> nor the next:
>
> > *Turl Son of Thucydus @ Eunice Tomy*
> > *born Jun 1833 yr stars fell Fathers will*
>
> and nothing more, no tedious recording filling this page of wages day by day and food and clothing charged against them, no entry of his death and burial because he had outlived his white half-brothers (257)

The twins may not have questioned their father's $1,000 legacy to Tomey's Turl, but surely they must have deciphered the connection between Eunice's death and the birth of Tomasina's son six months later; or, short of that, they clearly understood from their father's will and his bequest to Tomey's Turl that he was also their father's son, even if they could not accept that she was also their father's daughter. The act of the father, perhaps known to the twins only as miscegenation rather than also as incest, may be interpreted as having a bearing on Buck and Buddy's decision to live differently from their father: to remain outside the bounds of adult sexuality and to avoid women—white or black. Tomey's Turl, living with them, would be a constant reminder, then, of the sins of their father and a source for their adherence to a lifestyle reflecting their anxieties over heterosexual manhood and social order in the slaveholding, patriarchal culture.

Like Buck and Buddy, Tomey's Turl does not escape the cultural formation of roles, even though the trauma of enslavement is not a part of his representation in the text. He is, however, labeled "nigger" (9, 10) and objectified outside of the expected code of behavior of (white) men, whose racialization is assumed: "Because, being a nigger, Tomey's Turl should have jumped down and run for it afoot as soon as he saw them. But he didn't; maybe Tomey's Turl had been running off from Uncle Buck for so long that he had even got used to running away like a white man would do it" (8–9). The boundary of race is an already existing social condition in the games on which the narrative depends, in the binary oppositional of freedom, and in the social interactions among the players. The frequency with which Buck refers to Tomey's Turl as "my nigger" fixes his racialization within the economy of slavery and establishes his subordination to his owners' legal authority over him. It also routinizes the epithet and racist hierarchy and defines Buck as white. Despite the ridicule heaped on his racialized body and on his determined efforts to be with Tennie, Tomey's Turl is differentiated from the twins in the process of rejecting the label "boy" and of coming into a (sexual) maturity as a man.

Courtship is a crucial aspect of Tomey's Turl's maturation and masculinity. His courtship of Tennie is methodical and directed; it is also tied to the economics of power within the institution of slavery. Twice a year, he heads for her cabin on the Beauchamp plantation despite knowing that their enslavement represents an impasse, a stalemate, because neither of their owners will relinquish their property to a marriage: "Tomey's Turl would go there to hang around Mr Hubert's girl, Tennie, until somebody came and got him. They couldn't keep him at home by *buying* Tennie from Mr Hubert because Uncle Buck said he and Uncle Buddy had so many niggers already that they could hardly walk around on their own land for them, and they couldn't *sell* Tomey's Turl to Mr Hubert because Mr Hubert said he not only wouldn't *buy* Tomey's Turl, he wouldn't have that damn white half-McCaslin on his place even as a free gift, not even if Uncle Buck and Uncle Buddy were to pay board and keep for him" (5–6; emphasis added). The emphasis on buying and selling underscores the correlation between slavery and capitalism, between the market economics of chattel slavery and marriage and sexuality. The traffic in slaves would determine a market price for Turl and Tennie, but neither the McCaslins nor Beauchamp was willing to spend money to satisfy a slave's desire to marry. Marriage, after all, was a contract the three white men had not entered into themselves, and it was a contract that legally slaves could not make.

Beyond contractual prohibitions, monogamous sexual relations interfered with the master's right to control, to sexually exploit for their increase of property (in children), and to alienate slaves as property. At the same time, a point made by Karen Sanchez-Eppler in exposing antislavery fiction's evasion of the representation of blackness by focusing on miscegenation obtains here: "In defining the question of ownership of one's body as a sexual question, the ideal of liberty and the commercial concept of ownership attain not only an intimately corporeal appeal, but also an explicitly marital or domestic, dimension."[19] In "Was" the mixing of a marriage and domesticity narrative with an emancipation or freedom narrative delimits the out-of-bondage movement represented in games and modifies the intensity of the slave's desire for freedom from ownership not as a question of sexual oppression or denial of sexual maturity, but as extrication from the legal possession of his body under the laws of slavery. This admixture of conflicting narrative strategies of law and desire, emancipation and marriage heightens my awareness of the text as miscegenated and hybrid.

Tomey's Turl's tactic, however, is not merely recursive; it also allows for the development of responses to his repetitious actions. Buck, for example, can court Sophonsiba Beauchamp as a result of, and in response to, Tomey's Turl's running. By repeating his game of running to court Tennie, Tomey's Turl redefines the social life of the McCaslins to include interdependence and interaction, which open the potential for the brothers to understand that social life is also "about display, confrontation, exhibition and questions of tolerance."[20] In entering into white society and white cultural mandates through the process of courting in the guise of recapturing his runaway slave, Buck must confront on some level the harsh realities of the social world sustained by chattel slavery from which he has attempted to isolate himself. Buck's reluctant courtship is an indirect and evasive tactical game that functions in cooperation with Tomey's Turl's strategically repeated game.[21] In negotiating that courtship as "protection" (12) of his own, Tomey's Turl determines both his own future and that of his white owners, whose authority over him is legally complete and total.

The narrative privileges Buck's donning of a tie before chasing Tomey's Turl as a sign of his intention to court Sophonsiba, but it obscures the detail that Tomey's Turl dons his white Sunday shirt before beginning his run. In this act of dressing up, of dressing "white," of transforming himself into a "gentleman," Turl announces that a different set of rules are in motion from those that obtain while he remains on the McCaslin place. Already fixed visually as "that damn white half-McCaslin," Turl calculates the effect of whitening himself further and demonstrates the porous nature of racial barriers and caste, class, and economic boundaries. He provides a model of behavior that legitimates courtship as a medium of exchange and enables Buck to pursue Sophonsiba Beauchamp. Buck undergoes a similar process that changes his lived, everyday experience when he puts on the tie. Buck's tie and Turl's white shirt become more than articles of clothing; they are signifiers of the social status, economic worth, and gender identity of the two men. Though ordinary articles of dress, the tie and the white shirt function specifically in "Was" as ritualized and decorative, and as such can be read not merely as bodily covering but also as bodily adornment masculinizing, sexualizing, and racializing both Turl and Buck.[22] Turl's condition of enslavement is transformed when he wears the white shirt during his run to the Beauchamp plantation, and Buck's position as a man of property and class is indicated by his tie.

Both Tomey's Turl and Buck play out another existence through clothing. In their disguises, they become different men acting outside of their typical social and cultural realities. Producing through clothing an image of himself that is different from his everyday, asexual, subjugated self, Tomey's Turl suspends the boundaries and codes of that life and rewrites the script for the black male body. Concomitantly, he instigates the ritual that forces Buck into a similar transformation: "The only time he wore the necktie was on Tomey's Turl's account" (7), which is another way to indicate his participation in the social world of whites. Buck thus allows himself to become a suitor and a white man, and Sophonsiba Beauchamp to become the object of his sexual interest and offhanded courtship. Buck and Sophonsiba can then both participate in and accept white cultural scripts: the marriage game, the husband and the wife roles, the squire and landed-gentry conventions of ownership, money, and class.

The behavior of the player-characters (Buck, Buddy, Hubert, and Tomey's Turl) is predictable, based on what they have to win or lose by acting in a particular way. Moves and countermoves in *Go Down, Moses* are much like the strategy of the game of chess in *Light in August* (1932) and like the game of stalking that Charles Bon initiates in *Absalom, Absalom!* or the game of one-upmanship played by Thomas Sutpen in the same novel as he maneuvers to build his dynasty and plantation.[23]

Beginning with Freud's mention of chess in 1913, the game has been viewed psychoanalytically as a reenactment of the oedipal conflict, with the (unconscious) goal of patricide, which is manifested as "checkmate," trapping the king and thus committing father-murder. More recently, psychologist Reuben Fine followed the lead of Ernest Jones's classic psychoanalytic paper on chess and observed that chess involves a sublimation of homosexual impulses: "Chess is a contest between two men in which there is considerable ego involvement. . . . It touches upon the conflicts surrounding aggression, homosexuality, masturbation and narcissism which become particularly prominent in the anal-phallic phases of development." [24]

The McCaslin twins spend much of their adult lives in a contest with their father and his will. In their preoccupation with defeating their father's "boundless conceiving," they sublimate their sexual desires in their homosocial life style. Their unconventional household, made up of slaves, foxes, and dogs, involves oddly aggressive games and hyper-chases—hounds and foxes, slave-brother and white men. Similar to the movements on a chess board, their lives are represented as a strategic game. Chess has been described as a competitive sport of mental aggression in which the objective is to defeat the opponent's intellect or to crush someone's ego. [25] The strategies of chess as a contest of will, intellect, and memory, with already established and defined sequences of potential moves but with the added complexity of insolubility, inform the moves of the McCaslin twins in their contest with their father and their sublimation of sexual desire.

While similar to a chess player's intellectual strategies, Turl's action also retains the physical elements of the hunt and the tracking pursuit of prey. In predicting the moves of his pursuers and in his proclivity for playing well, for regulating his own moves skillfully, and for anticipating the moves of his opponents in the woods and making the necessary adjustments to his own movement, Turl prefigures Isaac McCaslin and his mentor, Sam Fathers, who engage in hunting and the rituals associated with it and the big woods in "The Old People" and "The Bear." At the same time, Turl's ability to play and his determination to play aggressively suggests a sublimation of hostile impulses toward his father-owner and toward his twin brothers as father-owner surrogates, so that his game playing may also be read as a means of working out the father-son rivalry and aggression. Turl, after all, made a decision to reject the

$1,000 left him in his father's will, which his twin brothers attempted to dispense. For his part, Turl is silent about his motives, in much the same way that chess players are penalized for talking, but his movement itself constitutes an articulation of his intent and strategy as a game player.

The main narrative of "Was" introduces Tomey's Turl and begins with a parodied hunt, a wild chase of a fox by a pack of dogs:

> When he and Uncle Buck ran back to the house from discovering that Tomey's Turl had run again, they heard Uncle Buddy cursing and bellowing in the kitchen, then the fox and the dogs came out of the kitchen and crossed the hall into the dogs' room and they heard them run through the dogs' room into his and Uncle Buck's room then they saw them cross the hall again into Uncle Buddy's room and heard them run through Uncle Buddy's room into the kitchen again and this time it sounded like the whole kitchen chimney had come down and Uncle Buddy bellowing like a steamboat blowing and this time the fox and the dogs and five or six sticks of firewood all came out of the kitchen together with Uncle Buddy in the middle of them hitting at everything in sight. . . . It was a good race. (4–5)

Obviously comedic and parodic, in part because Tomey's Turl assumes the symbolic determinants of the fox in the chase, this scene is a sort of crazy Beverly Hillbillies return home.[26] The narrative thus reduces Turl to the animal level, and the humorous tone cannot elide the gravely serious violation of his humanity.

The chase of the fox, with its reverberant issues of possession and property surrounding Tomey's Turl, is a parody of an early-nineteenth-century legal dispute involving the right to property in regard to a wild fox. Resolved by the Supreme Court of the State of New York in 1805, *Pierson v Post* is a sample case studied by first-year law students in property-law courses. The editor of one law casebook, evidently enjoying the opportunity to respond to a case about a fox, wrote: "There have been many foxes in song and fable—the masticator of the abdomen of the Spartan boy, Aesop's grape swindler, Uncle Remus's sly friend so useful as a soporific for the very young, to mention a few—but none has the sterling utility of the quarry in *Pierson v Post*. For more than half a century law students have teethed upon this particular mammal. He is to the law of property what 'Gallia est omnis divisa . . .' is to Latin; it is conceivable that a student might start somewhere else, but it would hardly seem right."[27] The case evoked, then, is so much a part of legal training in property law that its significant resonance in "Was" cannot be overlooked.

Pierson v Post is used to introduce the concept of possession and to examine the law governing the acquisition of title to wild animals, as well as to see how the case is put together. The facts of the case are that Post was fox hunting with his dogs on unowned land and had sighted, chased, and pursued a fox, when Pierson, aware that the fox was being hunted and pursued, killed it within Post's sight and carried it off. The case, regarding the killing and taking of a wild fox by someone other than the person hunting and pursuing it, depends on the idea of possession as the origin of property. Post maintained that his pursuit constituted his property right to the fox. The Court, however, ruled otherwise: "Pursuit alone gives no right of property in animals *ferae naturae;* and an action will not lie against a man for killing and taking an animal of this kind, pursued by and in view of the person who first found, started, pursued, and was on the point of taking it." Moreover, the ruling continued: "Occupancy in wild animals can be acquired only by possession, but this possession does not imply actual bodily seizure, but there must be some actual domination over the animals, as ensnaring them, or by other such means which will prevent their escape."[28]

Pierson v Post establishes what constitutes ownership in a wild animal. It dismisses pursuit but upholds possession, "some actual domination." Possession is, of course, one of the ways in which property rights have long been established. In classical property theory the labor and first-possession theses, associated with John Locke and Jeremy Bentham for example, "mask tensions in property law between alternative sources of property rights" (such as the initial possession by Native Americans of all land in the United States despite titles to that land dispensed by various colonial powers or such as the expropriation of labor from slaves without their accruing ownership or compensation).[29] In *Go Down, Moses,* pursuit, possession, and domination all are aspects of the representation of property, property rights, and personal rights. The substitution of Tomey's Turl for the fox in the analogous introduction of pursuit, capture, and possession, however, immediately transforms the analysis into an enquiry into persons as property or slave property and raises the issue of whether possession and domination, which according to *Pierson* guarantee a right to property, do so when that right conflicts with both the person's right to property claims in his own body (or labor) and the right of the individual to "life, liberty, and the pursuit of happiness."

Faulkner's clear evocation of *Pierson*'s central questions of property and ownership speak to the prominence of key legal discourses in "Was" and all of *Go Down, Moses*. In the opening section of "Was," for example, Faulkner introduces Isaac McCaslin as the person in whose "name . . . the title to the land had first been granted" and McCaslin Edmonds as "the inheritor, and in his time the bequestor" of that same land (3–4). This very brief section establishes the centrality of rights to property and the familial or relational identity based in property rights. Both then segue into the fox hunt and its human analog, the owned property Tomey's Turl, whom Faulkner aligns quite prominently and unequivocally with the question of ownership in the second section of "Was," in which possession as physical control impels the narrative.

It is fairly safe to speculate that Faulkner most likely knew of the *Pierson* case through his friend and mentor Phil Stone who studied law at Yale and who in 1918 was Faulkner's host in New Haven.[30] Subsequently, Stone not only practiced law in Oxford but was appointed assistant United States district attorney for the northern district of Mississippi in 1921. Although Faulkner's relationship with Stone was often conflicted and complicated, it did foster his reading of modern literature and his interest in the legal profession.[31] In addition to Faulkner's having a great-grandfather and a grandfather who were lawyers (as were an uncle and a first cousin), his circle in Oxford, Mississippi, included a relatively large number of lawyers in his age group and in his father's and grandfather's generations, any of whom may well have shared comments on *Pierson v Post* with him.[32] Certainly, he manifested a keen interest in legal matters and demonstrated a fair working knowledge of the law, as has been observed by readers of his fiction.[33] The point, however, is not so much how Faulkner may have come to know about *Pierson v Post* but how much "Was" is enriched by a knowledge of that case and its discourse on property and possession. Faulkner's allusions to *Pierson* are layered onto the surface of the text. For instance, when Uncle Buck says, " 'Damn the fox. . . . Tomey's Turl has broken out again" (5), he in effect signals a connection between the wild fox, contained but running loose within the house, and Tomey's Turl, enslaved but also depicted as running and hunted; his words signal as well a concern with containment and possession that is central to the economic issues at stake in ownership.

Carol M. Rose sees *Pierson v Post* as "the act of establishing individual property for one's self simply by taking something out of the great commons of unowned resources. The common law of property, through its variously named doctrines of 'first possession,' recognizes such self-created entitlements, but . . . the necessary moves add up to a great deal of persuasion—or, some might say, bluff."[34] Her reading of the case suggests a linkage to Faulkner's more direct theorizing about property in "The Bear" and his use of the bluff in the game of stud poker that determines the possession of Tomey's Turl and Tennie in "Was." Rose concludes, "*Pierson* . . . presents two great principles for defining possession, but they are seemingly at odds: (1) notice to the world through a clear act and (2) reward to useful labor. The latter principle . . . suggests a labor theory of property: the owner gets the prize when he 'mixes in his labor' by hunting. On the other hand, the 'clear act' principle suggests at least a weak form of the consent theory, insofar as the world at large might be thought to acquiesce in individual ownership when the claim is clear and no one objects."[35] In considering the "clear act" principle, Rose states that it "suggests that the common law defines acts of possession as some kind of *statement*," and she refers to William Blackstone's *Commentaries on the Laws of England* for the explanation that "the acts must be a *declaration* of one's intent to appropriate."[36] The rhetoric or narrative of possession, then, articulates property as a legal claim "that will be enforced by society or the state, by custom or convention or law."[37]

During a time when she was studying the contract sale of her great-great grandmother as personal property, Patricia J. Williams received a six-year-old's interpretation of *Pierson v Post* from the perspective of the fox: "it resembled Peter Rabbit with an unhappy ending; most important, it was a tale retold from the doomed prey's point of view, the hunted reviewing the hunter." It caused Williams to rethink *Pierson v Post* from the angle of the voiceless, the hunted and contested wild fox, whose situation is comparable to Tomey's Turl's. The reinterpretation prompted her realization that both her great-great-grandmother and "the fox shared a common lot, were either owned or unowned, never the owner. And whether owned or unowned, rights over them never filtered down to them; rights to their persons were never vested in them. When owned, issues of physical, mental, and emotional abuse or cruelty were assigned by the law to the private tolerance, whimsy, or insanity of an external master. And when unowned—free, freed, or escaped—again their situation was uncontrollably precarious, for as objects *to be* owned, they and the game of their conquest were seen only as potential enhancements to some other self." Williams keeps the comparison to *Pierson v Post* clear. "In *Pierson*," she continues, "the dissent described the contest as between the 'gentleman' in pursuit and the 'saucy intruder.' The majority acknowledge that Pierson's behavior was 'uncourteous' and 'unkind' but decided the case according to broader principles of 'peace and order' in sportsmanship. They were fair game from the perspective of those who had rights; but from their own point of view, they were objects of a murderous hunt."[38] Williams foregrounds the way in which the right to claim the fox and right to ownership of the fox was never at issue; rather both parties in *Pierson* had the right to make a claim under the law because the fox was a thing to be owned and claimed as property. Similarly with Tomey's Turl, his right to be free was never a consideration; instead, both the McCaslin twins, who are his brothers, and Hubert Beauchamp assumed they could claim Turl as property—the twins by inheritance from their father and Hubert by winning in a poker game.

The chase of the fox in "Was" depends overtly, and to some readers distastefully, on sport and play and humor, but it also obliquely and oppositionally raises the questions fundamental to *Pierson v Post:* how do things get to be owned and what constitutes ownership? Physical capture, possession, at the heart of the case, raises the issues of Tomey's Turl as slave captured within the narrative chase but for whom first possession already was vested in his owners. Can Turl, a human being, be a thing owned? What constitutes a property right in his being? Is property in persons possible? What rights does Turl have that would effectively limit the rights of his pursuers? These questions, although they do not outweigh the offensive joke at the center of "Was," accommodate an oppositional reading of the chapter.

The fox chase is contained within the McCaslin house and inscribed as a "good race," though it is clearly intended to be slapstick humor, full of bodily comedy and absurd movement, at the expense of the white twin brothers. When viewed as sport or play, this kind of hunting—fox hunting—emphasizes a leisure, classed activity that both adheres to and dismisses everyday societal rules. It is a culturally inflected "sport" that, like the duel and hospitality, signals social ritual and expresses southern honor.[39] However, this particular fox hunt and the incidents that follow it resist the expected cultural symbolic, and not merely because the hunt is linked to the issue of possession and occupancy signified by *Pierson v*

Post. It resonates with the condition of owned human beings, with enslavement and Tomey's Turl. Turl assumes the object position and the symbolic determinants of the fox in the chase, and though he similarly runs within a confined and defined area, he is running away from his own enslavement. Ultimately, Tomey's Turl outwits and outruns both dogs and men. The dogs chasing him function as devices that contain human beings and as extensions of human control (i.e., law and order), but the fact that Turl subdues them defeats the expected outcome. "The contract between play and seriousness is always fluid," because the "inferiority of play is continually being offset by the corresponding superiority of its seriousness."[40] The parodic play of "Was" extends to the title, which, as Daniel Hoffman notices, Faulkner uses despite saying: "There is no such thing as *was*—only *is*. If *was* existed, there would be no grief or sorrow."[41] The "was" that exists in the parodic play of this text, then, constitutes a lack of "grief" and "sorrow," emotions erased and replaced in a reconstituted past by a naively utopic vision of a challenge to authority and containment as necessarily victorious and good natured.

However, the privileging of humor at the expense of the characters racialized as black promotes and maintains racist cultural stereotyping, which then reverberates throughout the remainder of *Go Down, Moses*, troubling thereafter both the constructions of race and gender, as well as the production of textual coherence. It is a cruel extension of the destabilization of black identity and subjectivity explicit in slave law and in slavery (ownership of blacks as property without will) and in the circumstances of Tomey's Turl's birth (the death of his mother and his grandmother and the rejection by his father). The farcical, cruel sleight of hand in "Was" proceeds uninterrogated in the narrative.

Yet, as a runaway, Tomey's Turl represents the fluidity of boundaries between "real" life and make-believe or play. While the absurdity of a fox hunt in a house is underscored by the absurdity of "the dogs' room" inside that house, the relationship between the house and family remains unmarked, so that the absurdity of a hunt for a family member (albeit a subservient one) within a space defined as family goes without commentary. No matter how broad their comic gestures or unorthodox their living arrangements, Buck and Buddy naturalize racial distinctions, racial hierarchies, and racial power. They own the runaway Tomey's Turl just as they possess the fox. The elusive silence in the text has to do with the relationship between the white men and the black object of their hunt: they are brothers. Although family slaves were held to be "special" under slave law, slaves without such connections were ruled on differently: "No sacrifice of feeling, no consideration of humanity, are involved. These were not family slaves, but strangers to the plaintiff,—bought from a distance, and casually purchased at a public sale; no statement that they were peculiarly valuable for their character, qualities, or skill in any trade or handicraft; or that the plaintiff bought them cheap, and would be injured by the loss of his bargain."[42] While Tomey's Turl may receive special consideration because of his public identity as a family slave (with the attendant ties of sentiment to him), he receives none as a family member. That concealed and suppressed identification is disallowed under the law, and thus rendered invisible and nonexistent.

Tomey's Turl turns the "run" of slaves into a mockery of escape: if bondage is physical then the additional implication is that marriage, the result of the game of courtship, will further the bondage and negate any possibility of escape from enslavement. As one slaveholder wrote, "It is necessary that Negroes have wives, and you ought to know that nothing attaches them so much to a plantation as children."[43] The role of women in the enslavement of men is implied; the cabin of Tennie and the bed of Sibbey are implicated in the capture of Turl and of Buck, respectively, both being domesticated spaces allotted to women and into which men fall helplessly entrapped. Turl, however, acts with volition in persistently running to Tennie's cabin, and although Tennie's response to his courtship goes unarticulated, her cabin becomes the site associated with his capture. In Buck's case the issue of will is complicated; for example, Hubert Beauchamp restates Buck's walking into Sophonsiba's bedroom using the metaphor of a bear and a bear's den:

> "You come into bear-country of your own free will and accord. All right; you were a grown man and you knew it was bear-country and you knew the way back out like you knew the way in and you had your chance to take it. But no. You had to crawl into the den and lay down by the bear. And whether you did or didn't know the bear was in it dont make any difference. So if you got back out of that den without even a claw-mark on you, I would not only be unreasonable, I'd be a damn fool. After all, I'd like a little peace and quiet and freedom myself, now I got a chance for it. Yes, sir. She's got you,

ONE HUNDRED DOLLARS REWARD—Ran away from the subscriber, living in Port Gibson, Miss., on the 15th of March last, a mulatto slave, aged about 16 years, named HARRY, sometimes called ZIP, a good looking boy and well grown for his age; no scars remembered except a cut on the first toe of the right foot, which causes the toe to turn down; when spoken to is much in the habit of casting his eyes to the ground. I will give $50 for the apprehension and delivery of said boy to me, in Port Gibson, if taken in the State of Mississippi; and if taken, out of the State,—$100. It is very probable said boy may have a pass or free papers—if so, they are not genuine. He has a fine head of hair, not kinky, but black and wavy. He will perhaps endeavor to make his way to some free State.
SAMUEL MARTIN.
Port Gibson. April 25, 1856.   ap29—1m ¶

TWENTY-FIVE DOLLARS REWARD—Ran away from Richland Plentation, near New Carthage, parish of Madison. La., on the 4th inst., the black boy EDWARD, belonging to the estate of Robert Dunbar. The said Edward is about 18 years old, about 5 feet 6 inches tall. The above reward will be paid for his apprehension and lodging in jail, or delivery to the overseer on plantation. Address agent of said estate at Natchez, Miss., or
GEO. CONNELLY, 43 Carondelet street,
ap9—1m   New Orleans

REWARD—One Hundred and Twenty-Five Dollars Reward for the apprehension of the griff boy named DANIEL, aged about 18 years; has weak or inflamed eyes, and thick lips; had on a blue check shirt and cloth pantaloons; left his owner's domicil on Sunday morning, 27th inst. The above reward will be paid for the proof, to conviction, of the party or parties who have the said boy harbored, or twenty-five dollars for his delivery to the subscriber. It is verily believed that the boy has been kidnapped for the purpose of taking him out of the State, as he was purchased from a trader from Mobile. All masters of steamboats are hereby cautioned against taking said boy away, as they will be prosecuted accordingly.
ap28—6t ¶   THOMAS FELLOWS, 7 Camp street.

TWENTY DOLLARS REWARD For arresting the slave HENRIETTA, a griffe girl, aged about thirty years; has a mark upon her arm from a burn;—walks very quick; was heard of last March, 29th, [hunting for a master; was last on Duplantier street; speaks English alone. The above reward will be paid upon her being lodged in jail, and information left at the lumber yard, Common street, No. 347, or Gasquet street, No. 14, between Canal and Common.
ap19—tf ¶

ONE HUNDRED AND FIFTY DOLLARS REWARD—Ran away on the night of the 19th February, the mulatto girl MARY MACKENDISH, aged about 32 years, of small stature, round face, long hair, and not curled; her upper teeth are out. The above reward will be paid to any person who will lodge her in the city jail, or deliver her at No. 64 Toulouse street, corner of Royal.
☞ Captains of steamboats are hereby cautioned not to receive said girl on board, as it is supposed that she will try to go up the river.   ap20—1m

TWENTY-FIVE DOLLARS REWARD—Ran away from the subscribers, the griff boy WILLIAM, a native of the city, pockmarked, aged about 36 years, a well known hack driver, speaks French and English. He is probably lurking about the city. The above reward will be paid to any person lodging him in jail and returning him to us.
H. M. ROBINSON & CO.,
ap24—tf ¶   100 Gravier street.

TWENTY DOLLARS REWARD—Ran away from the subscriber, the boy TOM. Said boy is black, 5 feet 7 or 8 inches high, has a piece out of one ear, is about 26 years old. The above reward will be paid if he is lodged in any jail in the State; if caught in a free State, I will pay $500 if he is brought to me in New Orleans.   JOHN ERMON.

Advertisements for runaways were commonplace in Mississippi and Louisiana newspapers by the 1850s. From *New Orleans Daily Picayune* (April 1856).

'Filus, and you know it. *You run a hard race and you run a good one, but you skun the hen-house one time too many.*" (21–22, emphasis added)

Buck, the seemingly reluctant suitor, becomes linked linguistically to the animal imagery and the ritual hunt. Buck and Tomey's Turl form a mirror image in their roles as suitors and in their running of a race in which women represent a danger zone disruptive of the male domain.

Law functions implicitly in the same space as the card game, which becomes a contest for possession of blacks and women—for blacks in the "legal" bondage of slavery, which in elevating property denies or circumvents the existence of the person, and for women in the legal institution of marriage in which coverture erases their separate existence and submerges their personality (property) with their husbands'. Ultimately, the contest is also for agency, for control, and for subjectivity. Unlike the game of running invented by Tomey's Turl out of a cruel necessity, the games of chance and sport are not only gendered masculine but racialized white. Their outcomes directly affect women and blacks, as in the case of women's fates (both white Sophonsiba's and black Tennie's) and in the case of the enslaved man and brother, Tomey's Turl.

Playing to Win

The contests in hunting, in cards, dice, and courting depicted in *Go Down, Moses* all signify challenges to a transcendent social order. The convoluted games signify the convoluted economics of slavery. The economic motive of the players is never far from the surface of the play. In the two poker games between Hubert Beauchamp and first Buck, then Buddy McCaslin, the intersection of laws and games occurs, much as it does in Faulkner's 1931 novel, *Sanctuary*, in which clubfooted lawyer Eustace Graham's skill as a poker player is excellent preparation for his role as district attorney.[44] The wagers in *Go Down, Moses* reflect the "undifferentiated individualism" that Mark Tushnet has identified as the motivating principle of bourgeois law, which "embodies a strong presumption that all transactions involve completely fungible commodities. Thus, where some transaction goes awry, the law presumes that things can be set straight by a monetary award of appropriate damages, for the parties are presumed to be unconcerned about the transaction itself so long as they receive the profits, whether from the transaction or from some other source."[45] But slave law differs fundamentally from bourgeois law in its "undifferentiated communalism," which depends on a reluctance to treat slave property "as reducible to a common measure in money" and which depends as well on "an acceptance of social control of the master's choices."[46]

In the first game of draw poker the stakes are Tennie and Turl, the slaves, and the white woman, Sophonsiba Beauchamp. The card table as a space is linked to the slave market and the marriage market; the interactions among the players at Warwick, the Beauchamp plantation, may be read as marketplace transactions. Hubert Beauchamp designates the game and the stakes in an effort to avoid paying Buck McCaslin five hundred dollars wagered on capturing Tomey's Turl in Tennie's cabin.[47] Hubert loses the bet because, although Buck finds Tomey's Turl at the cabin, he is unable to catch him there. Without the cash to pay his debt, Hubert then calls for a game of poker to settle the matter: " 'One hand,' he said. 'Draw. You shuffle, I cut, . . . Five hundred dollars against Sibbey. And we'll settle this nigger business once and for all' " (23). When Buck fails to understand the wager, he receives Hubert's impatient explanation: " 'Wins Sibbey, damn it!' . . . 'Wins Sibbey! What the hell else are we setting up till midnight arguing about? The lowest hand wins Sibbey and buys the niggers' " (23). It is a reminder of the nature of the economic exchange in a slave-holding society, in which Hubert can equate unequal values: "Sophonisiba will always be 'equal' to 'niggers and acres of land,' just as 'niggers and acres of land' themselves have been equated to the money that 'bought' them."[48] Buck "wins" Hubert's sister, but before he can propose, his twin Buddy arrives for a second chance at a wager and a fresh game of poker.

Despite being the passive object of the wager in the poker games, Tomey's Turl becomes the active dealer in the second game of poker represented in the text, just as he has been the initiator of the game of running/courting. Due to his status as enslaved and outside the limits of bourgeois law, he should not function as an agent capable of influencing the outcome of a game between white card players; yet Tomey's Turl's desperate gambit succeeds. He understands the necessity of intervening in the game of chance; his future with Tennie hangs in the balance, and he cannot depend on either his owners or Tennie's for his psychological well-being or emotional satisfaction. When Hubert Beauchamp calls for "the first creature that answers, animal mule or human, that can deal ten cards" (25), he does not notice that Tomey's Turl responds to the call. He fails to notice, in part, because within the institution of slavery one slave is interchangeable with another inasmuch as a slave is defined as "labor" rather than as "laborer," and, in part, because Hubert is concentrating on defeating a superior card player, Buddy McCaslin, who is playing to reverse Hubert's opportunity to rid himself of his sister by marrying her off to Buck McCaslin.[49]

The hand of stud poker that Tomey's Turl deals for Hubert Beauchamp and Buddy McCaslin renders relative the rules of the game and its stated objective. His move outwits Beauchamp as an opponent who would neither buy Tomey's Turl so that he could marry Tennie nor have "that damn white half-McCaslin on his place even as a free gift" (6). Tomey's Turl's move places him in collusion with Buddy, who in his position as twin to Buck had been committed to capturing the runaway and to retaining a woman-free existence on the McCaslin place. In the game of five-card stud, the wager is "Buck McCaslin against the land and the niggers," promised as Sophonsiba's dowry (25). What is at stake is race continuity in either the game of draw or of stud poker. Whether Buck, Buddy, or Hubert wins, the wager is all the same: the white men against the land, the slaves, and the white woman. The card games are not only gendered masculine but racialized white, because they are a means of maintaining hegemony and of exerting social control. They constitute another display of the power of ownership.

Tomey's Turl as a racial hybrid controlled by the mandates of property becomes both a signifier of the race, individualism, and power of the card players and a determinant of their fate, masculinity, and fallibility. His racial status as "that damn white half-McCaslin" has been an issue from the beginning of his run. Invisible and unobserved because unanticipated as an intervening force or player, he deals the cards: "Still neither he [Hubert] nor Uncle Buddy looked up. They just sat there while Tomey's Turl's saddle-colored hands came into the light and took up the deck and dealt, one card face-down to Mr Hubert and one face-down to Uncle Buddy, and one face-up to Mr Hubert and it was a king, and one face-up to Uncle Buddy and it was a six" (26). Tomey's Turl when put under the light, confounds the observer's expectations: " 'Who dealt these cards, Amodeus?' Only he [Hubert] didn't wait to be answered. He reached out and tilted the lamp-shade, the light moving up Tomey's Turl's arms that were supposed to be black but were not quite white, up his Sunday shirt that was supposed to be white but wasn't quite either, . . . and on to his face; and Mr Hubert sat there, holding the lampshade and looking at Tomey's Turl" (28). In this moment Tomey's Turl, whose arms "were supposed to be black but were not quite white," is a trope of hybridity calling into question a black-white racial binary, and he is as well a signifier of the whiteness of the observer and card player, Hubert Beauchamp, and a portent of his defeat. Turl has negotiated a space in which he becomes a viable economic actor, despite both his race and his condition of enslavement.

Tomey's Turl disrupts the visual components of normative whiteness, but the observation of his difference constitutes at the same time a reminder of the presence of the card players as racially defined, as white men. Race is not self-evident without the mediating presence of an other. Hubert may construct Turl visually as "that damn white half-McCaslin," but he sees him socially and culturally as "a nigger" in order to distinguish his own precarious social condition from the legally defined one of the slave. That is, for Hubert, being white, even without money, is infinitely better than being black and a slave. Foregrounding a racial concern with discontinuity, instability, and disjuncture suggests that the moment when Hubert lifts the lamp shade to reveal Tomey's Turl as dealer can be understood as ancillary to a concern with how to represent whiteness within the social, historical, and literary narrativity magnified by moving, shifting light. The dichotomous black-white racial divide clearly dictates the terms for being white and not black. The black dealer and the white card players can be understood as significations of the mutually defining aspects of race in the text. In lighting Turl, Hubert unmasks whiteness's hidden neutrality, though he also opens up the latent threat of the black dealer to determine the winning hand and to undo the power resident within the white players.

The light on Tomey's Turl extends outward to the card players—Buddy and Hubert in this second poker game, Buck and Hubert in the first game—all three being white men and slaveholders, active in the white social, political, and economic world of the antebellum South. The light encircling the players is suggestive of the circle that property draws between private and public power. Charles A. Reich puts it this way: "Property draws a circle around the activities of each private individual or organization. Within the circle, the owner has a greater degree of freedom than without. Outside, he must justify or explain his actions, and show his authority. Within, he is master, and the state must explain and justify any interference."⁵⁰ Within the circle of light and of property in the scene depicting the game of poker, it becomes possible, then, to suspend the external world and focus only on the whims or wishes of the owners.

As a result of the disruption within the lighted space that Tomey's Turl represents to the outcome of the game, and perhaps symbolically to racial distinctness, Hubert can merely say, "I pass" to his white opponent (28). Hubert's passing acknowledges defeat and, implicitly, Tomey's Turl's part in that defeat. As Cornel West remarks: "Without the presence of black people in America, European-Americans would not be 'white'—they would be only Irish, Italian, Poles, Welsh, and others engaged in class, ethnic, and gender struggles over resources and identity. What made America distinctly American for them was not simply the presence of unprecedented opportunities, but the struggle for seizing these opportunities in a new land in which black slavery and racial caste served as the floor upon which white class, ethnic, and gender struggles could be diffused and diverted. In other words, white poverty could be ignored and whites' paranoia of each other could be overlooked primarily owing to the distinctive American feature: the basic racial divide of black and white peoples."⁵¹ Tomey's Turl's presence interjects racial difference into the tableau of card players. His condition as a "black" slave dispels Hubert's "illusion of control," because as Ellen Langer and other psychologists have proposed, "To the extent that one perceives choices, one tends to think of outcomes as caused."⁵²

Faulkner's characters in the tableau of the card game are raced subjects. While race is not self-evident without the mediating presence of an Other, the dichotomous black-white racial divide clearly dictates the terms for being white and not black. Race is always an unstable category of analysis, but it can be understood as a relationally derived construct. Racial formation, as Michael Omi and Howard Winant remind us, "is always historically situated," and thus "our understanding of the significance of race, and of the way race structures society, has changed enormously over time."⁵³ Indeed, the danger in using race as a category of analysis remains its fluidity. Henry Louis Gates Jr. states, "The sense of difference defined in popular usages of the term 'race' has both described and *inscribed* differences of language, belief system, artistic tradition, and gene pool, as well as all sorts of supposedly natural attributes such as rhythm, athletic ability, cerebration, usury, fidelity, and so forth."[54] Without falling into the traps Gates outlines or essentializing race and promulgating biological determinism, it is possible to consider race a significant category of analysis, albeit a slippery one. Berlin suggests that "the meaning of race itself changed as slavery was continually reconstructed over the course of two centuries."[55] White raciality for Hubert, Buddy, and Buck, within the slave-holding South, is inherent in the solidification of their white social identities. In owning and bequeathing property, in legitimating matrimony through contracts and patrimony through wills, they exercise their difference from the black Others, just as they do in casting an ironic eye on the staged performances of Turl, from whom the trope of minstrelsy is never far.[56] Yet the reader comes to know the social identities of the white twins because of Tomey's Turl, a point further inflected by a central conclusion drawn by Walter Johnson in his study *Soul by Soul: Life Inside the Antebellum Slave Market:* "slaveholders often represented themselves to one another by reference to their slaves."[57]

The winning of the hand is ultimately a white man's game. As a resolution, the winning of the hand signifies at once a hand of cards and a hand in marriage, and thus a continuation of the social body that is the status quo. In the two poker games is a contest for the possession of blacks and women—for blacks in the legal bondage of slavery and for women in the legal institution of marriage. The black dealer and the white card players can be understood as significations of the mutually defining aspects of race in Faulkner's text. Tomey's Turl returns to enslavement within the McCaslin land and as McCaslin property, but with a difference. Not only does he return with the woman he has courted, Tennie, who will become his wife, but also he returns marked as an adult. The game has been a rite of passage and of personhood (marriage serving as the province of the adult, fully matured body). However, because emancipation is not the objective of his run, Turl cannot facilitate social reconstruction. His "win," because it is mediated through the win of the white, slave-holding Buddy as a superior card player, does not constitute an abolitionist blow to the institution of slavery, and it does not facilitate his personal freedom. Mary Frances Berry reminds us that those enslaved blacks who did not rebel, revolt, or run "were not necessarily 'docile'; they lived in the grip of a system of violent control institutionalized under the Constitution."[58] Yet meditating on Tomey's Turl's black male, but visually white male body, I am at a loss to connect him to the likes of Ellen Craft, to the visually white enslaved people who escaped slavery by running and who affected their escapes by making a game of visible whiteness. Ellen Craft and her husband, William—like Harriet Jacobs, Moses Roper, John Anderson, and William Wells Brown, who were in "real life" property who rejected remaining owned—understood freedom, bodily freedom, physical freedom as the only possible antidote to enslavement. But, as represented by Faulkner in "Was," a slave escapes and runs *not* for the purpose of attaining his freedom, not with the intention of being and remaining bodily free, but rather only to "visit" a neighboring plantation.

In Faulkner's construction Tomey's Turl cannot seek his own freedom. He does, however, achieve something unanticipated in Faulkner's scenario: Tomey's Turl's run, culminating not in the freedom plot but in the marriage plot, constitutes the willful institution of a legally recognized black family with an economic stake in the social order and with a traceable genealogy. This founding of a legal black family is an unexpected outcome of investing Turl with agency and will in this reading of the text.

Thus, there are no intrinsic winners or losers; each positionality depends on the perspective from which such an outcome is viewed. For example, Buddy is the winner of the poker game in "Was" only if one assumes that the maintenance of order in a slave economy depends on preventing slaves from running away. But the confusions of the wagers, added to the positionality of Sophonsiba as "bear" and object of humor (as well as of repressed desire) and made through two layers of language to appear ludicrous, aged, and demented (21), and the positionality of Tomey's Turl as "fox" and object of the hunt and indirectly of the wager through the fates assigned to him and to Tennie as a result of their being negotiated pieces of property, all blur the seriousness of the game and its stakes into a seemingly benign joke, expressive of nothing more than a bit of rural male fun. And yet, Turl's very participation in the game marks a level of agency all too frequently obscured in the existence of enslaved people. As Ira Berlin observes: "For while slaveowners held most of the good cards in the meanest of all contests, slaves held cards of their own. And even when their cards were reduced to near worthlessness, slaves still held that last card, which, as their owners well understood, they might play at any time."[59]

The objectives of game players are rational and strategized on the basis of knowledge and expectations of the behavior of opponent game players. In neither of the two poker games in "Was"—the first between Hubert and Buck and the second between Hubert and Buddy, the superior player who is clearly abetted by the dealer Turl, whose fate is the object of the card game and of the draw of cards—is winning a matter of luck. In a coalitional game, Buddy and Tomey's Turl are allied players with what can be called a "transferable" payoff.[60] Buddy, though known for his ability to play poker (7), is functioning in a coalition with Tomey's Turl as card dealer, which because the interests of Buddy and Tomey's Turl cohere, positions Tomey's Turl as a player. That Tomey's Turl occupies the pivotal space of dealer realigns his subservient position. The joint action they undertake—the defeat of Hubert and his wager—has less economic impact than sociopersonal impact. To defeat Hubert frees Buck from the outcome of his previous loss to Hubert, reinstates the twins as inseparable (at least temporarily) in their domestic space, assures Buddy of the company of his twin, and obligates Buddy and Buck to purchase Tennie to become the wife of Tomey's Turl. While Hubert's defeat frees neither Tennie nor Turl, it does void the stalemate that had prevented either of them as pieces of property from being moved to the location of the other. Because both Tennie and Tomey's Turl retain the status of property, they remain as well the objects of the game and of the social bargaining that is explicit in the game of cards.

The poker game of "Was" is related to the craps game in "Pantaloon in Black," the chapter of *Go Down, Moses* in which Rider, as a gambling man and a black laborer, violates not the rules of the dice game but of the social configurations governing the interactions between black and white men. Unlike Tomey's Turl who is enslaved, Rider is nominally free; that is, "Pantaloon in Black" is set in the early-twentieth-century South—a South modern enough to have motion pictures ("pictures shows") as a form of entertainment but still reflecting the post-Reconstruction era in which blacks were held in economic peonage and social subordination and still controlled by law though unprotected by law.[61] Rider, whose remarkable physical strength and agility signify his athleticism, can be read as a runaway from the material reality of his life after his wife Mannie's death and as a game player attempting to cross the physical barrier between death and life that is actuated by his experiential reality as a game player. His return to the dice game at the saw mill where he worked is less a signal of a desire to win something and more an indication of game-playing to avoid boredom, to express grief, and a debilitating sense of emptiness and powerlessness.[62] Rider was powerless to prevent his beloved wife's death, and her loss leaves a void in his existence that only a reunion with her can adequately fill. He experiences both forgetting his loss and remembering what he has lost in the process of mourning, but he cannot detach himself from both desiring Mannie and expecting her return. His complete devotion to Mannie and his instant love for her reconstituted his entire way of being in the world; her death reconfigured his attachment to life. Her absence resounds in all aspects of his new life as a physical absence, lack, void, emptiness, which, while connected to the libidinal gratification prominent in Freud's analysis of mourning, is more closely aligned with object recovery. Rider does not seek to achieve the letting go; his word to Mannie's fading shade is "Wait" (136), but when that proves impossible, he states, " 'Den lemme go wid you, honey' " (136). His "artistry of consciousness and bodily presence," to use Joseph Mihalich's phrase for the lived experience of sports and athletics, is bracketed by "spontaneity and inventiveness (without arbitrariness)" and signals his attunement with the experiential world; in this existential state, Rider as athlete "does not think about space and time in the world," he "lives space and time in the world in his . . . acute expression of consciousness-in-the-world-with-a-body."[63]

In contrast to the "mute click and scutter of the dice" (147), Rider gives voice to the cheating in the game, articulating the crime against blacks even in games of chance (148), where cheating increases the arbitrary power over them. The narrative description emphasizes the racial identity of the white gambler Birdsong, whom Rider kills: "still smiling at the face of the *white man* opposite, then, still smiling, he [Rider] watched the dice pass from hand to hand around the circle as the *white man* covered the bets, watching the soiled and palm-worn money in front of the *white man* gradually and steadily increase, watching the *white man* cast and win two doubled bets in succession then lose one for twenty-five cents, the dice coming to him at last, the cupped snug clicking of them in his fist" (148; emphasis added). The hierarchy of power in the relations between the black workers and the white foreman remains intact in the dice game; the societal rules governing race are not suspended because of the nature of the game, its false rules, the rigged, crooked play of the white supervisor, Birdsong. Here the power relations also reflect the imbalance in the economic order. Exploited in their labor and victimized in their entertainment, the black workers accede to the hierarchy of power.

When Rider catches Birdsong with a second pair of dice, secreted in his shirt sleeve, he levels the accepted imbalance of power:

> "Shoots a dollar," he [Rider] said, and cast, and watched the white man pick up the dice and flip them back to him. "Ah lets hit lay," he said. "Ah'm snakebit. Ah kin pass wid anything," and cast, and this time one of the negroes flipped the dice back. "Ah lets hit lay," he said, and cast, and moved as the white man moved, catching the white man's wrist before his hand reached the dice, the two of them squatting, facing each other above the dice and the money, his left hand grasping the white man's wrist, his face still fixed in the rigid and deadened smiling, his voice equable, almost deferential: "Ah kin pass even wid miss-outs. But dese hyar yuther boys—" until the white man's hand sprang open and the second pair of dice clattered onto the floor beside the first two and the white man wrenched free and sprang up and back and reached the hand backward toward the pocket where the pistol was. (148)

Rider situates himself as "snakebit," as poisoned, out of the ordinary, and, consequently, as outside the realm of daily racial experience within the game. As outsider with nothing more of value to lose after his wife's death, Rider no longer holds either to the ethic of work, of getting along within the exploitative economy for the sake of providing for his family, or to the distractions of avoidance and the escape from knowing the extent of racial oppression. Rider's response to the white player's cheating is also an assault on the economic subjugation of blacks in the workplace and in the larger culture. Fueled by his recognition of the consequences of his breaking out of the racial and social codes, Rider acts aggressively, certain of white retaliation and punishment for attacking a white man.

The white sheriff's deputy, presented as "officially in charge of the business" related to Rider's capture and lynching for killing Birdsong, is representative of the uncomprehending legal system—"the law" that is incapable of recognizing a free black man's humanity. Seemingly without irony, the deputy states, "Them damn niggers. . . . I swear to godfrey, it's a wonder we have as little trouble with them as we do. Because why? Because they aint human. They look like a man and they walk on their hind legs like a man, and they can talk and you can understand them and you think they are understanding you, at least now and then. But when it comes to the normal human feelings and sentiments of human beings, they might just as well be a damn herd of wild buffaloes" (149–50). The law, of course, cannot recognize unenforceable rights, so the sheriff's deputy is at a loss to recognize Rider's private grief. He assumes that two aspects of the legal inheritance of slavery obtain: blacks as property not as persons and therefore inhuman; and blacks as immoral and therefore as not subject to the moral codes of whites. What has occasioned his conclusion is not only his mistaken perception of Rider's failure to grieve for his dead wife but also his inability to recognize the extraordinary nature of the game in which Rider engaged.[64] According to the sheriff's deputy, "the same crap game where Birdsong has been running crooked dice on them mill niggers for fifteen years, goes straight to the same game where he had been peacefully losing a probably steady average ninety-nine percent of his pay ever since he got big enough to read the spots on them miss-out dice" (151). That Birdsong had been cheating for so long a period of time and that the players knew that he had a second set of dice up his sleeve would be appropriate conclusions to draw. What these two pieces of information would suggest, then, is that a different set of rules applied to this particular craps game based on its significant deviations from other craps games that were not routinized as crooked, and that this specific craps game images white-black power relations in the social world but with the difference of Rider's intensified awareness of his material condition—"snakebit" and seeking reunion with his dead wife. In *Beyond the Pleasure Principle* (1920), Freud presents his theory of the compulsion to repeat as an instinct for mastery over unpleasant realities. He labels this compulsion a prior force to pleasure and an urge to restore an earlier state of things, which is an instinct toward death. Rider's death instinct is transparent and ambulatory in the various contexts in which he finds himself after Mannie's death.

Rider's renewed courtship of Mannie in death is part of the overlay of courts of law as a game. In pursuit of Mannie, Rider does not run; he wants to be captured and killed. His mantra is " 'Ah'm snakebit and bound to die' " (147); " 'Ah'm snakebit now and pizen cant hawm me' " (144). That his story involves him in a form of play that has rules of its own is suggested when Rider shovels dirt into Mannie's grave with a shovel that in his hands "resembled the toy shovel a child plays with at the shore" (131). This reconfiguration of the adult Rider signals his out-of-the-ordinary state, just as his aunt's calling him "Spoot," rather than

Rider, signifies his regression after Mannie's death: "And for a space he could hear . . . her voice crying after him across the moon-dappled yard the name he had gone by in his childhood and adolescence" (146). His response, then, to Mannie's death is to recover the lost object; it is like children's responses to separation and to their unconscious urge to recover what they have lost. Mourning Mannie's loss for Rider necessarily means seeking her recovery. From mourning, he moves to a self-induced death.

Rider's night movement is a contest with nature, against the white moonshiner and his gun. It is a contest with the symbols of power and control in his society: " 'Ha,' he said. 'Dat's right. Try me. Try me, big boy. Ah gots something hyar now dat kin whup you' " (143). His movement is also represented as a contest of wills in his interaction with his aunt's husband, Unc Alec, who cries out for the fast-moving Rider to wait for him: " 'You cant keep up,' [Rider] said, speaking into the silver air, breasting aside the silver solid air which began to flow past him almost as fast as it would have flowed past a moving horse" (144). In both cases, Rider is in a contest against containment and against the societal and familial barriers that would prevent his reunion with his dead wife. The repetition of contestatory acts becomes a replacement for his remembering of Mannie. In his race against the confines of the natural world, he acts out his wish to be free of his body. Rider recognizes his freedom "in the night's infinitude": "his shadow and that of the dog scudding the free miles, the deep strong panting of his chest running free as air now because he was all right" (144). The emphasis on "free," along with that on his shadow, calls attention to Rider's emancipated psychological state, to his experience as out of body and out of servitude. This condition anticipates his reunion with the vision of Mannie who could not wait at Rider's command and who disappeared too fast for him to apprehend and accompany her.

Rider's freedom, like Turl's is a moving out of the place assigned to blacks in the antebellum and postbellum South. Abnegation of place is as dangerous to the social order as is race-mixing or miscegenation. More than initiating a change in psychology, both produce physical threats to economic stability and to societal exclusiveness. In "Pantaloon in Black," just as in "Was," the freedom from containment initiates a series of calculated moves, a series that ends in the player's winning, in his achievement of his desired outcome; in the two narratives, however, those outcomes assume very different relationships to the prevailing social order.

In the second part of "Pantaloon in Black," the wife of the sheriff's deputy is short-tempered when her husband tries to tell her Rider's story because "she had attended a club rook-party that afternoon and had won the first, the fifty-cent, prize until another member had insisted on a re-count of the scores and the ultimate throwing out of one entire game" (150). The wife's loss results in her ill-temper and impatience, as well as in her desire for diversion and escapism in the form of a moving-picture show. The economics of loss interrupts the emotion of loss being interpolated by the sheriff's deputy, who is unable to comprehend either shame (his own) or grief (Rider's) in the narrative he tries to tell his wife. The interjection of an invalidated game as an explanation of attitude here serves a familiar purpose: it restates that a different set of rules operate for a game and that attention to those rules alone will result in winners and losers, even though the results may impinge on the larger social world external to the game.

That the games in *Go Down, Moses* are imbricated with issues of marriage, property, and possession signifies the way in which the Faulkner represents the interactions between the races and between the sexes as inherently legal; that is, as market relations or contractual relations. In writing about "the body as property," Alan Hyde has pointed out, "Legal discourse powerfully and relentlessly translates all other and earlier ways of describing human relations into its preferred formulations. Thus, love becomes marriage, which is conceptualized as a *contract;* intrafamily relations become described as a clash of parental and children's *rights,* and so on."[65] In connecting games and the winning of games to the legal issues and language related to property and the imposition of will, Faulkner raises the stakes connected with Tomey's Turl, the seeming object of property.

Objecting to Ownership

Tomey's Turl's identity is incomplete in "Was," and his identity is equally incomplete in my subversive reading of his subjectivity as game player. Tomey's Turl is owned. He is property, whose "rightful" owners Buck and Buddy McCaslin also happen to be his brothers, sons of the same father, Carothers McCaslin who "held [human beings] in bondage and in the power of life and death" (*Go Down, Moses*, 243). While Turl exercises his agency by running at will and by courting the woman of his choice, he is represented neither as an autonomous being nor as a serious subject, and this lack fractures any attempt to read *Go Down, Moses* as a unified, coherent project. He is "that damn white half-McCaslin." His construction as visually white though he should be black and as relationally half McCaslin when both his father and mother are McCaslins argues for the slippage between discrete categories of race.[1] Nonetheless, against the logic of experience, the categories are maintained by slavery as bipolar and impenetrable, and Tomey's Turl is racialized as black and abstracted as fatherless. He is chattel, the enslaved black "thing" who can be denied paternity and thus fraternity, precisely because relations can exist only between persons, not between a person and a "thing." Tomey's Turl is the object of property.

As offensive as the concept is to contemporary sensibilities, in the legal discourses of nineteenth-century America, particularly the American South, the slave was constructed as an object of property. Orlando

Patterson, however, argues in *Slavery and Social Death* that property is *not* one of the constitutive elements of slavery, despite his insistence that he does consider slaves to be property objects. "The problem, rather," Patterson states, "is that to define slavery *only* as the treatment of human beings as property fails as a definition, since it does not really specify any distinct category of persons. Proprietary claims and powers are made with respect to many persons who are clearly not slaves. Indeed any person, beggar or king, can be the object of a property relation. Slaves are no different in this respect." His view removes the specificity of slaves as objects of property, without denying the material reality of enslavement. He concludes, "The fact that we tend not to regard 'free' human beings as objects of property—legal things—is merely a social convention."[2] Patterson tends toward the "doctrine of *dominium*," which transforms slavery into a condition of powers, but his argument does not convince me that being the object of property is not a distinct category of "things." The slave as an object of property claims is integral to the relationship between slavery and law.

There are several reasons why the relationship between property claims, slavery, and law is overlooked. One of the most obvious is that property law does not apply exclusively to enslaved persons, so that property claims in persons is a difficult concept to grasp, precisely because of the disjuncture between personhood and "thingness." Placing slaves within the category of property, Thomas D. Morris contends, "involved a legally backed right to use the 'property' in certain ways. It also involved rights to transfer the slave to someone else, and to name someone to succeed to the ownership on the death of the owner. The notion of the person as property is so ethically repugnant that even scholars who mention the slave as a 'thing' often drop it in order to get on to the ways law governed the slave as a person." Morris concludes that the property element in the slave was nonetheless " 'juristically' significant" and that "one of the essential 'incidents' of slavery was that the slave was an object of property rights, he or she was a 'thing.' "[3]

Property is an inscription of the hegemony of the male symbolic. In *Go Down, Moses* questions about property involve law and originate in the perspective of white male southerners, the McCaslins, the Edmondses, and the Beauchamps, who possess, own, inherit, and hold "property," and whose right to dispose of it as they choose is protected by law. Their property rights encompass their right in and to persons as property. Property, thus constituted, is about power, despite the fact that the meaning of property does not remain constant but changes over time, both because of the institution of property itself and because of the way individuals view property. According to C. B. Macpherson, property "is both an institution and a concept," but despite the common usage of property to mean things, in law property is rights rather than things: "rights in and to things."[4] The obvious slippage between things and rights in the matter of definitions of property and of slaves creates disjunctures and fissures in the discourses and narratives constructed in law.

Property rights, according to one of the foundational theories, originate in possession and labor. John Locke pointed out that "every Man has a *Property* in his own *Person*," so that the "*Labour* of his Body, and the *Work* of his hands . . . are properly his."[5] Characterized as a labor-desert theory, Locke's conception includes the notion that individuals must deserve to own the items mixed with their labor; for example, the work individuals put into land and crops entitles them to property rights. Although following different emphases from Locke's labor theory, the major classical theories of property—the personality theory of Hegel and the utilitarian theory of Bentham—depend on an embodiment theory of personhood in which the body is personal property.

Property in *Go Down, Moses* specifically includes slaves, whose labor was expropriated without compensation, so that their labor could not be a source of property rights. The slaves themselves constituted property. Faulkner's central white character, Ike McCaslin, recognizes the unjust nature of ownership and property when he considers that his ruthless grandfather, old Carothers McCaslin had not only bought the land "with white man's money from the wild men whose grandfathers without guns hunted it, and . . . believed he had tamed and ordered it for the reason that the human beings he held in bondage and in the power of life and death had removed the forest from it and in their sweat scratched the surface of it . . . to grow something" (*Go Down, Moses*, 243–44). In *Principles of Political Economy* John Stuart Mill wrote:

> Besides property in the produce of labour, and property in land, there are other things which are or have been subjects of property, in which no proprietary rights ought to exist at all. But as the civilized world has in general made up its mind on most of these, there is no necessity in dwelling on them in this place. At the head of them,

is property in human beings. It is almost superfluous to observe, that this institution can have no place in any society even pretending to be founded on justice, or on fellowship between human creatures. But, iniquitous as it is, yet when the state has expressly legalized it, and human beings, for generations, have been bought, sold, and inherited under sanction of law, it is another wrong, in abolishing the property, not to make full compensation.[6]

While observing that slavery, "property in human beings," does not belong in a just society, Mill nonetheless accepts the right of individuals to hold slaves if states have legitimated that practice by law, and thus he believes that were property in human beings abolished, then compensation would be required for those claiming slave property. In economic terms, compensation is required even if the practice is abhorrent. The concept of compensation became one of the primary tenets of legal decisions in slave law when owners sought compensation for the loss of service of their slaves.

In 1848 Mississippi incorporated the element of race specifically into its legal compilations: slavery as the "Institution of *African* Service."[7] That law conflated slavery and race, so that anyone of African descent in Mississippi after 1848 was presumed to be a slave. The complicity of law in oppression and enslavement is linked, in one respect, to its shaping originary in the protection of property and the rights of the property owner following from the logic Jeremy Bentham set forth in the utilitarian theory that law originated for the protection of property and has continued to exist for that purpose.[8] The McCaslin and Edmonds characters in *Go Down, Moses* not only own property inherited from old Carothers McCaslin, but they also control the boundaries of that property and, in effect, also control law and the legal discourses constructed to protect their holdings, both real estate and enslaved people.

Cass Edmonds debates with his cousin Ike McCaslin the ethics of ownership and the definition of property. He links the ownership of land and slaves in their plantation tradition to biblical authority and the right to property according to "divine law." His claim is that their grandfather, old Carothers, "did own it. . . . Not alone and not the first since, as your Authority states, man was dispossessed of Eden. Nor yet the second and still not alone on down through the tedious and shabby chronicle of His chosen sprung from Abraham, and of the sons of them who dispossessed

Sketch showing persons as property along with paintings and other goods. From W. H. Brooke, *Sale of Estates, Pictures, and Slaves in the Rotunda* (1854). Courtesy of Historic New Orleans Collection.

Abraham, and of the five hundred years during which half the known world and all it contained was chattel to one city as this plantation and all the life it contained was chattel" (246–47). Ike answers with his own reading of another mandate from the Bible, in which he disputes even the possibility of ownership: "Bought nothing. Because He told in the book how He created the earth, made it and looked at it and said it was all right, and then He made man. He made the earth first and peopled it with dumb creatures, and then He created man to be His overseer on earth and to hold suzerainty over the earth and the animals on it in His name, not to hold for himself and his descendants inviolable title forever, generation after generation, to the oblongs and squares of the earth, but to hold the earth mutual and intact in the communal anonymity of brotherhood, and all the fee He asked was pity and humility and sufferance and endurance and the sweat of his face for bread" (246). Ike's vision is suggestive of Jean-Jacques Rousseau's *Discourse on Inequality*, which blamed private property for the loss of equality and thus for envy, jealousy, slavery, and war: "You are lost if you forget that the fruits of this earth belong to all and the earth to no one."[9] In Faulkner's text there is no reconciliation of these divergent views of property and their appeals to various philosophical concepts of ownership.

Although between the 1830s and 1840s Mississippi codified and solidified the relationship between race, slavery, and slave property, the state initiated a slight loosening of the connection between gender identity and property restrictions in the same period, when property in the developing state was primarily slaves and land. Mississippi enacted the Woman's Law of 1839, which in an enlightened and radical move under common law protected and preserved the rights of married women to retain their own property; notably, however, the property protected was for the most part not real estate but slaves.[10] Although attacked as an "indelicacy," degrading and disgraceful to women (to own and manage their own slaves), and a "stupendous" fraud "calculated to sow discord into the domestic and social relations," the statute was an attempt to revise both law and custom related to the persons and property of married women.[11]

In *Go Down, Moses* the law is "a vast and multidimensional affair," as Jay Watson has observed of the law throughout Faulkner's texts, "at once a deeply normative cultural system, a vehicle of ideology (in its constructive and destructive manifestations), a force of social stability and control, an entrenched and often blindly self-interested institution."[12] Invested in public displays of order and stability, law takes on visible areas of public concern, and these, as Faulkner shows in *Go Down, Moses*, typically reflect the concerns of white men. As a discourse of power expressive of the interests of men, law has not attended well to those traditionally controlled, defined, and silenced by "private recesses of society," for example, blacks as the object of property and of slave law.[13]

In the matter of rights, the arbitrariness and contradictions of legal discourses and juridical decisions regarding ownership can be seen especially in the treatment of slaves as property. Courts were fundamental to the implementation and application of slave law and to the preservation of masculine domains of exclusion. Courts functioned both to uphold the law but also in effect to make the law and to sustain the boundedness of existence for individuals who were black and enslaved. Not only in the now famous *Plessy v Ferguson* case, which upheld racial segregation, but in all of the court rulings that essentially created law through the interpretations rendered, the precedents were set and not challenged or vacated. Early in the nineteenth century in Mississippi, for example, slavery was "condemned by reason and the laws of nature," when the state supreme court ruled in favor of a petition for freedom in the case of *Harry and Others v Decker and Hopkins*.[14] The laws of nature or natural law become, along with reason, part of the objection Ike McCaslin has to ownership of land, which takes shape because of his association of his grandfather's holding of land in ownership and violation of human beings as personal property. While *Harry v Decker* may well have spoken more precisely to the theory rather than to the practice of the law in Mississippi, it nonetheless maintained a legal objection to and condemnation of slavery. Within a few years of that 1818 ruling, however, the legality of slavery in Mississippi changed and without legal challenge.

According to the Supreme Court of Mississippi in *State v Jones*, slaves were "reasonable and accountable beings," but they were nonetheless lawfully "deprived of [their] freedom."[15] Without questioning the legality of depriving the slave of freedom or of holding a reasonable, accountable being in bondage, the court upheld the delimited "rights" of a slave as "all those rights, of which he is not deprived by the positive provisions of law," and the court ruled, in a decision written by Justice Joshua G. Clark, that murder could, in fact, be committed against a slave, even though as a "reasonable being," the slave is comparable to "a lunatic, an idiot, or an unborn child": "It would be a stigma upon the character of the state, and a reproach to the administration of justice, if the life of a slave could be taken with impunity, or if he could be murdered in cold-blood, without subjecting the offender to the highest penalty known to the criminal jurisprudence of the country."[16] A white man, Isaac Jones, accused of murdering a slave was thus condemned to death by hanging on 27 July 1821, and the legal rights of those enslaved in Mississippi were established. Nevertheless, those rights were limited by the condition of bondage, and they were increasingly circumscribed by extensive legal encroachments, which in turn reflected law as "constitutive of *and* derivative of social and political changes."[17]

Although *State v Mann*, the case that has become the classic in analysis of slave law in both the nineteenth and twentieth centuries, was set in North Carolina rather than Mississippi, it upheld "the dominion of the master over the slave"; however, in effect, it also made clear that law regulates market transactions rather than other relations. *State v Mann* became the precedent cited in states such as Mississippi for the denial of rights to a slave. Lydia, a slave belonging to Elizabeth Jones but hired out to John Mann was at the center of the case. Mann attempted to punish Lydia for a minor offense, whereupon she ran to avoid being beaten. He shot and wounded her in the back. Convicted of assault and battery, Mann appealed. Judge Thomas Ruffin contributed the court's opinion, which reversed the conviction: "The hirer and possessor of a slave, in relation to both rights and duties, is for the time being, the owner" who has "uncontrolled authority" over the slave; therefore, the hirer has a contractual obligation for the safety and welfare of the slave during the contract for hire to the owner, not to the slave "who has no will of his own, [and] who surrenders his will in implicit obedience to that of another."[18] This case was cited by Harriet Beecher Stowe in *A Key to* Uncle Tom's Cabin (1859), in part because *State v Mann* placed "feelings" and "duty" in counterpoint ("the feelings of the man and the duty of the magistrate"), so that despite the feelings of the man, the magistrate concluded that "public tranquility" required the slave's complete subordination.[19] In the same year, 1859, the Mississippi Supreme Court declared slaves to be "artificial persons" who were not subject to common law that applied to "natural persons."[20] The slave's surrender of will and the master's exercise of control reflect the earlier definition of property under common law as stated in *Blackstone's Commentaries:* "the right of property is that sole and despotic dominion which one man claims and exercises over the external things of the world, in total exclusion of the right of any other individual in the universe. It consists of the free use, enjoyment, and disposal of all a person's acquisitions, without any control or diminution save only by the laws of the land."[21]

Despite the requirement of subordination to external structures, slaves possessed both inner lives filled with innate, inchoate needs and external interactions with a physical environment not delimited by slaveholders. Slave testimony in the form of letters, diaries, autobiographies, memoirs, narratives (such as *The Narrative of the Life of Frederick Douglass* [1845] or *Incidents in the Life of a Slave Girl* by Harriet Jacobs [1861]), and interviews with former slaves have all presented encounters of enslaved people with their interior and exterior worlds.[22] And recent critical studies of slave narratives and histories of individuals and social networks under slavery have revised notions of how domination affected the enslaved.[23] Neither absolute subordination nor complete resistance would accurately describe their response to their condition. Although there may have been more silences than voices to express the various registers of slave existence, what is abundantly clear is that the rationalization of property in persons resulting from the category of artificial person could not and would not hold.

There is, of course, ample evidence of "slave property" breaking through the imposed silence and voicing a response to the pattern of forced subordination. One such case is Henry Bibb, who wrote *Narrative of the Life and Adventures of Henry Bibb, an American Slave* (1849). After his escape from Shelby County, Kentucky, in 1840, he made his way to Detroit, where he actively campaigned for black rights. While there, he wrote the following in a letter to William Gatewood, one of his six previous owners:

> Dear Sir:—I am happy to inform you that you are not mistaken in the man whom you sold as property, and received pay for as such. But I thank God that I am not property now, but am regarded as a man like yourself, and although I live far north, I am enjoying a comfortable living by my own industry. If you should ever chance to be traveling this way, and will call on me, I will use you better than you did me while you held me as slave. Think not that I have any malice against you, for the cruel treatment which you inflicted on me while I was in your power. As it was the custom of the country, to treat your fellow men as you did me and my little family, I can freely forgive you.[24]

With the enactment of the Fugitive Slave Act of 1850, Bibb left Detroit for Canada, where he was not threatened by slavecatchers and was free to write to Albert G. Sibley, another of his former owners: "It has now been about sixteen years since we saw each other face to face, and at which time you doubtless considered me inferior to yourself, as you then held me as an article of property, and sold me as such; but my mind soon after became insubordinate to the ungodly relation of master and slave and the work of self-emancipation commenced and I was made free."[25] Bibb's purpose over the course of several letters was to take Sibley to task for being a hypocrite who, though active in the Methodist Church, kept and misused slaves including Bibb's mother and siblings. With signal clarity, Bibb wrote, "The idea of a man being a slave—of being subjugated to the will and power of a master, is revolting to his very nature."[26] One significance of Bibb's letters to his former master is that they reveal the way in which a former slave understood "property" and its distinction from his "self," his personality, and being, which could undertake emancipation as an act of agency. Bibb rejects the property designation and "the ungodly relation of master and slave."

Between the decision of *Mann v State* in 1829 and the election of Abraham Lincoln in 1860, southern state laws and legal codes consistently renegotiated and delimited the rights of the enslaved while advancing the dominion of the master. Mississippi's Revised Codes of 1857, for example, contained numerous strict prohibitions codifying the state's slave laws and prohibiting slaves from marriages, contact with free blacks, defense or testimony against whites, learning to read or write, and travel without a pass.[27] The legal ploys of the 1857 codes were designed to vex the relation of slaves to any conception of themselves as other than property, just at the very moment when the larger political climate was beginning to turn against slavery. Many such strictures were in response to fears and rumors of revolt, which from Nat Turner's Rebellion in 1831 right up to the eve of the Civil War in 1861 increased in frequency. Although the major slave rebellions took place far from Mississippi (in Virginia and South Carolina), Mississippi was not without slave revolts that bubbled up to disturb any complacency about black acquiescence to enslavement. In July 1835, for example, Mississippi experienced a slave insurrection in which blacks and whites plotted to take the town of Vernon, Madison County, kill the white residents, take their guns and ammunition, and proceed to Livingston, the adjoining town, and from there eventually to Natchez. The insurrectionists anticipated, mistakenly, that all other slaves in the area would join them along the way.[28]

Mid-nineteenth-century American apologists for slavery attempted to redefine both property and slavery in legal discourses by focusing the claim to property rights in slaves on a claim to their labor. E. N. Elliott's 1860 collection of proslavery writings, for instance, stated that "slavery is the duty and obligation of the slave to labor for the mutual benefit of both master and slave, under a warrant to the slave of protection, and a comfortable subsistence, under all circumstances. The person of the slave is not property, no matter what the fictions of the law may say; but the right to his labor is property, and may be transferred like any other property, or as the right to the services of a minor or an apprentice may be transferred."[29] This clear abstraction of "the person of the slave" from the category of property on the eve of the Civil War is an attempt to negate the harm done to a person enslaved and to disassociate slavery from the physical human body by only associating slavery with the effort or energy expended by the body in the act of working. Thus disembodied from the concept of property, the slave becomes analogous (falsely) to any wage laborer.

Within "Was" and the culture it represents, Tomey's Turl is objectified as a body in slow motion, expending little energy, and thus challenged as a laborer. The stereotyped, slow-moving body of the actor Stepin Fetchit would fit the visualization "nobody had ever known Tomey's Turl to go faster than his natural walk, even when riding a mule" (8). Not only his bodily movements but also his verbal expressions are minimal and coded. " 'And nem you mind that neither. I got protection now. All I needs to do is to keep Old Buck from ketching me unto I gets the word' " (12). Riddle-like and echoing his ambiguous birth and complicated positionality within the McCaslin household, his words must be deciphered. Tomey's Turl's position resonates with the legal conception presented in 1827: "the cardinal principle of slavery—that the slave is to be regarded as a thing,—is an article of property,—a chattel personal,—obtains as undoubted law in all these states."[30] Tomey's Turl's enforced subordination demands silences so that his private injuries cannot become the subject of legal or social appeals, and neither can they disrupt the comic facade of storytelling in "Was."

Neither revealing his motives nor addressing his desires, Tomey's Turl alludes nonetheless to his condition of powerlessness: " 'I gonter tell you something to remember: anytime you wants to git something done, from hoeing out a crop to getting married, just get the womenfolks to working at it. Then all you needs to do is set down and wait. You member that' " (13). His words to young Cass Edmonds, the narrator of "Was," introduce a concept of gender difference that is unlike his twin brothers' fear of women. Rather than constructing women in terms of social conventions, Tomey's Turl equates women with social action. How his socialization could have allowed for this conception is unclear, particularly given his initiation and execution of running; nevertheless, his retreat behind the action of women for "protection" and accomplishment renders him passive and submissive. In fact, the first words he speaks in "Was"—" 'Whut they doing now?' "—distance him from active participation in the events, as well as from immediate, firsthand observation of them. He directs his words and his advice about women to young Cass, whom Faulkner represents as the narrator of the past events in "Was." Perhaps Faulkner envisioned Tomey's Turl as a signifier of Cass's education into the ways of his society and as a corollary to Sam Fathers, the mentor of Isaac McCaslin. It is Cass after all who later becomes both teacher and surrogate father to Isaac Beauchamp McCaslin, the son of his Uncle Buck and Sophonsiba Beauchamp. Perhaps, then, Tomey's Turl cannot tell a story, because a story "allows the addressee to participate in and to share in an evaluative social negotiation," which cannot occur between Cass and Turl since they cannot be linked as resident in the same interpretive community or within the same narrative constituency.[31]

Turl remains fixed in an object position that does not allow him to negotiate meaning himself or to articulate his own meaning. The right to property (public/social, ownership, and entitlement) necessarily competes with the right to subjectivity (privacy, "life, liberty, and the pursuit of happiness"). Tomey's Turl's oppression and exploitation are contingent on his being silent and verbally unintelligible as the object of property toward whom the exercise of discourses of legal authority and social power is complete.[32] Nonetheless, the confidential and mysterious nature of his utterance points to the dualism inherent in slavery: "slaves were at the same time both objects and subjects, human property held for the purpose of enriching the masters and *individuals with lives of their own.*"[33]

While Tomey's Turl's language may suggest that he is positioned in the text as a cipher, his actions define the concreteness of his effort to win the woman he loves and thus remove the opaque veil enveloping him because of his inarticulate state. In a highly stylized, comic moment in *Go Down, Moses,* Tomey's Turl speaks back to ownership and moves (quickly) to challenge Buck and Buddy McCaslin's property claims, and therein lies his "story"—the interpolated silent story. He is neither controlled, defined, nor silenced as he breaks the rules of proper subordination and compliant subjugation expected of a thing. Turl runs over Buck, escapes a trap set to capture him, and races to a temporary freedom: "Tomey's Turl ran right clean over him. He never even bobbled; he knocked Uncle Buck down and then caught him before he fell without even stopping, snatched him up under one arm, still running, and carried him along for about ten feet, saying, 'Look out of here, old Buck. Look out of here, old Buck,' before he threw him away and went on" (18).

Turl's resistance to being reduced to a thing is determined, resolute, and persistent. He does not defer to Buck, does not call him "mister" or "master," and does not hesitate to throw Buck to the ground—all as part of his effort to remain free to court Tennie, free to be a man. However limited his legal rights may be, Tomey's Turl empowers himself to act as an intentional and righted subject. In that sense, then, he can be repositioned as a figure who transgresses the boundaries of slavery and society. His very body becomes a space defined as resistant to easy categorization or domination. His location as a largely voiceless black man within *Go Down, Moses*, a text of talk and telling by white men, primarily by the white McCaslins and Edmondses, reminds me of the lesson Patricia J. Williams learned in law school: "the best way to give voice to those whose voice had been suppressed was to argue that they had no voice."[34] She suggests that when rights are reconfigured to include those who have been presumed to be rightless, then that broader configuration will have as a consequence giving "voice to those people or things that, by virtue of object relation to a contract, historically have no voice. Allowing this sort of empowering opens up the *egoisme à deux* of traditional contract and increases the limited bipolarity of relationship that characterizes so much western civilization."[35] In particular, in terms of black people held in slavery, this perspective challenges and changes the paradigms and the hierarchies of power, and begins an assertion of the right to voice.

What narrative, then, might Tomey's Turl also be telling in his advice to get the womenfolks on anything that needs doing? How might his unarticulated story provide another angle from which to view his own condition and that of the Beauchamps and McCaslins? In effect, his words are clearly indicative of a covert but active cooperation between himself, Tennie, and Sophonsiba Beauchamp. The three become linked in a narrative one can both imagine and authorize because the three—the enslaved black man and woman and the free white woman—join together out of an expressed need and an unarticulated recognition of their intersecting oppressions. This multivalent, symbolic, hybrid narrative forms the angles that force the dominant discourse of property and ownership into an explosive confrontation with the consequences of its legal fictions.

Gendering Ownership

The ultimate act of ownership is bodily control, especially of women because they have the capacity to reproduce. *Go Down, Moses* is predicated on the hierarchical location of men as owners. The McCaslin and

Edmonds men contribute to a gendered ownership that controls women and that is perhaps most efficiently regulatory in eliminating the presence and influence of black and white women in the text through their deaths in childbirth. The slave-holding class assured its absolute authority not merely by oppressing all women but by controlling reproductive females. Patriarchy established the patterns of subjugation that became more pronounced with slavery.[36] While the symbolic similarity between the condition of women and that of slaves was often evoked by nineteenth-century abolitionists, particularly by feminist abolitionists, the difference in the condition of slaves gendered female is remarkable.

Black women in slavery faced unrestrained domination of their reproductive lives both as property and as labor, because from 1662 onward, the children of enslaved women followed the condition of their mothers. The Virginia statute cited for the determination of status, *partus sequitur ventrem*, was initially an attempt to regulate sexual relations between whites and blacks: "1662. Act XII. Children got by an Englishman upon a Negro woman shall be bond or free according to the condition of the mother, and if any Christian shall commit fornication with a Negro man or woman, he shall pay double fines of a former act."[37] There was an economic motive in the child's following the condition of the mother, rather than the condition of the father as was the precedent in English Common Law.[38] A. Leon Higginbotham observes, "Once it was established that the black woman's child took the mother's status, the master class gained a crucial economic advantage—its labor force reproduced itself."[39] With an inherent economic incentive to expand both the labor force and the dollar value of property holdings, slave-owners exercised unrestrained control over black women's reproduction and procreation, especially after 1808 and the suppression of the foreign slave trade. Sanctioned by law and custom, the reduction of slave women to objects of property who could be sexually assaulted, abused, raped, and bred went largely unchallenged by the social order, though the precise legal grounds for such treatment did not remain fixed over time.

For enslaved women who, like Tomasina and Eunice, are so controlled by their masters, to reproduce is not just to duplicate themselves as property but to reproduce the image of the owner. "Reproduction," master-slave intercourse leading to offspring or issue, is a narcissistic act, in addition to being a declaration of the legal authority of patriarchy (the law of the father) and of the law of the land. Sexual assault upon the bodies of enslaved women becomes a mark of their oppression and domination within the political, economic, and cultural institution of slavery. Such assault or rape "bears a direct relationship to all of the existing power structures in a given society. This relationship is not a simple, mechanical one, but rather involves complex structures reflecting the interconnectedness of the race, gender, and class oppression that characterize that society."[40] It is part of the overall outrageous and merciless attempt to extract the humanity from enslaved women and to render them abstract mechanisms of profit.

According to the ruling in *State v Mann*, which in 1829 upheld a master's right to "uncontrolled authority" to inflict any kind of punishment, short of death, on a slave:

> The end [of slavery] is the profit of the master, his security, and the public safety; the subject, the one doomed in his own person and his posterity to live without knowledge and without the capacity to make anything his own, and to toil that another may reap the fruits. What moral consideration shall be addressed to such a being to convince him, what . . . the most stupid must feel and know can never be true—that he is thus to labour upon a principle of natural duty, or for the sake of his own personal happiness. Such services can only be expected from one who has no will of his own, who surrenders his will in implicit obedience to that of another. Such obedience is the consequence only of uncontrolled authority over the body. There is nothing else which can operate to produce the effect. The power of the master must be absolute to render the submission of the slave perfect.[41]

Extended into the legal realm and the legal processes in effect during slavery, "the control the court sought was the total submission of blacks."[42] Necessarily, then, the sexual submission of enslaved women in forced intercourse or rape manifests an exercise of white male power, not desire, intended to demonstrate absolute control and will and to assert complete power and authority over blacks.

Significantly, white men often allowed themselves to believe the legal fictions and functioned as if blacks literally were without will and totally submissive. In an 1855 Missouri case, *State v Celia, a Slave*, an eighteen-year-old enslaved female was tried, found guilty, and executed for murdering her master, Robert Newsom, who as a sixty-year-old widower had purchased the fourteen-year-old girl to serve his sexual needs. According to Melton A. McLaurin, "from the moment he purchased Celia, Newsom regarded her as both his property and his concubine."[43] He raped her and used her for his sexual gratification for five years, during which time she bore him two children. Newsom's insistence that a pregnant Celia continue to have sex with him despite her objections led to her resistance, his death in her cabin, and her execution. McLaurin concludes that "Celia's challenge to her master's power over her sexual integrity was personal, violent, extreme, and unacceptable to a slaveholding society. It was unacceptable because gender mattered in both the social conventions and in the laws that upheld slavery. To have empowered slave women in the domestic area, to have recognized their right to control their sexuality, would have undercut the power of the master to a degree that would have threatened the very survival of the institution."[44] Newsom acted out of a belief in his total control of Celia and his absolute right of ownership of her body. She, on the other hand, acted out of the desperation and rage brought on by abuse and the relief and strength engendered in fighting back in order to have a measure of control over her own body. Ultimately, *State v Celia, a Slave* demonstrates that the "total control" or "uncontrolled authority" that whites sought to exercise over blacks could neither exist perfectly nor be sustained effectively because the bodily domination of slaves could not control an enslaved person's psyche. In their constantly traumatized state, enslaved people possessed the always already apparent will and volition to resist.

Even more than rape or sexual assault on an unrelated enslaved woman, incest both guaranteed the exclusive right to property and manifested the absolute power masters attempted to exert. By his representation of incest in *Go Down, Moses*, Faulkner links the sexual economy and the slave economy. In the father-daughter incest that Ike McCaslin deduces in his familial history, old Carothers McCaslin legally possesses the body of his daughter, Tomasina. He demonstrates "uncontrolled authority over [her] body," just as Chief Justice Ruffin wrote in the *State v Mann* decision: "This discipline belongs to the state of slavery. It constitutes the curse of slavery both to the bond and free portion of our population."[45] Carothers exercises absolute power in an incestuous narcissistic violation. As his property, Tomasina must surrender her will in obedience to his. Her body is thus marked incest victim and is re-marked a second time as doubly the property of the father, though this specific incest narrative is generally left out of the critical discourse on Faulkner's usage of incest in his fiction.[46]

Carothers McCaslin's sexual conquest of Tomasina is an act of staving off competition for property already owned and marked as owned. Yet in the game of competitive acquisition, Tomasina is always vulnerable to being the object of domination not merely because she is female but because she is chattel, the racialized object of property. According to the legal codes of the time, were another white man to assault Tomasina, Carothers could charge him with "trespass." In his *Inquiry into the Law of Negro Slavery*, for example, Thomas R. R. Cobb states: "the violation of the person of a female slave, carries with it no other punishment than the damages which the master may recover for the trespass of his property."[47] Though he acknowledges "person" in his formulation, Cobb construes sexual violation or rape of an enslaved woman as an "offense not affecting the existence of the slave" and thus limits the personhood of a slave.[48]

In marking his daughter Tomasina's body as his exclusive property, then, Carothers does not violate legal codes regarding the right to hold property and to protect property from seizure by trespassers or transgressors; nevertheless, he does transgress the religious, moral, ethical, cultural, and societal codes of individual and communal conduct or behavior. In the nineteenth-century South, incest, as Peter Bardaglio explains, "confused the roles and duties of individuals and eroded the stability of the family, thereby weakening its effectiveness as an institution of social control. To commit incest was to violate one's responsibility to the family and to the society at large."[49] Any legal restrictions were formulated in terms of the social order; for example, in *Ward v Dulaney* (1852), the Mississippi Supreme Court ruled that failure to punish those who commit incest "would undermine the foundations of social order and good government."[50] Incest involving miscegenation, however, was not held to the same moral or ethical standard—in terms neither of the social order nor of familial good. This brutality passed virtually ignored for generations among the white ruling class.

Reinhold Niebuhr in his study of ethics and social conflict reminds us of "the brutal character of the behavior of all human collectives, and the power of self-interest and collective egoism in all inter-group relations," and he insists that it is important both "to recognize the stubborn resistance of group egoism to all moral and inclusive social objectives" and to understand "the easy subservience of reason to prejudice and passion, and the consequent persistence of irrational human egoism."[51] Niebuhr suggests that the failure to recognize and appreciate "the power, extent and persistence of group egoism in human relations" allows us to overlook the difficulty of establishing just relations between individuals within a group "purely by moral and rational suasion and accommodation," and the near impossibility of just relations in intergroup relations because the proportion (specifically disproportion) of power that each group possesses is overlooked or denied: "It is not possible to determine exactly how much a party to a social conflict is influenced by a rational argument or by the threat of force."[52] Niebuhr's commentary on human egoism recalls the enormous power exerted by slaveholders. "Some planters of the Old South were notoriously promiscuous, sexually extravagant men who took advantage of vulnerable beings, black or white, women or girls, men or boys, and yea even the beasts of the fields. By its very nature slavery created commanding imperious persons. Slaveholding planters saw themselves as the lords of their little earths, and of all the bodies that dwelt thereon. Slavery required the absolute mastery of masters."[53]

What Faulkner terms Carothers's "own vanity's boundless conceiving" (251), though linked literally to his unfinished plantation house, also fittingly describes his incestuous abuse of Tomasina. His violation successfully staves off all competitors for his "property" Tomasina and produces yet more property (their son Terrel)—property that in its "white" maleness is even more the image of the father-owner Carothers than Tomasina could ever be in her femaleness. "There had already been some white in Tomey's Terrel's blood before his father gave him the rest of it" (259), Ike McCaslin remembers from his own boyhood observation of Tomasina's son. Here is a confounding point: miscegenation that is also incestuous is a move toward the legal destruction of blacks as racially marked. With the erasure of bodily difference, then, the issue of property and ownership becomes more problematical and more subjective. Concomitantly, with the erasure of difference, slavery as the condition of the "Black Other" would challenge and disrupt the conventional social fabric, and slavery as "African Service" would be dismantled. In this sense, incest is antisocial, much as in psychoanalysis where Freud accounts for incest on the ground that it is antisocial.[54]

The Owner of the following named and valuable Slaves, being on the eve of departure for Europe, will cause the same to be offered for sale, at the NEW EXCHANGE, corner of St. Louis and Chartres streets, on *Saturday*, May 16, at Twelve o'Clock, *viz.*

1. SARAH, a mulatress, aged 45 years, a good cook and accustomed to house work in general, is an excellent and faithful nurse for sick persons, and in every respect a first rate character.

2. DENNIS, her son, a mulatto, aged 24 years, a first rate cook and steward for a vessel, having acted in that capacity for many years on board one of the Mobile packets; is strictly honest, temperate, and a first rate subject.

3. CHOLE, a mulatress, aged 36 years, she is, without exception, one of the most competent servants in the country, a first rate washer and ironer, does up lace, a good cook, and for a bachelor who wishes a house-keeper she would be invaluable; she is also a good ladies' maid, having travelled to the North in that capacity.

4. FANNY, her daughter, a mulatress, aged 16 years, speaks French and English, is a superior hair-dresser, (pupil of Guillac,) a good seamstress and ladies' maid, is smart, intelligent, and a first rate character.

5. DANDRIDGE, a mulatoo, aged 26 years, a first rate dining-room servant, a good painter and rough carpenter, and has but few equals for honesty and sobriety.

6. NANCY, his wife, aged about 24 years, a confidential house servant, good seamstress, mantuamaker and tailoress, good cook, washer and ironer, etc.

7. MARY ANN, her child, a creole, aged 7 years, speaks French and English, is smart, active and intelligent.

8. FANNY or FRANCES, a mulatress, aged 22 years, is a first rate washer and ironer, good cook and house servant, and has an excellent character.

9. EMMA, an orphan, aged 10 or 11 years, speaks French and English, has been in the country 7 years, has been accustomed to waiting on table, sewing etc.; is intelligent and active.

10. FRANK, a mulatto, aged about 32 years speaks French and English, is a first rate bostler and coachman, understands perfectly well the management of horses, and is, in every respect, a first rate character, with the exception that he will occasionally drink, though not an habitual drunkard.

☞ All the above named Slaves are acclimated and excellent subjects; they were purchased by their present vendor many years ago, and will, therefore, be severally warranted against all vices and maladies prescribed by law, save and except FRANK, who is fully guaranteed in every other respect but the one above mentioned.

TERMS—One-half Cash, and the other half in notes at six months, drawn and endorsed to the satisfaction of the Vendor, with special mortgage on the Slaves until final payment. The Acts of Sale to be passed before WILLIAM BOSWELL, *Notary Public*, at the expense of the Purchaser. *New-Orleans, May* 13, 1835.

1835 advertisement for a group sale of mainly bilingual mulatto or mixed-race slaves, with excellent skills and character, several of whom were related, and all of whom were said to have been "purchased by their vendor many years ago." Two little girls, ages ten or eleven and seven, and two young women, one a teenager, are offered in the sale. Courtesy of Louisiana and Lower Mississippi Valley Collections, Louisiana State University Libraries.

That Carothers's "violation" ends in Tomasina's death (as well as the death by self-drowning of her mother, Eunice) makes him neither guilty of a crime nor any more culpable under the law. "Law privileges objectivity, individualism, and rights over their binary opposites, subjectivity, collectivity, and responsibility, and this privilege is identified with the more general male privilege over females."[55] When ownership is added to the legal discourses of objectivity, individualism, and rights, the result is a vacating of any legal censure of Carothers's behavior. He acts out of privilege and right, and he has behind him the full sanction of law.

Women within the law are treated in four ways, according to Zillah R. Eisenstein: "as a sex class, as different from men—reproducers and gendered mothers; as the same as men, like men, and therefore not women; as absent but a class different from men; and as absent but as a class the same as men. The phallus is centered in all these conceptualizations but in different formulations."[56] The black women in slavery do not fall within any of these categories, because they are also represented as different from the class of women. Thus, it is not unimaginable that to Carothers McCaslin whatever protections women as a class or caste may have enjoyed were not extended to slave women, not even to those black women directly related to him by blood.[57]

Put another way, race influenced conceptions of womanhood and of sexual expression. Black women, excluded from protections as women under the law yet remanded bodily to the category of property, could be exploited sexually with impunity. In *Scenes of Subjection* Saidiya Hartman cautions, however, that "the decriminalization of rape not be understood as dispossessing the enslaved of female gender, but in terms of differential productions of gendered identity or . . . the adequacy or meaning of gender" in the specific context of "property relations, the sexual economy of slavery, and the calculation of injury."[58] While excluded as women under law and dismissed from the protections afforded white women, enslaved women nonetheless possessed and produced gender identities as women.

Southern ideology fostered the conditions that made the exploitation of enslaved women possible. Power and with it physical and psychological domination enabled an acceptance of social and sexual practices that brutalized black women. As Catherine Clinton concluded, "Within the complex sexual scenario of plantation society, power eclipsed other themes. It is not excessive to speculate that domination shaped erotic imagination, arousal, objects of desire, and modes of gratification. Slaveowners incorporated violence, actual or implied, into their pattern of sexual satisfaction."[59] Rape, in particular those cases brought into legal discourse, conveyed not a story of a victim's abuse but one of male power and indulgence in sustaining the social order. On the basis of her reading of nineteenth- and early-twentieth-century rape cases brought to trial, Mary Frances Berry suggests, "Rape enhances our understanding that patriarchy is the subtext underlying race, class, gender. We may think the story is race, but when we look at race dead-on we are looking at a socially constructed distinction used to maintain hierarchical relationships in the society." Berry goes further and concludes from those cases that "every child and incest case brought into the courtroom a drama in which judges, lawyers, and defendants protected male sexual proclivities and power."[60] The exercise of legitimized sexual violence and the social power behind it resulted in the protection afforded by the judiciary composed of white men who understood the necessity of maintaining the status quo.

Ultimately, Tomasina's trauma, or that of her son or of her mother, is so disguised by the method of storytelling that seemingly it merely figures the project Faulkner places at the narrative center of the discourse on ownership: Isaac McCaslin's trauma, which is sexual as much as social. While old Carothers may have exercised his power over his daughter with impunity, his grandson Ike responds to that power with both shock and shame. Ike thinks of his grandfather's sexual use of Tomasina as unimaginable in the context of raw force and domination: *"But there must have been love. . . . Some sort of love. Even what he would have called love: not just an afternoon's or night's spittoon"* (258). Ike would like there to be something more than old Carothers's casual gratification, but once he understands the father-daughter relationship existing between Carothers and Tomasina, Ike is hard pressed to excuse his grandfather's exploitation and "ruthlessness" (260). His speculation about "some sort of love" is not so far removed from the interpretation Eugene Genovese places on sex between slave owners and enslaved women: "It would be hard to live with a beautiful and submissive young woman for long and to continue to consider her mere property or a mere object of sexual gratification. . . . it would not be astonishing if many of the fancy girls, like their famous quadroon sisters in New Orleans who entered into an institutionally structured concubinage with wealthy white men, *often ended by falling in love with their men and vice versa."*[61] Genovese suppresses the power imbalance in such relations and ignores the sexual exploitation inherent in relations of unequal power and exercise of will.

What love could possibly have existed in scenarios in which slave children were purchased by adult white men for sexual gratification? Patricia J. Williams uncovered documents from which she was able to piece together the narrative of her great-great-grandmother's violated childhood. When only eleven years old, her great-great-grandmother was purchased and raped by Austin Miller, a thirty-five-year-old bachelor and lawyer in Tennessee. In the county census two years later, she was listed as a "slave, female," thirteen years old and the mother of an eight-month-old child, the first of those she bore her owner.[62] He subsequently became a prominent judge and the father of sons who also became lawyers, and she became invisible, producing his children-slaves who became his house servants when he later married and began his white family. The narrative is inflected with power and abuse of a child, which cannot be mistaken for love. Williams concludes that the story has inspired her "interest in the interplay of notions of public and private, of family and market; of male and female; of molestation and the law," so that she "track[s] meticulously the dimension of meaning in [her] great-great-grandmother as chattel: the meaning of money; the power of consumerist world view, the deaths of those we label the unassertive and the inefficient."[63] In her legal work, Williams counters her great-great-grandmother's erasure by seeing "her shape and his hand in the vast networking of our society, in the evils and oversights that plague our lives and laws. The control he had over her body. The force he was in her life, in the shape of my life today. The power he exercised in the choice to breed her or not. The choice to breed slaves in his image, to choose her mate and be that mate. In his attempt to own what no man can own, the habit of his power and the absence of her choice."[64] Her family history is an exposé of uncontrolled power and its exercise of sexual domination over girls as slave property.

In *Go Down, Moses* Ike, similar to Genovese, would like to inscribe a relational "paternalism" but not the racial domination that Williams exposes. Resistant to the explanation implicit in his speculative reconstruction of his grandfather, Ike does not want to confront the ideology of domination. "It would be a mistake to regard the institutionalized pattern of rape during slavery as an expression of white men's sexual urges," Angela Y. Davis has concluded. "Rape was a weapon of domination, a weapon of repression, whose covert goal was to extinguish slave women's will to resist, and in the process to demoralize their men."[65] In the case of Carothers and Tomasina, sexual relations reflect power relations manifested in coercion, not love. Coerced sexual "assaults" upon the person of an enslaved and powerless woman "would remind the women of their essential and inalterable femaleness. In the male supremacist vision of the period, this meant passivity, acquiescence and weakness"; it did not mean love.[66]

What Ike "reads" into the plantation commissary ledgers constitutes the narrative mortar and power and trauma of race and storytelling in *Go Down, Moses*. Ike "reads" the homosocial: the absolute power of whiteness within a slave holding society. His interpolation of meaning lifts the narrative from the initial comic and tragicomic stance. The text of the ledger, multiply inscribed by Carothers and both of his twin sons, Buck and Buddy, may be deciphered as the ultimate heterosexual homosocial act—the incestuous "right" of the father-owner over life and body, the paternalistic power authorized in a masculinist culture to create and to destroy life. Ike recoils from the pages of the ledger even while turning them and thinking, "*His own daughter His own daughter. No No Not even him*" (259). He is, of course, thinking in terms of family and familial relations that would render Carothers's taking of his own daughter unimaginable; however, as Nell Irvin Painter pointed out, slavery and family are inextricably intertwined: "for the etymology of the word *family* reaches back to the Latin word *familia*, meaning a household, and *famulus/famula*, meaning servant or slave, deeply embedding the notion of servitude within our concept of family."[67] By means of speculative reading and deep sensitivity to all aspects of his cultural environment, Ike concludes that the corruption implicit in the physical, psychological, and sexual enslavement of human beings did indeed extend into the family, into his own family.

The evidence for that corruption within families does exist, not only in fictive ledgers but also in actual legal documents, one example of which is a will written in the late 1850s by a slave owner who, having fathered children by his slave Louisa, directed his white sons and legal heirs to make certain that only family members and no strangers would own his slave children: "Nor would I like that any but my own blood should own as Slaves my own blood or Louisa. . . . Do not let Louisa or any of my children or probable children be the Slaves of Strangers. Slavery *in the family* will be their happiest earthly condition."[68] Perhaps even more problematical in this case of the abuse of familial bonds is that the testator, Senator James Henry Hammond of South Carolina, after having sexually used Louisa from the time she turned twelve and her mother, Sally, with whom he also had children, deeded the two women to his son, Harry, who also exploited the daughter sexually and fathered a child by her.[69] As slaves, neither mother nor daughter could protect their bodies or their relational bond from violation by the powerful and politically prominent

Hammond men with their paternalistic notion of keeping their enslaved concubines and children all in the family.

Ironically, while the family was viewed progressively throughout the nineteenth century as "the spiritual and moral hub of society" and as a "morally superior place," the family under slavery enjoyed no such place.[70] In legal terms, the family gained new definition in the nineteenth century. Laws emerged that "recognized the family as an organic, autonomous legal entity, and established the framework for the public governance of private life."[71] These laws became the cornerstone of what today is known as family law; however, the slave family "was constructed outside of legal developments governing family relationships. The notion of legal autonomy within the private sphere had no meaning for the slave family . . . [which] could not be an organic unit of permanently linked, interdependent persons. In the eyes of the law, each slave stood as an individual unit of property and never as a submerged partner in a marriage or family. The most universal life events—marriage, procreation, child rearing—were manipulated to meet the demands of the commercial enterprise."[72] In both rhetoric and in practice, as the Hammonds' abuse of slave women and their children demonstrates, whites constructed a different standard of family and morality in relation to slaves.

In what has become one of the best-known nineteenth-century diaries, Mary Boykin Chesnut responded to the sexual abuses perpetrated within families by male slaveholders with anger against the perpetrators for what white women like herself had to endure and with contempt for the black victims ("these beastly Negress beauties are only animals"); she observed, "We live surrounded by prostitutes. God forgive us, but ours is a monstrous system, a wrong and iniquity. Like the patriarchs of old, our men live all in one house with their wives and their concubines; and the mulattoes one sees in every family exactly resemble the white children. Any lady is ready to tell you who is the father of all the mulatto children in everybody's household but her own. Those, she seems to think, drop from the clouds."[73] Chesnut's usage of *family* is another reminder that the Latin origin of the word also means "all those included in a household—slaves, women, and children—who were subject to the master's supreme will."[74] These examples all open a space for critically interpreting Ike McCaslin's rejection of his inherited right (by virtue of his white, male, son positionality) to land (and the legal and commercial traditions of the plantation) as also a rejection of his right to power in masculinity and to the heterosexual prerogatives figured in Carothers's sexual domination of his daughter.

Joel Williamson in *William Faulkner and Southern History* exposes an aspect of the Faulkner history that adds another dimension to the miscegenation narrative and white owners' sexual exploitation of their female slaves and to the often hidden crossing of racial boundaries in Faulkner's fiction. Williamson recounts the liaison between Colonel William C. Falkner, Faulkner's great-grandfather, and his "shadow family," the slave family of Emeline Falkner, who was the colonel's slave and the mother of two daughters, Delia and Hellen, by her first owner, Benjamin E. W. Harris, and of two additional surviving children, Arthur and Fannie. Born in 1837, Emeline was twenty-one years old when Falkner advanced Harris $900 for Emeline and her two daughters and moved them to the safety of his yard in 1858. Once under Falkner's protection, the three were never again pawned for credit by Harris, who had repeatedly used the three as collateral for loans and passed them from one creditor's household to the next. The mother, under the name "Mrs. Emeline Lacy Falkner," and the two oldest daughters are all buried in the Ripley (Mississippi) Cemetery.[75] Williamson terms Emeline's story "amazing," the "saga of a slave woman and her children, fathered by the white men who owned her, and how they passed out of slavery and beyond in to the broad stream of black life in America."[76] While Williamson is struck by the eventual social mobility of Emeline and her children, he discloses without amazement what is so striking to me: that Benjamin Harris exercised such "uncontrolled authority" over his slave mistress and his own two daughters that he routinely made them vulnerable to physical (including sexual) abuse as the human collateral for debts that he knew could not be repaid.

With the spread of market capitalism in the nineteenth century and with its increased opportunities for accumulating wealth, individuals took greater risks in pursuit of fortunes and incurred greater debt as a part of the process. Benjamin Harris repeatedly mortgaged Emeline and her daughters by him to finance his schemes for making money in Mississippi. Not only was he participating in recognizable ways in capitalistic ventures, but he was also using the legal concept central to the marketplace: contract, "a promise that the law will enforce. 'Contracts and promises are essentially risk-allocation devices'. . . [originating in] an 'advanced level of economic development.' "[77] Harris's mortgaging of his slaves is a form of contract for high-risk ventures; they provided him with capital, but as chattel mortgages, they faced the possibility that they could be sold to satisfy Harris's creditors, as they were held in mortgages that were essentially trust deeds. The legal boundaries between trust deeds, mortgages, and conditional sales were not distinct, particularly when the contract involved slaves whose status was devolving throughout the nineteenth century and whose value was escalating at a greater rate than real estate as property.

These general conditions of an expanding marketplace made it possible for Harris to pawn his shadow family of three females to cover his debts and to acquire additional cash for his expenses. (His action is not so far-fetched considering that in the case of *Bryan v Walton* [1853] Judge Joseph Henry Lumpkin in drawing an analogy between American slavery and that existing in early republics linked slaves to cattle in that they both might be sold or mortgaged.)[78] The three females, very white in appearance, were used as objects without will and without rights. Commodities in a new marketplace, the women were more valuable than land or immovables. Perhaps more importantly, Williamson concludes, "It is a story that resonates marvelously with William Faulkner's depiction in his fiction of that same vast and vital phenomenon in Southern — and American — culture. The kinship between fact and fiction is not coincidental. Through Emeline and her children, Faulkner was personally intimate with a real story, a historical happening, fully as powerful as any that he ever conceived in his imagination."[79] For the writer William Faulkner, the resonance between his family history and his fictional plots may have been particularly powerful because, after ending the cycle of mortgaging of Emeline and her daughters, Col. Falkner fathered the youngest of Emeline's surviving children, Fannie Forrest Falkner.

The commissary ledgers in "The Bear" become texts within a text, and thus they facilitate understanding and knowledge (perhaps empathy as well) of those enslaved and their enslavers on the McCaslin plantation. Faulkner wrote "The Bear" after the other McCaslin stories, and the fourth section, which interpolates intertextual ledger entries, constitutes a movement in the text away from social comedy and toward personal tragedy.[80] There, the fates of the fictional Eunice and her daughter, Tomasina, like that of the actual Emeline and her daughters, are intricately connected with the will of white men.

In *Incidents in the Life of a Slave Girl* (1861) Harriet Jacobs concludes a chapter of her narrative devoted to the abuses of will and overreaches of power by slaveholders with the experiential reality she has known as one who was held in slavery for twenty-one years.

> No pen can give an adequate description of the all-pervading corruption produced by slavery. The slave girl is reared in an atmosphere of licentiousness and fear. The lash and the foul talk of her master and his sons are her teachers. When she is fourteen or fifteen, her owner, or his sons, or the overseer, or perhaps all of them, begin to bribe her with presents. If these fail to accomplish their purpose, she is whipped or starved into submission to their will. She may have had religious principles inculcated by some pious mother or grandmother, or some good mistress, she may have a lover, whose good opinion and peace of mind are dear to her heart; or the profligate men who have power over her may be exceedingly odious to her. But resistance is hopeless.[81]

The written narrative that Jacobs herself produced, however, constitutes an act of resistance and suggests that there are various modes of resistance recognized and utilized by enslaved women in their struggle for bodily integrity. Jacobs testifies from her own experience and observation, as other contemporary nineteenth-century observers have, "that slavery is a curse to the whites as well as to the blacks. It makes the white fathers cruel and sensual; the sons violent and licentious; it contaminates the daughters, and makes the wives wretched. And as for the colored race, it needs an abler pen than mine to describe the extremity of their sufferings, the depth of their degradation."[82] Jacobs ably articulates the specific horrors of slavery for women whose bodies are always vulnerable to sexual assault and its physical and psychological consequences.

Within the fictional narrative of "The Bear" in *Go Down, Moses*, Ike McCaslin's subjective experience while reading and deciphering the ledgers is powerful, life-altering, and transformative. In reading the ledgers, he intuits his social and familial history and its human consequences: "page followed page and year year; all there, not only the general and condoned injustice and its slow amortization but the specific tragedy which had not been condoned and could never be amortized" (254). Because of this experience, Ike will not fall victim to the abuses Jacob delineates. As a result, he functions at the intersection of power and resistance. Knowledge of the subjective experience of others fosters not simply understanding but community; it is what Robin West says makes both justice and society.[83]

Ike subjectively and patiently understands the message that Faulkner transmits through the pages of the plantation ledgers: Property as a concept is transformatively connected to the embodied, oblique, elliptical story of trauma, rape, transgression, incest, betrayal, shame and rage. That multifaceted story with its center in persons as property has consequences so devastating that its telling can only occur in fragments, between spaces, in silence.

Ike recognizes that he is impotent to repair the damage done to Tomasina and her son, Terrel, as well as to her mother, Eunice, but he does not draw the logical conclusion that Tomasina has rights, that she and her son deserve justice. According to Oliver Wendell Holmes Jr., "A legal right is nothing but a permission to exercise certain natural powers, and upon certain conditions to obtain protection, restitution, or compensation by the aid of public force."[84] Ike understands that his own rights, protected by law like his grandfather's, are a source of oppression, transgression, and violation; thus, he renounces his rights and repudiates his grandfather's exercise of rights. At the same time, Ike does not see that Tomasina is a righted subject; in his view, she remains, like Tomey's Turl, the object of property and without rights. His position is not the position taken, and challenged, in the nineteenth century when the issue of rights for emancipated black people and for white women was a dominant legal and social discourse. Even after Emancipation, for example, Sojourner Truth would remark to a mixed audience, "I want women to have their rights. In the courts women have no right, no voice; nobody speaks for them. I wish woman to have her voice there among the pettifoggers. If it is not a fit place for women, it is unfit for men to be there."[85]

Patricia J. Williams has said that "rights are to law what conscious commitments are to the psyche. This country's worst historical moments have not been attributable to rights *assertion* but to a failure of rights commitment. From this perspective, the problem with rights discourse is not that the discourse is itself constricting but that it exists in a constricted referential universe. The body of private laws epitomized by contract, including slave contract, is problematic because it denies the object of contract any rights at all."[86] Williams seeks to expand "private property rights into a conception of civil rights," because rights should "reflect a larger definition of privacy and property: so that privacy is turned from exclusion based on self-regard into regard for another's fragile, mysterious autonomy; and so that property regains its ancient connotation of being a reflection of the universal self."[87] The discourse of rights that Williams suggests would turn the conventional notion of rights on end, reverse the negative and hierarchical connotations, and open a space for reconsidering property rights as civil rights.

What would that look like in the case of Tomey's Turl as offspring who is positioned in *Go Down, Moses* as the object of property? Perhaps it would look somewhat like the story of Tomey's Turl as a game player who achieves his righted subjectivity out of his own agency and his brothers' recognition that he is a man and a brother, who has the right to enter into a legal contract. Turl's social history, interpolated from games, creates the narrative discourse of rights and (dis)empowerment. But Ike McCaslin sees Tomey's Turl's case quite differently.

Ike objectifies Turl as the tangible sign of his grandfather's act of will and power in his sexual violation of Tomasina. What Ike recognizes and rejects is the active masculine and aggressive heterosexual role played by his grandfather, old Carothers, whom Ike envisions as "that evil and unregenerate old man who could summon, because she was his property, a human being because she was old enough and female, to his widower's house and get a child on her and then dismiss her because she was of an inferior race, and then bequeath a thousand dollars to the infant" (281). Tomey's Turl becomes the embodiment of the contested site of power, and he figures a transgressive move against that very power. Thus, Ike confronts power by means of Tomey's Turl. With his construct of Turl, Ike struggles against the legacy, the sexuality, and the psychology of his grandfather. Like his father and uncle before him, Ike attempts to repudiate the societal expectations of human and land ownership and of the sexual prerogatives of an aggressive masculinity that are intricately embedded in societal customs and laws regulating property. His experience interpreting the ledger and the history of his family (and of the larger slave-holding culture) renders him a sexual victim of the impact of slavery and links him, psychologically, to Tomey's Turl, and thus both of their existences can be read as social death. "The essence of slavery is that the slave, in his social death, lives on the margin between community and chaos, life and death, the social and the secular. Already dead, he lives outside the mana [*sic*] of the gods and can cross boundaries with social and supernatural impunity."[88] Ike assumes, like a stigmata, the material condition that links him to Tomey's Turl.

Sexual crime, as it is read into the ledgers, is linked to property and also to death. The enslavement of issue, Turl, and the death of his mother and grandmother are penultimate. It is a scenario that Anna Julia Cooper, a teacher and former slave, knew all too well, as she acknowledged in speaking to the World's Congress of Representative Women in 1893: "Yet all through the darkest period of the colored women's oppression in this country her yet unwritten history is full of heroic struggle, a struggle against fearful and overwhelming odds, that often ended in horrible death, to maintain and protect that which woman hold dearer than life. The painful, patient, and silent toil of mothers to gain a fee simple title to the bodies of their daughters, the despairing fight, as of an entrapped tigress, to keep hallowed their own persons, would furnish material for epics."[89] In remarking the "painful" and "silent" work of black mothers "to gain a fee simple title to the bodies of their daughters" and "to keep hallowed their own persons," Cooper references the struggle of black women against sexual victimization and degradation because their bodies were not their own. Slave women's relationship to their own bodies was even more vexed precisely because they could not control reproduction and their pregnancies were often the result of forced cohabitation. Writing in *Killing the Black Body* about the importance of reproductive liberty to women's equality, Dorothy Roberts concludes, "Every indignity that comes from the denial of reproductive autonomy can be found in slave women's lives—the harms of treating women's wombs as procreative vessels, of policies that pit a mother's welfare against that of her unborn child, and of government attempts to manipulate women's childbearing decisions through threats and bribes."[90]

The representation of women's otherness or alterity in *Go Down, Moses* is largely connected to reproduction and women's capacity for bearing children. "Women are both biological sexual selves and selves engendered through their bodies. Sex and gender play back on each other through a complicated process. The woman's body is particularized as female, but it is inevitably associated with the mother's body, which is more than female because it embodies institutionalized gender 'difference.'"[91] Eunice, a slave, has no legal recourse. But Eunice is also a woman and a mother. Although Zillah Eisenstein worries over conceptions of the female body that would omit the dynamic of change and engender the meaning of the mother's body in essentialist terms, she may have overlooked the legal deprivation of black women's right to be mothers, even though as slaves they could be bred.[92] Not only could the children of slave women be sold away from them at any time convenient to the owner, but the children, born and unborn, could also be bequeathed separately from the mother. For example, in *Nelson v Nelson*, an 1849 North Carolina case, Judge Thomas Ruffin decided that Leah, a slave woman, could be given to one person and her increase (that is, her first born or second born or all of her children) could be given to a different person. "The court ruled that this applied only to children Leah had in the lifetime of the testator and held that afterborn children went with Leah. If there had been 'plain words' to the contrary, they would have been respected, but there were not."[93]

Eunice may be without an identity that would allow her access to the law, but she is not under the absolute control of old Carothers, her owner and, according to Ike's interpretation of the ledgers, her lover. Configured as a mixed-race woman bought in New Orleans to be a concubine, Eunice is embodied in the text to the extent that she is a mother who commits suicide by drowning herself. Literally, she erases her body from the patriarchal text of domination and subjugation. What remains is the conception of Eunice as mother, specifically as Tomasina's mother, as a mother who cannot avenge her daughter's rape but who can register her own grief and guilt and her daughter's pain in the act of bodily annihilation. As Wilma King states, "Slave parents had unusually heavy responsibilities. They had to ensure that they survived and, at the same time, that their children survived. All too often, these responsibilities fell disproportionately upon slave mothers, who provided the initial nurturing and were the basic anchors for the young children."[94]

Both Eunice, brought to Mississippi as an exotic sexual property, and Tomey, born into chattel slavery as her master's property, child, and concubine, are subjects only of the laws of property, not of morality or family. That Tomey bears her father-owner's child is not open to discussion, not within the text where the act of incest can only be deciphered by Ike McCaslin out of a sense of his own sexual inadequacies. Ike remembers that "Tomey's Terrel was still alive when the boy [Ike] was ten years old and he knew from his own observation and memory that there had already been some white in Tomey's Terrel's blood before his father gave him the rest of it" (259). Nor is Turl's parentage open to discussion within current theoretical debates, when text-driven scholars ask: How do we know that Tomey is old Carothers's daughter? Neither disbelief nor incredulity nor empiricism requires such interrogation of the "facts" of sexual exploitation. And how do we know that old Carothers fathers her son, Terrel? Ike, in fact, thinks, that old Carothers "made no effort either to explain or obfuscate the thousand-dollar legacy to the son of an unmarried slave-girl, to be paid only at the child's coming-of-age, bearing the consequence of the act of which there was still no definite incontrovertible proof that he acknowledged, not out of his own substance but penalising his sons with it, charging them a cash forfeit on the accident of their own paternity; not even a bribe for silence toward his own face since his fame would suffer only after he was no longer present to defend it" (257–58). Perhaps Edward Said's conclusion in *Culture and Imperialism* has some bearing on this matter: "Culture is exonerated of any entanglements with power, representations are considered only as apolitical images to be parsed and construed as so many grammars of exchange."[95] But, more to the point, Noel Polk has, with his discovery of a letter from William Faulkner commenting on Tomasina's white paternity, acknowledged the critical interpretation of that paternity that has animated the reading of the text by race-invested scholars all along.[96] Ultimately, the debased Tomasina and Eunice together are the catalysts for the elevation of the narrative from the denial of humanity embedded in slapstick plantation humor to an eloquently painful renunciation of property and, with it, racial privilege and power.

Who is responsible for Eunice's death? If she is valuable because she is a slave, who will make compensation for her loss? Eunice's death has no meaning in the legal sense beyond the loss of property (though from today's vantage point it may be variously read as an act of resistance or rebellion).[97] In a relevant discourse on compensation, however, Adrian Howe argues that the distinctive aspect of women's experience to focus on in legal discourse is that of injuries: "we should value them, politicize them and, when necessary, demand that they become actionable."[98] Is Eunice's death actionable in a legal sense? Tort law or injury law is a product of the nineteenth century, but it did not develop as a response to the human suffering of slaves; instead, it developed around injuries resulting from industrialization. Mechanical power, machines, engines, whether in factories or railroads, involved a high risk of bodily injury, and along with this risk came the legal hazard of liability for such injury, although the expansion of industry and marketplace economics blunted the sense of moral responsibility for physical injury. Eunice's suffering, then, does not constitute a legal injury. The cause of her pain bears no liability and no compensation. Even in the twenty-first century, calls for reparations for slavery in the United States have not adequately taken into account the problematic legacy of tort law in the construction of discourses of injury.

Already socially dead within the system of slavery, Eunice commits suicide because, Ike surmises, her white owner and lover, the father of her daughter, commits incest and begets a child upon his own daughter. Suicide among slaves was dismissed as impossible, as the entries in the McCaslin ledger suggest: "*June 21th 1833 Drownd herself. . . . 23 Jun 1833 Who in hell ever heard of a niger drownding him self*" (256). Thomas D. Morris, in his massive treatment of slavery and law in the South, does not even have an entry for suicide. Yet, as Leslie Howard Owens observes in his work on "the logic of resistance," the frequency of suicide among slaves has been underestimated. Neither age nor designated labor, no matter whether skilled or unskilled, domestic or field workers, functioned as deterrents. Owens suggests that Emile Durkheim's term "fatalistic suicide" applies to the suicides of slaves, such incidents seemingly occurring with no warning: "Freds Negro woman took it into her hed that She had lived long enough and between 12 and 1 o'clock hung herself . . . for no known cause."[99] The words "for no known cause" resonate precisely because the condition of enslaved women, in fact, or in fictional narratives, always already exists as cause—however suppressed, denied, or ignored—of the desire for release and escape, even the escape of suicide.

What Ike McCaslin surmises and then sees has a compelling truthfulness about it. "In response to intimate violence, women usually learn a range of methods for disassociating from the immediate incident of abuse as well as from memories of the experience. When the abuse occurs women may alter their consciousness as a form of escape, by closing down some part of their psychic selves."[100] Ike envisions Eunice as having transcended feeling, as being outside the realms of emotion: "he seemed to see her actually walking into the icy creek on that Christmas day six months before her daughter's and her lover's (*Her first lover's* he thought. *Her first*) child was born, solitary, inflexible, griefless, ceremonial, in formal and succinct repudiation of grief and despair who had already had to repudiate belief and hope" (259).[101] Perhaps Ike is constructing Eunice's state of psychic annihilation and self-erasure because, despite the legal fiction of Eunice's marriage to Thucydus and the resulting official narrative of Tomasina as the product of that marriage, Ike surmises that Carothers did not travel all the way from north Mississippi to New Orleans in order to pay $650 for a bride for his slave Thucydus.

Ike's construction of a ceremonial Eunice is similar to that of Charles Bon's octoroon "wife" in Faulkner's *Absalom, Absalom!* Bon explains her origins and those of other mixed-race women involved in *plaçage* relationships as "flowers" created by the combination of white blood and the African "female principle which existed, queenly and complete, in the hot equatorial groin of the world long before that white one of ours came down from trees and lost its hair and bleached out" (145).[102] Yet Eunice is neither "flower" nor "female principle." Hortense J. Spillers has problematized such romantic constructions of sexuality as is evident in the case of the Creole women: "Sexuality as a term of power belongs to the empowered."[103] Eunice is a woman, enslaved, denied grief and despair, just as she has already been denied belief and hope. She is a woman abstracted from both justice and retribution. She is punished for someone else's sins and for society's larger crime because she is a slave and a woman.

And though Ike does not mention anger in his imagining of Eunice's walking into the creek to drown herself, surely a further speculation might well be an anger so profound that the only imaginable outlet was destruction. Because she cannot retaliate against Carothers or speak out against his violations, Eunice may have turned her anger at the severity of her racial and gender subjugation inward, deflected from Carothers to herself. Eunice has not only been used sexually by Carothers, but she has been discarded as an objectified "thing"—an object for sexual gratification and sexual domination. In going all the way to New Orleans and paying $650 for her (a Creole exotic in Mississippi), he separates himself from the ordinary white men within his community. In marrying her off to one of his slaves when he finds it convenient, Carothers has demonstrated his sense of his superiority both to her and to Thucydus, her husband, and ultimately to her child. The deleterious consequences of his actions may be figured partly in Eunice's traumatized body walking into the creek and partly in the social isolation and anguish of her daughter. Eunice's anger may have been compounded by her sense of guilt and her untenable role as a slave mother, who, as Patricia Hill Collins concludes about black mothers of daughters and the "troubling dilemma" they face,

> on one hand, to ensure their daughters' physical survival, mothers must teach them to fit into systems of oppression. . . . Mothers also know that if their daughters uncritically accept the limited opportunities offered Black women, they become willing participants in their own subordination. Mothers may have ensured their daughters' physical survival, but at the high cost of their emotional destruction.
>
> On the other hand, Black daughters with strong self-definitions and self-valuations who offer serious challenges to oppressive situations may not physically survive.[104]

Eunice's outrage at Carothers's taking not a young replica of herself, but the child of her own flesh and of his must have been without bounds. Her own daughter! His own child! Yet because Eunice is enslaved and thus accustomed to suppressing her anger, she does not attempt to destroy Carothers McCaslin; instead she destroys herself. Anger, of course, is not allowed to property. Slaves were forced to repress their anger. My construction of Eunice's suicide as an expression of anger in no way ameliorates the responsibility of Carothers and the legally sanctioned institution of slavery, or endorses the social and legal discourses that would configure Eunice as without feeling. As bell hooks has said, "I understand rage to be a necessary aspect of resistance struggle," because the repression of rage has functioned to perpetuate white supremacy and black victimization: "black rage [is] something other than sickness. . . . [It is] a potentially healthy, potentially healing response to oppression and exploitation."[105]

There is no way of separating Eunice's race-specific and gender-specific injuries, the kind of injuries Robin West has called "legally unrecognizable" but in need of phenomenological description to "communicate its magnitude" and lift it to "legal recognition."[106] The "social injury" caused by "hidden injuries"—those that are specific to race-oriented and gender-oriented societies—as Adrian Howe has observed, is indeed a *social* and not a "privatized," personal injury. Yet, Eunice's injuries, pain, and trauma are systemic, endemic to slavery as a legally condoned institution. Or, put another way, "the entire community is morally culpable for the deleterious consequences of male sexual and physical assault on women," and therefore "women's anguish is a communal problem."[107] In reading Eunice's death, Elisabeth Muhlenfeld concludes that her suicide "not only shames the race who so wronged and dehumanized her but also empowers her descendants," but in reading the larger impact of slavery on what she terms "the symbolics of female gender," Hortense J. Spillers recognizes the marks of brutality not only on the slave woman's body but on all facets of her relationship to sexuality and reproduction.[108]

And what of Tomasina? Her resistance to sexual domination by Carothers may finally be measured in her refusal to live, which may be an act of agency comparable to Eunice's act of will in committing suicide. Despite the fact that Tomasina's death occurs in childbirth, it may be read as a response to her victimization, her rape by a white man, owner, and father, who in the very markers of his identity personified all the entitlements that she was powerless to fight legally or emotionally. Her death, then, may be seen as self-induced, a manifestation of grief at the loss of her mother and a mourning of her own shameful violation at the hand of her father—but surely, it is also murder, because just as certainly the trauma she suffers is life-destroying. While rape was defined as "carnal knowledge of a woman forcibly and against her will," slaves were defined as without will, and therefore, according to this perverse logic, slave women could not be raped. In the 1859 Mississippi case of *George, a Slave v State*, Judge William L. Harris ruled that slaves were outside of common law and a young slave girl under ten years of age, who was a victim of rape by the slave George, could not have a suit brought because the provisions of English Common Law were "inapplicable to injuries on the slave here" and the state's general rape law did not apply to slaves.[109] Indeed, George's lawyer had argued, "Our laws recognize no marital rights between slaves; their sexual intercourse is left to be regulated by their owners. The regulations of law . . . do not and cannot apply to slaves; their intercourse is promiscuous, and the violation of a female slave by a male slave would be assault and battery."[110] Black girls and women in slavery, even when evidence supported their just claims were removed from the protection of law.

A white man could not be charged with sexual assault or rape of a black woman, whether slave or free. The prevailing belief among Mississippi jurists was that "by their very nature 'African' slaves copulated freely. . . . Blacks were randy and that was that."[111] Sexual aggression against a black woman was absolved as impossible. Thus, semantically, logically, and legally, the condition that Tomasina endures is denied and erased, so that she is alienated from her own body. And with Eunice's suicide occurring six months before Tomasina gives birth, Tomasina is also isolated from her mother and estranged from the maternal, by both circumstance and guilt. Death in childbirth may be read as a psychological, as much as a physical, response to her condition. Her shame, in particular, may have weighed as heavily on her as her mother's guilt. Traci West suggests that "while guilt is directed toward an action and can be assuaged through penalty or reparation, shame is invariably directed inwards."[112] The pain, isolation, and deprivation Tomasina suffered along with humiliation, shame, and ultimately death as the object of property cannot be fully calculated or recompensed.

This may be why Thucydus, cast in the public role of father to Tomasina and husband to Eunice, does not accept land from Carothers McCaslin's will. "*Thucydus Roskus @ Fibby Son born in Callina 1779. Refused 10acre peace fathers Will 28 Jun 1837 Refused Cash offer $200. dolars from A. @ T. McCaslin 28 Jun 1837 Wants to stay and work it out*" (254–55). Thucydus cannot overtly express his disgust or rage at Carothers McCaslin's "uncontrolled authority" over the bodies of Eunice and Tomasina. As a slave, he is without legal protections and rights; that is, he has no legal right "to own any property, marry, or raise children."[113] He may have understood the bequest in McCaslin's will to be payment for his silence. In Faulkner's text he is rendered silent about his reaction to his family's treatment and his own subordination, unlike the historical figure Henry Bibb, whose escape from slavery enabled him to articulate his pain in being unable to protect his wife and child: "To be compelled to stand by and see you [his former master] whip and slash my wife without mercy, when I could afford no protection, not even by offering myself to suffer the lash in her place, was more than I felt it to be the duty of a slave husband to endure. . . . This kind of treatment was what drove me from home and family, to seek a better home for them."[114] With freedom comes the right to speak. Thucydus remains in silence and in bondage that is psychological as well as physical.

The arranged marriage between Thucydus and Eunice duplicates the marriage between one of the slave men inherited by the Chickasaw Ikkemotubbe, called Doom, and the pregnant quadroon he brought from

New Orleans. As represented in "The Old People," Doom himself marries the pair just after he becomes chief ("the Man") of the Chickasaw by displacing the rightful heir; he sells the couple and the child two years later to Carothers McCaslin. Apparently, having introduced slavery to his people, Doom has no objection to selling his own son into slavery. That act is part of his consolidation of power. That son, Sam Fathers, whose Chickasaw name was "Had-Two-Fathers," repeats the discourse of race, concubinage, enslavement, white fathers, and black property central to *Go Down, Moses*. Both the unnamed quadroon and Eunice, bought and traded exotic bodies whose sexuality is defined by the men who own them, are inscribed into the text as sexual commodities, linked by their raced and gendered fate in chattel slavery and arranged marriages, and especially by their origin in Creole New Orleans, the city Faulkner feminized as hedonistic, "opulent, sensuous, sinful," courtesan, and foreign.[115]

Although he is himself enslaved by Carothers, Thucydus has already been rendered complicit in the concealment of Tomasina's parentage. Implicitly, he may have felt morally culpable for his wife's sexual ordeal and emasculated by his lack of protective power. Or, in an even more complicated scenario, Thucydus may have been Carothers McCaslin's own brother, as Nancy Dew Taylor speculates, and may thus have felt even more keenly his inability to stand up against Carothers.[116] In his state of powerlessness combined with guilt and shame, he cannot assume responsibility for his wife's pain, just as he cannot protect and defend his daughter. "Black women, unfortunately, proved to be mirrors for black men," Deborah Gray White observes. "Each time the former was abused, the latter's own helplessness was reflected."[117] Challenged in his masculinity and his subjectivity, Thucydus resorts to work, to the blacksmith's forge and hammer, which would as a matter of course also contradict conceptions of his inferiority, dependency, and weakness by demonstrating his strength and skill. He finds a space in which to resist becoming a thing, a space in which he can repair the damage done to his personhood. Over nearly a five-year period, his efforts to buy his freedom are recorded in the pages of the commissary ledgers:

> the slow, day-by-day accrument of the wages allowed him and the food and clothing—the molasses and meat and meal, the cheap durable shirts and jeans and shoes and now and then a coat against rain and cold—charged against the slowly yet steadily mounting

sum of balance (and it would seem to the boy [Ike] that he could actually see the black man, the slave whom his white owner had forever manumitted by the very act from which the black man could never be free so long as memory lasted, entering the commissary, asking permission perhaps of the white man's son to see the ledger-page which he could not even read, not even asking for the white man's word, which he would have had to accept for the reason that there was absolutely no way under the sun for him to test it, as to how the account stood, how much longer before he could go and never return, even if only as far as Jefferson seventeen miles away) on to the double pen-stroke closing the final entry. (255)

Thucydus is "the slave whom his white owner had forever manumitted by the very act from which the black man could never be free so long as memory lasted," and resident within his memory is the almost unimaginable act that would never allow him to be free of the consequences of his own enslavement.

The very name Faulkner chose for Thucydus, "Thucydides," references the Greek general and historian who chronicled the Peloponnesian Wars, and an aspect of bearing witness to experiential reality and human behavior. According to Lillian Feder, in the opening of his history, Thucydides states that he is writing "with exactness and objectivity about events he witnessed; he regards his history not as an ephemeral work but one that will last forever, for his purpose is to suggest historical principles through an account and an analysis of contemporary events. Thucydides's accuracy, his effort to suggest a clue to the future through the history of the present, and his method of employing speeches, incidents, documents, and records of oracular prophecies make his history both a fascinating account of events in ancient Greece and a commentary on the behavior of men."[118] Coincidentally, the historian Charles Joyner used a long quotation from The Peloponnesian War as an epigraph to his essay "Texts, Texture, and Context: Toward an Ethnographic History of Slave Resistance."

> With regard to my factual reporting of . . . events . . . I have made it a principle not to write down the first story that came my way, and not even to be guided by my own general impressions; either I was present myself at the events . . . or else heard them from eye-witnesses whose reports I have checked with as much thoroughness

as possible. Not that . . . the truth was easy to discover: different eye-witnesses give different accounts of the same events, speaking out of partiality . . . or else from imperfect memories. . . . My history will seem less easy to read because of the absence . . . of a romantic element. It will be enough . . . if these words . . . are judged useful by those who want to understand clearly the events which happened in the past and which (human nature being what it is), will, at some time or other and in much the same ways, be repeated in the future. My work is not . . . designed to meet the taste of immediate public, but . . . to last forever.[119]

"Thucydides" thus in Faulkner's nomenclature may signify a commentary by a living witness whose name calls attention both to the significance of the ledgers as textual evidence and to the behavior of Carothers McCaslin and the McCaslin men in the matter of slavery.

Thucydides's determination to take nothing from the McCaslins may have to do with his already having taken too much. His marriage to Eunice is a subterfuge, because he is given Eunice when clearly she is Carothers's concubine and perhaps when she is already pregnant with Carothers's child. That very marriage was vulnerable to legal challenges; for example, in North Carolina in the 1830s, "Slaves lacked the necessary 'will' to enter into a marriage contract, and slave jurisdiction universally refused to recognize any slave marriage."[120] In *State v Samuel* (1836), Chief Justice Thomas Ruffin of the North Carolina Supreme Court offered as explanation of the law's denial of slaves' right to marry a legal tenet more foundational to the prevailing social order: the master's protected right to hold slaves as private property and therefore his "continuing licence" to separate slave spouses at will.[121] If marriage could not be permanent, then no contractual legal requirement of permanence could be entered into, which meant that because slaves "had no civil existence, they could not assume the civil benefits and burdens of husband and wife."[122] Such legal rulings were intended to sever bonds between enslaved men and women in order to strengthen their bondage to their owners.

Yet, slave marriages did take place and often with the insistence or approval of slaveholders.[123] And in the case of Eunice and Thucydus, the marriage endured for over twenty years. Though it is impossible to gauge the nature of the affection between Eunice and Thucydus, it seems that after their marriage and the birth of Tomasina, Eunice does not bear other children. One reason may be that slave women attempted forms of birth control to prevent introducing more children into slavery. However, even as Deborah Gray White concludes, "The jury will have to remain out on whether slave women were guilty of practicing birth control and abortion," she nevertheless states that there were sufficient reasons why they might: "they had reason not to want to bear and nurture children who could be sold from them at a slave master's whim. They had ample cause to want to deny whites the satisfaction of realizing a profit on the birth of their children. But they also had as much reason as any antebellum woman, white or free black, to shun pregnancy and childbirth. As long as obstetrics had not yet evolved into a science, childbirth was dangerous." [124] Perhaps, it is that Eunice does not bear other children because in this narrative Faulkner has no interest in those possible children, the black and enslaved offspring of a marriage between enslaved blacks.

Ultimately, too, despite being the social father of Tomasina, Thucydus is rendered powerless to protect her from the sexual aggression of her biological father Carothers, whose transgressive acts compromise all familial bonds. According to juridical ruling in *Frazier v Spear* (1811), "The father of the slave is unknown to our law." [125] Thus, from birth the slave child is alienated under law. As young Carothers Edmonds puts it: "*Old Carothers got his nigger bastards right in his back yard and I would like to have seen the husband or anybody else that said him nay*" (112). Certainly, a husband who was also a slave could not say "nay." He was reduced to "social irrelevancy" and his social relationship to his offspring vitiated.[126] Thucydus suffers, too, under the "almost perverse intimacy in the bond resulting from the power the master claimed over his slave," because both his wife and his daughter are his owner's property and sexual concubines; that situation exposes Thucydus on a personal level to the degree of bodily invasion and control that results from a slave's life being only through and for his master.[127] Owned, dominated, and debased himself, Thucydus cannot act according to the logic of the patriarchy as father or as husband. Although he may well have been outraged by his wife's concubinage and his daughter's rape, Thucydus would have been able to take no action against Carothers; any retaliation or retribution on his part would have ended with further suffering or death for himself and Eunice and Tomasina.

One such instance occurred in 1859, when Alfred, a man enslaved on a Mississippi plantation, killed an overseer who had raped Alfred's wife, Charlotte. Neither rape nor sexual assault entered into the legal deliberations over Alfred's fate; instead the court focused on the overseer's "adultery." The court ruled in *Alfred, a Slave v State*, "[A]dultery with a slave wife is no defense to a charge of murder. A slave charged with the murder of his overseer can not introduce as evidence in his defense, the fact that the deceased, a few hours before the killing had forced the prisoner's wife to sexual intercourse with him."[128] When Charlotte's victimization, her being forced to submit to sexual intercourse with the overseer, can be negated and substituted with the perpetrator's "adultery," Alfred's righteous outrage and justifiable motive can be erased completely, and both wife and husband become mere objects, without will. Similarly, with Thucydus, objectified into an inert state of nonbeing, he can do nothing against Carothers's "uncontrolled authority" not merely over his wife's and daughter's bodies but over his own black male body as well. Thucydus, like Ike McCaslin, functions within a space delineated by shame. His response to his cultural and racial and familial positions is not wooden but instead animated by his emotional shaming and his powerlessness to confront old Carothers.

That same pain of humiliation and shame that has no calculation or recompense suffered by Tomasina is probably why Ike fails even when attempting to make amends for his ancestor. It is no wonder that the words of Eunice and Tomasina's descendant, Fonsiba, the daughter of Tomey's Turl and named for Ike's mother, in response to Ike's question " 'Fonsiba. Are you all right?' " reverberate with such force and power: " 'I'm free,' she said" (268). Free is a word her grandmother and great-grandmother were not able to utter. It is a word that her father Tomey's Turl could utter only within the games he devised to challenge the boundaries of enslavement.

CHAPTER 3 | The Game of Boundaries

Interlocking Spaces

In *Go Down, Moses* boundaries may be read as interlocking circles. There is, for example, the trope of locked circles from "Was," in which Tomey's Turl follows a fixed pattern of movement that he charts to and from and within the Beauchamp plantation. "Tomey's Turl had doubled and was making a long swing back toward the house" (17). His doubling back on his own trail, and thus on his own self, confounds and confuses his pursuers, though they assume a superior knowledge of both the terrain and of Turl himself, the enslaved subordinate. The self-referentiality in his act mirrors the loop of the narrative involution. What the white owners fail to comprehend, however, is that strategically Turl is a master of logic and maneuver because at stake for him is life-altering and life-affirming experience, an appropriation of public space and with it an incursion into public visibility.

Tomey's Turl functions within a logic that moves him toward "winning," which means that he seeks the optimal course of action for himself. "Tomey's Turl was still making his swing. But they never caught him. . . . They hunted the banks both ways for more than an hour, but they couldn't straighten Tomey's Turl out" (17). He predicts how they will read his "swing" and adjusts his movement accordingly. Not only can they not "straighten" him out, but they face the inevitable conclusion that their optimal reasoning regarding his behavioral pattern fails. Tomey's Turl contradicts and confounds. He can be as random in his choice as he can be deliberate. In assigning equal probabilities to his different possible courses of action, he "thinks on his feet" and acts in keeping with an obvious point in game theory: "Intuitively, each player seeks to prevent the other from predicting his strategy choice and nothing can be harder [to predict] than a choice made at random."[1]

Turl's periodic moves represent a planned sequence in which he leaves the McCaslin plantation, enters the Beauchamp plantation, and eventually returns to his starting point after tracking a new circle around and within the Beauchamp place. Within the interlocked circles of movement and behavior, he accomplishes a deregulation of the ownership claims and property rights in a person that were central to the slaveholding society. Without using his own words to tell his story, he nonetheless articulates a narrative by means of motion and action. Using games rather than speech to project himself into a different space, he frees himself from the physical and psychological containment of slavery. His ritualistic manipulation of temporary freedom by putting on the clothing of a white man, and with it the attitudinal stance of the white "masters" that matches his white skin, demonstrates the performativity of identity and the constructedness of race. At the same time, Turl's defiance of boundaries is an intentional strategy of individual agency in which he calculates how, within the given paradigms of bondage and containment, he can most actively, and to his own desired outcome, manipulate the economic system that lays claim to his body and his labor without the expectation or demand of compensation.

Turl's game of boundaries in "Was" becomes a template for *Go Down, Moses.* The relational space allotted to human beings who are property is played out in games (such as gambling, hunting, courting) in which blacks are positioned within the legal system of chattel slavery and its aftermath in delimiting legal codes of segregation, and in which women —most typically nameless in the text—are situated in extralegal spaces and defined by the boundaries of lawful marriage and codified domesticity. Both are bound by the subjectivity of white southern males and their right to property, which encompasses protection under the legal system and restrictive, obligatory behavior under the social codes. The interpenetrating discourses on race and gender are dispersed through the confinements of legal spheres, the boundaries of law and property, and the records of law and property, which in *Go Down, Moses* are actuated in the interpolated McCaslin plantation ledgers. The ledgers function as the interlocutor between property, the body of Tomey's Terrel inscripted with a figuration of his mother, and heir, the body of Ike McCaslin haunted by an image of violated kin and humankind. Within the resultant dialogic is a critique both of power and passion as ideologies. In these discourses the court is a system of managing judgments and challenges, so that the narrative becomes a linking of domestic space to two divided but intersecting spheres that represent themselves as bipolar, polarized, and oppositional.

Turl's game of boundaries is a reminder that within the text is what Peter Brooks identifies as "a system of internal energies and tensions, compulsions, resistances, and desires."[2] Turl's "doubling," taken from the realm of his literal motion and into the context of his psychological self, maps a process of tracking, crossing, and returning central to the strategies of detection, discovery and location of subjectivity in the text, and these in turn both energize and complicate the narrative. "Doubled," Turl reconfigures the boundaries of exploitation, dependence, and desire marking his place in slavery so that they become control, independence, and fulfillment identifying his free space within the game and within the making of narrative story. He is doubled: both himself, the enslaved, property in person; and his other self, the McCaslin son and brother free within himself. In that free capacity he assumes the privileges of whiteness. While what constitutes a solution to a game is rarely straightforward, Turl achieves a solution that, despite the reductio ad absurdum inherent in "Was," is intricately connected to his condition as a human being whose behavior is rational, self-conscious, individualistic, and self-interested, and is therefore oppositional to the aims and formulations of chattel slavery.

Turl's crossing of boundaries negates the bonds of enslavement but also of interpretation inherent in the construction of the slave as property. If enslavement may be categorized as a condition of psychological fragmentation in which embodiment in bondage does not constitute a whole self, then Turl's boundary crossing may be seen as a movement toward wholeness or a movement out of discontinuity and natal alienation. He challenges the expectations of ownership and of possession by negotiating two incipient forms of contract: an agreement to make clear the lines and direction of his self-emancipation; and an agreement to seek out Tennie as a marital partner at the Beauchamp plantation. These two form the basis for the major contracts that ultimately will not only disrupt the system of slavery but dismantle it entirely: blacks as part of the social contract of the founding of the nation and thus entitled to all of its rights and privileges, including freedom and suffrage; and blacks as persons who can enter into the legal agreement of marriage and within that contractual state establish family and legitimate kinship bonds.

Turl's game strategy for boundary crossing and his particular signifying practices inform a reading of his nephew Ike McCaslin and a way of thinking about Ike's "civil death" and self-induced removal from the social contract, the political life and the marital life, which insure the continuation of the state, the community, and the family. In a more familiar configuration of interlocking circles, in part 1 of "The Bear," a young Isaac McCaslin undergoes a purifying ritual. Linked analogously to the game of boundaries and freedom that Tomey's Turl maps onto the southern landscape, Ike's "game" renounces the fixed positions of hunter and game and initiates a fluid interaction between the real and the ideal that will push him toward the same mythic but free realm his uncle Turl occupies in "Was." After abandoning his gun, his watch, and his compass, Ike "realized he was lost" and "did as Sam [Fathers] had coached and drilled him: made a cast to cross his back-track" (199). Because he desires to see the bear, Ike begins to reshape his world through the usage of signs. After several attempts to find his starting point, he was still lost, "so he did next as Sam had coached and drilled him: made this next circle in the opposite direction and much larger, so that the pattern of the two of them would bisect his track somewhere" (199). Eventually in "a seepage of moisture somewhere between earth and water," he sees a crooked print, follows it, and then in an instant "the wilderness coalesced . . . the tree, the bush, the compass, and the watch. . . . Then he saw the bear" (200). Free of the instruments of destruction (the gun) and location in time and place (the watch and compass), he functions at the intersection of the natural and the primordial. He achieves his desire and perpetuates it in the transmission of his experience in narrative, the expressive discourse shaping the interlocked circles.

In part Ike acts in response to his training, and in part he turns inward to his own intuition. He doubles back on himself, on his own interiority, and calculates the probability of certain outcomes to his actions. His doubling back on his own tracks, those footprints that mark his location in space, forces him to confront his own subjectivity and the behavioral patterns upheld in his social realm. As with his uncle Turl before him, at stake is his masculinity, his development as a man within or against the proscriptions of his culture. His relocation there in his own interiority intersects with his own various paths to illumination, sight, and vision ("the pattern of the two [circles] . . . would bisect his track somewhere"). These interlocking circles—at once closed and contiguous—function as a figural reminder that narrative is "a system of understanding that readers engage in negotiations with reality and temporality, what Peter Brooks terms "man's time-boundedness, his consciousness of existence within the limits of mortality."[3] The interlocking circles as dynamic movement also open a critical space for reading what has not been seen in *Go Down, Moses:* the centrality of Tomey's Turl's origins and his existence to the Mississippi civilization and wilderness and their mutual histories in the contest for property and ownership foregrounded in Faulkner's narrative of Ike McCaslin.

Ike's initial location in "Was" as an old man who has divested himself of property and ownership serves to emphasize his simultaneous suspension in narrative circularity as both teller and listener to the tale of Tomey's Turl rendered from the retrospection and memory of McCaslin Edmonds: "this was not something participated in or even seen by himself [Ike], but by his elder cousin, McCaslin Edmonds" (3), "not something he had participated in or even remembered except from the hearing, the listening, come to him through and from his cousin McCaslin born in 1850 and sixteen years his senior and hence, his own father being near seventy when Isaac, an only child, was born, rather his brother than cousin and rather his father than either, out of the old time, the old days" (4). Within the central circles of narrated memory and familial history, Ike both constructs and deconstructs Turl's story, that of an enslaved McCaslin, and within it places his own story of the renunciation of inherited McCaslin land. This process situates Ike from the beginning of the text in an interior space of reflection and recollection, which he shares through narrative with Tomey's Turl. This interior space allows Ike the freedom to double back on his desire to dismantle property and redress the "sin" of ownership and its embodiment in Turl.

Property, as a powerful symbol of rights, is inextricable from the idea of boundaries, of marking off and delimiting access. In American constitutionalism, property "both reflects and exacerbates the problems of boundary as a central metaphor in the legal rhetoric of freedom," Jennifer Nedelsky theorizes.[4] The protection of property intrudes on the issue of rights, so that the concept of boundary cannot be overlooked in the discourse on property. Because the Constitution as scripted by whites only acknowledged rights for blacks piecemeal rather than whole cloth, it created an imbalance in rights for blacks. "Perhaps the predominance of that imbalance," Patricia J. Williams argues, "obscures the fact that the recursive insistence of those rights is also defined by black desire for them—desire fueled . . . by knowledge of, and generations existing in, a world without meaningful boundaries—and 'without boundary' for blacks has meant not untrammeled vistas of possibility but the crushing weight of total—bodily and spiritual—*intrusion.*"[5] Being without boundary then has signaled the way in which blacks could be intruded on, bodily and psychically invaded, because they were unprotected by boundaries that could ordinarily protect and encircle their rights. This state of being without boundaries is one of the legacies of slavery and the possession of black bodies as property. Generations of blacks, then, inherited a desire for constitutional rights and rights protection. This specific desire is evident within Tomey's Turl and his descendants, as they interpolate their own meaning, needs, and rights into the otherwise degraded, right-less spaces to which they are legally and culturally consigned.

The interlocking circles may be an alternative way of approaching what Peter Kolchin points to as "a dualism inherent in slavery: slaves were at the same time both objects and subjects, human property held for the purpose of enriching the masters and individuals with lives of their own."[6] The boundaries that would contain Tomey's Turl and his ancestors and descendants as only property and without self-interest invariably intersect with those that contain these same individuals as persons and as subjects. Turl's individuation becomes apparent when he makes his way through the woods, traveling twenty-two miles to circle around the plantation where Tennie is held in bondage. In crossing through the barriers that separate them from each other and from their own personhood, Turl resembles Rider in his quest for a reunion with Mannie. Unlike either Rider or Ike, however, Turl traverses the wilderness as a passageway to his future life; he chooses life over death. It is a manifestation of a self-interest vested in transforming the world of the living. Turl's collapsing of boundaries that both separate and contain becomes the model for reading the actions of his son, Lucas, in the next generation of blacks and of his nephew, Ike, in the corresponding generation of whites.

Much has been written about the representation of the wilderness in *Go Down, Moses*.[7] The diminishing space of the untamed land reiterates an elegiac tone in "The Old People" and "The Bear" and the lament for that which has been lost, or a mourning for that which never was in "Delta Autumn."[8] The boundaries that demarcate the wilderness as land distinct and separate from property owned and subdivided into familiar economic spacializations become increasingly permeable and contiguous with the civilization created out of slave labor and then free market labor of blacks coerced into menial and inadequately compensated work. Although coming to terms with the limits placed on the wilderness, or the "Big Woods," by the encroachment of industry and machinery occupies the foreground of the text, the bounded spheres of the plantation, the owned and cultivated land distinct from the once unbounded wilderness, function as a trope for property and propertied individuals, who also are bounded and whose personal actions must conform to the boundaries within which they are placed. Orlando Patterson, in *Freedom*, argues that "freedom was generated from the experience of slavery. People came to value freedom, to construct it as a powerful shared vision of life, as a result of their experience of, and response to, slavery or its recombinant form, serfdom, in their roles as masters, slaves, and nonslaves."[9] This view seems applicable to Ike and to his mentor Sam Fathers, whose homage to freedom and the woods stems from a mutual heritage of enslavement, though experienced from different ends of the owner-owned relationship: "I am free," Ike says, and he later explains, "Sam Fathers set me free" (285, 286). Patterson's view of freedom as generative from slavery also seems especially relevant to the representation of Ike and of Turl's son, Lucas Beauchamp, the two surviving direct male descendants of old Carothers, who are related by collateral consanguinity.

Ike understands the wilderness as his life. It gives birth to him, but it also exacts as retribution his death. Doreen Fowler has pointed out that when Ike voluntarily relinquished his gun, his watch, and his compass and surrendered to the wilderness, "he permitted all boundaries between self and other to collapse; he willingly accepted self-extinction."[10] Ike's self-extinction functions in opposition to Tomey's Turl, whose desire is both for life and for continuance, and who, in relation to the woods, "slowed down and he and the dogs all went into the woods together, walking, like they were going home from a rabbit hunt. And when they caught up with Uncle Buck in the woods, there was no Tomey's Turl and no dogs either" (14). Turl vanishes, not as part of self-extinction, but rather in a strategy to maintain life and to secure life's fullest possibilities. Living for Turl is engagement, active engagement with all the forces, negative and positive, that shape and inform his social world. On the other hand, "Ike's wilderness refuge, as Sam Fathers always knew, is not a retreat from death but a retreat to death."[11]

In a different lexicon, however, Ike renders himself "civilly dead." The condition of being dead in law, *civilter mortuus*, stems from the withholding of civil rights from criminals under British Common Law. According to Blackstone, "For when it is now clear beyond all dispute, that the criminal is no longer fit to live upon the earth, but is to be exterminated as a monster and bane to human society; the law sets a note of infamy upon him. . . . He is then called attaint, *attinctus*, stained, or blackened."[12] Corruption of blood, extinction of civil rights, and forfeiture of property are the three major consequences of civil death, which is also the condition of enslavement. Ike freely assumes an analogous condition, perhaps out of shame and a desire to extricate himself from the exercise of privilege given to white men under law. His sense of "defilement" (a term his mother uses regarding her brother's mixed-race concubine) and his desire for "illicit hybrid flesh" are both repressed but nonetheless resident within the ways in which he responds to his grandfather's sexual violation of Tomasina and to his uncle's sexual relations with a woman "even lighter in color than Tomey's Turl" (289). His obsession with servitude, racial and sexual, with being sonless or without an heir, with sterility and the opposing notion of virility, all speak to the unspoken drives in Ike's personality. (For all their concern with inheritance, the McCaslins are not a reproducing lot—with a few exceptions and with the prominence of their mixed-race offspring. Corruption of blood may have more implications than may be immediately apparent.) Banishment under civil death is similar to Ike's self-imposed exile from the legal "rights" that govern his society and the inheritance rights that secure his family's land.

And because Ike has determined that "the woods would be his mistress and his wife" (311), he can be linked to Rider, who moves through the woods in an effort to recapture and reunify with Mannie as wife. The attitudinal difference toward the woods may be linked to their different views of life and death: death as life for Rider and life as death for Ike. Ike wants only containment, that is, a gravelike space in which to retreat; Rider wants only to be free, though in the idealized state of unity of person (with his wife).[13]

Ike's sighting the bear as a part of the ritual of hunting resonates with the game of hide-and-seek Tomey's Turl initiates in "Was." The verbal tone is different—Ike's finding of himself and finding his way while tracking the bear is presented in high, dignified seriousness. Tomey's Turl's hiding and seeking comes on the verbal lip of high comedy. Both, however, function as games adults initiate in order to displace the normal boundaries constricting their lives. Hide-and-seek, of course, is not only a children's game but also one of the oldest, perhaps dating back to a Greek game described in the second century by Julius Pollux.[14]

The game of hide-and-seek initiated by Tomey's Turl in "Was" reverberates throughout *Go Down, Moses* with its discontinuous narratives and disappearing characters and collapsing genealogies. That it is a game associated with children does not, however, reduce Turl to the level of a child, because his games (runaway and hide-and-seek) have as their mature objective the obtaining of Tennie Beauchamp as wife and, through that conjoined state, his own manhood. He functions within the space of games, but his objective is exterior to the limits set by games, which are "largely teleological, shaped by a purpose, in that they are an ordering agency, a means not an end, a process that seeks to impose on the exterior, visible world of society a patterned model of an internal reality."[15] By means of his oppositional game playing, Tomey's Turl attempts to reorder the slave-holding world governing his material condition to institute a conception of rights for a black man. Specifically, hide-and-seek is one of the most popular and familiar games. In it a player closes his or her eyes for a specified count while the other players hide. Tomey's Turl inverts the game, so that when he hides, he sets in motion a series of seekers: Buck and Cass for him, for his literal slave body; but also Buck for a wife, the body of Sophonsiba; Hubert Beauchamp for Turl and also for a husband for his sister. In a variation of hide-and-seek called sardines, one hider may be joined surreptitiously by seekers as they find him; coincidentally, in the plotting of "Was," Cass, then Buck, and finally Buddy, all join Turl as hider and all cooperate in his objectives. Considered a folk game responding to the developmental needs of children and fostering the social values of adults within the society, hide-and-seek persists in several variants because it offers commonly known traditions important to the physical, social, and cognitive development of children. "The framed stage of play also allows children to act out adult roles in society accompanied by various strategies of competition, cooperation, and achievement. On this stage of play, children typically feel more tolerance for unusual behaviors, and children use games to experience other roles and test social limits."[16]

Games map society's values. Not merely play but an interactive guide, folk games typically follow the narrative structures of specific cultural rites of passage (for instance, birth, marriage, or death). They demystify life's major transitions and enable social maturation. Games frequently inculcate the patterns of ritual central to social development: separation, transition, and incorporation. "In many games, a player is separated from the group and then performs a task or goes through a ceremony, rejoining the group later with a new status. . . . As cultures have rites of passage to mark transitions from one stage to another, so games on an everyday basis offer children the reassurance of their passage through a period of rapid development."[17] The use here of "game," however, is invested with added meaning. In their influential *The Theory of Games and Economic Behavior* (1944) Von Neumann and Morgenstern made the discovery "that both parlor games and real-life games pose similar problems and that an analysis that works for the former may very well be relevant to the later.[18] That Faulkner so transparently uses games and the traces of games to facilitate the development of character and societal traits points to his understanding of the way games are implicated in cultural rituals and the manner in which they become revelatory of societal values and mores.

A son of Tomey's Turl and Tennie, Lucas Beauchamp, provides a way of accessing the continuation of games as sacrifice in the lives of blacks in the text. Lucas replicates, in the free labor market of the postbellum South, his father's determined efforts for personhood in spite of enslavement. Born in 1874, Lucas has assimilated the experience of his white grandfather, old Carothers McCaslin, in acquiring possessions and material wealth as accomplishment and assertion of manhood, as well as a mask of protection against the shame he associates with being a "nigger" in his society. At the same time, nevertheless, Lucas reenacts in his generation the calculated risks and maximum individuation of the game theoretic mode of his father, because racism after slavery in Mississippi still demanded a crafty response for black social advancement.

"The Fire and the Hearth," the chapter introducing Lucas, functions at the intersection of law and commerce. It relies on both legal and business words and phrases, such as *interdict, reprieve, justice, partnership, recompense, Law* (with a capital "L"), *revenue, money, competitor,* and *business,* all of which appear in the text and mark Lucas's conception of himself as a man cut from the same cloth as his grandfather. His understanding of manhood is embedded in the conjoined discourses of law and commerce. The rhetoric of law and business elevates Lucas Beauchamp's attempts to entrap his competitor and his daughter's suitor, George Wilkins, above comic buffoonery to parody. Five years before the narrative present, Lucas had taken care of another competitor in the illegal business of running a still by scheming to have him incarcerated at Parchman, the state penal farm. Lucas plots to have George suffer the same fate because he understands how the Law operates, particularly in relation to the monetary claims of business.

When he maneuvers to have his economic competitor legally jailed for the same crime that he himself is actively committing in making liquor for commercial sale and profit, Lucas appeals to his "rights" under law. What happens however is that rights—legally defined—become another part of the game for Lucas, because he understands precisely how the Law plays games with the lives of blacks. If he can turn their game back on them and play it to his own advantage, then he will "uphold" the legal system—laud it and attest to its justice because its beliefs and practices, to which he has himself been subjected, adhere to his momentary goals and desires. " 'So a man's kin can't tell on him in court" (*Go Down, Moses* 67). Although Lucas contemplates this legality as a ploy to protect his secrets, he discovers the flip side when his daughter's marriage to George Wilkins foils his plot to send George to prison. That a woman and a wife is so situated within the legal sphere nonetheless becomes another way of understanding Lucas's own position under the law as "head" of the family, patriarch and businessman.

From the beginning of "The Fire and the Hearth," Lucas uses the law in a game theoretic model of self interest for revenge and for the control and elimination of his competition, which he accomplishes with the unwitting assistance of Roth Edmonds, the white owner of the land he has farmed for forty-five years. Lucas plays the game of tightrope. His clever self maximizing strategies in "The Fire and the Hearth" place him in a direct relationship to his father's games in the initial chapter "Was." Involving Roth in his subversive strategies signals Lucas's willingness to utilize the racial paternalism within the Law to his best advantage. He walks a narrow line over which is an abyss or a prison, and on either side are actual dangers constructed by the demands of racial segregation and competitive capitalism. Thus, legal terms abound in the narrative introducing Lucas; moreover, much of the section uses the language of contracts law, and several of the main ideas are related to contractual obligations, whether those obligations stem from the authority of the Law, from that of the patriarchy (head of the family, Lucas himself), or from that of the plantation system.[19] Within the traditional narratives of law, especially contracts, Lucas attempts an intervention in the legal stories constructed by elite and powerful whites. He represents himself in performance, as part of the theatrics of law and its connections to monetary power.

Lucas understands the political and arbitrary nature of law regarding black people, and he knows the complicity of law in racial oppression. He knows from experience that "the law can be irrational and prickly in the hands of its enforcers."[20] Lucas accepts the irony of engaging that law in his contests with George over primacy in illegal activity. He skillfully plays the absurdities of the legal system and its racial politics against his own desires and will.[21] "Part of a man's life has always been spent playing games, with his family, with his friends and enemies, with institutions and organizations, with his own life. Some are deadly serious. Some are not; rather, they are fun, sport. A man may play for money, for national advantage, for pure delight, and out of spite."[22] Lucas clearly plays from a variety of motives. His play conforms to the paternalism of Mississippi's legal practices, but it also attempts to channel the paternalistic racism into service beneficial to his purpose. In maintaining playfulness within the constraints of the authoritarian conditions of his segregated society, Lucas adheres to what Theodor Adorno contends is a crucial part of intellectual productivity.

Lucas, whose values regarding competition and business and money have been shaped by the organization of the plantation, as well as by the conception of patrimony, operates within an ethics of business. As John Matthews puts it, "Lucas seeks to enter and occupy the social arrangements that have been founded on his exclusion."[23] (Or, put another way, founded precisely on and because of his very presence.) Capitalism and competition enable Lucas's response to challenges from his daughter's suitor. His code of honor and of conduct stems from his belief in the necessity of manhood, the primacy of age, and the legitimacy of acquisition, all of which are partly formed out of the plantation system and partly out of Lucas's response to the place of blacks in the plantation world. He recognizes the incarceral nature of the plantation and tenancy worlds and the resultingly bounded existence of poor blacks.

He perceives his own rights outside of an exploitative capitalism and in terms of the fairness of competition. For example, the competitive motive is evident in one of the defining moments in the text. In his youth Lucas determined that he must kill his kinsman Zack Edmonds, the white man who had appropriated Lucas's wife to care for his motherless infant. Lucas tells Zack, " 'You tried to beat me. And you wont never, not even when I am hanging dead from the limb this time tomorrow with the coal oil still burning, you wont never' " (52). Lucas functions within the economics of capitalism, but because of the legacy of slavery and servitude, he walks a fine line, his tightrope, between being an entrepreneur with capital and being the expendable capital. Within the competitive mode of the marketplace, he challenges Zack for his right to both a marital contract and a recognition of his black manhood; his challenge is a duplication of his father's desire for marriage and manhood. His response to Zack reveals an anxiety and shame about cuckoldry which as a racial inferior he is powerless to prevent, yet as a familial equal (that is, descended from the male line rather than the distaff side of Carothers McCaslin's family, as is Zack), he can resist both domination and submission.

Lucas knows the immediate meaning of compensatory justice for blacks, but he knows also that if he is to avail himself of justice, he must do so in the terms understood and practiced by whites, because only those demand respect. Lucas appeals to the notions of patriarchy and to the rights of the propertied when he faces down Zack Edmonds, his competitor, who is white and kin. Zack's response is a confirmation of Lucas's ability to circumvent the codes oppressing blacks and to use them to assert himself: " 'By God . . . I never thought to ever pass my oath to a nigger' " (47). Always at stake is race and the ability of a racial definition to determine behavior and cultural affinity. In the next generation of McCaslin-Edmondses, Zack's son Roth configures the source of Lucas's power in terms of white patriarchal lineage and masculine power: "*He's more like old Carothers than all the rest of us put together. . . . He is both heir and prototype simultaneously of all the geogra-*

phy and climate and biology which sired old Carothers and all the rest of us and our kind" (114). Lucas carries a double impact of resemblance resulting from Carothers's incestuous act. That resemblance allows him a property claim in old Carothers's whiteness. What Roth does not know is that Lucas is not only Carothers's grandson but his great-grandson as well, and that added dimension, the doubled aspect of resemblance, also constitutes an embedded moral claim that would assuage the shame associated with Carothers's sin against Lucas's father. The erasure of Lucas's mixed-race father, Tomey's Turl, here elides the negative and excessive aspect of ownership and power, but, recalling him, foregrounds the claim of racial connection central to Lucas's representation in the text.

But Lucas Beauchamp's own relation with his white kin is such that he himself is a dependent and inferior in the court of law. The racism expressed in the condescension of the court to blacks as "wards" or "infants" can be seen most visibly in legal cases in which at the deaths of blacks "claims against others passed on to their guardians, such as a 'discreet white citizen' appointed by the courts, rather than to their heirs."[24] The Mississippi Supreme Court had held in *George, a Slave v State* that "because slaves had 'no right prior to legislative enactments,' only statutes could make slave activity a crime."[25] Mississippi's highest court merely followed the decision of the Supreme Court of the United States in the 1857 ruling in *Dred Scott v Sandford:* "it is fixed and universal in the civilized portion of the white race" that blacks have "no rights which the white man [is] bound to respect."[26] This is the legal heritage that Lucas acknowledges and fears.

At the same time, there is another legacy at work in Faulkner's representation of Lucas. It encompasses the notion of participatory democracy as a marker of freedom. For example, Orlando Patterson links democracy and civic freedom, "the capacity of adult members of a community to participate in its life and governance": "The existence of civic freedom implies a political community of some sort, with clearly defined rights and obligations for every citizen."[27] This conjunction of rights and obligations in the civic sphere as freedom is Tomey's Turl's, not Carothers McCaslin's, legacy to Lucas. It is Turl who attempted to exercise his right to enter into contract and to constitute himself in civic freedom. Yet Lucas assumes a right to participate in governance, the maintaining of rules and regulations applicable to stills and illegal liquor (selectivity here for he also has a still), because he is a McCaslin descendant and from the white progenitor's male side of the family, and a man himself living within the community of his birth and having a defined place in that community. Like his kinsman Ike, Lucas sets out compensatory boundaries within which he necessarily functions.

"The boundaries so central to American law are the boundaries that feel desperately necessary to the separative self," according to Jennifer Nedelsky, who suggests that keeping "the threatening others at bay" is an impossible task "whose impossibility only fuels the desperation."[28] Her observation is reminiscent of the desperate scene at the end of "The Bear" when Boon Hoganbeck, a mixed-race Chickasaw Indian like Sam Fathers, fends off those who would shoot the squirrels he claims as his property. "At first glance the tree seemed to be alive with frantic squirrels. There appeared to be forty or fifty of them leaping and darting from branch to branch until the whole tree had become one green maelstrom of mad leaves" (315). Boon, however, is unprepared to shoot any of the squirrels he claims belong to him. "Then he [Ike] saw Boon, sitting, his back against the trunk, his head bent, hammering furiously at something on his lap. What he hammered with was the barrel of his dismembered gun, what he hammered at was the breech of it. The rest of the gun lay scattered about him in a half-dozen pieces while he bent over the piece on his lap his scarlet and streaming walnut face, hammering the disjointed barrel against the gun-breech with the frantic abandon of a madman. He didn't even look up to see who it was. Still hammering, he merely shouted back at the boy in a hoarse strangled voice: 'Get out of here! Dont touch them! Dont touch a one of them! They're mine!' " (315). Dismembered and disjointed, the gun signifies an impotency in male sexuality and virility. Manhood as signaled by property claims is problematized and dismantled. Boon's claim of possession made to Ike McCaslin recapitulates all of the problematic aspects of ownership and manhood as well as their manifestation in real estate and chattel slavery as rehearsed and debated in "The Bear." With Boon, Faulkner illustrates the protection of one's supposed property from intruding others as a hysterical, impotent act, bordering on madness. The scene undermines the conception of "possession," echoing as it does the *Pierson v Post* issue of ownership or title to wild animals, and coming as it does following the death of Sam Fathers as a freeing of the person of the old man. Through Ike's eyes, Boon's lunacy in his claim and in his words is magnified in his frenzied state, which duplicates that of the squirrels.

Ike McCaslin, however, in his final appearance in "Delta Autumn," represents a different instance of boundary usage to maintain racial distinctions, racial identifications, and racial property in his exchange with his black kinswoman, Turl's descendant. In responding to her, Ike suggests an intensive version of what Nedelsky describes as ineffective efforts to maintain boundaries: "We fear being 'invaded,' 'taken over,' not just by threats but by demands—the overpowering demands of those in pain and hunger all around us. We wall ourselves off from their cries—genuinely do not hear them most of the time, even though we 'know' they are there—by telling ourselves that we are 'within our rights,' that rights define our obligations as well as our entitlements, and that as long as we have violated no one's rights, we are doing nothing wrong in our daily nonresponsiveness."[29] Ike would point to his kinsman Roth as being the source of the problem. But Ike would identify not Roth's cruelty in abandoning the woman and their son, but rather his irresponsibility in violating the fixed boundary between the races when he begins an affair with a woman with black ancestry. Ike, of course, overlooks his own culpability in keeping others at a spatial distance and thus his failure to act responsively within a community of human needs, including those residing on the other side of the color line.

In *Go Down, Moses* boundaries become a compensation for the exclusivity of property rights and ownership. Compensatory boundaries can be seen in the extralegal spaces occupied by runaways or family servants, such as Tomey's Turl, and freed blacks, such as Lucas Beauchamp, who uses the arbitrary nature of laws governing property and rights to his advantage. These boundaries include both property lines, property descent through wills, property ascent through inheritance and the excluded—those people and spaces outside of the definition of property.

Lucas in plotting his strategy thinks through his possible courses of action. "At first, on his return home this morning, his plan had been to notify the sheriff himself, so that there would be absolutely no slip-up, lest Edmonds should be content with merely destroying George's still and cache and just running George off the place. In that case, George would continue to hang around the place, merely keeping out of Edmonds' sight; whereupon, without even any farm work, let alone the still, to keep him occupied, he would be idle all day and therefore up and out all night long and would constitute more of a menace than ever" (43). Implicit in Lucas's plan is an understanding both of human psychology and of the threat of imprisonment in race control. Lucas thinks, "The report would have to come from Edmonds, the white man, because to the sheriff Lucas was just another nigger and both the sheriff and Lucas knew it, although only one of them knew that to Lucas the sheriff was a redneck without any reason for pride in his forbears nor hope for it in his descendants. And if Edmonds should decide to handle the matter privately, without recourse to the law, there would be someone in Jefferson whom Lucas could inform that not only he and George Wilkins knew of a still on Carothers Edmonds' place, but Carothers Edmonds knew it too" (43). His understanding of race in law and in justice is based on the biased practices of the system in operation; justice becomes two-tiered and race-conscious.

Much like his white grandfather, Lucas capitalizes on the law and on social practice for power. Much like his father, Tomey's Turl, Lucas attempts as a game player to manipulate an oppressive legal system to his own ends. Although he is constructed by means of the play of comedic situations, that construction is outside of the minstrel tradition that marked the representation of his father in "Was." Lucas is crafty and thoughtful, and Faulkner represents his intricate thinking and planning as part of the plotting of the story. When Lucas recognizes that the offending George Wilkins might be useful to his search for gold he believes buried on the plantation, he abandons his plan to send George to prison. "So, George Wilkins was reprieved without knowing his . . . danger. . . . [Lucas] even thought of taking George into partnership on a minor share basis to do the actual digging; indeed, not only to do the actual work but as a sort of justice, balance, libation to Chance and Fortune, since if it had not been for George, he would not have found the single [gold] coin" (39). His peremptory acts of benevolence make a curious appeal to justice.

Lucas's sense of justice extends mainly to what is fair to himself. In whatever arrangements he makes and in whichever linguistic pattern he chooses, he reveals his concern for what he himself deserves due to his position as the oldest living McCaslin descendant on the plantation, his wisdom about financial and business matters, and his position as head of the Beauchamp family. Therefore, he quickly dismisses the thought of sharing with George "before it even had time to become an idea" (39). His logic, intricate but persuasive, is based on his distinction: "He, Lucas Beauchamp . . . who actually remembered old Buck and Buddy in the living flesh, older than Zack Edmonds even if Zack were still alive, almost as old as old Isaac who in a sense, say what a man would, had turned apostate to his name and lineage by weakly relinquishing the land which was rightfully his to live in town on the charity of his great-nephew;— he, to share one jot, one penny of the money which old Buck and Buddy had buried almost a hundred years ago, with an interloper . . . whose very name was unknown in the country twenty-five years ago. . . . Never. Let George take for his recompense the fact that he would not have to go to the penitentiary to which Roth Edmonds would probably have sent him even if the Law did not" (39–40). Lucas works on probability. He calculates the risks involved in his actions, and he adjusts his behavior according to the expected outcomes. His "wins" then are fully within the potential gains he can anticipate.

Although Lucas may exaggerate his ability to turn situations to his best advantage, he sees himself both as a worthy descendant of old Carothers and as protected by that position of male privilege despite his race. In fact, were he not subject to legal exclusion because of his race, Lucas would, under common law, be in the direct line of inheritance from old Carothers if no lineal descendants survived. "Brothers were preferred to sisters, with the eldest brother inheriting all. If there were brothers, however, the sisters or their issue took equally with one another. . . . If there were no siblings or issue of siblings, the realty would be inherited by the issue of the decedent's paternal grandfather, the eldest male of the nearest degree succeeding first. All relations on the decedent's father's side were preferred, regardless of how distant, before those on the mother's side."[30] Lucas levels inequities of power not by seeking social justice but rather by calling on the power inherent in a white racial ancestry. Within his limited situation, he negotiates power in the manner he associates with whites who own land and access to the Law, and who by means of that ownership amass power and stature in the community and under the institutions of law. Nowhere, however, in his musings on lineage and heritage does he incorporate his father, Tomey's Turl. Here, Faulkner represents the driving force in Lucas's existence as his white ancestor, while erasing his tie to the *black* part of his family and history. Racial heritage figures on the surface only in Lucas's coloring and his social condition; however, the subsurface carries the trace of Tomey's Turl and his way of dealing with the white-dominated world.

At the same time, however, Lucas is aware that the plantation system represented by his grandfather entraps all blacks and negates his individual manhood. For example, before depositing his inheritance, he has to ask, " 'Will the bank keep it for a black man same as for a white?' " (106). He knows full well the system of economic exploitation and domination, and he understands the systemic inequities inflicted on blacks in the Jim Crow South. Even with Roth's affirmative answer, the paternalism is apparent, because he adds, "*I will* ask them to" (106; emphasis added). The devaluation of blacks inherent within the southern social order produces shame in those like Lucas who nonetheless have to fight the negative judgment and resist internalizing the racist construction of black inferiority. Money is for Lucas one of the primary signifiers of manhood, and the vulnerability of blacks without access to the system of money and banking is evident to him.

After his confrontation with Zack, Lucas poses another significant question, which renders in microcosm the place assigned to blacks and the prerogative assured whites: " 'How to God . . . can a black man ask a white man to please not lay down with his black wife? And if he could ask it, how to God can the white man promise he wont?' " (58). Lucas understands the restrictions placed on him by the racial codes of his society, and he understands the unlimited exercise of power on the part of whites within southern society. The connection between the economies of race and sex is reiterated. Abuse stems easily from the corruption of power, and exertions involving sex and money are the most frequent manifestations of corrupt power. Lucas even admits that the law is "rich white lawyers and judges and marshals talking to one another around their proud cigars, the haughty and powerful of the earth" (70). Haughty and powerful, white lawyers, judges, and marshals make up the legal elite whose discourses control and dictate the terms of living for the others in Mississippi society. Nonetheless, Lucas still believes that as "the oldest living McCaslin descendant still living on the hereditary land" (39), he can circumvent racial restrictions by evoking his connection to Carothers McCaslin and his power over the land. Despite Lucas's belief, he cannot escape the truth of the material condition and historical treatment of blacks in Mississippi and its literal repercussions in his own life. Moreover, as construed by Faulkner, he has to accept "sacrifice" as the ultimate recourse and saving grace.

Lucas is forced into racial submission, to accept sacrifice and a different authority, when his wife, Molly, threatens to divorce him because of his obsession with acquisition, with obtaining buried money from the land. Unlike Lucas, Molly believes that the land belongs to God who has the power of authority over it and that, therefore, it cannot belong to any human being. ' "Because God say, 'What's rendered to My earth, it belong to Me unto I resurrect it. And let him or her touch it, and beware' " (99). Both in Molly's explanation and in the spiritual "Go Down, Moses" from which Faulkner took his title, there is a sense of God's power to seek retribution for transgressions against his will, his law. Though she speaks about the buried treasure, Molly also reminds Lucas that the land is defiled by human exploitation, and she draws him away from the egocentric and destructive ways of his grandfather. Ironically, however, she also causes him to accept sacrifice—to abandon his hopes for a change in his condition and to acquiesce to his subordinate place as a black on the McCaslin plantation. Molly becomes the instrument that will tie Lucas to a reality he longs to subvert. Linked symbolically to Ike McCaslin's wife as women who in their desire for an ideal clash with the contrapuntal and antagonistic ideals of their husbands, Molly is as well a tool of white society. Faulkner creates a resonance that foregrounds a profound antagonism to women, their epistemology, and their desires not only in "The Fire and the Hearth" but also in the larger text.

The narrowly assigned and rigidly defined social conventions affecting a black male, descendant of slaves, overcomes any possibility of Lucas Beauchamp's being able to create a new subjectivity for himself, a different and equally significant subject position for himself. Each of the several times he constitutes himself as subject, his moves are contested. To be linked, as he is in the final segment, to Molly and to the class of black women poses problems of subject location for Lucas, who is a black desiring male subject.

Lucas is not ultimately free. His life, as Molly reminds him, has progressed in a certain prescribed way in spite of his efforts to make it otherwise. At sixty-seven, he cannot change it, as he admits: " 'Man has got three score and ten years on this earth. . . . He can want a heap in that time and a heap of what he can want is due to come to him, if he just starts in soon enough. I done waited too late to start' " (127). What goes unarticulated here is that despite his claim to a white ancestor, Lucas has no claim himself in the privileges, possibilities, and rights of white men. His makeshift masculinity is a make-do black manhood. It is not within his power to remake his life and receive his share of the spoils of the earth.

He and Molly and Roth will remain tied to one another as social creatures in a particular social world, one that is not only racially but gender
stratified. The burden of their past is stronger than the possibilities for
a reordered future.

Unexplored or unexplained in Faulkner's text is the social reality, a
legacy of enslavement that would motivate a black man like Lucas to so
respect his wife and his married state as to extinguish his own dreams.
Historically marriage was denied blacks in Mississippi. With Emancipation, blacks entered into marriage as a legal contract that marked them
as free people who were not objects under the whimsical or predatory or
economic interests of slaveholders. Between April and November 1864
(after the Emancipation Proclamation but before the end of the Civil
War), over 1,500 marriages were recorded for recently freed blacks, and
although in the period after the war Mississippi law attempted to circumvent black desire for legal marriages, that state saw unprecedented
numbers of impoverished blacks paying for marriage licenses, so that by
1870 black marriages in thirty-one counties exceeded whites: 3,427 to
2,204.[31]

Lucas's marriage to Molly is one of the viable signs of his freedom
and manhood. It is a tangible mark of his equality with whites in the
execution of a contract that carried the same obligations and expectations for a white or black person. Significantly, too, it is suggestive of
the unlimned marriage between Lucas's parents, Tomey's Turl and Tennie, which begins *Go Down, Moses* and continues to circulate in the text
around the conjoined issues of marriage and freedom, contacts and contractual rights. Love, for a male slave, as John Blassingame remarked,
"represented one of the major crises of his life," because of the inability
of enslaved men to choose their partners or to protect them from insult,
abuse, rape, beatings, overwork, or sale.[32] Not only did the condition
of ownership make slaves subject to the slave market and separation
through sale, but it also meant that, because the father of slave children was unrecognized by law, any children of the union belonged to the
owner of the mother, who decided their fate. Moreover, as Turl's own
parentage and the helplessness of Thucydus reveal, black women were
ever at risk from the sexual attacks of white men, and black men were
powerless to prevent them.

The importance Tomey's Turl placed on marriage to Tennie reverberates in Lucas's attitude toward his marriage to Molly. Marriage for Turl,

obviously, was a public acknowledgment of his rights and his duties.[33] Under the regulations of secular legislation, marriage "created a public relationship, the terms of which were preset by law."[34] The intersectional relationship of marriage as both public and legal locates the institution within a desired, optimal space for individuals denied their humanity and reduced to property in persons in societal spheres of law and community. This combined public and legal aspect made the marriage contract even more significant to blacks after slavery because it constituted their identity within the visible (white) spheres that had previously delimited their existence and humanity.

Lucas's acquiescence is finally to his legal union with Molly, to his moral responsibility toward her, and to his inherited place on the McCaslin-Edmonds plantation. It is, nevertheless, also a taming of his will to resist and rebel. His sacrifice signals a necessary renunciation of "egocentric" dreams, but the cost is his hope for a different future, a future that would, through the acquisition of wealth, level the racial bars delimiting his existence and mediate the property right of whiteness in his society.

Lucas's relation to marriage as a legal contract and as a moral bond not so dissimilar to bondage reflects the materialist boundaries resident from the outset of the narrative in the interlocking concepts of slavery and marriage in "Was." There, in constructing the slapstick humor of the mad chase to the Beauchamps' plantation, elevated to the likes of an English manor estate and in a romanticized fantasy named Warwick, Faulkner elides the pain of the bounded lives of both Turl and Tennie and reduces the racial bondage of chattel slavery to an amusing outing by a lovesick suitor. Humor, especially physical comedic humor, is a way of expressing shame and articulating the repressed issues resident within that emotion. Both boundedness and bondage are linked to the concept of textual boundaries, which are always in the process of being violated or broken, so that "Was" dissolves into "The Bear," part 4, in which Turl's earlier determined and strategic but comic behavior, embedded in traditions of both romance and myth, is contextualized within the ledgers' factual recordings of his birth, his mother's death, his grand-mother's suicide, and his father-grandfather's cruel destruction of the sanctity of human existence for Turl and his maternal family. The enactment of the courtship in "Was" as a frantic and humorous escapade disguises the humiliating circumstances of Turl's enslavement, his existence as property, and the denial of a relational ethic in his brothers' treatment of him; however, that enactment also is always already reinterpreted by the layers of new knowledge and by the dynamic of human behavior. Patriarchal and paternal ideologies collide in a seemingly humorous and innocent time. Freedom, according to that logic, is nothing more than the bumbling courtship game men play; loss of freedom is nothing less than the prize of successful courtship (either welcomed and sought—as in the case of Turl—or unwelcomed but nonetheless sought—as in the case of Buck).

The interplay of courts and courtship in the text intersects both with systems of law and justice, rights and morality, and with binding decisions protecting spatial designations and property rights. While the configuration of courts of law in "The Fire and the Hearth" manifests the way in which legal courts contributed to the condition of oppression, "courts" also echo courtship, courting. There is a connection initially between law (courts) and love (courting) in the story "A Point of Law," in which a wife cannot testify against her husband in a court of law.[35] Lucas Beauchamp's daughter, Nat, and her suitor, George, Lucas's competitor in the moonshine business, are the courting couple. Lucas makes a game of entrapping George, just as George and Nat make a game of concealing their courtship and marriage, thereby entrapping Lucas. Their concealed relationship extends the trope of detection—manifested in Lucas's divining machine and his search for gold—into the marital and legal discourses of the text. The multiple concealments resident within the relations of men and women encourage the tropic work of textual detection, particularly around the hidden ideologies of property—slaves as property, land as property, gold as property, and, in Nat's utilitarian terms, a water well and a back porch as property. All of the searches for property echo Tomey's Turl's game of hide-and-seek. The repetition of property carries with it a repeating of the crimes against property as well as an apprehension of the interlocked circles of motion, space, independence, and agency—which is to say, freedom.

Freedom is necessarily bounded in a world in which divisions and separations constitute a system of legal ownership. Within the text, hunting and sport within a wider natural world (the wilderness, the big woods) and within a bounded domesticated world (the plantation, commissary, house, and cabin) collide with duty and obligation or responsibility under competing systems of law. The plantation, commissary, house, and cabin are figurations of property, differentiated from the wilderness of "Indians" and the big woods of "hunters" by legal definitions of the rights of owners. The society of hunters with Sam Fathers as its chief is not race blind, nor does it level race. Instead it establishes a racial hierarchy that inverts the one existing in the larger society. Sam, as a surviving Chickasaw and a trained woodsman-hunter, is at the top of the social order, while Ash is the black cook who cannot become a hunter and remains outside full intimacy with the Indian-White group of hunters. Sam accepts Ike into what Lee Jenkins labels the "mythic brotherhood of the people of color," which retains a problematical and unresolved place for blacks.[36] Nevertheless, the usage of *brotherhood*, gendered male, is particularly appropriate, because, as Elisabeth Muhlenfeld has observed, "*Go Down, Moses* is a novel of the game, the con, the hunt, the quest. Its world is a man's world; its voices, male voices."[37] It is a world in which freedom is challenged and delimited.

The masculinity of the text, nevertheless, has not been fully remarked, despite the noticeable absence of women and particularly the steady erasure of white women as wives and mothers after their very brief, and often nameless, appearance in the text.[38] One possible reading of the disappeared and vanishing women of the text is that legally they become submerged in the personality of the husband. Coverture makes one legal identity out of two people, and the man's identity becomes the only one visible under law. In his *Commentaries*, Blackstone observes, "The very being or legal existence of the woman is suspended during the marriage, or at least is incorporated and consolidated into that of the husband; under whose wing, protection and cover, she performs everything; and is therefore called in our law-french *a feme covert* . . . and her condition during her marriage is called her coverture."[39] Coverture makes possible a particular kind of negation of white women and especially wives in *Go Down, Moses.*

Married women, both black and white, such as Sophonsiba in "Was" or Molly and her daughter Nat in "The Fire and the Hearth," are constructed as without property yet linked to the disposition of property. Because of their coverture, they are obscured under the paternalistic legal system that would suppress their identities as active agents or unique legal subjects but instead position them as the objects of protection. Ironically perhaps, they share a location with other forms of property under the law—for example, plantation, land, house, machinery, slaves, animals (dogs, mules, horses). Beyond coverture, Nat, the un-named mother of Sam Fathers, the unnamed descendant of James Beau-champ, and all of the black women are especially vulnerable to the laws and beliefs of the society regarding women and race. Molly Beauchamp, a free woman, has no legal standing beyond the protection of the white man she has nursed. Molly is doubly treated as property—by the white McCaslins for whom she is both wet nurse to the white infant and an unspoken but implicit gratifier of "other" sexual needs of the white man (*rite de seigneur*). A vessel, an object, Molly belongs as property also to her legal husband Lucas Beauchamp whose hearth has a fire signifying conjugal, marital love but whose treatment of Molly reduces her to in-animation and boundedness within an "impervious" tranquility, which is perhaps the extreme understanding of coverture by the otherwise legally unrighted black man. While the black women in *Go Down, Moses* are ex-cluded by race from certain legal protections, the white woman Sophon-siba Beauchamp McCaslin as a married woman does have her prenup-tial property protected by the Mississippi Married Woman's Property Law of 1839, which allows her to retain ownership after marriage of any property including slaves she inherited, bought, or acquired prior to her marriage.[40]

Most prominent in the textual masculinity, however, are the inter-twined discourses on hunting and community that occupy the fore-ground of *Go Down, Moses*. The hunt functions as a masculine form of ritualized play in which male bonding generates community. Obviously, hunting as a game or sport is a central means of turning boys into men and of molding social values: "Sports are highly significant, but not as simulation, not as reflection or sublimation, not as example, not as a diversion, but as a relevant and complex institution."[41] That sense of belonging and of sharing in a fraternity continues into the old age of those initiated into the hunt. In "Delta Autumn," for instance, an aged and alienated Ike feels at home only in the tent used for the hunt, "be-cause even this tent with its muddy floor and the bed which was not wide enough nor soft enough nor even warm enough, was his home and these men, some of whom he only saw during these two November weeks and not one of whom even bore any name he used to know—De Spain and Compson and Ewell and Hogganbeck—were more his kin than any" (335). The special nature of the bond continues and defines the rela-tional and subjective identity of men. Even as the old society of hunters is disappearing along with the wilderness in "Delta Autumn," the hunt continues as masculinized ritual play—the sport of men who remember the big woods and old Ben, and who alleviate their sense of aloneness by formalizing a community.

The society of hunters is not only a brotherhood but also a play community with economic implications. In "The Old People," "The Bear," and "Delta Autumn," Ike, Sam Fathers, and the hunters represent a formation of a male-centered play community. Johan Huizinga states that play communities tend "to become permanent even after the game is over," because there remains a feeling of "apart together," the sharing of something important—"mutually withdrawing from the rest of the world and rejecting the usual norms retains its magic beyond the duration of the individual game."[42] Hunting is a form of male-defined cultural play throughout *Go Down, Moses*; as a cultural phenomenon, it allows for male hunters as signifiers of society to express their interpretation of life and the world.[43] The men who hunt together forge bonds within the woods that they then carry with them as loyalties into business, economic, and legal interests in society. Their business dealings are not necessarily idealistic. Men from the hunting brotherhood, for example, sell the Big Bottom and deplete the wilderness for the profit from lumber sales.

In "The Old People" and "The Bear," Ike and Sam are drawn to rituals of the woods, the hunt and the society of hunters. They accept the boundaries and the freedoms imposed by the code of hunting. The "apart together" aspect of their association is particularly poignant because, similar to Tomey's Turl, Sam Fathers, black and native, has been enslaved by his own father and suffers the separation as a father's loss, though he blames his mother not simply for his African heritage and his mixed-race status but primarily for the loss of his father—that same father who sold him and his mother for a horse. Ike's story, though less dramatic, is nonetheless a product of his induction into the valorized world of hunting. Ike derives his identity as an asexual son from the hunter's ideology and from the teachings of his surrogate father, Sam.

Biological fathers are displaced from connection with sons in *Go Down, Moses*, but in their places are surrogates who appear to raise the sons and ameliorate their loss. These surrogates are most prominent within the society of hunters, but they exist as well within the community of enslaved men. Sam's Chickasaw name, "Had-Two-Fathers," is one indication of the addition of surrogates to biological fathers in the text, but Thucydus, Tomey's Turl's surrogate father, is not to be omitted from the list.

In "Was" Buck and Buddy derive pleasure from the ritual play of fox hunting and the exclusion of women from the masculine world constructed around their games. But Tomey's Turl is also excluded, and although there may seem to be an equivalence between Turl and the fox in terms of their being the objects of the hunt, the equivalence is not only unequal but outrageously unnatural, challenged by Turl's humanity and his singular refusal to be reduced to an economic or market value. He is located outside of their normative community, yet the reference points for his identity stem from the white family. As he can, in fact, only be object of their game, not part of its created society, Tomey's Turl constructs his own game—running—in order to create a social world that is not dependent on a male community of hunters but integrates women into its larger, procreative community.

Importantly, however, in the context of the hunt, Turl's felt presence pervades the symbolic logic of the text, as in "Delta Autumn" when Ike assumes he sees the shadow of one of the blacks in the hunting group: "The shadow of the youngest negro loomed. It soared, blotting the heater's dying glow from the ceiling, the wood billets thumping into the iron maw until the glow, the flame, leaped high and bright across the canvas. But the negro's shadow still remained, by its length and breadth, standing, since it covered most of the ceiling, until after a moment he [Ike] raised himself on one elbow to look. *It was not the negro, it was his kinsman;* when he spoke the other turned sharp against the red firelight the sullen and ruthless profile" (336; emphasis added). The melding of the shadow of the black into the profile of his "kinsman" speaks not only to the racial instability engendered in the text and figured by Tomey Turl's hybridity, but also to the racial blending of black/white (as well as native) people of which Turl himself rather than Sam Fathers is the most emblematic. The words "It was not the negro, it was his kinsman" also displace the negative value attached to "the negro," because Ike's kinsman then is *not* the negro. This issue of black kin and race mixture is precisely what has troubled and worried Ike throughout his life. Sam, after all, denies race and thus rejects the most important identification marker of his formative experiences: his racialization as black rather than Indian, as slave rather than free.

The looming shadow calls into question racial certainty and racial exclusivity. Ike's unconscious fear from the moment he reads into the ledgers the violent, ruthless miscegenation that produced Turl and precipitated the death of his grandmother, Eunice, and his mother, Tomasina, rears itself once again in the shadow that is both the young black man and his younger cousin, Roth Edmonds. Edmonds in profile is "sullen and ruthless"; the transfiguration of the two shadows does not elide the dynamic of power imbricated in Edmonds's profile. The symbolic figure of the racially interconnected shadows gives way to the bodily appearance in the tent of the mixed-race woman who is both the mother of Edmonds's child and his relative via her descendancy from Tomey's Turl. A reconfiguration of Turl, she is a substantive apparition, called up by Ike's own nightmares and conjured up by Legate, one of the hunters, as a "doe," a "light-colored" doe (321).

The hunt for the "doe" is very different from the hunt for the bear, Old Ben, which is also a hunt for the ancestors, for the lost fathers who in owning their sons as property use not spatial but legal boundaries to separate themselves into a hierarchy of arbitrary power in which they never admit a paternal bond. "In hunting games there are no boundaries . . . , and the feature of games without boundaries is that those being pursued must give some indication of the direction they have taken, which they do, according to the game being played, by shouting, by showing themselves, by showing a light, by leaving a trail, or by providing a guide. . . . In hunting games those who are pursued may, and often do, make use of cover; but the game is not over if they are seen, named, or even touched; the quarry has to be effectively captured, sometimes, as in Seeking Games, by ritual action of the body."[44] In the hunt for Tomey's Turl's literal body in "Was," just as in the hunt for his figurative body in the ledgers and "The Bear," is the narrative equivalent of hunting games and their resolution in the "ritual action of the body." Importantly, in a major point of difference from the hunt for the bear, the hunt initiated by Turl in "Was" is not for a father but to become a father, not for the past but to create a future. This distinction between the past for back-looking, ancestor-obsessed whites and the future with its risks and uncertainties for the blacks marks a crucial difference between the races in the text. Certainly, the figuration of the mixed-race female body as represented in "Delta Autumn" becomes a message to the future — a message thickly resonant with the presence of fatherless sons.

The departure from the containment of the plantation "civilization" results in the freedom of the wilderness. That freedom may be variously defined as lack of ownership, melding of gender roles (e.g., Ike), and melding of racial constructions without the imposition of a white male sexual aggressor (e.g., Sam Fathers). Ike engages in what Leo Frobenius calls "playing at nature" in the hunt/forest/wilderness sequences.[45] The suspension of the legal and social codes of the plantation civilization results in the necessity of a new set of codes of conduct that can be taught only in the sport of the hunt, which is transformed from a game into a ritualization of birth, life, initiation, maturation, death. Indeed, "The Old People," the chapter that marks the shift to the dominant rituals of hunting in the wilderness, opens with echoes of primordial beginnings, creation myths, and the rhetoric of Genesis: "At first there was nothing" (157). That the hunter and the hunted are represented as similarly apportioned to the interpretation of the hunt revises the stakes of domination and conquest, and that the sightings and gazes are variously enacted and reversed mediates the difference between human and animal. The sightings of Old Ben, the bear, are apocryphal—as rare as the gaze of women, who for the most part are outside the boundaries of the woods and the communal spirit and sport it signifies.

On Ike's last hunt, not only does he confront the gaze of Tomey's Turl's female descendant ("he saw again that grave, intent, speculative and detached fixity like a child watching him" [342]; "She regarded him, almost peacefully, with that unwinking and heatless fixity—the dark wide bottomless eyes" [343]), but he also acknowledges his understanding of women's alterity: "But women hope for so much. They never live too long to still believe that anything within the scope of their passionate wanting is likewise within the range of their passionate hope" (335). Women, then, disrupt the fatalism that is part and parcel of the aesthetics of the hunt. Women can replace men/hunters as the "watchers," those calculating the moves and behavior of the "other"—the prey. Thus, within the interlocking circles of life, death, and desire, women, and black women in particular, because of their removal from the active space of recognized physical agency, become the ocular, the sighted, and the seeing—those who occupy an alternative space of psychic agency that is not the moral sphere typically allotted to women in the domestic sphere or in the cult of true womanhood.

At the same time, however, the gambit, an opening in chess in which a piece is sacrificed to gain an advantageous position, may also under-gird Faulkner's representation of gender in the text. Analogous to the masculinist beliefs and values of Sam and Isaac as hunters is the idea of sacrifice, which as Reuben Fine concludes is the essence of gambits: "the essential question to be answered on both sides [of a gambit] is: Is the advantage in development sufficient compensation for the material given up or not? Normal moves in gambits are those which help to answer this question."[46] As Ike and Sam practice the cultural life of a hunter, that existence is intricately connected to sacrifice—the giving up of the trappings of modern civilization in order to become pure and untainted as a hunter, as a man. In *Go Down, Moses*, however, hunting, sacrifice, and games operate not without a significant degree of irony and out of a large measure of shame. "For gamesters, strategists of sports, it is usually wiser to manipulate less intractable facets of the real."[47] Clearly, for both Sam and Ike, the ritual of the hunt is much easier to master than the shame they associate with their heritages.

Ike McCaslin rejects his own physical needs (warmth, food, water, shelter, sex) and meets his social needs (companionship, acceptance, love) within the community of men, the hunters. There he can also enjoy a certain amount of security (freedom from danger and deprivation) and of esteem (self-respect, recognition, importance). Moreover, Ike can relive his self-actualization, his initiation into the society of hunters and his training in the ways of the woods by Sam Fathers. Through this relived self-actualization, he finds the creative and expressive achievements that signify his sense of personal fulfillment and well being.[48] As a boy becoming initiated into the rituals of the woods and hunting, Ike sleeps next to Sam Fathers: "the two of them wrapped in the damp, warm, negro-rank quilt while the wilderness closed behind his entrance" (187). Interpreted by Ike himself who remembers the "fluid circumambience, drowsing, earless, almost lightless" as "at the age of ten he was witnessing his own birth" (187), the scene comforts and contains an Ike already lost in the process of memorializing the disappearing physical world. Ike situates Sam as the maternal force engendering his birth. In this moment, too, as Judith Sensibar has suggested, is Faulkner's "encoded version of his African-American mother," Caroline Barr.[49] Ike, then, becomes irretrievably linked to blacks, to slavery, and to social death. Sam's mixed-race status as part black and part Chickasaw seemingly would place him in a doubly objectified and oppressed position; however, Faulkner represents him as a noble subject (savage) and a free agent within the woods, where he functions on the margins of the modern world, on the edges of property claimed as owned—the domesticated and tame spaces of the town and farm. Racial inheritance becomes another of the boundaries by which Faulkner refocuses narrative attention in *Go Down, Moses*.

Inscripting Will

The words carrying the weight of obligation, interpretation, and law in *Go Down, Moses* are "father's will," which occur twice in the portion of the commissary ledgers represented. In the first instance, the words appear as "*fathers Will*" (254), in the second as "*Fathers will*" (257). The difference is slight but significant. In the first instance, the "w" in *will* is capitalized, placing an emphasis on it as a noun with some of the naming capacity of proper nouns. In the second, the "f" in *fathers* is capitalized, placing the emphasis on the proper noun-like, naming capacity of this noun in its possessive form. The two words signal the dominant legal authority and ideology inscribed in the text. These words, signifying the transmission and the succession of property, also gesture toward the narrative transformations in *Go Down, Moses* and the intergenerational transference of story.

Definitions of *will* from legal discourse all link the term to the idea of property and death. A will is ordinarily a description of a testamentary disposition of either real property or personal property (linked formerly to a testament rather than to a will). *Atkinson's Handbook of the Law of Wills* provides the simple statement, "A will is a person's declaration of what is to be done after his death."[50] *Black's Law Dictionary* treats the term *will* in multiple contexts. In the first, *will* is defined as "Wish; desire; pleasure; inclination; choice; the faculty of conscious, and especially of deliberate, action. When a person expresses his 'will' that a particular disposition be made of his property, his words are words of command, and the word 'will' as so used is mandatory, comprehensive, and dispositive in nature."[51] In the second context, the disposition of property, *Black's Law Dictionary* defines *will* as "an instrument by which a person makes a disposition of his real and personal property, to take effect after his death, and which by its own nature is ambulatory and revocable during his lifetime." In a third definition, *will* is "the legal expression or declaration of a person's mind or wishes as to the disposition of his property, to be performed or take effect after his death. A revocable instrument by which a person makes disposition of his property to take effect after his death." In the final of the definitions in *Black's Law Dictionary*, *will* is "a written instrument executed with the formalities required by statutes, whereby a person makes a disposition of his property (real and personal) to take effect after his death."

These various definitions converge in one aspect—will as the freedom of testation granted and respected. That freedom is explicit in what nineteenth-century legal scholars termed "the third great natural right," "the right to acquire, possess, and transfer property."[52] In *Go Down, Moses* the document left by Carothers McCaslin as a will is neither presented as a legally probated instrument nor as registered literally into the pages of the text. Nevertheless, his will as his uncontested directions for the dispensation of his property on his death is executed by his sons, Buck and Buddy, and subsequently by his grandson Ike. In two successive generations, the three attempt to carry out the terms and intent of Carothers McCaslin's will, but they also suggest the necessity of modifying and ameliorating the oversights implicit in his will. They actualize Carothers's desire for determining succession by inscripting editorial commentary on the will into the textual narrative, the plantation ledger. In the process, they add to the transmission their own stories of Carothers's "will" and his "rightful" heirs. While the three McCaslins acquire property by descent, they also use property to express a generational conflict over the very nature of will. The notion of will follows the Common Law of England as modified by the Statute of Wills, so that in the United States, the "power of the testator to dispose of his realty, as well as his personalty [personal property], by last will and testament, has always been recognized."[53] There has been, however, a marked tendency from the earliest period "to regulate the law of wills and testaments by legislation, to make the rules for passing land and personal property substantially the same, and to require a greater degree of form for the testament of personalty than was required as the ecclesiastical law of England; a tendency which resulted ultimately in statutes in force in most states which require the same form for wills of land and for testaments of personal property."[54] *Will* in its current usage "denotes the entire testamentary instrument, a place formerly said to be occupied by *devise*."[55] The strength of the will as testament links *will* in *Go Down, Moses* to narration as human desire: "the need to tell as a primary human drive seeks to seduce and subjugate the listener, implicate him in the thrust of desire that . . . never can quite come to the point—but that insists on speaking over and over again," in a "dynamics of exchange."[56]

The words "fathers Will"/ "Fathers will" resonate throughout *Go Down, Moses*. In particular, they emphasize the difference between the will of the forcefully desiring subject, the father and his right, and the antiwill attributed to the enslaved son, Terrel. Orlando Patterson insists that a slave has to be defined in terms of natal alienation, an absence of all rights.[57] Separated at birth from all claims of rights and heritage, the slave enters life alienated from the claims of birth. *Will* in the slave economy substitutes for the rights that remain even in the period of Turl's children and grandchildren elusive and problematical. In the text "fathers Will" carries with it testamentary freedom for Carothers and his white sons and heirs. The connection between testate rights and ownership rights are irrevocable in the matter of proprietary rights over enslaved people.

The question of property and the dispersal of property, and proprietary rights linked to paternal rights are, from the outset of the narrative and its "dynamics of exchange," embedded in the attention to blacks and to racial difference, which confuses the inheritance process with "families." Old Carothers and Ike are the two main, and controversial, sources of property exchange within the family represented in the text. Carothers, whose story of migration to Mississippi reflects the spread of capitalism and market economics in the first quarter of the nineteenth century, wills his accumulated wealth and property. Ike, two generations removed, continues the process of execution of the will begun by his father and uncle because, despite his devaluing of capitalism, competition, and possessions, he values family.[58] In particular, Ike attempts to amend family formation by seeking out the black Beauchamps, the children of Tomey's Turl, to give them their legacy and to atone for his own inheritance by acknowledging their familial connection to old Carothers and thus to himself.

Central to Ike's understanding of property is the shame connected with it. Shame is an emotion he has come to place in a binary opposition to heroism and courageous conduct. As a boy of twelve under the guidance of Sam Fathers, then a man of seventy, Ike shoots his first buck and stands marked by the blood. *"I slew you; my bearing must not shame your quitting life. My conduct forever onward must become your death"* (334).

While the emphasis on shame is consistent with that emotion's centrality in the text, it also functions to redirect attention to the heritage of sins against kin and the crimes against the natural world in reducing people to chattel and the wilderness to real estate with which Ike struggles even as he constructs an ideology of atonement. Ike's conduct, produced out of his own morality, which is laced with an almost hypersensitive awareness of shame, links him not only to the heroic bear but also to his debauched grandfather. Just as Robin West remarks that alienation in Kafka characters may be accounted for by a "disjunction between a system that formally and outwardly insists upon the legitimating function of consent and a human personality that inwardly and persistently seeks the security of authority," so Ike's alienation from the shameful practices of capital accumulation through property in person and the resultant shame of sexual violation across racial but within familial lines may also be viewed.[59]

The text of the Carothers McCaslin's will is inscribed into the text of the commissary ledgers, but it is not visually reconstructed within "The Bear." The construction of texts, books, ledgers, and documents within the novel functions in the space of will as a form of cohesiveness. The ledgers gain significance as the narrative burrows deeper into the quagmire of relationships—economic, social, and familial—in the antebellum South. At sixteen, when Ike takes the ledgers down to read, he remembers the fascination they held for him as a child: "he would look up at the scarred and cracked backs and ends but with no particular desire to open them, and though he intended to examine them someday because he realised that they probably contained a chronological and much more comprehensive though doubtless tedious record than he would ever get from any other source, not alone of his own flesh and blood but of all his people, not only the whites but the black ones too, who were as much a part of his ancestry as his white progenitors, and of the land which they had all held and used in common and fed from and on and would continue to use in common without regard to color or titular ownership" (256). For Ike, ideally, the ledgers create his identity by means of their records of his history. As written memory, the ledgers connect Ike to white and black people and to the land to which they are all tied and which economically forges their kinship. Ike's attitude toward the records is both fear and awe. He is reluctant to acquire the knowledge that he knows resides within the pages: "it would only be on some idle day when he was old and perhaps even bored a little since what the old books contained would be after all these years fixed immutably, finished, unalterable, harmless" (256).

Part of the inscription of wills, deeds, and commissary ledgers as texts that confer or deny identity in *Go Down, Moses* relates to records of property and ownership: "the books which McCaslin kept did not include obituaries: just *Fathers will* and he had seen that too: old Carothers' bold cramped hand far less legible than his sons' even and not much better in spelling, who while capitalising almost every noun and verb, made no effort to punctuate or construct whatever" (257). Inheritance as a process, assured through the legal instrument, the will, connects the discourse on family with that of capitalism. The will was in the nineteenth century the primary instrument "the elite as well as the average wealth-holder had for influencing the transmission of property."[60] The ledgers, in turn, trace the process of succession and transmission of property. These recordings of exchanges and contracts are part of the legal and commercial languages that while validating the family nonetheless function to commodify human beings. This commodification includes their production from their labor, so that a market value can be scripted. The ability to will property, to pass it intact into the next generation creates a major adjunct of capitalism and family stability. As adjuncts of capitalism, wills and deeds represent a textual authority that imprisons Ike McCaslin and McCaslin Edmonds within a defining heredity and a crippling conception of transmission and succession in the racially closed space of "family."

"There is nothing," William Blackstone remarks in his *Commentaries*, "which so generally strikes the imagination and engages the affections of mankind, as the right of property; or the sole and despotic dominion which one man claims and exercises over the external things of the world, in total exclusion of the right of any other individual in the universe."[61] He maintains that while property is an absolute right, property is acquired and maintained by law and not out of natural right, as law determines what can be owned and how that property can be transferred.[62] The notion of sole dominion activates Carothers McCaslin's bequeathing of his property. It legitimates his freeing of slaves, his leaving of land, his allotting of money, but more importantly, it secures his right to property and a consolidation of his family. Carothers assumes the right of dispersal and with it the perpetuation of his lineage, just as Thomas Sutpen in Faulkner's *Absalom, Absalom!* presumes the necessity of dynasty, that he must produce both a legal heir, one who is white and male, and an estate or cultivated land with a house such as his Supten's Hundred, in order to authenticate himself within Mississippi society.

As a relation of power between persons, property is part of the private sphere in which the individual assumes control over "things," over personalty, despite the fact that property when mixed with personhood also functions within the public sphere. Morris Cohen, for instance, argues for a distinction between the branches of law engaging property and sovereignty: "Sovereignty is a concept of political or public law and property belongs to civil or private law. . . . The distinction between property and sovereignty is generally identified with the Roman distinction between *dominium*, the rule over things by the individual, and *imperium*, the rule over all individuals by the prince."[63] Within the concept of slavery is the commingling of the *dominium* and *imperium*, because the type of absolute control owners sought over slaves and the denial of will in those enslaved produced owners with the powers of a prince and property in persons reduced to "thingness."

Wills signal the inevitable, but they also construct a continual power dynamic. They evoke both death and succession of property, and out of a respect for both, "in giving a construction to a will the leading rule is that the intention of the testator shall govern."[64] A will, in other words, is the legal ability of a person to alter a relationship to others with respect to rights. To circumvent the authority of the will, to break its binding contract, is a transgression of the expected order and the rationale behind that order. It is as well a denial of the textual authority of patriarchy and of the expressed intent of the patriarch. The paternal line is clarified and strengthened by the enactment of a will, which makes the family visible and its members distinct. At the same time, those excluded and disinherited from the transmission of property are rendered invisible and disconnected under law.

In *Threads Cable-strong* Dirk Kuyk Jr. constructs an elaborate chart that shows that the McCaslins actually both share and relinquish in regards to the land, beginning with old Carothers, who, Kuyk maintains, "shares" the land and his property by leaving ten acres to Thucydus and $1,000 to Tomey's Turl.[65] However, this reading does not come to terms with differences in the category of property held and elides the difference between inert property—money and land—and human beings who have rights that are not recognized in the bequests. That is to say, Tomey's Turl is "son," not simply family retainer as is Thucydus. A confusion of rights and obligations marks this reading. Since there is no way of attributing motive to old Carothers's act, it seems impossible to determine whether he acted out of a sense of obligation to his human property or out of his right to dispense the property—material goods—as he saw fit. What is clear, however, in the reconstruction rendered by Ike is that Carothers McCaslin does not acknowledge Tomey's Turl as his son. His sin of omission is not merely part of "the general condoned injustice and its slow amortization but the specific tragedy which had not been condoned and could never be amortized" (254). Importantly, both Thucydus and Turl refuse the land and money that Carothers willed to them. Both refuse the "sharing" of property that does not acknowledge their humanity.

Property, when considered in terms of rights, includes inheritance, which is at the core of Ike McCaslin's spiritual and moral dilemma, and which, for instance, is disrupted in Hubert Beauchamp's symbolic ious left in place of the gold coins that he bequeathed to his nephew Ike. Over a period of years, Hubert avails himself of the gold he held in trust for Ike's majority, until ultimately he decimates the entire amount and leaves in its place a few scraps of papers, ious with his signatory and promise to pay. The promissory notes are, of course, as worthless as the cheap paper they are written on and as emblematic of Hubert's delusional self-conception as the British title, the Earl of Warwick, to which he lays claim, and thus signifies his location outside the institution of capitalism and his figurative association with feudal despotism. A contested right to that title and with it ancestral lands leads to Hubert's presumption of a prerogative right to the gold coins he has already given to his nephew. But because Ike has as a child merged his gaze and identity with Hubert's (289), Ike's own claims of title are equally empty, as light as the paper scraps in the coffee can. What is important, however, is that Ike desires his claims to property to be so. Conflicted about any relation to the my-thy/mine-thou distinction that children learn in the process of identity formation and ambivalent about relations to rights that human beings cannot easily unbundle, Ike has no lasting way of relating to his culture—except in the uncivilized wilderness and its mythic space.

Faulkner also represents the right to property as one most subject to abuse because of human personality traits, including aggression. A morality that would relegate property to a subordinate place in social interaction has traumatized Ike into a retreat from engagement with the material world and into a static contemplation of expunging the literal record and expiating the meaning of the commissary ledgers. He is unable to extricate himself from the competing systems of law and morality signified by the spiritual "Go Down, Moses" and its three levels of authority and sources of law.

Legality, then, is connected to the language of rights and courts; it is implicit in such notions as entitlement, which Lucas Beauchamp holds when he searches for gold or when he names himself a descendant of old Carothers McCaslin and constructs himself in his image. Hunting for gold, like hunting for game and hunting for Tomey's Turl, is sport and a way of life connected both to nature and to domestic spaces. It allows for an experience of agency and freedom, and it forms the masculinist core of the interconnected narratives. The authority of the past motivates or actuates both Lucas and his McCaslin kin, Ike, so that both, in relation to property and inheritance, define themselves as autonomous and whole subjects.

Lucas shares with Cass Edmonds the vision of an ancestor "who saw the opportunity and took it, bought the land, took the land, got the land no matter how, held it to bequeath, no matter how, out of the old grant, the first patent, when it was a wilderness of wild beasts and wilder men, and cleared it, translated it into something to bequeath to his children, worthy of bequeathment for his descendants' ease and security and pride and to perpetuate his name and accomplishments (245). In valorizing old Carothers as a man among men, Cass's description establishes the narrative perspective of masculine power that pervades the text and motivates Lucas. Though his own father, Tomey's Turl, was one of Carothers's slaves, Lucas believes in the ethical right of ownership and in the principle of occupation making the right to property. These he links to a viral masculinity, yet he also understands it bodily as conflicting interests. He sees industry in acquiring land and power in holding it, yet he discounts both need for the land and need for labor performed on it. The latter, of course, applies most directly to the McCaslin blacks, as viable claims to property and ownership. Lucas does not seem at all aware of the circumstances surrounding the birth of his mixed-race, nearly white father, Turl.

Yet there may be a conscious repression of Turl at work, because on his twenty-first birthday Lucas asks for the money old Carothers left for his father in his will. Turl had refused to accept a thousand dollars in payment, not inheritance, from a man who did not acknowledge him as son. Lucas removed from the unarticulated but nevertheless dramatic struggle for a father's recognition, can declare, " 'I'm a man now. I can do what I want. I want to know I can go when I decide to' " (105). Unlike the pre-Emancipation period that marked much of his father's life as enslaved and delimited his physical mobility, the Jim Crow era in which Lucas exists acknowledges, without encouraging, the possibility of black mobility. The money provides Lucas with the opportunity for choice. He can choose to stay or leave the McCaslin plantation because money establishes his manhood in economic independence. "Money makes white" in nonracist societies, Alan Watson concludes, but in a racist society, having funds makes it easier for freed slaves and their descendants to incorporate into society.[66] The patrimony rejected by his father becomes an added measure of freedom for Lucas, despite his having been born during Reconstruction and having lived through the repressive nadir of race relations in the turn-of-the-century South: "a lightless and gutted and empty land where women crouched with the huddled children behind locked doors and men armed in sheets and masks rode the silent roads and the bodies of white and black both, victims not so much of hate as of desperation and despair, swung from lonely limbs" (278). Lucas knows that as a black in a racist society he has a finite set of options, and he attempts to design a strategy of behavior that will protect his interests and allow him to make decisions.

For Lucas, money is intricately connected to his construction of manhood. Having turned twenty-one, he defines himself through the legal discourses of majority and inheritance as constitutive of male gender identity and adulthood. However, his acceptance of money as a legacy acknowledges old Carothers's right to property and bequeathal of it. In asking for his inheritance, Lucas also asks that a contractual obligation be met. His understanding of rights is primarily in terms of the plantation as a business derived from acquisition, possession, and dispensation, which are protected by law. From that knowledge, Lucas recognizes how money circulates out of business and its contractual protections, including wills as legal documents with contractual status. His freedom and his manhood depend on his access to and use of money, which in turn enhances his ability to enter into legally binding contracts, whether in marriage or in business, from which his enslaved parents were excluded.

In one of the major silences in the text, Lucas makes no reference to his father's position as slave property and son on the McCaslin plantation. That silence suggests in Faulkner a disinterest in the immediate paternal legacy, for what concerns him is not what passes from one black person to another but rather what passes between whites and blacks. Legacies, patrimony in particular, in *Go Down, Moses* stand for interracial mediation. Tomey's Turl's refusal of the money left him by his white father initiates the circulation of money from whites and the cycle of resistance from blacks that together signify a response to property and law.

Lucas Beauchamp in hunting for gold, in standing up for himself as a man, seeks to occupy a subject position that is different from the one ideologically expected and culturally demanded. He may ultimately be subsumed in a discourse of patronization and reductive race relations that turns linguistically on readings of texts that are external to any of the sections of *Go Down, Moses* in which Lucas appears. The narrowly assigned and rigidly defined social conventions affecting a black man, descendant of slaves, overcome any possibility of Lucas Beauchamp's being able to create a new subjectivity for himself. Yet he attempts to constitute himself as subject in several moves that are at each point contested. One of the most revealing is his relationship with his wife, Molly, which he understands as a contractual union, and thus he makes use of the empowering notion of rights—his legal right to enter into a contractual agreement which carries with it obligations along with entitlements. Equally revealing and perhaps obvious is his relationship to money, because it is in the economic sphere that Lucas and his kin have been exploited and denied rights.

Read back through the actions and motivations of his son Lucas, Turl's game playing takes on added possibilities for interpretation. For instance, a game of a different sort places Tomey's Turl at its center: the detection of crime in the past; or, to put it in the more moralistic terms of the detective, the deciphering of sin and corruption in the past that must be expiated in the present. Linking the detection to crime functions to emphasize the civil legal system and its shortcomings—its inability to recognize rights for those enslaved. The legal negation of rights, then, makes it possible for crimes to occur but for no victims of crimes to materialize. By the time Ike extrapolates meaning from the ledgers, all the principals are dead, but Carothers's descendants on both sides of the racial boundary remain. Thus, within the religious and moral symbolic of "sin," the potential for wrongdoing and the enactment of wrong (as opposite to "right" and "rights" within the legal system) occur not against a righted victim but against a religious or moral authority, against God and the moral commandments that, in effect constitute the making of "wrong."

In the deconstructed messages in the ledgers, Faulkner launches a potent assault against property, ownership, and the laws protecting both, by means of Ike's challenge to his grandfather's cultural authority and his social identity. Ike may well discursively expose Carothers's wrongdoing and dissect his power; however, Ike also capitulates to the "will" of old Carothers when he attempts to disperse to Tomey's Turl's children their monetary legacies. In private, he recognizes what cannot be acknowledged in public: that sexual bonds can generate economic relationships. According to Adrienne D. Davis, "It is the task of private law to determine which relationships will give rise to enforceable (or permissible) obligations. . . . Succession law sorts and ranks relationships that stem from sexual or companionate bonds between men and women, or biological ones between generations."[67] Ike makes these determinations. Despite the tensions he uncovers between his epistemology and ideology, he dispenses what he believes to be just. He consolidates his own racial self, however, and remains indebted to inheritance as evident in biology, psychology, and law. He acts out of an acceptance of common law entails in will and deeds. To circumvent the authority of Carothers's legal will, or to break its binding contract, would be a transgression of the expected order and the rationale behind that order. Historically, some of the American colonies sought to make entail in wills and deeds "an effective dynastic tool by putting obstacles in the way of those who wished to reverse the actions of an ancestor," even going so far in a Virginia statute of 1705, for instance, as to make a special act of the assembly necessary to break an entail, and going still farther in redefining slaves as real property in order to make entailing of slave property legal.[68]

To vacate a will is to disrupt patriarchy in the site of patrimony and property. Such disruption rarely occurred, not even when interracial transmission of wealth was sought. Mary Frances Berry has pointed out not only that in numerous inheritance cases, "Southern state supreme courts between 1868 and 1900 upheld the power of propertied white men to leave estates to their African American mistresses and children," but also that "courts insisted on affirming the power of wealthy white male patriarchs": "white fathers provided for their children whether they acknowledged them or not. The judges routinely upheld the father's will, with only a very occasional rhetorical outburst to show that some understood that these relationships were disapproved, though they might be tolerated."[69]

Several prominent cases have become the subjects of recent books. In *Woman of Color, Daughter of Privilege: Amanda America Dickson, 1849–1893*, Kent Anderson Leslie reveals how one planter pampered his daughter by a slave woman throughout his life and at his death left her a half-million dollar estate. When he was a forty-year-old bachelor, David Dickson, called "the Prince of Georgia Farmers," forcibly took twelve-year-old slave girl Julia Frances as his sexual concubine. Within the year of the rape, Julia Frances bore his daughter, Amanda America Dickson.[70] From her birth on 20 November 1849, Amanda Dickson was accepted by her father, whom he raised and educated as his daughter in direct opposition to the racial customs and legal restrictions of mid-nineteenth-century Georgia. In his will Dickson made Amanda his heir and the wealthiest black woman in the pre-Civil War South; in so doing, he set the stage for a legal battle over the right of a mixed-race daughter to inherit from her white father. That will was contested by his white relatives, who fought any concession of bequeathed property or paternal identity to the mulatto daughter of a slave woman, but on 6 July 1885, Probate Judge R. H. Lewis upheld the will.[71]

The white family's appeal went to the Georgia Supreme Court. The trial testimony (including examination of Julia Frances Dickson) became part of the legal records of the State of Georgia. Of interest here is the conclusion Leslie draws: "Before David Dickson left his estate to his outside family, his behavior was sometimes censured but more frequently, judging from this testimony, ignored, tolerated, or accepted. But after Dickson left his fortune to his outside kin, his heirs-at-law portrayed his behavior as illegal, immoral, and even more shocking so they could gain control of his estate."[72] Dickson's right to disperse his property across race lines was the actual challenge, but because his white relatives could only contest his will on the basis of his immorality and not on the basis of his testamentary freedom, they had little legal grounds for vacating his will. At stake was also the hidden discourse that, as Adrienne Davis concludes after a study of testamentary transfers, posited the fear of black accumulation of wealth that would disrupt the economy in the South and its racial and social hierarchies.[73] In the period after reconstruction, that fear was still a determining factor in legal decisions.

The Georgia Supreme Court upheld the decision of the lower court on 13 June 1887. Chief Justice James Jackson and Associate Justices Samuel Hall and Mark Blanford heard the appeal, but when Jackson, who is quoted as saying "I would rather die in my place than uphold the will," indeed died after contracting pneumonia, his successor Logan E. Bleckley in choosing not to rehear arguments in the case, moved Justice Hall to issue a decisive thirty-two page ruling settling the case and upholding the will and the lower court.[74] Hall based his decision on the legality of the Fourteenth Amendment, which gave citizenship and the rights pertaining to citizenship in the United States and in the state in which they resided to "colored persons," so that "all distinctions as to the rights pertaining to citizenship between the two races are abolished, and as to their civil rights, they stand upon the same footing. . . . Whatever rights and privileges belong to a white concubine or to a bastard white woman and her children, under the laws of Georgia, belong also to a colored woman and her children, under like circumstances, and the rights of each race are controlled and governed by the same enactments on principles of law."[75] In the final analysis, David Dickson's will, the document and the desire of a wealthy white man, carried enough weight to counter and transgress the prevailing codes of strict racial purity and racial separation ordering the post-Civil War world in familial and social matters.

The Supreme Court of Mississippi, however, ruled in the case of *Mitchell v Wells* that Nancy Wells, the emancipated daughter of a white Mississippian living in Ohio, could not inherit $3,000 and personal property left to her in her father's will, because although Edward Wells had freed her in Ohio in 1846, on his death in 1848, Nancy Wells remained "a slave" who could not acquire rights, "civil or political, within her limits, by manumission elsewhere."[76] The decision went against Nancy Wells because she had returned to Mississippi a year and a half after her manumission and had remained in the state first as a servant in the home of her former owner and then as the wife of a free barber in Jackson, Mississippi, before returning to Ohio in 1851. Used against her was an 1842 amending act to Mississippi legislation mandating that slaves taken from Mississippi and emancipated may not return and that free blacks may not emigrate to Mississippi.[77] In a dissenting view that did not alter the court's determination in *Mitchell v Wells*, Edward Wells's unlimited right to dispose of his property was remarked and with it a "fundamental and controlling idea upon which property in slaves rests . . . the right of absolute disposition." Even when legal elites did not uphold the right to inherit of emancipated people, they did not ignore the right of white men and property owners to exercise their dominion over their property.

During the much more stridently anti-emancipation period of the 1850s, a Mississippi jurist upheld the bequest and will of James Brown in *Shaw v Brown*. A Mississippian, Brown took his two sons to Ohio in 1850, freed them, and purchased land for them in Indiana, where they resided except for visits to their father in Mississippi in 1852 and 1854. When Brown died in 1856 while visiting the mother of his sons in Indiana, he left behind a will directing his executor to sell his land and slaves. His white next of kin, John Brown, attempted to attach to the estate the freed sons and their lands, because of a fraudulent emancipation and a restriction against blacks inheriting property, but Justice Alexander Handy ruled against him by supporting what he believed to be the clear intention and desire of the testator. Handy maintained that though Brown was "infatuated or debased" in freeing and providing for his sons, the emancipation was not a fraud and that the freed man was not "an outlaw, a banished person or natural enemy of our people, against whom any man's hand may be raised with impunity, and as wholly without the protection of our laws."[78]

In his will Carothers McCaslin does not free Tomey's Turl. The state of Mississippi in 1822 "outlawed manumission except by will, and only as a reward for meritorious service."[79] In freeing Thucydus Roskus, Turl's supposed father, and Thucydus's parents, Roskus and Fibby, Carothers adheres to Mississippi law, as their manumission could have been argued on the basis of meritorious, long service. The elderly Roskus and Fibby, having come with Carothers from Carolina, are his long-term family retainers; they accept their freedom but remain on the McCaslin place. Thucydus, however, rejects the gift of manumission and prefers to work out his freedom so as not to accept anything from Carothers who had so compromised his status as husband, father, and man. To his enslaved son, Turl, Carothers leaves a thousand dollars, but not his freedom. The monetary legacy, as Ike remarks, *"was cheaper than saying My son to a nigger. . . . Even if My son wasn't but just two words"* (258).

Turl's patrimony, then, is embedded in the twisted logic that substitutes property for paternity. Were Turl not enslaved, he still would be unable under American law to inherit an equal son's share of Carothers's estate because he would be deemed illegitimate. In his will Carothers "made no effort either to explain or obfuscate the thousand-dollar legacy to the son of an unmarried slave-girl, to be paid only at the child's coming-of-age, bearing the consequence of the act of which there was still no definite incontrovertible proof that he acknowledged, not out of his own substance but penalising his sons with it, charging them a cash forfeit on the accident of their own paternity; not even a bribe for silence toward his own fame since his fame would suffer only after he was no longer present to defend it" (257–58). Nor did he need to explain. Carothers charges his sons with executing his will and "charging them a cash forfeit on the accident of their own paternity." The "cash forfeit" reiterates the issue of property and the legally protected rights of the owners of property.

Not only was manumission severely restricted in Mississippi in the 1830s and absolutely forbidden by 1842, but also the law presumed that black people were slaves unless they could prove otherwise.[80] In *Talbott v Norager* (1851) the Supreme Court of Mississippi rendered the opinion that "the laws of this state presume a negro *prima facie* to be a slave."[81] Mississippi had enacted laws to prevent a free black population from existing within its borders. Considered a bad example for those enslaved, free blacks were expected to leave the state. By 1857, the legal, social, cultural, and economic hostility to free blacks had become codified in the official Mississippi Code: "it shall not be lawful for any free negro or mulatto, to emigrate to, and become a resident of this State."[82] There were, however, no legal impediments to manumission under the condition that any freed person would not remain in the state.[83] In *Hinds et al. v Brazealle, et al.* (1838) John Munroe Brazealle sought to inherit from his white father's estate. Emancipated in Ohio, he had returned to Mississippi with his father, but the state chose not to recognize his free status, not to award him the inheritance, but to treat him as part of the property of his father's estate.[84] Because of the issue of residency in free territories, *Hinds v Brazealle*, much like *Mitchell v Wells*, has echoes of the more famous Dred Scott case, which became the bellwether of legal attempts to restrict the possibilities of black emancipation, and of the frequently cited British case of *The Slave, Grace* (1826). In *Grace*, a woman enslaved in Antigua was brought to England in 1822, but after returning the following year to Antigua, she petitioned for freedom on the basis that her residency in England constituted emancipation.[85] Her petition was denied. Unlike *The Slave, Grace*, however, the Hinds and the Mitchell cases were both connected to the execution of wills and rights of inheritance.

Faulkner locates Carothers McCaslin's death in 1837, a year before the *Hinds v Brazealle* decision, although that case may not have been known to him. What Faulkner would have known about the late 1830s is that by then Mississippi had hardened its position on slavery and on manumission. Thus Carothers, of course, does not attempt to free Tomey's Turl in his will, but rather only leaves him a thousand dollars. In refusing to accept the bequest of money from his father's estate, Turl refuses to acknowledge the authority or will of his father. His white brothers, however, not only accept their father's will but go out of their way to enact its terms: "when in the early fifties old Carothers McCaslin's twin sons, Amodeus and Theophilus, first put into operation their scheme for the manumission of their father's slaves, there was made an especial provision (hence a formal acknowledgment, even though only by inference and only from his white half-brothers) for their father's negro son. It was a sum of money, with the accumulated interest, to become the negro son's on his verbal demand but which Tomey's Turl, who elected to remain even after his constitutional liberation, never availed himself of. And he died" (102). Turl does not ask for the money, does not make the "verbal demand" for that willful omission. He circumvents his father's "flinging almost contemptuously, as he might a cast-off hat or pair of shoes, the thousand dollars" as a payment for his parentage (258). The repetition—"He never asked for it. He died" (103)—places a stress on Turl's stubborn resistance to the will, the document and the desire, of the father.

Subsequently, after Ike McCaslin "had retained of the patrimony, and by his own request, only the trusteeship of the legacy which his negro uncle still could not quite seem to comprehend was his for the asking" (103), he misreads Turl's relationship to the legacy while he was enslaved: "the thousand dollars which could have had no more reality to him under those conditions than it would have to the negro, the slave who would not even see it until he came of age, twenty-one years too late to begin to learn what money was" (258). What Ike misses is that perhaps like Thucydus, his surrogate father before him, Tomey's Turl consciously and willfully refuses to accept a legacy from Carothers McCaslin because he will not give the McCaslins the satisfaction of absolution through alms-giving.

When Ike relinquishes his claim to a paternal inheritance, he does not deny the authority of Carothers's will and its assertion of right over his black progeny. The questions of property and the dispersal of property, and proprietary rights linked to paternal rights, that Ike raises, are, from the outset of the narrative, embedded in the attention to race and to racial difference, and to economic and social power particularly relevant to whites. Ike's efforts to execute his grandfather's will in relation to Tomey's Turl and his children are also efforts to assuage his own shame at his ancestor's behavior. For example, the lone daughter of Tomey's Turl, Fonsiba, named Miss Sophonsiba for Sophonsiba Beauchamp, is the object of another search, the hunt for the inheritor of property, the flesh of property bequeathed a monetary boon that becomes especially important to Ike because of his failure to locate Tennie's Jim in Tennessee: "his [Ike's] secret golden girdle like that of a disguised one of the Magi travelling incognito and not even hope to draw him but only determination and desperation, he would tell himself: *I will have to find her. I will have to. We have already lost one of them. I will have to find her this time.* He did" (265).

Not merely a property object, Fonsiba is also the object of marriage. In both instances, she functions in dialogic relationship to the laws and legal codes initiated by men. Married, she is bound, but not despairingly, to a husband who fully assumes his place as patriarch. When Ike finds the cabin in Arkansas in which Fonsiba and her husband reside, he "saw, crouched into the wall's angle behind a crude table, the coffee-colored face which he had known all his life but knew no more, the body which had been born within a hundred yards of the room that he was born in and in which some of his own blood ran but which was now completely inheritor of generation after generation to whom an unannounced white man on a horse was a white man's hired Patroller" (265). Although recognized as a "coffee-colored face" and "the body," Fonsiba has been folded into her husband's identity and conception of the world. Under coverture, she no longer has a distinct social history or subjectivity. She has become, according to Ike, like her husband, "the man himself, reading—sitting there in the only chair in the house, before that miserable fire for which there was not wood sufficient to last twenty-four hours, in the same ministerial clothing in which he had entered the commissary five months ago and a pair of gold-framed spectacles which, when he looked up and then rose to his feet, the boy [Ike] saw did not even contain lenses, reading a book in the midst of that desolation" (266). Ike wishes to bind Fonsiba's husband to his conceptions of appropriate behavior for black men in the postbellum South. The man is made to seem a lazy nonprovider for his wife: "that muddy waste fenceless and even pathless and without even a walled shed for stock to stand beneath: and over all, permeant, clinging to the man's very clothing and exuding from his skin itself, that rank stink of baseless and imbecile delusion, that boundless rapacity and folly, of the carpetbagger followers of victorious armies" (266).

Ironically, Ike may protest too much. His response to Fonsiba's marriage and husband foreshadows Ike's own dysfunctional relationship with his wife and their contest over not merely property but dominance in their marriage. As he and Fonsiba's husband argue about how he will provide for his wife, Ike notices "she had not moved, she did not even seem to breathe or to be alive except her eyes watching him; when he took a step toward her it was still not movement because she could have retreated no further: only the tremendous fathomless ink-colored eyes in the narrow, thin, too thin coffee-colored face watching him without alarm, without recognition, without hope" (268). Fonsiba does not express hope or gratitude in being rescued by Ike. She articulates a different level of awareness of her situation when Ike asks, " 'Fonsiba, . . . Fonsiba. Are you all right?' " (268). Her response is only that she is free. And the meaning of freedom for those formerly enslaved is what Ike cannot fathom.

Ike's conception of what freedom should be for the couple intrudes on their freedom and their ability to exercise will and rights in an emancipated state. Ultimately, Ike circumvents the husband's will by leaving money in a bank with directions to pay Fonsiba directly three dollars a month. By his calculations, "multiplied three dollars by twelve months and divided it into one thousand dollars; it would stretch that way over almost twenty-eight years and for twenty-eight years at least she would not starve" (268). Ike's caregiving is an exemplary paternal bequest passed on from the property claims of his grandfather. His attempt to give Fonsiba an economic personality is figured against the context of a husband, house, and farm, which he deems inadequately productive and protective.

Because wills relate directly to bequests, the structure of property in the text includes houses, money, material spaces, land, wells, porches, as well as the systems of laws and courts that execute wills. These are all linked to Carothers McCaslin's act of will and to the theory of wills that supports and contains property rights as foundational to an orderly society. House as property is crucial to Lucas's defense of his domestic space and with it his defense of his masculinity, his proprietary "right" to his wife's physical body within his house and within his bed. The house, as a symbol of power and manifestation of property, is key to Ike's rejection of all domestic space, even the "jerrybuilt house" his wife's father leaves to them. Ike nonetheless responds to an aggressive encompassing masculinity that reverberates in the ledgers and in the phrase "fathers will." His ambivalent response to his grandfather's will positions him in opposition to his society because he literally rejects its conception of sustaining an orderly society through clearly defined and uninterrupted succession.

Masculinity is fraught with tensions for Ike; sexuality is burdensome precisely because it is bound up in a heritage of ownership, slavery, and property. The choices of action and belief render him immobile for much of his life. Ike deciphers a homosocial message in the ledgers and the "will" of his grandfather. Connected to Tomey's Turl in his refusal to accept the interpretation of slave property as a thing, Ike is both freed by and encumbered by being motherless and fatherless, as is Turl. His absence of parents emancipates him from the prevailing models of chattel slavery. Within the ideology informing this text, it is a short step from a recognition of the problematic of slave ownership, to that of land ownership; the explicit connection is the state or condition of the materiality. Ike's choice of the society of men, Sam Fathers and the hunters, in the masculine space of the big woods, for example, is not necessarily a displacement of male heterosexual erotic desire, but it can be read as homoerotic attraction to the Other of Tomasina, or Eunice, or the various unnamed white women who reproduce McCaslin heirs; that is to say, it is an attraction to the other as configured by Sam Fathers and by the men of the big woods. Foucault theorizes, "It is through sex—in fact, an imaginary point determined by the deployment of sexuality—that each individual has to pass in order to have access to his own intelligibility (seeing that it is both the hidden aspect and the generative principle of meaning), to the whole of his body (since it is a real and threatened part of it, while symbolically constituting the whole), to his identity (since it joins the force of a drive to the singularity of a history)."[86] Ike textualizes the "sin" as sexual and reads into the ledgers his own sexual awakening and his fear of a biological danger implicit in any recognition of self as a sexual being. It is also a fear, not unlike Buck's and Buddy's, of being fully socialized as white—given the full implications of whiteness within their culture. The repression of Ike's sexuality and masculinity positions Ike on the fringe of his culture. His rejection of hereditary rights and proprietary rights seals his fate as one dead to his society. He may attempt to live as a hermit or monk, but he cannot escape the gender definitions and identifications of his society. Foucault concludes, "Sex is worth dying for. It is in this (strictly historical) sense that sex is indeed imbued with a death instinct."[87]

Ike rejects his wife and with her his prospect for a son, progeny, and continuance within his society. Unable to relate to his wife sexually, he does not understand the economic and material drives that urge her to trade, unsuccessfully, her body for his farm. This is why he gives property to the son of a black Beauchamp and of a white Edmonds, both descendants of Ike's own grandfather and, an important point that the narrative does not make well, all three (mother, father, and child) are relational to Ike himself.

Ike justifies his loss of a son as being a salvation for that unborn son who would be freed from the shame and wrong inherited from Carothers and passed down to the male McCaslins:

> in repudiation and denial at least of the land and the *wrong and shame* even if he couldn't *cure the wrong and eradicate the shame*, who at fourteen when he learned of it had believed he could do both when he became competent and when at twenty-one he became competent he knew that he could do neither but at least he could repudiate the *wrong and shame*, at least in principle, and at least the land itself in fact, for his son at least: and did, thought he had: then (married then) in a rented cubicle in a back-street stock-traders' boardinghouse, the first and last time he ever saw her naked body, himself and his wife juxtaposed in their turn against that same land, that same *wrong and shame* from whose regret and grief he would at least save and free his son and, saving and freeing his son, lost him. (334–35; emphasis added)

Ike attempts to absolve that potential son from guilt but mainly from shame (connected to wrong and reiterated four times) which he has hidden in the repudiation of an inheritance. It is that act of selflessness which ultimately leaves him bereft of a future.

Ike's complicated decision to become free of his grandfather's legacy and live as a simple carpenter, "not in mere static and hopeful emulation of the Nazarene," masks an underlying sexual tension: "Isaac McCaslin's ends, although simple enough in their apparent motivation, were and would be always incomprehensible to him" (295–96). His life, "invincible enough in its needs," nonetheless is as vulnerable to sexual desire and its conjunction with masculine power as was his grandfather's. In a lengthy scene that is perhaps the most erotic and sexually graphic in all of Faulkner's texts, Ike's wife, "an only child, a small girl yet curiously bigger than she seemed at first, solider perhaps, with dark eyes and a passionate heart-shaped face" (297), intuits the desire for sex underlying his multiple renunciations.[88] Ike inscribes her with the text of bodily presence and sexuality that objectifies her and all women as sexual instruments. "*She already knows more than I with all the man-listening in camps where there was nothing to read ever even heard of. They are born already bored with what a boy approaches only at fourteen and fifteen with blundering and aghast trembling*" (300).

For her part, the unnamed wife attempts to use her knowledge to gain dominance over him so that he will accept the ownership of property and inheritance of wealth—the means to a solid economic base and class position for them both. Her act, while satisfying Ike sexually and transporting him out of his morbid self-referentiality, recalls the physical manipulations and unbounded desire of his grandfather to which ultimately he cannot yield. Thus, he projects onto her body the normative condition which defines his own spiritual depression and his determination to lose his body. "*She is lost. She was born lost. We were all born lost* then he stopped thinking and even saying Yes, it was like nothing he had ever dreamed, let alone heard in mere man-talking until after a no-time he returned and lay spent on the insatiate immemorial beach and again with a movement one time more older than man she turned and freed herself. . . . 'And that's all. That's all from me. If this dont get you that son you talk about, it wont be mine:' lying on her side, her back to the empty rented room, laughing and laughing" (300–301). Her laughter mocks his desire for progeny and his self-righteous renunciation of his birthright, because the production of an heir, a son in particular, is always already implicated in property and property rights. But her laughter also mocks her own desire for property and possession, so that both wife and husband are defeated by the complexity of their desires and frustrated by their inability to love, and especially to love life over death and the body itself along with abstractions or chimera. In this sexual encounter, "the most passionate" and "the most tragic" in Faulkner's fiction, as Elisabeth Muhlenfeld puts it, Ike has willed himself into a state of "dispossession and disempowerment," while his heart-faced wife longs for "possession and authority" in which she might "accede to the place of power."[89]

Their conflicting wills reconfigure the concept of will in the text. Will then becomes a reminder of both the desire for property and not simply the testament for the dispersal of property after death. The struggle of Ike and his wife is over will and over the right to inherit and hold property, as well as the right to determine lines of inheritance and succession. He holds their sexual union in a romantic remembrance that only vaguely infers their tense conflict: "that one long-ago instant at least out of the long and shabby stretch of their human lives, even though they knew at the time it wouldn't and couldn't last, they had touched and become as God when they voluntarily and in advance forgave one another for all that each knew the other could never be" (104). But until her death, she views Ike with "pity" and "regret," which she expresses in a "tense bitter *indomitable* voice" (104; emphasis added). In the absence of conjugal relations, they both recognize that their struggle is thus about power and a continuation of the discourse on power emerging from the example of old Carothers McCaslin. It is only coincidentally about love, the vacated emotion for the white McCaslin descendants.

When in "Delta Autumn" the young woman descendant of Tomey's Turl asks Ike, " 'Old Man . . . have you lived so long and forgotten so much that you don't remember anything you ever knew or felt or even heard about love?' " (346), her words may be read in relation to the higher value placed on love (with the attendant suggestion of the transcending spiritual). Love in the abstract ameliorates the necessary sexual (bodily and materiality) component of the intercourse that produced yet another biracial Edmonds-McCaslin-Beauchamp child. She exerts on the scene a reconfiguration of Tomey's Turl: a configuration of Ike's own absent and long-vacated desire for either love or sex; each has been replaced by a desire for death, but without a specific mechanism or mode of transport to death, and thus also with an all-compelling motive for death. Even before the woman's appearance in "Delta Autumn," Roth Edmonds has linked Ike's condition to death: " 'So you've lived almost eighty years. . . . And that's what you finally learned about the other animals you lived among. I suppose the question to ask you is, where have you been all the time you were dead?'" (329). If configured in the ledgers of "The Bear" is a propelling toward death (read multiple deaths—Eunice, Tomasina, eventually Carothers) in the aftermath of sex and specifically sex across racial lines, then Ike is attracted to death but repulsed by the sexual component he identifies with it. Sexuality is power, and power is gendered masculine. But power is also threatening as figured by the sexual aggression and power plays of old Carothers, whose masculine virility is transgressive, destructive, and enduring.[90]

The young woman in "Delta Autumn," however, puts a different face on power. If the nature of power is reconsidered in terms of the complexity of games, then power shifts to the unnamed woman with the child. As great-granddaughter of Tomey's Turl, she reclaims both familial connection across race lines and individual names for her black kinsmen. When Ike McCaslin "cried, not loud, in a voice of amazement, pity, and outrage: 'You're a nigger!'" he receives her unequivocal response: "'Yes,' she said. 'James Beauchamp—you called him Tennie's Jim though he had a name—was my grandfather. I said you were Uncle Isaac'" (344). Her grandfather, the eldest son of Tennie and Terrel,

> ran away before he became of age and didn't stop until he had crossed the Ohio River and they never heard from or of him again at all—that is, that his white kindred ever knew. It was as though he had not only . . . put running water between himself and the land of his grandmother's betrayal and his father's nameless birth, but he had interposed latitude and geography too, shaking from his feet the very dust of the land where his white ancestor could acknowledge or repudiate him from one day to another, according to his whim, but where he dared not repudiate the white ancestor save when it met the white man's humor of the moment. (102)

Her recitation of her grandfather's heritage situates the land itself in the construction of race and discourses of racial inferiority that forced James Beauchamp to run away. But her memory of his will to be free suggests another facet of power.

James Thucydus Beauchamp's history in "The Fire and the Hearth" is different from that represented in the ledgers of "The Bear" and is written in Ike's handwriting, which resembles his grandfather's: *"Vanished sometime on night of his twenty-first birthday Dec 29 1885. Traced by*

Isaac McCaslin to Jackson Tenn, and there lost. His third of legacy $1000.00 returned to McCaslin Edmonds Trustee this day Jan 12 1886" (261). The version in "The Fire and the Hearth" contains verbal clues that Faulkner may have intended to suggest a racial passing in James's flight, which also has resonance with Eliza's across the Ohio River in *Uncle Tom's Cabin*, but the version in "The Bear" places James's birth during the Civil War and after the Emancipation Proclamation: *"Born 29ᵗʰ december 1864"* (260).

James's granddaughter, the visibly white woman in "Delta Autumn," represents the return of the repressed black side of Ike's family and with it the erotics of race difference, but she acknowledges her own hybridity. Freedom of identity for her is possible. Subjectivity and race can be self-constructed—rather than culturally constructed. She owns her identity and her self-possession unnerves Ike and his racial ideology. She is verbally prepared to anticipate her opponent's response and to speak in self-aware, self-confident words that were not given to her ancestors. "If meaning must be conceived as dialogic," Peter Brooks contends, "dialogue represents a centerless and reversible structure, engendering an interminable process of analysis and interpretation, a dynamics of transference in which the reader is solicited not only to understand the story, but to complete it."[91] Within her linguistic command and verbal expression, James Beauchamp's granddaughter enables the reversal of the expected narrative and its potential meaning.

Her affair with the white Roth Edmonds produces a child, but her articulation of her own condition, combined with her knowledge of her white kinsmen and their history, creates her equality to and her dominance over Ike.[92] In the tableau in which they meet, she stands up, he lies down; she knows both their histories, he knows only his own; she is life-giving, he is dying. Her knowledge and his ignorance signal a break in the old dynamics of power between the two families that are in fact one. While her near-white body as a visual reminder of Tomey's Turl may be a site of sexual and racial politics in the text, it is fully hers and an epistemological sign of her control of her reproductive rights even against the logic of sexual involvement with a member of the McCaslin-Edmonds family.

She introduces an almost inconceivable concept to Ike: a statement of individual will and active desire on the part of a black person. Ike has conditioned himself to accept the wholesale victimization of blacks under the exploitative institution of slavery and its abusive legacies. As a result, he has inadvertently bought into the notion of black nonwill, of blacks being without will, and with it, he has accepted the concept of the absolute control of whites over black life. While the woman may be complicit in Roth's sexual use of her body, she is not finally a victim of his will. And that amazing revelation forwards a necessary reconsideration of the subject of property.

Owning the Subject

Tomey's Turl does not reappear in "The Bear," but references to him abound there. In particular, Terrel, as Faulkner chooses to identify him in the later section of *Go Down, Moses*, signifies the bequeathing of property, the inheriting of property, and the limits of responsibility regarding property. He becomes the visible sign of the corruption of the plantation system and the contested site of meaning. Not merely the name Tomey's Turl but also the psychology of the game-player who would risk his life to court Tennie and to become a sexually active adult male is largely absent from "The Bear." There, Terrel is the decipherable trope for the fall of the South (the sins of various men like Carothers McCaslin) and the deterioration of the South (the wilderness of the literal landscape). Yet, it is also Terrel's story that allows his nephew Ike McCaslin to become a natural lawyer in arguing the case for reparations for the unspeakable act that produced Terrel and the abuses inherent in the very core assumptions of the institution of slavery.

The connection between the discourse on ownership of land and the discourse on property in persons is implicit throughout *Go Down, Moses* and explicit in the debate central to "The Bear." This linking of land and slavery has an underpinning in legal analysis. According to Lawrence M. Friedman, "The slave was a capital asset. He belonged to the land. A law of colonial Virginia (1705) . . . declared slaves to be real estate, not personal property. Kentucky in 1798, and Louisiana Territory in 1806, had similar laws. In those jurisdictions, a single set of rules governed transfer and inheritance of the estate as a whole—that is, both the plantation or farm and the slaves who labored on the land."[1] In Louisiana, for instance, according to the *Black Code* of 1806, "Slaves shall always be reputed and considered real estates"; however, that classification of slave property was complicated by later designations of slaves as immovables (*"immeubles"*) as in the *Digest of 1808:* "Slaves in this territory are considered as immovables by the operation of the law, on account of their value and utility for the cultivation of the lands."[2] Although the Virginia law was repealed in 1792, legal practice in that state and in Louisiana and in general maintained the connection between slaves and the land. In some instances, and well into the nineteenth century, slaves were treated under law as real estate. Without first exhausting all other personal property, selling a slave to satisfy a debt was prohibited, which resulted in slaves being situated under law "halfway between the legal position of land, which could not be levied on until *all* personalty had been sold, and that of ordinary chattels."[3]

When Terrel's white kinsmen, Ike McCaslin and his cousin McCaslin Edmonds begin their debate in "The Bear," they function as two lawyers embroiled in a contest over land and slaves. On the one side, Ike is obsessed with the tragedy of a diminishing wilderness and the shame of slavery. He has dreams of an idealized world, but he sees the land he occupies as "Cursed" (*Go Down, Moses*, 284). On the opposite side, McCaslin insists on a level-headed practicality regarding property relations: " 'Habet then.—So this land is, indubitably, of and by itself cursed' " (284). McCaslin, described as showing a "thin and bitter smiling," with his eyes having a "faint lip-lift which would have had to be called smiling" (284), has committed his attention to the here and now and to the ironic import of the debate. Ike responds, " 'Habet too. Because that's it: not the land, but us. Not only the blood, but the name too; not only its color but its designation" (285). He turns the focus once again to the issue of enslavement and violation of human beings, both linked to the land and the question of ownership.

Their long discourses in "The Bear" may be read as lawyerly testimony before two competing courts of law, both of which share the positionality of legal elites, the judges and lawyers in law cases, decisions, or narratives. "The natural lawyer's insistence that law, properly defined, incorporates the demands of morality, entails either a chivalric conclusion—the necessary morality of the current regime—or the revolutionary conclusion—the immorality and hence illegality of the regime," Robin West maintains. "Whereas the comic natural lawyer sees virtue in existing power relations, the tragedian finds such virtue only in his dreams of an idealized or future world."[4] No simultaneously binding judgment or comprehensive ruling can be made or reached on hearing the two testimonies from Ike and Cass, "the two of them juxtaposed and alien now to each other against their ravaged patrimony, the dark and ravaged fatherland still prone and panting from its etherless operation" (284). Yet separately, the two refigure a performative dialogic with testimony and witness, though not for a defense and a prosecution, but rather for two defenses for two very different cases and perhaps even different trials harnessed together in an inescapably paternalistic performance. Ike argues for a combined notion of natural and human rights and makes his case for the inclusion and protection of both his grandfather and blacks, along with the land they occupy.

Although championing a wilderness free of the taint of ownership and held in a kind of sacred trust for all to use, Ike nonetheless seems to accept the two main suppositions of chattel slavery: lifetime servitude and inherited slave status. As Joseph William Singer points out, "property and sovereignty in the United States have a racial bias. The land was taken by force by white people from the peoples of color thought by the conquerors to be racially inferior. The close relation of native people to the land was held to be no relation at all. To all the conquerors, the land was 'vacant.' Yet it required trickery and force to wrest it from its occupants. This means that the title of every single parcel of property in the United States can be traced to a system of racial violence."[5] Ike implicates Native Americans in the tainting of the land and in the practice of slavery. " 'He saw the land already accursed even as Ikkemotubbe and Ikkemotubbe's father old Issetibbeha and old Issetibbeha's fathers too held it, already tainted even before any white man owned it by what Grandfather and his kind, his fathers, had brought into the new land' " (248). In overlooking the introduction of slavery by whites who entered and took the land by various means, Ike absolves his ancestor from part of the blame for the corruption and violence of slavery. He argues that there was " 'no hope for the land anywhere so long as Ikkemotubbe and Ikkemotubbe's descendants held it in unbroken succession' " (248), and that " '[m]aybe He saw that only by voiding the land for a time of

Ikkemotubbe's blood and substituting for it another blood, could He accomplish His purpose'" (248). Less obvious is that he also insinuates Ikkemotubbe and his people in the competitive economic practices of capitalism that gave rise to the plantation system and the abuses of slave labor.

Ike McCaslin equates the experience of his grandfather with possession of the land and of slaves. His equation is negative and encompasses his own shame at his ancestor's aggressive rapacity. He reasons that when old Carothers bought the land from Ikkemotubbe, he

> believed he had tamed and ordered it for the reason that the human beings he held in bondage and in the power of life and death had removed the forest from it and in their sweat scratched the surface of it . . . in order to grow something . . . which could be translated back into the money he who believed he had bought it had had to pay to get and hold it and a reasonable profit too: and for which reason old Carothers McCaslin, knowing better, could raise his children, his descendants and heirs, to believe the land was his to hold and bequeath since the strong and ruthless man has a cynical foreknowledge of his own vanity and pride and strength and a contempt for all his get. (243–44)

Ike envisions his grandfather as a ruthless man who misappropriates the land and abuses human beings because he assumes the right to property, the plantation itself as well as its chattel slaves. His right to property accrues from purchase, on the one hand, and from labor on the other. Based on Locke's conception of property in his *Second Treatise of Government*, individuals own their own bodies and thus their labor and whatever they mix their labor with they also own. But in the McCaslin case, the "human beings he held in bondage" work the land and add value to it, but they own neither their bodies nor their labor, and hold no property rights in the things they produce by their labor. Old Carothers assumes all rights to their production and the property rights so that he can bequeath his land and, with it, a better life as the landed gentry to his white children.

Ike desires to replace the rapacity of his grandfather and his patrilineal bequests with a culture free of both slavery and capitalism. He naively constructs his grandfather as an exception by representing him as one who forgets the truths God makes manifest in nature and thus commits crimes of excess in a basically good social order. Ike reasons, "'Maybe He [God] chose Grandfather out of all of them He might have picked. Maybe He knew that Grandfather himself would not serve His purpose because Grandfather was born too soon too, but that Grandfather would have descendants, the right descendants; maybe He had foreseen already the descendants Grandfather would have, maybe He saw already in Grandfather the seed progenitive of the three generations He saw it would take to set at least some of His lowly people free—'" (248). Just as Judith Lockyer suggests, however, "The romantic idea of a pristine natural world extant for human needs belies its own genesis in the very culture it seeks to transcend."[6] Implied within Ike's configuration is a notion of natural rights within a natural world—those rights justified for social stability and human dignity.

Having been born in 1867, Ike has a personal history that coincides with the difficult period of rebuilding and reconstructing the postwar South. "1874 the boy; 1888 the man, repudiated denied and free; 1895 and husband but no father, unwidowered but without a wife, and found long since that no man is ever free and probably could not bear it if he were" (269). At twenty-one, Ike repudiates the plantation tradition of his grandfather by renouncing his birthright, ownership of the McCaslin land, because he believes that God "created man to be His overseer on earth and to hold suzerainty over the earth and the animals on it in His name, not to hold for himself and his descendants inviolable title forever, generation after generation, to the oblongs and squares of the earth, but to hold the earth . . . in the communal anonymity of brotherhood, and all the fee He asked was pity and humility and sufferance and endurance and the sweat of his face for bread" (246). He adopts his terms from the language of plantation life: God as master, man as overseer, earth and animals as dominated or controlled. In his effort to understand those disturbing aspects of his cultural heritage, Ike effectively produces and occupies a psychological space in which his grandfather as oppressor and his uncle Terrel as victim conjoin. Central to this subjectification is Ike's presumption of the wilderness as the embodied culture, functioning in tandem with the oppressor-victim in his dialectical argument. In setting up the paradigm of no ownership and thus no property, Ike occludes the possibility of slavery.

Faulkner seems to base Ike's philosophy on Jean-Jacques Rousseau's *Discourse on Inequality*: "The first man who, having enclosed a piece of ground, bethought himself of saying 'This is mine,' and found people simple enough to believe him, was the real founder of civil society. From how many crimes, wars, and murders, from how many horrors and misfortunes might not anyone have saved mankind, by pulling up the stakes, or filling up the ditch, and crying to his fellows: 'Beware of listening to this imposter, you are undone if you once forget that the fruits of the earth belong to us all, and the earth itself to nobody.' "[7] Rousseau's philosophy made its way into other discourses, including law. That the earth and its fruits are not owned exclusively but shared by all is also the position taken in late-nineteenth-century U.S. law books. Thomas Smith's *Elements of the Laws* (1882), for example, states, "At the commencement of the existence of man . . . the earth, with all things thereon, became his by the gift of God; but the rights of property which he thus acquired were held in common. That is, the earth and its fruits were not parcelled out in distinct portions to each individual, but the whole was given to all mankind, to be distributed and enjoyed according to their necessities." Thus, in Smith's "legal" narrative of property, the main premise is that the "Creator gave to all created things the right to use and enjoy the fruits and productions of the earth, whether animate or inanimate, according to their several wants and necessities"; however, "rules by which individual rights to property are regulated result from the customs and institutions of civil society."[8] These civil rules ultimately may well conflict with the conception of the initial gift of the earth held in common.

Ike acts in philosophical opposition to the ethics of keeping blacks in bondage and in opposition to his own white race, "the very race which for two hundred years had held them in bondage and from which for another hundred years not even a bloody civil war would have set them completely free" (244). His bondage is directly connected to the image not merely of his grandfather but of Terrel whose image is both visual (what Ike remembers seeing) and textual (what Ike remembers reading). As a result, he rejects ownership of any personal goods in order to free himself from even the smallest accumulation of property, which would be a reminder of his heritage and the shame of his part in Terrel's fate. By divesting himself of ownership, Ike attempts to expiate the sins of his grandfather and "the whole plantation in its mazed and intricate entirety . . . that whole edifice intricate and complex and founded upon injustice and erected by ruthless rapacity and carried on even yet with at times downright savagery not only to human beings but to valuable animals too" (284–85). In reality, freedom is no more Ike's than it is his black kinsman's. " 'I am free' " (285), he insists. " 'Yes, Sam Fathers set me free' " (286). But Ike in the property of his white skin color already carries with him all the rights and privileges of freedom.

The point that Ike repeatedly considers is that his grandfather acts on a belief that he has the legal right to do what he wishes with his property. The key words in "Was," the chapter introducing Ike, are references to this recurrent concern with the right to property: "bequestor," "inheritor," "title," "patent," "owned," "property," "will," and "land." But these words do not fully signify what old Carothers's proprietary right has encompassed: his begetting of a child, Tomey's Turl, upon his own slave daughter; his allotting a thousand-dollar cash legacy to his slave son to be paid by his legitimate sons and white heirs, the twins, Amodeus and Theophilus. Nor do they allow for the moral conclusion that Ike reaches: that Carothers values property but not human life; that he finds dignity in possession but not in the human beings possessed. Race, according to Frances L. Ansley, is "at the heart of property law."[9] And the configuration of blacks as inferior, or, as McCaslin argues, " 'The sons of Ham. You who quote the Book: the sons of Ham' " (249), whom he links to " 'Promiscuity. Violence. Instability and lack of control. Inability to distinguish between mine and thine' " (281). McCaslin then relegates blacks to property transactions and objects of property—not unlike, as he insists, mules and dogs in undermining the virtues (endurance, pity, tolerance, forbearance, fidelity, and love of children) that Ike attributes to blacks (282). Even Ike himself argues that the vices of blacks " 'are vices aped from white men or that white men and bondage have taught them: improvidence and intemperance and evasion—not laziness: evasion: of what white men had set them to, not for their own aggrandisement or even comfort but his own' " (281).

Isaac McCaslin discovers and verifies in reading the plantation ledgers the truth of his grandfather's values and power; he intuits and reasons the actual facts of use and ownership, and with these the superiority and dominance of his white relative over others. For Ike, the vision and the memory of Tomey's Turl's literal body, his near whiteness and his enslavement, constitute the reality of his grandfather's corrupt power. The ideal of natural rights in a natural world is not possible once the land has been held by the Chickasaw, occupied by them, thus giving them possession and the right to assume ownership of it, until finally they sell the land to Carothers McCaslin. The ledgers as records of the plantation's business dealings provide Ike with one truth about his grandfather's treatment of his chattel, his incestuous relationship with his daughter, which is a transgression of the natural law Ike espouses.

Perhaps even more significant is that he discovers that the ledgers themselves are not simply a record of purchases, expenditures, debits, and credits for the plantation, but that they are, in effect, an index to the codes of the land and the society: "strong as truth and impervious as evil and longer than life itself and reaching beyond record and patrimony" (285–86). As an index, the ledgers contain the regulations, the rules, the contracts, and the customs of the plantation owners in regard to their property. They are also the record of human expenditures and profits, for debits and credits. Essentially, the evidence Ike needs to understand his heritage is in "that chronicle which was a whole land in miniature, which multiplied and compounded was the entire South, twenty-three years after surrender and twenty-four from emancipation—that slow trickle of molasses and meal and meat, of shoes and straw hats and over- alls, of plowlines and collars and heel-bolts and buckheads and clevises, which returned each fall as cotton—the two threads frail as truth and impalpable as equators yet cable-strong to bind for life them who made the cotton to the land their sweat fell on" (280–81). The phrase "threads frail as truth . . . yet cable-strong," recurrent especially in "The Bear," is suggestive of the language in Jeremy Bentham's discourse on law and property in *Principles of the Civil Code* (1802).[10] Bentham's cost/benefit analysis of property rests on utility, the principle of the greatest hap- piness for the greatest number. Property then is constituted by a legal claim and by the rhetorical articulation of that claim. That property is the construction of law, according to Bentham, means that there is no such thing as "natural" property.

Ike cannot accept the legacy of his grandfather because he has a differ- ent conception of himself as a human being and of property as a concept. He will respect the land and its inhabitants, but he will not accept owner- ship of the land. Unlike old Carothers, Ike acknowledges that harm has been done to others in the securing of his birthright:

> he couldn't speak even to McCaslin [his older first cousin Cass], even to explain his repudiation, that which to him too, even in the act of escaping (and maybe this was the reality and the truth of his

need to escape) was heresy: so that even *in escaping he was taking with him more of that evil and unregenerate old man who could summon, because she was his property, a human being because she was old enough and female, to his widower's house and get a child on her and then dismiss her because she was of an inferior race.* (281; emphasis added)

Whereas Carothers neither recognizes the wrong that he perpetrates on his daughter ("because she was his property") and their progeny, nor admits responsibility for the damage and trauma he causes in the lives of his slaves, Ike can only acknowledge by repudiation and shame; he cannot escape. He sees himself and Lucas as "the last . . . of old Carothers' doomed and fatal blood in which the male derivation seemed to destroy all it touched" (280). From this perspective, Tomey's Turl becomes the tangible evidence of the enormity of the transgressions against human beings committed during slavery and because of the prevailing notion of property.

Though Sam Fathers, the black Indian who was himself sold by his father Ikkemotubbe, sets Ike free within the wilderness by teaching him the positive values of the natural world, Sam Fathers cannot provide a place for Ike in white society. Sam remains raced in a way that Ike is not, because Sam is "inheritor on the one hand of the long chronicle of a people who had learned humility through suffering and learned pride through the endurance which survived the suffering, and on the other side the chronicle of a people even longer in the land than the first, yet who now existed there only in the solitary brotherhood of an old and childless Negro's alien blood and the wild and invincible spirit of an old bear" (282). Though Cass Edmonds teaches Ike the practical realities of plantation life, Cass cannot join those practicalities of money and goods to Ike's ideals. Buck and Buddy McCaslin, his father and uncle, show Ike by their example that they object to the treatment of slaves; that is, they quarter their slaves in the "big house," old Carothers's "tremendous abortive edifice scarcely yet out of embryo" (251), and they refuse to secure the slaves at night or to have slaves build a house for them and perform the household chores. Nevertheless, Buck and Buddy cannot show Ike how to change the economic system of slavery for they remain complicit in it, and they do not acknowledge Tomey's Turl as their brother. Ike cannot escape the complexities of ethical and moral conduct in a society whose laws reinforce the ruthless proprietorship of his grandfather and reduce his father's and uncle's circumvention of ownership to humorous eccentricity.

The past with its living legacies, particularly the embodied descendants of Turl, combines with reason, intuition, and emotion in the present to destroy both innocence and simplicity and to deflate moral action and ideals. The reality is that the land is not, as Ike had supposed, "held and used in common and fed from and on and would continue to use in common without regard to color or titular ownership" (256). Racial color and trust deeds continue to have divisive and hierarchical meaning in matters of land and ownership. The ledgers and Ike's experience, as well as that of his grandfather and Tomey's Turl, deny the image of community and of brotherhood without regard to race or ownership.

The land is divided and owned. The owners declare, as one Mississippi legislator did in 1840, that "the institution of domestic slavery . . . [is] not a curse, but a blessing, as the legitimate condition of the African race"; or as the Supreme Court of the United States did in *Dred Scott v Sandford*, that it is "fixed and universal in the civilized portion of the white race" that blacks have "no rights which the white man [is] bound to respect";[11] or as an observer reported of conditions in Mississippi in 1865, "that the negro exists for the special object of raising cotton, rice and sugar *for the whites*, and that it is illegitimate for him to indulge, like other people, in the pursuit of his own happiness in his own way. Although it is admitted that he has ceased to be the property of a master, it is not admitted that he has the right to become his own master."[12] *Dred Scott v Sandford* was a concerted defense of slavery and "the precept of black inferiority"; the decision used legal theory to justify both racial oppression and black enslavement.[13] Chief Justice Roger B. Taney in writing the opinion was adamant: "the negro might justly and lawfully be reduced to slavery for his benefit."[14] The rhetoric and logic of this opinion would undergird legal decisions and separate blacks from the rights of the larger citizenry for more than a century.

Against such division and ownership, Ike has only a broad social idealism. He has rejected emotional ties along with his inheritance. Unlike Lucas Beauchamp who loves Molly and accepts his responsibility toward her, Ike fails to respond to individuals. He forgets that even the custodians of the earth have an obligation to assume responsibility for their caretaking, just as in the system of ownership that he opposes and repudiates owners must assume responsibility for their actions. While he may have followed Fonsiba, the daughter of Tomey's Turl to Arkansas, in order to give her a share of her father's inheritance, or traced Tennie's Jim to Tennessee to give him money as well, Ike does not understand that he can protect blacks neither with idealism alone nor with money alone, given the realities of their subjugation and oppression. Although his intention is to give his black kin, Tomey's Turl's heirs, their rightful share of the property left to them by their father's failure to accept a monetary legacy from his father, old Carothers, Ike does not recognize that his action replicates his grandfather's act of leaving a thousand dollars to Tomey's Turl, an act that Ike himself condemned: "*So I reckon that was cheaper than saying My son to a nigger*" (258). He acts out of a sense of compensatory justice, but the compensation or reparation is, as it was for his grandfather, only money. While Ike feels a moral obligation to compensate for the injustice done to Tomey's Turl, he does so with money, since property retains meaning for him. So central is his belief in the negative meaning of property that he cannot rid himself of measurement in terms of it. When Lucas goes to claim his inheritance from Ike, his request and his presence force Ike to reflect on his own situation: "*Fifty dollars a month. He knows that's all. That I reneged, cried calf-rope, sold my birthright, betrayed my blood, for what he too calls not peace but obliteration, and a little food*" (105). He suspects that despite his high ideals, his action has resulted in "obliteration." In effect, Ike brings no meaningful change into his environment because he has given up his opportunity to sustain contact with it.

"A static being," Melvin Rader observes, "cannot be moral because he is not confronted by choice. It is the temporal and ongoing character of life that poses problems: our existence is charged with concern because we must look before and after."[15] In the last encounter between black and white descendants of L. Q. C. McCaslin, Ike has become as static as his grandfather or his society. Not only has he missed his opportunity to love, but by the end of his life in the 1940s, love alone is not enough.[16] Even limited actions such as those of Lucas, Mollie, and Miss Worsham argue for the necessity of human beings to act in society and to do so according to a principle of justice and a guiding moral authority of ethical behavior that is higher than the cultural norm and that is invested in the social nature of property. Ike's movement is, to the contrary, inward and further away from the demands of living in the world: "the territory in which game still existed drawing yearly inward as his life was drawing inward" (320). He looks inward and backward not only to a time before ownership and possession and property and law, but also to his own finest moment in the wilderness with Sam Fathers and the bear; however, he cannot go back, for Sam and the bear are dead, and the wilderness always already "owned" in the text is now destroyed by a new generation of Carothers McCaslins. His memories and his models are not enough to foster new disciples; his truth and his experience will die with him and the disappearing wilderness. Ike's crying in the wilderness—not for what has been lost but for the moment of potential reformation that he has been unable to sustain—will be to no avail. The issue of property and ownership goes unresolved in the text.

During the period in which he wrote *Go Down, Moses*, Faulkner's fortunes were at a low point. Yet his desire to own land, to purchase more property, to become the landed gentry is clearly manifested in his acquisitions in the late 1930s. Karl F. Zender concludes that "Faulkner helped to create the difficulties he faced by his willingness to take on responsibilities within his family and by his eagerness *to acquire property*." In his reading of Faulkner's financial burdens and "impoverishment at the time of writing *Go Down, Moses*," Zender points to Faulkner's psychological need for property as a means of "actualizing a deeply cherished vision of his proper role in the world": "a paterfamilias, the owner of a mansion, the master of a plantation," who by acquiring and holding property participates in "acts of memorialization" of values entrenched in the southern past.[17] This need for property, to become the titled owner of land, Greenfield Farm, and the manor house, Rowan Oak, as well as the patriarchal master of the family, configured specifically as dependent women and black servants, is an expression of Faulkner's self-definition and self-actualization, of his game- and role-playing, of his linking himself to a passing social order.

Both Zender and John Carlos Rowe connect Faulkner to an imaginative identification with his troubled character, Roth Edmonds. As head of the family and farm, Roth is overburdened, nearly overwhelmed, and to Zender "driven almost to distraction by the demands, both social and economic, being made on him by the people among whom he lives."[18] At the same time, in Rowe's reading, Roth defends himself "from the more terrifying vision of an African-American authority different from that of the Southern patriarch."[19] In both case scenarios, the linkage between Faulkner and Roth places additional stress on property and patriarchy in *Go Down, Moses*.

Tracking Faulkner's dealings with real estate also may be read in terms of the psychological effects of ownership. Hegel, for instance, writes that "it is only through owning and controlling property that [an individual] can embody his will in external objects and begin to transcend the subjectivity of his immediate existence."[20] In a sense, Hegel suggests that property provides an individual with a way of putting his personality into the world. Similarly, William James, in explaining "the Empirical Self," believed that the line "between what a man calls *me* and what he simply calls *mine* . . . is difficult to draw. . . . In its widest possible sense . . . a man's Self is the sum total of all that he can call his, not only his body and his psychic powers, but his clothes and his house, his wife and children, his ancestors and friends, his reputation and works, his lands and horses, and yacht and bank-account. All these things give him the same emotions." James concludes that an "instinctive impulse drives us to collect

Faulkner role-playing as "lord of the manor" in formal riding gear and hosting a breakfast at Rowan Oak after a hunt, Sunday, 8 May 1938. Photographed with his wife, Estelle, and daughter Jill, friends, and servants, all dressed for the party. Ned Barrett, serving as butler with a tray of shot glasses of bourbon, had been owned by Faulkner's great-grandfather, W. C. Falkner (the "Old Colonel"). Barrett remained with the Faulkner family after emancipation and was the model for Lucas Beauchamp in *Go Down, Moses* and *Intruder in the Dust*. Photograph by Jack Cofield. Courtesy of the Cofield Collection, University of Mississippi, Southern Media Archive, Special Collections, University of Mississippi Libraries.

A brick, tree-lined walkway leads to Rowan Oak, the home in Oxford, Mississippi, that Faulkner purchased in 1930. Built in 1848 by Robert Shegog, it is surrounded by the land and woods Faulkner acquired during the 1930s.

property; and the collections thus made become, with different degrees of intimacy, parts of our empirical selves." And the corollary is that the loss of possessions produces a sense of the diminishing of personality, or what James terms "a partial conversion of ourselves to nothingness."[21]

Faulkner began acquiring property in 1930 when he purchased Rowan Oak. He next purchased Greenfield Farm in 1938 following the sale of

Faulkner and Andrew Price, the handyman, groom, gardener at Rowan Oak, posing with Faulkner's horse Tempy. Photograph by Jack Cofield. Courtesy of the Cofield Collection, University of Mississippi, Southern Media Archive, Special Collections, University of Mississippi Libraries.

the film rights to *The Unvanquished,* for which he received $19,000. He also used a portion of that money to purchase Bailey's Woods in Oxford. He had already bought three lots adjoining Rowan Oak in 1933. This period between 1930 and 1938 coincides with Faulkner's initial successes as a husband, father, and novelist, and indeed it is most often considered the major creative period for his fiction. It may well have been that the acquisition of property enabled his sense of himself and concretized his achievement in terms well known within a southern society that valued land and property.

Intermittently between 1932 and 1937, Faulkner wrote scripts for Hollywood films and lived in California for a part of each year. The toll was punishing because he missed both Mississippi and his daughter, Jill, but the work enabled him to continue his acquisition of land and to make payments on his mortgages and property taxes.[22] After his return to Mississippi, he attempted to publish a book a year in order to satisfy his financial obligations and to avoid a return to Hollywood.[23] The pace he set for himself in producing new fiction was as punishing as his Holly-

Andrew Price, Faulkner's helper and man-of-all-work, splitting wood outside his cabin. Photograph by Martin J. Dain. Courtesy of the Martin J. Dain Collection, University of Mississippi, Southern Media Archive, Special Collections, University of Mississippi Libraries.

wood years, and despite his best efforts, he remained constantly in debt. His brother Dean's widow and daughter; his own wife, Estelle, and her two children from her first marriage; their daughter, Jill; his mother; and the blacks he employed to maintain his house in town and his farm all added to his dire financial straits and, thus, to the increased pressure to produce and to his prolonged bouts of heavy drinking which culminated in his collapse in 1940.

Michael Grimwood calls this an extended period of exhaustion, "the onset of a spiritual menopause."[24] True, but it was also a game of ego-rebuilding through fantasies of power, racially and militaristically based, manifested in narratives of games, sport, and play, because Faulkner was at such a low point in his career and life that he desperately needed a psychic boost. Grimwood's assessment, based on his psychological interpretation of Faulkner's November 1940 collapse after a bout of drinking while on a hunting trip to the Mississippi Delta, makes plausible a reading of the connection between this period of Faulkner's life and *Go Down, Moses*. Indeed, in one of the key scenes in "The Old People,"

McCaslin Edmonds says to Isaac McCaslin: " 'But you cant be alive forever, and you always wear out life long before you have exhausted the possibilities of living' " (179). Having worn out life, Faulkner seemed intent on finding an elixir to enable him to continue living and writing.

After analyzing Faulkner's wrecked physical health following his alcohol-induced collapse, Daniel Singal remarks that "*Go Down, Moses*, a work undertaken during those crucial years of 1940 and 1941, sits precisely astride this watershed in Faulkner's life, which accounts for its puzzling nature. Part of the time brilliant, but in places conspicuously flawed, it seems to consist almost of two books, written by the same author at different stages of his career."[25] Perhaps the miscegenated text is also mired in the author's own shame at falling ever closer to the stereotypical personal shortcomings (e.g., drinking or alcoholism) and economic failures (e.g., insolvency and dependency) that white southerners of his generation associated with black people. Faulkner's shame may also have been exacerbated by the echoes of his father's failures in his own life.[26] At the same time, Faulkner's diminished capacity as a writer seems to have propelled him to find his "fresh" material in the fictionally underexplored world of southern blacks, particularly at a moment when he was exercising authority over the funeral and burial of Caroline Barr, the black woman who had been his nursemaid. That performance of familiar power supported a renewed freedom, control, and mastery over the materials of his fiction. However, it did not necessarily return him to his full creative abilities, those having been permanently damaged by his physical and mental deterioration after his collapse in 1940.[27]

Faulkner's own personal history, then, complicates an interrogation of property in *Go Down, Moses*, because that history suggests his reduction of human society to market relations and his elevation of political society as the protective strategy for property and the orderly exchange of property. However, in this view those who are "proprietors" dominate both society and law. In Faulkner's case, this placed him in a position of dominion over both his white family—particularly the women as dependents—and his black servants, as the paternalistic funeral sermon for his "mammy" and his dedication of *Go Down, Moses* to her would suggest.[28] The significance of the words: "To Mammy . . . Who was born in slavery and who gave to my family a fidelity without stint or calculation of recompense and to my childhood an immeasurable devotion and love" rests on an interpretation of "a fidelity without . . . recompense."

Caroline Barr, to whom *Go Down, Moses* is dedicated, holding Faulkner's niece, the baby Dean Faulkner, named for her father, Faulkner's youngest brother killed in a plane crash, 3 November 1935. Courtesy of Dean Faulkner Wells. Print from University of Mississippi, Southern Media Archive, Special Collections, University of Mississippi Libraries.

In a succinct reading John Carlos Rowe observes, "The real sacrifice is the one recorded in Faulkner's somewhat stilted dedication," because "it is Caroline Barr's century that frames the narrative, even if Faulkner can only 'name' her with the slave name, 'Mammy,' and the white paternalism inscribed in his testament to her 'nobility' for 'fidelity without . . . calculation of recompense.'"[29]

Minrose Gwin has suggested that the dedication to Caroline Barr inscribed in *Go Down, Moses* "may be seen as open" based on its shape and the space it occupies, and that it thus "becomes the foyer leading into the novel. On the other hand, it summons the closed equation: black mammy

In 1937 Faulkner took this photograph of Caroline Barr and his four-year-old daughter, Jill, outside his storeroom for horse equipment and riding gear at Rowan Oak. Courtesy of Mrs. Dean Faulkner Wells. Print from University of Mississippi, Southern Media Archive, Special Collections, University of Mississippi Libraries.

equals love (devotion, fidelity), the figure of 'mammy' and the ideological construction of mammy equals love."[30] Beyond that, however, the closed ideological space in which Caroline Barr becomes "Mammy" and a signifier of slavery, service, and subordination is rarely observed. The linkage to slavery, named in the dedication ("born in slavery"), often becomes a gloss rather than the identifying trope for "Mammy"—the emblematic presence and absence in the text. Ownership or possession is very much resident within the space, the terms, and the ideology of Faulkner's dedication. "Mammy" is as much a function as a naming. It is also an inscripted memorialization of enslavement, as well as its legacies of proprietary claiming of servant bodies in the South.

According to Judith Sensibar, Caroline Barr's relatives objected to

Faulkner's appropriation of her funeral service and to his claiming of her body as his and his family's.[31] He held the main funeral in his parlor at Rowan Oak and spoke the eulogy there. Afterward, he accompanied Barr's body to the Negro Baptist Church and on to the black section of St. Peter's Cemetery for burial. Faulkner's role in Barr's funeral was performative; it was an enactment of his relationship to her and a performance of his ability to naturalize her place as a race-marked mammy who attended to the white Faulkner family. Beyond her raced bodily functions and symbolizations, Faulkner cannot go. In considering the epitaph Faulkner had carved on Caroline Barr's grave ("MAMMY / Her white children / bless her"), Sensibar points out that it "signifies her white children's exclusive ownership, even in death and even in the black cemetery. But such claims, which ignore black kinship ties, also reveal the dehumanization that ownership of other human beings necessitates. This dehumanization is a constant and constantly conflicted subject of Faulkner's fictional texts."[32] The inscription of "white" to identify "her children" according to race may also be read as a magnification of race that makes racial difference much more pronounced. Sensibar's main argument is that *Go Down, Moses* "offers the clearest genealogy of its author's own racial unconscious" (109), but she also raises the issue of ownership of the black woman's body and, implicitly, the subject of property.[33]

Is it possible, then, for a white southerner of Faulkner's generation, steeped in history and tied to "Mammy . . . born in slavery," to escape the connection between the ownership of human bodies and the ownership of land parcels? On the page, the dedication appears in four distinct sections. The first section comprises the two words "TO MAMMY." The second bears the name "CAROLINE BARR." The third appears in a two-line segment: "Mississippi" and beneath that word, the bracketed dates "[1840-1940]." The fourth section of the dedication is the text which has been the focus of most commentary: "Who was born in slavery and who / gave to my family a fidelity without / stint or calculation of recompense / and to my childhood an immeasurable devotion and love."

The positioning of "Mississippi" is significant. While the lone word "Mississippi" follows Caroline Barr's name, it is separated from her name into the third section. That section encompasses not only the word "Mississippi"—that is the state, the land, the place, the geography—but also the material condition, the social formation, the political economy, the experiential reality that Faulkner, like Caroline Barr, knew and lived. And the third section also includes the bracketed dates "[1840-1940]," the years of Caroline Barr's life or her life span, but also the period of Mississippi history and heritage about which Faulkner wrote and constructed his narrative. Although he attributes 1840 as Caroline Barr's birth year, Faulkner did not know the exact year of her birth. He was aware that by her own calculation she was about sixteen at Emancipation and about twenty-five at the time of the 1870 Census, which would place her birth year close to 1845, but it was most likely between 1845 and 1849.[34] His attribution, however, rounds out her life to the span of a century.

There is an emblematic link between Caroline Barr and Mississippi as Faulkner positions them in the dedication. Mammy and Caroline Barr and Mississippi are covalent, all codependent and intricately connected to Faulkner's prevailing vision of slavery, maternity, and emotional space, psychical space, in the dedication and the text. The configuration of the triad, "Mammy/Caroline Barr/Mississippi," is preceded by the dedicatory "TO," which functions to memorialize all three while also collapsing all three names into one symbolically remembered unit. This memorializing becomes symbolic testimony in a refiguration, a refigurative process that is not unlike the psychoanalytic methodology of building interpretation on the relationship between a disembodied or disappeared figure and a remembered or symbolically recovered figure. The reconfiguration allows access to both the remembered and the repressed. It seems no accident, then, that Faulkner entitled his 1954 autobiographical essay "Mississippi" or that he includes in it extensive personal recollections of Caroline Barr.[35]

Was Faulkner finally using "race" as a game of self-identification and self-aggrandizement? Was he playfully or painfully inscribing himself into the text of Go Down, Moses as "nigger," the wished-for, irresponsible, manipulative presence? Was he answering those who disparaged both his fiction and his place in Oxford, Mississippi? Or was he figuring himself as a Tomey's Turl, a hybrid construction produced within a restrictive environment yet able to invent a game within which freedom obtains? There is a revelatory moment in the text when Ike McCaslin gazes at his landlady, "looking at her as peacefully as he had looked at McCaslin that first night in this same room, no kin to him at all yet more than kin as those who serve you even for pay are your kin and those who injure you are more than brother or wife" (296–97). Within this gaze, Faulkner seems to speak back to both his own family and his servants—

to his wife and his brothers and their families for the injuries associated with demands placed on him, and to the blacks like Caroline Barr who through their service to him become identified as kin.

Not long after the death of Caroline Barr on 31 January 1940, Faulkner wrote a letter describing his family's and his own relationship with the woman he called Mammy. He detailed in four and a half pages of typescript Caroline Barr's life and traced her interaction with the Faulkner family. The letter ends with the observation, "I cannot hope to express the sense of grief and loss which she has left us, but I would like to have drawn a picture of the admirable woman whom it was my fortune to know. People dont know so many of them in a lifetime."[36] Faulkner expresses not only a kinship and a debt to Caroline Barr but also admits to an inexpressible grief and loss across race lines. This latter may well be connected with his sense of himself as an artist who had been nourished by the stories and tales of Caroline Barr.

Faulkner's self-consciousness as a white, male southerner entrapped within an unsatisfying and costly domesticity and his expressed desire for attention and acclaim as an author during the period in which he produced *Go Down, Moses* has been documented. At the same time as the declaration of war in Europe in 1939, Faulkner began an obsessive consideration of war that masked more immediate and personal concerns. His brooding caused him to repeat several times in his writings the conclusion reached by Harry Wilbourne in *The Wild Palms: "Between grief and nothing I* will *take grief."*[37] Not only was the world changing, but Faulkner's conception of himself, in particular, of his potential as a writer was changing. By late 1940, he could write, "I still have the novel in mind, may get at it when . . . I become better adjusted mentally to the condition of this destruction-bent world."[38] Like the looming overcast of the war, the pressures of his own life were not easily erased; contracts and legal arrangements, Hollywood scriptwriting, business and family responsibilities, love affairs and marital troubles, money and debts, all compounded his frustration with the novel-in-progress, *Go Down, Moses.* Certainly, at the end of the 1930s and into the early 1940s, Faulkner worried over his failure to achieve the kind of combined artistic and commercial success that he desired. He was acutely sensitive to his lost potential, and this sensitivity spilled over to fuel his desire to be better than he was. In this period, which culminated in the death of Caroline Barr, may well have arisen his realization that try as he might he could neither love

At the time of the publication of *Go Down, Moses* in 1942, Faulkner was in his mid-forties and facing a stalled career and financial instability. Photograph by Jack Cofield. Courtesy of the Cofield Collection, University of Mississippi, Southern Media Archive, Special Collections, University of Mississippi Libraries.

black people nor consider them his equal (or the equal of white people); and with that realization may well have come an inexpressible shame that ignited his discursive shifts in *Go Down, Moses*, particularly evident in the debate between Ike and Cass in "The Bear."

Go Down, Moses may be read in terms of hybridity as an autobiographical act distanced and protected by games (masculine), forms of entertainment ("nigger stories," in Faulkner's own words), distraction, and relief (hunts, cards, dice-playing, gold-digging). The ideological constraints of games and the textual constructions of race (and gender) function as a mask for the construction of a writerly self, autonomous and authoritative. There is little doubt that during the period from the late 1930s to the early 1940s Faulkner was at a point of sheer frustration with both his position as a writer, his lack of recognition and income, his position within the family, and his multiple dependents, mainly female relatives but also blacks who worked and lived on his property. Thus, while the narrative may appear to be an intervention against racial aggression—a dual attempt at accommodation (Ike, McCaslin, Roth) and resistance (Ike, Sam Fathers, Lucas, Rider)—and against female devaluation (Molly, Mannie, and Miss Worsham), it may also function as retribution, challenging the material support of family and the morality of family structure, even while assuming responsibility for their existence and continuance (Ike, Gavin Stevens). The narrative may well be Faulkner's accommodation to and contestation of cultural rituals and ideologies that ultimately as a white racial southern male subject he cannot dissemble.

Owning Whiteness

So much attention in *Go Down, Moses* revolves around racialized Others (those of African, Indian, and mixed-race descent) that it is easy to overlook the prominence of the discourse on whiteness that is also central to the representation of race and of property in the text. In the midsection of "The Bear," the white father–black daughter incest and the sexual domination figured as the defining trope of both the slave economy and its economic legacy, tenancy, magnify race and racial difference in the systemic imbalance of power. In particular, it demonstrates that whiteness within this historical and economic condition is impervious to any attempted constraints on its desires and appetites. Whiteness from this perspective functions as privilege and property in *Go Down, Moses*.

The law not only protected a property interest in whiteness but also established whiteness within the identifying characteristics and philosophical descriptions of property. In "Whiteness as Property," Cheryl L. Harris maintains that the disparate formulations of property in legal discourse all can be brought to bear on placing whiteness within the realm of property.[39] Harris's conception of whiteness is revelatory because she sees it as more than a property interest. "Whiteness has functioned as self-identity in the domain of the intrinsic, personal, and psychological; as reputation in the interstices between internal and external identity; and, as property in the extrinsic, public, and legal realms," she maintains. "According whiteness actual legal status converted an aspect of identity into an external object of property, moving whiteness from privileged identity to a vested interest." The important point that Harris emphasizes is the crucial role of law in constructing whiteness. The law "defined and affirmed critical aspects of identity (who is white); of privilege (what benefits accrue to that status); and, of property (what *legal* entitlements arise from that status)."[40]

This postmodern understanding of whiteness as privilege, property, and entitlement is linked to the very conception of "an actual pecuniary value" in whiteness that the counsel for Homer Plessy argued in *Plessy v Ferguson*, the law case that attempted to assess the value of a white racial identity in a world of legal segregation and discrimination:

> How much would it be *worth* to a young man entering upon the practice of law to be regarded as a *white* man rather than a colored one? . . . Nineteen-twentieths of the property of the country is owned by white people. Ninety-nine hundredths of the business opportunities are in the control of white people. . . . Probably most white persons, if given a choice, would prefer death to life in the United States as colored persons. Under these conditions, is it possible to conclude that the reputation of being white is not property? Indeed, is it not the most valuable sort of property, being the master-key that unlocks golden doors of opportunity?[41]

The argument of the value of whiteness as a property did not, of course, convince the court in the Plessy case, but it has since become a significant way of understanding the subtle benefits of white racial identification and its privileges in the United States.

Faulkner's idea of race in *Go Down, Moses* and his subsequent fiction has everything to do with whiteness and its privileges and power. These ideas appear early in the literature of the South, even among its more racially sensitive practitioners. George Washington Cable, for instance, in *The Grandissimes: A Story of Creole Life* (1879) writes an explanatory comment on whiteness for one of his central characters, an outsider who is unaware of the nuances of racial references in Louisiana.

> When we say, "we people," we *always* mean we white people. The non-mention of color always implies pure white; and whatever is not pure white is to all intents and purposes pure black. When I say the "whole community," I mean the whole white portion; when I speak of the "undivided public sentiment," I mean the sentiment of the white population. What else could I mean? Could you suppose, sir, the expression which you may have heard me use—"my down-

trodden country" includes blacks and mulattoes? What is that up yonder in the sky? The moon. The new moon, or the old moon, or the moon in her third quarter, but always the moon! Which part of it? Why, the shining part—the white part, always and only! Not that there is a prejudice against the negro. By no means. Wherever he can be of any service in a strictly menial capacity we kindly and generously tolerate his presence.[42]

Although Cable sets his scene in 1804, he articulates sentiments current during the Civil War and Reconstruction period, as well as in the late 1870s when his novel appeared.

Importantly, whiteness is not fixed and stable over time. Ian F. Haney-Lopez concludes, "Being white is not a monolithic or homogeneous experience, either in terms of race, or other social identities, space or time. Instead Whiteness is contingent, changeable, partial, inconstant, and ultimately social. As a descriptor and as an experience 'White' takes on highly variegated nuances across the range of social axes and individual lives."[43] While this conception is quite encompassing and accurate, it lacks some of the narrative and imagistic power of Patricia J. Williams's description of whiteness in *Seeing a Color-Blind Future: The Paradox of Race*.

> The very category of something called 'whiteness' is revealed as a kind of collective neural toboggan run, encouraging good people to slide, to *shush* at high speed right on through the realm of reason. Whiteness is a kind of sociological clubhouse, a weird compression of tribal and ethnic animosities, some dating back to the time of the Roman invasions, all realigned to make new enemies, all compromised to make new friends. . . . The notion of whiteness as any kind of racial purity is a cognitive blind spot blocking out the pain . . . of such histories as the Thirty Years' War, massacres in Scotland and tyranny in Transylvania. Buttressed by aesthetic trends that feel ever-so-inherent, we can't slow down to think to save our lives.[44]

Of course, it is fast becoming not merely trendy but clichéd to formulate discourses on whiteness as a long-overlooked racial category and as a response to Toni Morrison's call for studies "in which an African-ist character is used to limn out and enforce the invention and implication of whiteness."[45] But some redress corrective is necessary—for the time being—because literary studies and Faulkner studies, as they were conventionally practiced, though not articulated as such, as an all-white aesthetic enterprise, as a primarily white cultural project, could not adequately contain or accommodate racial difference when that difference was not erased in the creative product or silenced in the critical methodology of a person maintaining a racially marked identity as intricately informing the project. Linda Wagner-Martin has identified an important shift in Faulkner scholarship regarding race and "the view of Faulkner's melding of white narratives with black. No longer seen as charming or sentimental, primitive or embarrassing, the racial bifurcated story of the McCaslin lineage was understood to be the book's center." Wagner-Martin provides a reassessment of *Go Down, Moses* directly connected to race, specifically to issues of whiteness: "I would propose that this 1942 novel is, in some ways, a new start. In it, Faulkner begins to attempt expressing what it feels like to be the heir of white patriarchal power in a slave state, what it feels like to be the wellborn son, the wellborn *white* son, of a family hardly memorable for its stability or sanity."[46]

"Society is suffused," Michael Omi and Howard Winant conclude, "with racial projects, large and small, to which all are subjected. This racial 'subjection' is quintessentially idealized. Everybody learns some combination, some version of the rules of social classification, and of [his] or her own racial identity, often without obvious teaching or conscious inculcation."[47] In "The Fire and the Hearth," the second chapter of *Go Down, Moses*, for example, Faulkner constructs a primary narrative of racial formation when the white boy Carothers moves into his white male adulthood: "one day the old curse of his fathers, the old haughty ancestral pride [read: race pride] based not on any value but on an accident of geography, stemmed not from courage and honor but from wrong and shame, descended to him" (107). Inserted into and inserting himself into a social structure that is comprehensively and rigidly racialized, young Carothers becomes *white*.

In taking possession of his whiteness, he accepts a central tenet, a "conceptual nucleus" that whiteness shares with property: "the right to exclude."[48] When Carothers refuses to allow Henry, his foster brother, to share either the sleeping pallet or the bed with him, he assumes the right of racial exclusion. He can exclude Henry simply because Henry is black and not white; he can exclude Henry because Carothers is white and not black. In his white racial identity he can thus control and dictate the space he occupies. The exercise of exclusion on the basis of race is an exertion of power, an enactment of privilege.

Lost to him is the black family, Lucas and Molly and their son Henry, whom he had known since his infancy. "Still in infancy he had already accepted the black man [Lucas] as an adjunct to the woman [Molly] who was the only mother he would remember, as simply as he accepted his black foster-brother [Henry], as simply as he accepted his father as an adjunct to his existence" (106–7). Lost to him is the interchangeability of two houses, two families, and an expansive occupation of a nonhistorical world, the one represented in the text as "the two houses had become interchangeable: himself and his foster-brother sleeping on the same pallet in the white man's house or in the same bed in the negro's and eating of the same food at the same table in either" (107). Carothers experiences in his racial whiteness what Heinz Kohut labels the grandiose self that "develops as the child's grandiosity (its feelings of power and of control over its environment) and exhibitionism (its pleasure in showing itself and in being seen and admired by others) are consistently confirmed by a responsible caregiver."[49]

A *white* racial identity becomes "common sense" for Carothers, what Omi and Winant term "a way of comprehending, explaining, and acting in the world. A vast web of social projects mediates between the discursive or representational means in which race is identified and signified on the one hand, and the institutional and organizational forms in which it is routinized and standardized on the other."[50] In his particular moment of racial acculturation, Carothers "knew, without wondering or remembering when or how he had learned that either, that the black woman was not his mother, and did not regret it; he knew that his own mother was dead and did not grieve. There was still the black woman, constant, steadfast" (107). More than a distancing from the maternal, the knowledge conveyed here is a necessary removal from blackness constructed as mother because, historically, the issue of slaves followed the legal condition of their mothers. Carothers must sever identification with Molly as mother, not merely so that he can emerge from childhood into manhood but, more significantly, so that he can become white. Without this racial separation, he cannot enter into his racial identity. His self-identification and personhood are invested in his whiteness. Masculinity and manhood are not unmarked by race in Carothers's culture, and therefore, in order to become an independent being within a racially explicit southern culture, he must distance himself from blacks and accept his racial identity as white.

The very term *white* as a racial designation did not even exist until 1680 when it replaced *English* and *free* to differentiate this group from enslaved Africans who were identified by their physical difference from the English. "From the initially most common terms *Christian*, at mid-century there was a marked drift toward *English* and *free*. After about 1680, taking the colonies as a whole, a new term appeared—*white*."[51] Africans, termed *Negroes*, were presumed to be slaves, while Englishmen, and subsequently other Europeans, were presumed to be white and free. But even people of African ancestry could become "white." A mulatto was defined by Virginia law in 1705 as "the child of an Indian, or the child, grandchild, or great grandchild of a Negro."[52] In 1785, however, the legal definition of a mulatto changed ("one-fourth part or more of negro blood") and transformed those with one-eighth Negro ancestry (one Negro great-grandparent), who were formerly considered mulatto under the 1705 law, into legal whites.[53] One hundred years after the appearance of *white* as an identificatory designation, the term remained unstable and subject to legal construction and redefinition. Yet, in looking back at the way in which law constructed race and the privileges obtained or denied on the basis of race, the logic of Alan Watson's conclusion becomes quite transparent: "Law is power. Law is politics. Law is politics in the sense that it is the persons who have political power who determine which persons or bodies create law, how the validity of law is to be assessed, and how the legal order is to operate."[54]

In the aftermath of *Go Down, Moses*, except for its polemical rewriting and rediscovery in *Intruder in the Dust*, Faulkner turned from the race binary in the construction of whiteness to class dynamics as it inscribes white raciality. Anticipated by *The Hamlet* and the Snopes clan, by Sutpen and Wash Jones in *Absalom, Absalom!*, this shift is also prefigured in Faulkner's discursive practice toward the end of *Go Down, Moses*. There one of the hunters observes in "Delta Autumn," " 'And what have you got left. . . . Half the people without jobs and half the factories closed by strikes. Half the people on public dole that wont work and half that couldn't work even if they would. Too much cotton and corn and hogs, and not enough for people to eat and wear. The country full of people to tell a man how he cant raise his own cotton whether he will or he wont, and Sally Rand with a sergeant's stripes and not even the fan couldn't fill the army rolls'" (323). The "people" here designates "white people," working-class white people, the racial determinant being apparent in the reference to fan dancer Sally Rand, a white woman who danced nude, though heavily painted, behind two white fans, because no black man could in safety be linked to such a textual reference—the sexual taboos, fears, fantasies, and threats of lynching would be too great. Thus, *people* is a term demarcating a group-distinguished race, that is, "white," which though subtle, nonetheless "retains its core characteristics: the legal legitimation of expectations of power and control that enshrine the status quo as a . . . baseline, while masking the maintenance of white privilege and domination."[55] Thus, while John Carlos Rowe concludes, "In *Go Down, Moses,* Faulkner realizes the impasse of his own fictional project, even as he struggles impossibly to transcend imaginatively his own white Southern heritage," I would suggest that Faulkner may also have attempted to reinvigorate his fictional project by becoming more vested in exploring rather than transcending his white racial heritage.[56]

Certainly in *Go Down, Moses,* for young Carothers, the rejection by his black family is the price he has to pay for becoming a white man— for entering into a racialized masculinity that leaves him "lying in a rigid fury of grief he could not explain, the shame he would not admit" (109). The inclusion of shame as a primary emotion is significant because it is rarely associated with white responses to blacks or to white treatment of black people. The recognition of shame as an inappropriate emotional response from the perspective of white culture marks both young Carothers, and, external to the text, Faulkner himself. The issue for both remains how to articulate an emotion that is not allowed by either their race or their gender, and if not articulated then how can shame be suppressed or eradicated. "Claiming a White identity additionally opens a deep chasm between the self and society," according to Haney-Lopez. "For Whiteness to remain a positive identity, it must remain free from taint. Thus, Whiteness can only retain its positive meanings through the denial at every turn of the social injustices associated with the rise and persistence of this racial category."[57]

For Carothers, the emotion of shame associated with his entry into racial identity causes him to suffer a new isolation. A month after claiming his whiteness and its prerogatives, he wishes to reverse his rejection of his foster brother Henry: "he knew it was grief and was ready to admit it was shame also, wanted to admit it only it was too late then, forever and forever too late" (109). A reversal may be his desire, but such a course of action is not a process he can control, dictate, or determine.

The turn in the text is that the black family, formerly his surrogate family and not racially segregated from him, excludes Carothers from their intimate circle. Denied familial intimacy, Carothers as the white boy is excluded on the racial ground he used against Henry. Henry and his parents will not allow Carothers to reenter his racially unmarked relation with them. When Carothers announces "lordly, peremptory: 'I'm going to eat supper with you all tonight'" (109), he believes that he will slip back into his old accustomed place within the family circle at their kitchen table. Molly's response is simply that she will cook him a chicken, and his former intimacy with the family seems once again assured and exclusion on the basis of race forgotten.

> Then it was as if it had never happened at all. Henry came almost at once; he must have seen him from the field, and he and Henry killed and dressed the chicken. Then Lucas came and he went to the barn with Henry and Lucas while Henry milked. Then they were busy in the yard in the dusk, smelling the cooking chicken, until Molly called Henry and then a little later himself, the voice as it had always been, peaceful and steadfast: "Come and eat your supper."
> But it was too late. The table was set in the kitchen where it always was and Molly stood at the stove drawing the biscuit out as she always stood, but Lucas was not there and there was just one chair, one plate, his glass of milk beside it, the platter heaped with untouched chicken, and even as he sprang back, gasping, for an instant blind as the room rushed and swam, Henry was turning toward the door to go out of it. (110)

The Beauchamp family in an unanticipated sleight of hand accords him the privilege of the differentiated place he asserted in sleeping alone in the bed and consigning Henry to the floor. The family both acknowledges his whiteness and undermines its hierarchical power.

Carothers cannot feel racially superior when he is denied familial bonding and left to eat alone. He, not Henry, suffers shame at the imposition of racial difference. "'Are you ashamed to eat when I eat?' he [Carothers] cried. Henry paused turning his head to speak in the voice slow and without heat: 'I aint shamed of nobody,' he said peacefully. 'Not even me'" (110). Henry has not internalized his rejection by Carothers as a humiliating flaw or a self-incriminating fault, so that in leaving the cabin, he is not fleeing Carothers's shaming gaze; instead he is leaving Carothers to experience his own emotions unmediated by Henry's black presence. Lee Jenkins reads Henry's response as a "mask of submission," marking him as "nonhuman, a thing, without rights or feelings, an object," because he seems neither hurt nor offended by Carothers and the severing of their fraternal relationship.[58] Certainly, the scenes involving Henry reveal little awareness that, under such circumstances, he might well have feelings that are equally as complex as Carothers's. Yet poised against the apparent lack of human response to the situation is the family's calculated answer to the white boy's claims of superiority. That representation argues for a knowing not simply of black submission to an assigned inferior or object space but rather of black retaliation in a withdrawal to a closed circle of family and intimacy inaccessible to whites.

Carothers is white and no longer able to foreclose its social implications: "So he entered his heritage. He ate its bitter fruit" (110). Carothers experiences a shame affect, which "is a highly powerful mechanism that operates to pull the organism away from whatever might interest it or make it content."[59] This scene is one of the most powerful and most race-conscious of whiteness in Faulkner's canon. One can only speculate about its relation to Faulkner's own youth and his experiences with Caroline Barr and whether the writing that went into *Go Down, Moses* after her death was a meditation on that relationship and shame.[60] As a boy Faulkner accompanied Caroline Barr to the homes of her relatives and spent time with her in spaces designated black and off-limits to whites. Faulkner did not record autobiographically precisely when and how his rules of conduct as a white youth dictated that he no longer spend time with Caroline Barr in the segregated black spaces in and around Oxford, yet he, like his boy characters, seems to have come to an awareness of "appropriate" race etiquette and relations in public and private spaces. His emphasis on shame in this text may be an acknowledgment of his failure to break the accepted social conventions and embrace his emotional attachment to Caroline Barr as an intimate. The transference of shame as a dominant affect to Carothers suggests Faulkner's biographical insertion, or what Terry Eagleton terms "authorial ideology," infusing southern racial dynamics with the added poignancy of the death of Caroline Barr.[61]

As a person who is white in his society, young Carothers should have nothing denied him on the basis of race. That is, the privilege of whiteness in the United States means inclusion and access. Yet the black Beauchamp family turns the tables on Carothers who is forced to face exclusion on the basis on his skin color and all that white skin signifies about his place in the social and economic order. He is denied reentry into the black family's world as an equal and the result for him is devastating. He is left to occupy the very position he forced on his excluded black brother. He comes to feel more deeply the knowledge that "the line between races exist as axes of power and privilege" and that there is a price to pay for his exercise of white privilege.[62] He is made to feel his race as otherness.

In reading the construction of whiteness as a significant enterprise in *Go Down, Moses*, it is not necessary to also remake Faulkner as a race traitor (to use the term currently associated with one part of the whiteness movement in the United States), although Ike McCaslin, despite his lapses and failures to move beyond his cultural conditioning, comes close to being a race traitor for a brief moment when he renounces his patrimony of ownership and aggression. In fighting against the mandates of racial supremacy, Mab Segrest, for instance—southern, white, activist, and lesbian—entitled her political autobiography *Memoir of a Race Traitor* in order to subvert the negative meaning assigned the term by white nationalists and white supremacists. She came to understand her title long after she had adopted it: "It's not my people; it's the idea of race I am betraying. It's taken me a while to get the distinction."[63] Segrest concludes her moving introductory chapter "Osceola's Head," in which she recounts her struggle to find a voice and her struggle against "the violence of annihilating ideas," alongside and by means of the grim story of Osceola, a Muskogee who in the 1830s led a band of Seminoles and escaped slaves against encroaching white settlers. (Osceola's wife, the quadroon daughter of a fugitive slave, had been captured by her mother's former owner and pressed back into enslavement; this situation contributed to Osceola's outrage at the proprietary practices of whites.) Segrest understands Osceola's fate as an emblem of the physical and psychological destructiveness wrought by the acceptance of racist ideology. Captured by Andrew Jackson, Osceola was beheaded by a white surgeon who tended him and claimed friendship with him while he was imprisoned in Charleston but used "his surgeon's saw to cut off Osceola's head" for a souvenir after his death.

Segrest finds the usage of the Indian leader's head disturbing. The surgeon placed it in the window of his drugstore in St. Augustine, Florida, and periodically placed it on his son's bedpost to frighten him into good behavior. This shocking scenario speaks directly to the betrayals and violences inherent in an American way of race. Such violence perpetrated on children and inevitably subsequent generations demands an active and vigilant dismantling to preserve a "safe" future for all.

Segrest raises the obvious but almost completely ignored issue: the underlying irony that white identity was a legal creation of late-seventeenth-century Virginia. "If we white folks were constructed by history," she reflects, "we can, over time and as a people, unconstruct ourselves. The Klan knows this possibility and recognizes those whites who disavow this history as *white niggers, race traitors,* and *nigger lovers.*" She then asks nonrhetorically, "How, then, to move masses of white people to become traitors to the concept of race?"[64]

The periodical *Race Traitor,* founded by Noel Ignatiev, whose research for *How the Irish Became White* helped initiate "white studies," attempts to foster a widespread rejection of white privilege and encourages activist racial stances with the slogan "Treason to whiteness is loyalty to humanity." However, the periodical is not unproblematical in the work that Ignatiev terms "New Abolitionist"; *Race Traitor* has published interviews with neo-Nazis and suggested that white militias can become allies in overturning the race system.[65] Yet Ignatiev has worried about the potential for whiteness studies to become apolitical, narcissistic, and nationalistic; both he and David Roediger, who authored *The Wages of Whiteness: Race and the Making of the American Working Class* (1991), have distanced themselves from the potential excesses implicitly validated by the concept of whiteness and the elevation of the category of whiteness. Roediger's title plays off the conceptual frame W. E. B. Du Bois presented in *Black Reconstruction* (1935). Du Bois pointed out that low-wage-earning white workers received an additional compensation, a type of public and psychological wage for being white, and that the wage of whiteness placed them in a superior position to all blacks, no matter the wage category to which blacks belonged.[66] Du Bois's notion of the non-monetary wages that accrue with being identified as racially white anticipates the current conception of whiteness as having property rights.

Raising the issue of whiteness in Faulkner's canon, is not to suggest that an outpost of Jeff Hitchcock's Cambridge-based Center for the Study of White American Culture be set up in Oxford, Mississippi, or based at the annual Faulkner conference. Manifestations of neo-white nationalism can after all achieve the reverse of the political call for leveling racial hierarchies. As West puts it, "Enforced social hierarchy dooms us as a nation to collective paranoia and hysteria," insofar as "the paradox of race in America is that our common destiny is more pronounced and imperiled precisely when our divisions are deeper."[67]

One measure of Faulkner's enormous literary achievement is his construction of race as central to his fiction, to his representation of characters, specifically his construction of white characters and whiteness, and to the metaphorical power of his language struggling with an interrogation of what it means to be white. That achievement is remarkable for its insistent race consciousness, for enabling discourses on race and racial transgressions and transactions not merely in the South but in the United States as a whole. This particular aspect of his achievement is not usually acknowledged primarily because most attention has been devoted to his construction of racial Others, the African Americans and to a lesser extent the Native Americans, who populate his texts. This discourse is particularly salient, not merely because it disturbs the notion that race only applies to people of color in Faulkner's writing, but also because it constitutes one of the possibilities for fresh conversations about Faulkner's particular achievement and the potential for future Faulkner scholarship.[68]

Go Down, Moses, given its social, structural, and historical context, provides a window for entering into, for observing, race and a discourse on whiteness. And what does *Go Down, Moses* representing race discursively allow one to observe? For one thing, how insistently Faulkner uses "white" as a designation of race. Throughout the text, "white" is the adjective of choice; it is an insistent marker of identity—even when its specific bodily referent is elided. In "The Fire and the Hearth" examples abound. Several relate to Roth Edmonds, a white child Molly Beauchamp nurses after his mother's death. Roth's father is Zack Edmonds, the son of the narrator of "Was," Cass Edmonds. Molly is the wife of Lucas Beauchamp, the son of Tomey's Turl (McCaslin) and Tennie Beauchamp. The emphasis on "white" is unmistakable: "And Molly, a young woman then and nursing their own first child, wakened at midnight by the *white* man himself and they followed then the *white* man through the streaming darkness to his house" (45); "Molly delivered the *white* child" (45); Lucas entered the house "to find the *white* man's wife dead and his own wife already established in the *white* man's house" (45); and "It was as though the *white* woman had not only never quitted the house, she had never existed—the object which they buried in the orchard two days later . . . a thing of no moment, unsanctified, nothing" (46, emphasis added). In the repetition of *white* in the interaction with blacks, Faulkner represents a racial ideology in *Go Down, Moses* that recalls James Baldwin's assessment that "America became white . . . because of the necessity of denying the Black presence and justifying Black subjugation. . . . It is the Black condition, and only that, which forms the consciousness of white people. It is a terrible paradox, but those who believed they could control and define Black people divested themselves of the power to control and define themselves." [69]

Racial difference forms the core of the tension between Zack Edmonds and Lucas Beauchamp, who are nonetheless described as lookalikes in "The Fire and the Hearth": "In age he [Zack] and Lucas could have been brothers, almost twins too" (46). What lies between them as antagonistic space is Zack's presumption of and exercise of white privilege. In the process of challenging Zack about his assumption of Molly, Lucas's wife, as wet nurse to his son and presumably as surrogate wife too, Lucas recalls his childhood closeness with Zack, "the man whom he had known from infancy, with whom he had lived until they were both grown almost as brothers lived. They had fished and hunted together, they had learned to swim in the same water, they had eaten at the same table in the white boy's kitchen and in the cabin of the negro's mother; they had slept under the same blanket before a fire in the woods" (54). Their closeness, prefiguring and resembling that between their sons, Carothers and Henry, does not, however, prevent Zack from claiming Lucas's wife in a presumption of power and control exercised out of an unexamined sense of racial superiority, white right and white will. Zack assumes a property right in Molly, in her labor, and in her body; her breast milk is not hers but his and his son's, and their entitlement to it presumed. Whether Zack uses Molly sexually as a surrogate wife as he has appropriated her body as a surrogate mother is not an issue; if he chose to do so, if he desired or willed to do so, he would and could with the selfsame presumption of a proprietary claim to Molly's body. It is this prerogative and custom of ownership and property rights to the black body that Lucas decries as a pervasive and ordinary aspect of the power of white men when he asks, " 'How to God . . . can a black man ask a white man to please not lay down with his black wife? And even if he could ask it, how to God can the white man promise he wont?'" (58).

The exercise of white male power in relations with black women is also an aspect of the representation of Hubert Beauchamp, Ike McCaslin's delusional and debt-ridden uncle, who moves his mistress into his house and lives with her, only to be forced by his sister to adhere to the prevailing public dictates of racial segregation and white superiority. Race comes into high comedic relief in the segment, but its implications in the post-Emancipation era of flux and transformation suggest the tragedy of a lost opportunity to disaggregate the function of race in southern life. It also provides another window for viewing Tomey's Turl's repeated, and refigured, appearances throughout the text and for observing his repetitious "white half-McCaslin" presence in Ike's formation and memory. Hubert, who is represented as so economically unstable that he would wager his sister in a poker game and later would replace his gift of gold coins to his nephew with paper IOUs (307), not only takes a black woman as his mistress but dresses her in his sister's best gowns.

(And he [Isaac McCaslin] remembered this, he had seen it: an instant, a flash, his mother's soprano "Even my dress! Even my dress!" loud and outraged in the barren upswept hall; a face young and female and even lighter in color than Tomey's Terrel's for an instant in a closing door; a swirl, a glimpse of the silk gown and the flick and glint of an ear-ring: an apparition rapid and tawdry and illicit yet somehow even to the child, the infant still almost, breathless and exciting and evocative: as though, like two limpid and pellucid streams meeting, the child which he still was had made serene and absolute and perfect rapport and contact through that glimpsed nameless illicit hybrid female flesh with the boy which had existed at that stage of inviolable and immortal adolescence in his uncle for almost sixty years; the dress, the face, the ear-rings gone in that same aghast flash and his uncle's voice: "She's my cook! She's my new cook! I had to have a cook, didn't I?" then the uncle himself, the face alarmed and aghast too yet still innocently and somehow even indomitably of a boy, they retreating in their turn now, back to the front gallery, and his uncle again, pained and still amazed, in a sort of desperate resurgence if not of courage at least of self-assertion: "They're free now! They're folks too just like we are!" and his mother: "That's why! That's why! My mother's house! Defiled! Defiled!" and his uncle: "Damn it, Sibbey, at least give her time to pack her grip:" then over, finished, the loud uproar and all, himself and Tennie and he remembered Tennie's inscrutable face at the broken shutterless window of the bare room which had once been the parlor while they watched, hurrying down the lane at a stumbling trot, the routed compounder of his uncle's uxory: the back, the nameless face which he had seen only for a moment, the once-hooped dress ballooning and flapping below a man's overcoat, the worn heavy carpet-bag jouncing and banging against her knee, routed and in retreat true enough and in the empty lane solitary young-looking and forlorn yet withal still exciting and evocative and wearing still the silken banner captured inside the very citadel of respectability, and unforgettable.) (289–90)

Watching this spectacle is Tennie, the wife of Tomey's Terrel, whose "inscrutable face" is linked to the "nameless face" of the observed, the watched. The spaces occupied by these two black women cause Minrose Gwin to ponder whether black women's locations for resistance, their "safe spaces," have been lost: *what lost stories are here?*[70] While Gwin's thoughtful interpretive questions cannot be answered, they help to refocus attention on several important aspects of the scene, all of them connected to issues of race and racial construction specifically in the post-Emancipation period.

Not to be overlooked is that both Tennie, the silent observer, and Ike, the reporter-observer, watch the spectacle. The distinction Lacan makes between the eye as a perceptual organ and the gaze as the vision of an objectively self-aware subject is useful here. "The gaze I encounter is not a seen gaze, but a gaze imagined by me in the field of the Other."[71] For Tennie, the scene may be one replete with an aspect of the gaze that involves a (self) identification of shame in the treatment of black women as property, as concubines, of black people as slaves. This shame involves her by the very "facts" of her race and gender, and her previous condition as property. The related markers of identity linking the two black women across a field of vision may suggest a "doubleness of experience," which, as Helen Block Lewis says, characterizes shame. "Shame is the vicarious experience of the other's negative evaluation. In order for shame to occur, there must be a relationship between the self and the other in which the self cares about the other's evaluation."[72] In Tennie's gaze may be a self-consciousness that produces a self-imaging concerned with defending against disapproval or shame.

For Ike, the spectacle is more than a scene of shame, it is a developmental moment in which his selfobject, to use Kohut's term, responds to and identifies with his uncle (in his public shame and his private sexual pleasure) as a part of his masculine self and does so through the body of the mixed-race woman, who for Ike immediately recalls Tomey's Turl ("even lighter in color than Tomey's Terrel's"), his measure of the actual meaning and cost of miscegenation.[73] It is the scene that destroys Ike's ability to negotiate public-private gender boundaries in his society, because forever after they are imbricated with race, with white-black interaction. Shame when bound with other drives or affects becomes especially powerful in regulating perceptions of and interaction with others and the environment. Ike mixes shame with curiosity and fascination with the illicit, the body of the mixed-race woman and thus with sexual intercourse that involves the crossing of social conventions and proprieties in his culture. His complex feelings of shame that subsequently motivate his renunciation of his patrimony are intricately connected with his recognition of his grandfather's involvement with what he has identified in the spectacle in his uncle's house as "exciting and evocative," a sexual excitement that Ike associates with hybrid flesh and forbidden sex.

The young woman represented as "free" and as "folks" becomes a free-floating signifier of race-marked blacks after the Civil War. Loosened from the boundaries physically marking her existence as slave and as property, she is also loosened from the restrictions of space that held her in bondage to the place of her owner. Though "black" in its various designations as "African" and later "Negro" had become legally equated with "slave" long before the Emancipation Proclamation in 1863, it had not yet achieved a new meaning in the period after 1865. Moreover, the woman is visually mixed-race, and though Hubert's statement implies that she is newly freed, it does not negate the possibility that she may have been one of the 773 free persons of color in Mississippi in 1860 (601 of whom were mixed-race). But assuming her recent emancipation, her life as a mulatto slave most likely was within the slaveholder's household, as only 36,618 of the 400,013 slaves in Mississippi in 1860 were mulatto, and mulattoes often had close blood ties to their owners and were often preferred on the basis of their color for work in proximity to the white family.[74] While enslaved the young woman may well have been a domestic servant, a cook, in her former life, but she was not compensated for her labor. In the free labor market that she enters after her emancipation, she expects to receive compensation for her work. Patricia J. Williams states, "After the Civil War, when slaves were unowned . . . they were also disowned: they were thrust out of the market and into a nowhere land that was not quite the mainstream labor market, and very much outside the marketplace of rights. They were placed beyond the bounds of valuation . . . ; they became like all those who cannot express themselves in the language of power and assertion and staked claims—all those who are nevertheless deserving of the dignity of social valuation, yet those who are so often denied survival itself."[75]

Unowned the light-skinned woman is in the position Williams identifies. She cannot express herself in the "language of power and assertion and staked claims" that Sophonsiba Beauchamp McCaslin can use in asserting her social valuation (her dress, her mother's house) as a white woman with a white family accustomed to owning things and people. Sophonsiba can assume the immorality and licentiousness based on the negative constructions of black women's sexuality during slavery, and she can commodify the woman into the proprietary relations defined by slavery that she expects. However, in her powerful rage, Sophonsiba goes beyond that and extends her racial preconceptions into the new, fluid, and unstable period after slavery. That the figure of the nearly white woman is associated with the potential and the fluidity of Reconstruction is hinted at with further hostility and suppressed rage at her using sex as a commodity; the hint is in the brief appearance in the text of "a United States marshal in Jefferson who signed his official papers with a crude cross, an ex-slave called Sickymo, . . . who had attained his high office because *his half-white sister was the concubine* of the Federal A.P.M." (279; emphasis added).

The connection of racial ideology and sexual morality as a justification of social segregation and Jim Crow laws was, Margaret Burnham contends, an "antebellum legal inheritance" of "tremendous contemporary significance."[76] In a sense, the young woman had to be prepared for her displacement based on the social and political landscape of the past and the legal construction determining her place and perceptions of her in that landscape. She cannot argue for her right to wages from Hubert Beauchamp or for her right to his "gifts" in exchange for her labor since he clearly is without money to compensate her (e.g., not only the dilapidated exterior and interior structure of Warwick, but also the "disappearance" of the furnishings). And she certainly cannot argue for their joint right to enter into a common law marital agreement, as interracial liaisons remained illegal even after the end of slavery. Her last appearance is on the road in movement and in flight, but symbolically looking ahead, not back, and in search of a place in which she can provide for herself economically and, importantly, define herself racially.[77]

The incident may be read as a site of memory that reenters Ike's consciousness when he reads of his grandfather's transgressions against his daughter-property. The childhood memory of his uncle and the mixed-race woman functions as a "screen memory," Freud's term for a memory that is associatively displaced onto another.[78] Ike remembers the incident at a moment of intense anxieties in his adulthood when he is engaged in attempting to explain his renunciation of his inheritance of property and his rejection of his wife's offer of sex in exchange for that property. Ike's vision of the face "young and female and even lighter in color than Tomey's Terrel's" (289) is conflated with a "nameless illicit hybrid female flesh" (289) and is later infused into his reading of the commissary ledgers in which not only the tally of profits and losses, buying and selling for the plantation is recorded, but also his grandfather's getting of Tomey's Terrel upon his own daughter, another example of "illicit hybrid female flesh." An underlying, already always resident emotion for Ike is shame. In the moment of his own vicarious sexual encounter with black female and forbidden flesh, Ike absorbs and assimilates, according to Albert J. Devlin, "the scene's sexual tenor," which he suggests, "should not be divorced from [Sophonsiba's] explosive reaction. Her violent dismissal of Hubert's mistress not only identifies the mulatto as a racially proscribed lover, but may also create for Isaac a more extensive system of association whereby sexuality is tinged with danger, violence, and fear of maternal disapproval."[79] His mother's insistence on racial purity and her conception of whiteness as invested with privilege and position function to heighten Ike's shame at being attracted to "illicit hybrid female flesh" like his uncle and his grandfather before him.

Hubert Beauchamp's insistence on the young woman's emancipated status ("free now") and on her being a human person ("folks too just like we are") may have been offered as a rather feeble excuse for his cohabitation with the woman, but it might also suggest a moment when freedom and personhood replaced slavery and property as a way of defining identity, thus allowing for a designation that did not insist on race first. It is a moment when the formulations of race and class are in the process of change, and when that fluency concretizes the conception put forth by Ira Berlin: "Race, no less than class, is the product of history, and it only exists on the contested social terrain in which men and women struggle to control their destinies."[80] Ike's mother, however, counters any claims of a new identity for the now free woman-person, because she insists on the conventions and the traditions of race propriety and race distinctions and race hierarchy, and decries the defiling of her ideals and her values. Despite the visual fact of the woman's coloration and her position in Hubert's house, Sophonsiba acts on the assumption that racial barriers are rigid, immutable, and permanent. The lost moment for redefinition is fully memorable and the young woman's reconfiguration ("the routed compounder," "routed and in retreat") is, according to Ike, unforgettable. "In largest part, racial identity is not directly a function of features and ancestry but rather of the context-specific meanings that attach to these elements of identity," Haney-Lopez concludes. "Context is the social setting in which races are recognized, constructed, and contested; it is here that race gains its life. Within a social context, racial systems of meaning, although inconstant and unstable, are paramount in establishing the social significance of certain features, such as skin color, and of particular ancestries, for instance European."[81]

Race, color, gender, female, illicit, flesh, sex, miscegenation, hybridity are all terms that reconfigure both in Ike's interpretation of the text of the ledger entries and later in his interaction with the young mother of Roth's son. Ike's memory of the young cook suggestively repeats the words "exciting and evocative" and links that memory with the two other instances of interracial sexual relationships: "routed and in retreat true enough and in the empty lane solitary *young-looking and forlorn* yet withal *still exciting and evocative* and wearing still the silken banner captured inside the very citadel of respectability, *and unforgettable.*" These memories are all part of the problem of property, ownership and commodification of black bodies, especially those sexualized as intimate with white men, that Ike carried through his childhood into adulthood. Adorno suggests that memory as "the only possession which no-one can take from us, belongs in the storehouse of impotently sentimental consolations that the subject, resignedly withdrawing into inwardness, would like to believe the very fulfillment that he has given up. In setting up his own archives, the subject seizes his own stock of experience as property, so making it something wholly external to himself."[82] Memory as property confounds and complicates Ike's maturation and socialization in white society.

The three "exciting and evocative" encounters with cross-racial connections of white men and black women take place at three distinct points in Ike's life, and each one is "unforgettable." The first, Ike's Uncle Hubert and his young near-white, emancipated "cook," occurs when Ike is still an impressionable child; the second, Ike's grandfather and his daughter, Tomasina, occurs before Ike is born but becomes a reality for him when he is a formative teenager reading the ledgers; the third, Ike's cousin Roth and his lover/distant cousin, occurs in Ike's old age. The three encounters serve to link race and illicit sex and power imbalances between his insider white male relatives and the outsider mixed-race, "hybrid," but "black" women, but they also function as the sources of shame that is racial and familial.[83] These recurrences construct a discourse of racial and sexual erotic and transgressive desire which is central to Ike's maturation and development. These three instances allow for a reconsideration of Ike from the opening of the first chapter "Was," and for a rethinking of his renunciation of property.

Beginning with the representation of white angst in an Ike McCaslin immobilized by inherited power and privilege, the text plays off Ike's refusal to exercise skin privilege and white power, while also examining his unwillingness to give up his assumptions of white racial superiority, as the narrative of "Delta Autumn" suggests. The Christian symbolism linking Ike's monklike appearance and existence to his response to ownership and domination may also be read through the lens of Gilles Deleuze and Felix Guattari's analysis of race and "racialities." Deleuze and Guattari argue that Christ's face has come to be identified with the white man himself. "If the face is in fact Christ, in other words, your average ordinary White Man, then the first deviancies, the first divergence-types are racial: yellow . . . black."[84] What they observe is that "the degrees of deviance from the White-Man face," are codified into "non-conforming traits" that are then considered "increasingly eccentric and backward waves," leading to the condition in which "ultimately there is no exterior, there are no people on the outside. There are only people who should be like us and whose crime is not to be."[85]

The opening of Go Down, Moses with its focus on the angst of old Ike McCaslin, "who owned no property and never desired to" (3), fixes the narrative historically and culturally defines Ike's whiteness—his prerogative to own property, land or slaves—his skin privilege that enables his right to inherit and to reject his inheritance: "his was the name in which the title to the land had first been granted from the Indian patent and which some of the descendants of his father's slaves still bore in the land" (3). Due to the racial marking of Indians and blacks, Ike's own race can go unmarked but nonetheless pronounced and visible. In part 4 of "The Bear," the same originary land acquisition names and racializes: "the tamed land which was to have been his heritage, the land which old Carothers McCaslin his grandfather had bought with white man's money from the wild men . . . [and] had tamed and ordered it for the reason that the human beings he held in bondage and in the power of life and death had removed the forest from it" (243). The formation of the plantation in the nineteenth century coincides with the consolidation of race theories, and thus Ike's refusal of patrimony and ownership because of their connection to slavery and white privilege resonates against a widespread acceptance of scientific racism.[86] Through the representation of Ike's "White-Man face," to use Deleuze and Guattari's term, as reflecting the face of Christ, the topic of celibacy can be joined to that of renunciation, of giving up the right to property. That as a child Ike felt compelled by the "exciting and evocative" woman, "a face young and female and even lighter in color than Tomey's Terrel's" (289), places him in a quasi-sexual position (of voyeur) in relation to the woman. Clearly he joins himself with his uncle, her lover, as "the child which he still was had made serene and absolute and perfect rapport and contact through that glimpsed nameless illicit hybrid female flesh with the boy which had existed at that stage of inviolable and immortal adolescence in his uncle for almost sixty years" (289). Ike's conjoining with his uncle Hubert over the body of the woman prefigures his melding with his grandfather over the bodies of both Eunice and Tomasina. His celibacy is over issues of property—bequeathed ownership and inheritance by progeny—but less readily observed is his repugnance of sex over the black female's flesh as sexual property, which he configures as the "illicit hybrid female flesh" already always linked to his childlike curiosity to see and his desire to know as intimately as his uncle.

Ike's father and uncle—Buck and Buddy, respectively—before him also attempt to resist the ideology and practice of racial hierarchies when they refuse residence in the Big House, the home begun by their father, old Carothers, as the seat of his power and progeny, and until their old age resist traditional sexual identities. Buck and Buddy vacate their inherited Big House, but in a conflicted gesture similar to Ike's in the next generation, they do not renounce their claim to it or ownership of the slaves who subsequently inhabit it.

In the one instance in which Buck and Buddy confront the response of a slave to enslavement, they are baffled. Percival Brownlee (listed as "Percavil Brownly" in the commissary ledgers) is the only slave Buck and Buddy appear to have purchased themselves. Theophilus purchased Brownlee from Bedford Forrest, then "a slave-dealer and not yet a general," for $265. The narrative of the purchase and of Brownlee's passive resistance to being enslaved and to producing for his owners fills seven months of entries in the ledger between March 1856 and December 1856. During that period, Brownlee proves himself incapable of reading, writing, bookkeeping, ploughing, herding, and tending livestock, but quite capable of frustrating the twins into freeing him because he cannot earn his keep and he costs them a hundred dollars for a mule, in addition to the initial investment in his purchase. Faulkner attempts to situate Brownlee as another Tomey's Turl in his resistance to the typical contours of slavery, but the narrative exposition, with its overtones of Melville's "Bartleby the Scrivner," is far too sketchy (252–53).[87] Brownlee emerges as neither comic nor tragic, as neither trickster nor gamester, but as a cipher whose actions may be interpolated as subversive rebellion and whose presence may be construed as a critique of even the most benign of those who would own slaves. Here Faulkner's attempt at humor, or at lightening the loaded contents of the ledgers, fails rather miserably, particularly because the twins, inexplicably, evoke their father as a model of advice on how to manage the slave, but the narrative construction of Buck and Buddy depends on their distancing themselves from the very practices, conceptions, and ideologies of their father regarding slaves. Even in a moment of exasperation, it is difficult to conceive of the twins seeking or following Carothers's advice. The Brownlee entries in the ledger attempt to satirize ownership and property rights in a person. The ledger entries addressing old Carothers McCaslin's intercourse with his slaves is anything but satirical.

The Brownlee story, however, continues in another sequence in "The Bear," which is linked directly to Emancipation and its aftermath in Reconstruction, and a narrative hostility to free black men. Brownlee reappears on the McCaslin place in 1862 when Ike's father is away in the war. For a month his presence is undetected, and during that time he is "conducting impromptu revival meetings among negroes, preaching and leading the singing also in *his high sweet true soprano voice*" (279; emphasis added). In this reappearance, Brownlee is seemingly feminized. As if the mere trace of a sexual identity that is gendered female were not enough, he is in his next appearance, in 1866, seen

> in the entourage of a travelling Army paymaster, the two of them passing through Jefferson in a surrey at the exact moment when the boy's father [Ike's father Buck] . . . also happened to be crossing the Square, the surry [sic] and its occupants traversing rapidly that quiet and bucolic scene and even in that fleeting moment and to others beside the boy's father giving *an illusion of flight and illicit holiday like a man on an excursion during his wife's absence with his wife's personal maid*, until *Brownlee glanced up and saw his late co-master and gave him one defiant female glance* and then broke again, leaped from the surrey and disappeared." (280; emphasis added)

The context for the sighting of Brownlee ("illusion of flight and illicit holiday") recalls Ike's vision of the mixed-race woman retreating from his uncle's house, and Brownlee's attitude, his "defiant female glance," links him more firmly with the feminization suggested earlier. Brownlee's homosexuality mirrors that implicit in the story of Amodeus, Ike's Uncle Buddy. Ultimately, the last report of Brownlee, from McCaslin Edmonds, is twenty years later, when he is "an old man now and quite fat, as the well-to-do proprietor of a select New Orleans brothel" (280). The placement of the continuation of Brownlee's story (that is, as Ike and McCaslin argue the case of ownership of slaves, property in the persons of blacks, and the characteristics of blacks as a race) suggests a second story: whiteness, race, and sexuality projected onto a black male body that Ike cannot tell and that Faulkner does not explore. The silences there are more pronounced than those in the narrative of Carothers's violation of his daughter, which is reiterated following the last report of Brownlee in New Orleans, the place also associated in the text with Eunice and exotic eroticism.

The incest committed by old Carothers and decoded by Ike, however, grounds a discourse on the whiteness of the McCaslin men (for example, their relation to the land and to slavery, their exercise of power or repudiation of it, their subjugation of blacks and women). This white male-centered focus is a way of reading identity, familial, or cultural formation and disintegration in the text, but it is also a way of inscripting the McCaslins as *white* within the political economy and social order representing whiteness in the text. Faulkner represents Ike McCaslin in the boundedness of his existence: walled off, violating nobody's rights, protecting no one, and convinced of his own righteousness. His repudiation of property, inheritance, enable his sense of righteousness and white racial difference. Thus self-constituted as righteous, Ike rejects identification with negative formations in his external world (slavery, economic exploitation, sexual aggression, incest, ownership, and consumerism). Patently antisocial, except in the closed society of hunters, he consciously rejects the white social world into which he was born and initially socialized; however, he ultimately recognizes that he has been able to escape neither the defining, race-marked social world nor its informing racial ideologies.

Ike cannot racially reinvent himself. He may relate to Sam Fathers as a mentoring Indian who teaches the rituals of the woods and hunting, but Sam Fathers is inescapably the slave imprisoned in the cage of his racial connection to blacks and bondage: "*He was old. He had no children, no people, none of his blood anywhere above the earth that he would ever meet again. And even if he were to, he could not have touched it, spoken to it, because for seventy years now he had had to be a negro. It was almost over now and he was glad*" (206). Sam suffers from the trauma of racial construction more than Ike does, yet even he cannot undo his connection to the cage.[88]

Ike may be linked symbolically to Tomey's Turl and to the social death of the enslaved, but he literally remains a white man, a subject constituted out of a specific social world and its ideologies. His move to negate his history merely reinscribes that history into the text for it is the always-already-remembered and to-be-remembered point of entry into his subjectivity. He does nothing to challenge directly the cultural integrity resonating in the present. The meditative strategy of the first part "Was" recurs in "The Bear" certainly, but even more so in "Delta Autumn" in which Ike's passive conciliatory memory conflicts with his contestatory, agitated, and aggressive actions. There, he would bequeath memorabilia from the game of hunt (horn) and offer property (money) to erase culpability and negate complicity, but in so doing, he resorts to the same legal codes that protect property and the propertied and that make some men white and whiteness the measure of civilization and culture.

Ike, who has had the moral vision and the potential for effecting social change within the modern World War II era, is finally an old man truncated by the inflexibility of his society and his own rigidity. Right moral decisions have negated his moral impact. He does not even appear as a reference in "Go Down, Moses," the final chapter of the novel, so that there is no closure to his story in the final chapter; instead the hybrid form leaves a gap between Ike's final appearance and the burial of Lucas's grandson. " 'There are good men everywhere, at all times,' " he tells his young kinsman Roth Edmonds in "Delta Autumn." " 'Most men are. Some are just unlucky, because most men are a little better than their circumstances give them a chance to be' " (329). But Roth replies, " 'So you've lived almost eighty years. . . . And that's what you've finally learned about the other animals you live among.' " (329). Ike is, Ross implies, inattentive to reality and figuratively dead to his society, a condition that recalls the verse from the spiritual "Go Down, Moses": "Let my people go; / If not I'll smite your first-born dead." Ike's "death" has resulted from the misalignment of race and power that has, particularly in the figuration of Tomey's Turl, disrupted both nature and nurture, leaving Ike immobile and "dead."

While the major virtues Ike espouses are, as he himself indicates, "pity and love of justice and of liberty," he does not act out of love, but out of love of abstractions, which remain abstract even though moral (282). Thus, when the young black woman descendant of James Beauchamp (the son of Tomey's Terrel) reveals that she is the mistress of Roth Edmonds and the mother of his son, she realizes that Ike cannot respond with love. Ike has not forgotten the existence of love, but rather he has not loved. The major burden of his heritage, its codes and values, is the inability to love. "The way of love may be the only way to justice," Reinhold Niebuhr states in his 1960 introduction to *Moral Man and Immoral Society* (1932).[89] Without love, Ike cannot attain the purity he seeks for himself, the justice he desires for blacks, or the differentiation he needs from his grandfather. He can forcefully resist evil in society only if he acts; passivity is no solution, because it cannot generate a social reformation. And within this novel, love becomes the most viable motivational force allowing individuals, such as Lucas and Mollie and Miss Worsham, to act according to "the dictates of the human heart," as Faulkner puts it in his Nobel Prize acceptance speech.

Unfortunately, when Ike recognizes that Roth's mistress is, in fact, black, not only does he once again offer money, but he also compounds his offense by advising her to go north and marry a black man. " 'That's the only salvation for you—for a while yet, maybe a long while yet. We will have to wait' " (346). He refuses to envision the possibility of change for whites and the white-dominated society. He concludes in a final admission of his helpless adherence to the rigid racial codes of his time and place: " 'Get out of here! I can do nothing for you! Cant nobody do nothing for you!' " (344). Though he gives the woman a boon of property for her son, he knows it is a useless relic, a hunting horn that will be mere memorabilia in that son's urban context. The useless gift, a castoff actually and a relic from times already past, will only signify that which was lost, though not the loss of the wilderness that Ike associates with the horn, but rather the lost opportunity for racial parity.

Ike does not finally believe in equality of the races: " 'You are young, handsome, almost white; you could find a black man who would see in you what it was you saw in him, who would ask nothing of you and expect less and get even still less than that, if it's revenge you want" (346). Implicit in this racist statement is the belief that Roth is the woman's superior because he is white and that the woman will be the superior of any black man because she is "almost white," as well as the even more invidious belief that what she saw in Roth was his whiteness, his race, just as any future black husband will see in her almost-whiteness, the visible sign of her almost-escape from an inferior race. The rigidity of Roth's racial exclusion of his black "brother" Henry so that he could become "white," along with his feeling of shame at the subsequent rejection by his surrogate black family, replays itself not only in Roth's behavior to the woman but in Ike's as well. Neither can encounter her gaze or engage her challenge to their way of making themselves "white men." The hierarchy of race remains intact. Whiteness retains its powerful currency. In one sense, property in the end is the property of blood, white racial lineage, and the right to humanity is defined once more according to possession. Ike has not been able to translate his strong moral convictions, his shame and outrage at old Carothers's treatment of slaves and kin, into social action, perhaps because the belief in property and ownership is too ingrained in himself and his community, or perhaps because his sense of individual justice, of renunciation and expiation by withdrawal, leaves him unengaged, suspended, and isolated.

CHAPTER 5 | Conclusion:
The Game of Compensation

Playing for Keeps

Tomey's Turl's story ends in two different narratives, both related to his kin and progeny: one, the narrative of the young woman in "Delta Autumn," and the other, the narrative of Samuel Worsham Beauchamp, or Butch, in "Go Down, Moses." Neither narrative, however, is a resolution to the maze of issues fomented in *Go Down, Moses*. Bracketed by textual instability, both characters are Tomey's Turl's relational descendants and the objects of property, and both transgress cultural codes and subvert social mandates.

Both of their narrative histories reconstitute the bodily and psychic importance of Tomey's Turl and, deploying clothing and attitude, enact dramas of property. The young woman continues the rejection of property and "law" in favor of the immaterial emotional, psychological connections that create society and family. She attempts to own her own body. She wears man's clothing, "a man's hat and a man's slicker and rubber boots" (340), and her appearance in the male domain of the hunting camp challenges expectations and transgresses boundaries. Butch is in full quest of all the materiality denied to him and his ancestors. In spite of the narrative sartorial judgment of "too much" and "too many," Butch dresses to attract external recognition of his black body and the value and worth denied him in a segregated, paternalistic society. "He wore one of those sports costumes called ensembles in the men's shop advertisements, shirt and trousers matching and cut from the same fawn-colored flannel, and they had cost too much and were draped too much, with too many pleats" (351). His flashy clothing is a marker of his individual and racial visibility, and a sign of his reclaiming his body and expressive culture as his own. These two narrative histories suspend speculation and reinscribe textual instability. The nameless woman disappears; the multiply named Butch dies. One is trapped within a narrative of miscegenation, the other within a story of black criminality. Neither survives in Faulkner's twentieth-century South.

Perhaps the woman disappears in "Delta Autumn" because, as Lee Jenkins suggests, she is constructed out of a white fantasy, a dream of wish-fulfillment and forgiveness.[1] Perhaps she disappears because she is also a reconfiguration of Tomey's Turl and because, together with her infant son, a sign of both Tomasina and Terrel who must confront the father and name his guilt and his sin (his rape and his lack of love or recognition). She is an iteration of the connection between the slave economy and the sexual economy of plantation society. She arrives at the hunting camp in the rain and via a skiff: "then the woman entering, . . . carrying the blanket-swaddled bundle on one arm and holding the edge of the unbuttoned raincoat over it with the other hand: and bringing something else, something intangible, and effluvium" (340). Visually white like Tomey's Turl, she is both recognizable in her familiarity and unrecognizable in her difference. Described as parts of a whole ("the face indistinct and as yet only young and with dark eyes, queerly colorless but not ill and not that of a country woman despite the garments she wore" [340]), she signifies the coalescing of the parts of the past into a sign of the future.

Once Ike McCaslin recognizes her race, he sees her differently: "pale lips, the skin pallid and dead-looking yet not ill, the dark and tragic and foreknowing eyes. *Maybe in a thousand or two thousand years in America,* he thought. *But not now! Not now!* He cried, not loud, in a voice of amazement, pity, and outrage: 'You're a nigger!'" (344). Ike focuses on her eyes as a racial sign. His emphasis on his ability to designate race by appearance resonates with the legal formulations of race as discernible, physical appearance set out in the early nineteenth century in Virginia and continued in the South long after Emancipation.

In *Hudgins v Wrights*, an early-nineteenth-century case that foregrounded the optical in assigning race, three enslaved women sued for their freedom and two remain in Virginia on the grounds that they were not "Negroes" but white with Indian ancestry and thus, according to Virginia law, could not be held in slavery because only Negroes could be slaves. Appearing before the Richmond District Court of Chancery to prevent Hudgins from removing them from Virginia, the Wright women claimed a free Indian maternal line of descent with some European ancestry. The presiding judge, Chancellor George Wythe, an opponent of slavery who had freed his own slaves, granted their freedom on the grounds that they had no visible traces of African features and thus were presumed to be free unless Hudgins could prove that one of their female ancestors had been enslaved. The grandmother—said to have long black hair and skin "the right Indian coppery colour"—the mother, and the daughter—observed to have "the complexion, the hair and eyes . . . the same as those of whites"—were found to be free not simply because of their skin color but because of their hair. The decision was upheld by the Virginia Supreme Court of Appeals in 1806. St. George Tucker wrote the opinion stating that, because "nature has stampt upon the *African* and his descendants two characteristic marks, besides the difference of complexion, which often remain visible long after the characteristic distinction of colour either disappears or becomes doubtful; a flat nose and woolly head of hair," a judge can depend on visual evidence to decide a person's race.[2] Tucker's judicial colleague, Chancellor Spencer Roane, observed emphatically, "The distinguishing characteristics of the different species of the human race are so visibly marked, that those species may be readily discriminated from each other *by mere inspection only*. This, at least, is emphatically true in relation to the negroes, to the Indians of North America, and the European white people."[3] Similarly, Ike becomes the signifying patriarch who envisions the young woman's face in terms of a black racial identity and a death mask, or her race as a death sentence. Although he believes he can look at her and know her race, it is his gaze that constructs her race.

The young woman's response to Ike is unequivocal: " 'Yes,' she said. 'James Beauchamp . . . was my grandfather. I said you were Uncle Isaac' " (344). She represents an emphasis on miscegenation and the miscegenated family/text. As the great-granddaughter of Ike's father's brother, whom she describes as "the one that had no name but Terrel so you called him Tomey's Terrel" (342–43), she is fully aware of the complicated interfamilial connections among the Beauchamps, McCaslins, and Edmondses. She insists on the name as a signifier of a relational identity that is different from ownership or the naming whites used for their human property. By invoking the proper names of her ancestors, she establishes a lineage both familiar and unfamiliar to Ike. She engenders the retelling of the McCaslin-Beauchamp narrative with Terrel at the center. Out of her relationship with Roth Edmonds, she has produced a son who duplicates the interconnectedness of the black and white descendants of Carothers McCaslin. Described as having "smooth young flesh where the strong old blood ran after its long lost journey back to home" (345), she duplicates the reproduction of a racialized and rejected progeny. Ike says to her, " 'It's a boy, I reckon. They usually are, except that one that was its own mother too.' " His riddle-like reference is to Tomasina, daughter of Eunice and Carothers and mother of Terrel by her father.

If Lucas Beauchamp could believe, "*Old Carothers*, he thought. *I needed him and he come and spoke for me*" (57), then perhaps it is possible to believe similarly that Terrel's female descendant comes back to speak for him, to talk back with the strength and passion that was silenced in Tomasina and unvoiced in Terrel. She provides the balance that offsets the destructive power of patriarchy and paternalism. In her brief exchanges with Ike, the young woman is articulate, self-aware, and clear-sighted, and as such, she removes the stigma of ownership from her Beauchamp lineage. She rejects shame as a controlling emotion, either in her individual or her familial experience, and she refuses to allow Ike to dismiss her as an object of shame. She explodes the narrative of will-less, erotic bondage. She transfigures her lineage from the paternal past (the law of the father) into the maternal present. Not simply a site of memory, what Pierre Nora terms *lieux de memoir*, she is a site of dream, or alternately nightmare.[4] She understands precisely Ike's implications by word and gesture, and she reads his motives with agility, facility, and insight. The synergism she represents is threatening. Marking herself and her son as agents and actors, she perceives a future unimaginable to Ike, yet one disturbing both his dreams and Faulkner's text.

The economics of integration and the sexuality of race-mixing are palpable in the bodily presence of the woman, and they are frightening to Ike, in part because they represent his own displacement, not merely the displacement of the egregious wrongdoers in his society.

This Delta, he [Ike] thought: . . . *This land which man has deswamped and denuded and derivered in two generations so that white men can own*

plantations and commute every night to Memphis and black men own
plantations and ride in jim crow cars to Chicago to live in millionaires'
mansions on Lakeshore Drive, where white men rent farms and live like
niggers and niggers crop on shares and live like animals, where cotton is
planted and grows man-tall in the very cracks of the sidewalks, and usury
and mortgage and bankruptcy and measureless wealth, Chinese and Afri-
can and Aryan and Jew, all breed and spawn together until no man has
time to say which one is which nor cares. . . . No wonder the ruined
woods . . . dont cry for retribution! he thought: The people who
have destroyed it will accomplish its revenge. (347)

A frantic image of money (wealth and poverty), interracial sex, and miscegenated offspring constitutes Ike's nightmare, his erasure of the material presence of the young woman and her son.

In the second of the two endings of Tomey's Turl's story, Samuel Worsham "Butch" Beauchamp dies perhaps because he is a cipher and in a
historical sense a signifier of a black man's fate between the wars. He is a
reiteration of the plantation society as carceral and disciplinary, but he
too rejects the construction of black bodies as controlled, will-less, coerced objects of labor. A description of Butch opens "Go Down, Moses":
"The face was black, smooth, impenetrable; the eyes had seen too much.
The negroid hair had been treated so that it covered the skull like a cap,
in a single neat-ridged sweep, with the appearance of having been lac-
quered, the part trimmed out with a razor, so that the head resembled a
bronze head, imperishable and enduring" (351). The racial emphasis is
clear, just as is the attitude toward racial difference inherent in the description. Despite the references to "imperishable and enduring," Butch
Beauchamp is about to go to his death in the electric chair. At twenty-
six, he faces electrocution for killing a cop, or, as he insinuates, for "getting rich too fast" (352). Unashamed and unapologetic, he embodies the
need for a modern cost-accounting of slavery. Butch's brief appearance
in "Go Down, Moses" catalyzes the systems of law, so that the residue
of property in twentieth-century society comes openly into play with
racial codes.

Butch's death initiates the involvement of Gavin Stevens, lawyer and
representative of the legal system, with the burial of an "outlaw."[5] In
the process, Stevens confronts the remainder of the old codes governing
race and morality. Stevens and Wilmoth, the newspaper editor, as well
as some of the townspeople and presumably Roth Edmonds, cooperate

in paying for the return of Butch's body from Chicago and for his burial. In the final analysis, they act out of duty to codes of conduct, primarily respect for an elderly white woman; they act neither out of any faith or belief that attention to blacks is ethical behavior, nor out of a belief that the law has functioned to control and subordinate blacks. Stevens even uses the assaultive language of his unregenerated culture when he collects money for the burial: "It's to bring a dead nigger home" (360). Playing off the white southern colloquialism, "The only good nigger is a dead nigger," his explanation is a reminder that in their contemporary society just as in the slave economy, there is no economic value in a "dead nigger." The implicit intent of the comment is ridicule and condescension; the expenditure is the object of derision. The unmistakable negation of Butch's "value" is systemic. Both Stevens, the lawyer, and Wilmoth, the newspaper editor, fail to recognize that for blacks the law has not primarily been a means of achieving justice, and that the law is partly to blame for the condition of an "antisocial" black such as Butch who was not "properly" socialized by the plantation system. In fact, the townspeople are mainly quite content to believe that somehow Butch is merely "bad," like his father before him, who abandoned his family and fled the community, but not that the duality of economic conditions compounded by legal, racial, and moral codes that are followed by their society (and which persistently dehumanize blacks or undermine the ability of blacks to be or to do) may be equally responsible for what Butch becomes.[6] They shift the burden of criminality to biological rather than social issues.

Entrapped and limited in living on the McCaslin-Edmonds place and working on shares just as his ancestors had, Butch rebels against modern bondage and commits crimes against the existing paternalistic and racist order. In stealing from the commissary he strikes out against the embodiment of power and control in the plantation system.[7] It is, after all, in the ledgers of that very commissary that the extent of the exercise of power over black life was revealed in the origins of his great-grandfather, Tomey's Turl. In his alienation from the law, Butch represents the consequences of legal abuse and racial domination. In his flight from the South, he sheds the way he is viewed. The cost to him is a larger alienation from feeling, but he does not internalize the shame of the contempt shown him by white society. His story makes clear the economic motive of slavery, tenancy, and racial exploitation and subordination.[8] And the narratives of law function as rationalizations for the economics of enslavement—chattel and modern.

It seems no accident that Faulkner initially conceived of Butch as an extension of another earlier production of chattel slavery. He first gave Butch the name Henry Coldfield Sutpen, thus linking him to *Absalom, Absalom!*, to miscegenation and incest, slavery and fratricide, as Eric Sundquist has pointed out.

> The abrupt, overbearing violence of that act [Henry Sutpen's murder of his brother Charles Bon] and Henry's later immolation . . . seemed to close the door on the Sutpen tragedy and its potential contagion . . . ; but Faulkner was soon . . . searching for . . . new ways to confront the act of miscegenation that might be, could be, had to be an act of incest. . . . The initial representation of Samuel Beauchamp as Henry Coldfield Sutpen is . . . an excursion into authorial fantasia, revealing that the contagion in blood has become a compositional contagion as well. The mixing . . . that this strategy and the preliminary figuring of Ike as Quentin would have entailed reflects the precarious extremity of Faulkner's own design, posed on the brink of collapse but . . . taking risks in every way equal to the emotional strain it is meant to express.[9]

When Faulkner abandoned that strategy, he renamed Butch, Carothers Edmonds Beauchamp, and in so doing connected him directly to Roth Edmonds, his conflicted relation to ownership and money, the farm and the bank, and the system of tenancy and black subjugation. But such direct collations held only briefly. Faulkner abandoned them and settled on Samuel Worsham Beauchamp, whom he made relational not only to Tomey's Turl through Lucas and Mollie, but also to Hamp Worsham, Mollie's brother, who could provide a conventional black male presence within traditional boundaries. Similar to the resolution of his brother-in-law Lucas Beauchamp's narrative, Hamp's is overshadowed by the ideology and will of his sister Mollie.

Mollie Beauchamp determines that her grandson must be reclaimed by the family and community. Thus, the ritual burial of Butch must be done in accordance with the wishes of two old women, one black and the other white, who act not in response to the legal codes but to moral codes and, ironically, to one set of racial codes as well. As Miss Worsham says, " 'Mollie's . . . parents belonged to my grandfather. Mollie and I were born in the same month. We grew up as sisters'" (357). Owner-ship from the historical system of slavery reconstitutes itself in the re-lationship between the women and in their sense of their bond to each other and, noteworthy here, to tradition. Both the white woman and the black woman assume what the role of whites must continue to be in the lives of blacks—that is, paternalistic and, in part, a moral response to the legacy of property. This culture, Faulkner concludes by his depic-tion of Mollie and Miss Worsham, has its limited but best hope in the women who function outside the dominant male codes of property, posi-tion, and ownership. He disassociates them from the masculinist values of their society by identifying them with an "old, timeless, female affinity for blood and grief" (358). Noticeably, shame is absent from the range of responses allotted them. In particular, Faulkner seems to place much of the possibility for change within the relationship developed between the two elderly women and within the realm of affective rather than systemic change, which given the valence of power in this society requires a *male affinity*. The ideal Faulkner may be memorializing in the representation of the two women's relationship is part of the personal and societal loss he experienced with the death of Caroline Barr and with her a genera-tion of black women whose primary existence was spent nurturing white lives to their fullest, richest, most creative and most moral. These same women are confined, nonetheless, to the most abject of dehumanizing conditions, grinding poverty, and illiteracy—and, ironically, confined to those conditions by the very white people whom they serve so faithfully.

The final alliance in the novel is primarily between the two elderly women, Mollie Beauchamp, widowed, and Belle Worsham, unmarried. As a single, older, white woman who is also poor and without property, but thus also significantly unencumbered by the coverture of her iden-tity, Miss Worsham is dependent on blacks for her livelihood; she lives off the truck garden of Hamp, Mollie's brother. Her alliance with Mollie, however, does not argue strongly for an alliance between the races that could move toward either social change or the common good, because, represented as a relic of the past ("the high, white, erect, old-time head" [363]), she is removed from the present-day social order. Mollie, too, is part of the traditional system as her and her brother's relationship with Miss Worsham suggests. The imbalance in that relationship is signaled by the hierarchical nomenclature: Mollie is always "Mollie." She can-not be "Mrs. Beauchamp" or even "Miz Beauchamp," though her white counterpart is always "Miss Worsham" (or "Miss Belle" to Mollie). The gender and race divide as represented in the narrative is too great to dismantle or mollify the powerful white male elites who control the economic, political, and social world. Nevertheless, Butch's death not only externalizes what Miss Worsham labels as "our grief," the familial experience she shares with Mollie, Hamp, and his wife, and from which Gavin Stevens is excluded, but it also produces an opportunity for limited communal reflection and action that includes the conscious mourners, as well as, potentially, the rest of the society. In the conclusion of the novel, however, that opportunity remains dormant, as static and catatonic and uncomprehending as Ike McCaslin in his final appearance in "Delta Autumn."

By insisting that Roth Edmonds sold her Benjamin (Butch) into slavery, Mollie is only partly aware of the reality that faced a young black man in a society still enmeshed in the old ways and attitudes. The image of slavery connected to the Exodus story Mollie rightly evokes speaks to the economic peonage to which Butch and blacks in his generation were subjected and against which they rebelled. Unlike Tomey's Turl whose tricksterlike activities subvert the process of white domination over him, Butch reaches his majority at a point in the 1930s when the claim of white blood or faithful service to a family of whites did not diminish the punishing aspects of rural poverty and segregation in Mississippi. Unlike Lucas, who is only allowed the primacy of an older race, not an equal one, Butch desires respect for his individual self worth but is entrapped in a system of economic and social peonage. In his social position as victim of modern bondage to the land, Butch retaliates against the existing order by breaking laws that are necessary for the common good but that do not factor his existence into their protective discourses. At the same time, his specific action—stealing from the plantation commissary—may also be read as a form of rebellion against the racist codes and laws that relegate him and his kind to their "place" and that deny him access to property and ownership—basically to a stake in the market economy that defines manhood. Two generations later, perhaps Butch would be one of the young southern black men sitting in at a segregated lunch counter or registering black Mississippians to vote in order to change their conditions.

Faulkner concludes that the North in the early 1940s was no better than the South for a black youth. There Butch falls into crime and is electrocuted, whereas in the South he is given a proper burial. However, Faulkner does not, and perhaps cannot, given the moral vision of the novel, address the lack of opportunity for manhood, for equal rights or economic parity in the southern world into which Butch was born.[10] Much like his ancestor Tomey's Turl in the nineteenth century, Butch would have remained challenged, oppressed, and exploited on the plantation. He would not have become a man but would have remained a boy, denied maturation and entrance into an economically viable world. Given Faulkner's own Lockean arguments about the land in "The Bear," Butch would have remained the "landless," working the land on shares and tied to it but denied the fruits of his labor. Just as Butch's criminal activity cannot be condoned, neither can the paternal, restricting social order into which he is born be condoned. No resolution can occur within the binary that Faulkner establishes.

Faulkner can only envision Butch Beauchamp as the bad seed of a bad father, who must be punished for leaving the South and transgressing its political economy and arbitrary morality. The discourse of black criminality replaces that of black minstrelsy in the movement from Tomey's Turl in "Was" to his great-grandson Butch in "Go Down, Moses." The representation of Butch, as well as his criminality, is replete with nostalgia for a lost past and sadness for an unfamiliar present. His very voice argues the unfamiliar and unsettling territory of the black emigre to the North: "answering in a voice which was anything under the sun but a southern voice or even a negro voice" (351). Created in the aftermath of Richard Wright's Bigger Thomas (*Native Son*, 1940), Butch Beauchamp is surely on one level, an apology for that treatment in the South of the Biggers of the 1930s—all the southern-born, southern-bred young black men who lost their way in Chicago, but who can come home again to the South for burial.[11] On another level, the subtext makes plain that the uppity niggers who go north in search of economic and social justice will receive their comeuppance—a reversal of fortune and a quick death.

Butch shares with the unnamed woman from "Delta Autumn" a material racial embodiment objectified in a narrative gesture toward the "dangers" of the world outside the traditional boundaries and mores of the South. Represented as a dual unruly coda rather than a conjoined resolution, the two characters extend the expressive possibilities of the fiction. With their supposedly race-marked appetites, desires, and needs that cannot be controlled by the dictates of the legal system and that are not sanctioned within the communal sphere, they signal a potential disruption of the public culture. That both Butch and the woman are relational residents in a text but do not come together as closure of that text recalls Tomey's Terrel's hybridity and the hybrid, miscegenated nature of the text itself. There is a sense in which Faulkner was playing for keeps in resisting a tidy conclusion for his multivocal narratives in *Go Down, Moses*. For instance, "play" itself is very much a part of the representations in the text: "the play element in human make-up . . . trains people to exercise self-control, because it develops a wider loyalty, because it sublimates aggressive tendencies, because it restores a sense of balance and proportion to those who tend to work too hard and in too limited a sector."[12] The suspension of the ordinary in play as in games at once allows Faulkner to back away from the vision of righteous old Ike McCaslin bested by the innate logic and morality of a woman historically branded immoral and irrational and to imagine momentarily an unsouthern future. That moment cannot be sustained, as Butch's fate makes all too apparent. Faulkner reverts to the known reality that catalyzes yet impedes his narrative. The ending is neither melodramatic nor utopian; neither "hopeless elegy, desperate nostalgia" nor "erasure."[13] It is merely, and perhaps irrevocably, a stay of dialogic and competing forces. The end of the game is not extinction, erasure, or death; it is merely the "*now*," when Gavin Stevens says, "*it's all over and done and finished*" (365). It is the moment when the ordinary, the everyday, resumes.

The ordinary aspect of family and belonging are inscriptions of the property rights of the black Beauchamps. Both the woman and Butch signify a homecoming and a reunification of the parts of the black body (a body figured both communally and familially in the text). Mollie's words, " 'Sold my Benjamin' . . . 'Sold him in Egypt' . . . 'Sold him to Pharaoh' " (362), are significant in this homecoming because they signify that slavery remains resident in the ideology of blacks and whites in the contemporary World War II South. The black family is sold off and separated but also denied and obscured as kin and as relatives because of the legal abstraction of fathers from their offspring and because of the legal usurpation of the issue of mothers. The subsequent clustering of blacks in supportive kinship units does not alter the fact that the black family remains victimized by the relational havoc wrought by the pernicious laws beginning in slavery and effective thereafter in Jim Crow segregation, its legal codes and social customs (as in the "illegality" of the young woman's union with Roth Edmonds). This specific devastation of slavery continued throughout the twentieth century with the separation of families and denial of familial bonds. It was exacerbated by a lack of compensation for black free labor, which compounded and extended black vulnerability and subservience in the white-dominated economic order.

In *Go Down, Moses* individual black males, like Tomey's Terrel in courting Tennie despite the containment of slavery and different owners and plantations, may attempt to create families of their own, but all are literally or figuratively orphans. In response to the census taker's query, " 'Parents,' " Butch replies, " 'Sure. Two. I dont remember them. My grandmother raised me' " (352). In "Pantaloon in Black," Rider too is raised by a surrogate mother: "She was his aunt. She had raised him. He could not remember his parents at all" (132). Mollie's wanting to put Butch's story, all of it, into the newspaper is a desire for the acknowledgment of the homecoming, a memorialization of the reunion of the black body, and an indictment of the legacy of enslavement. Mollie, no less than her grandson, refuses shame. She will not avert her eyes or the eyes of the community, white and black, from the spectacle of Butch's funeral cortege. Rather than allowing the whites to determine a response to Butch's life and death, she dictates the circumstances under which and through which gaze they must confront and see Butch, "the body," in Gavin Stevens's language (358). Mediating their projection of shame, Mollie recasts the lens through which they must filter their responses. Butch is not simply her grandson but " 'the only child of her oldest daughter, her own dead first child' " (38), and a metonymy for all the departed black children.

The homecoming for Butch is more than an elegy fueled by mourning. Like the spiritual it echoes, Butch's homecoming is a pronouncement of freedom and the right to bodily integrity, fueled by a desire to announce, to vocalize, and to textualize, to enter into the public sphere what is most often silenced, hidden, and secreted out of guilt or shame: the dehumanization of the black body and the separation of the black family. Unlike the speech act of Mannie's grave in "Pantaloon in Black" that is unreadable by whites ("marked off without order about the barren plot by shards of pottery and broken bottles and old brick and other objects insignificant to sight but actually of a profound meaning and fatal to touch, which no white man could have read" [131–32]), the newspaper account of Butch's story will be in a medium and in a language whites understand, and therefore they will be unable to ignore the story, even if they ridicule or misread it. Perhaps it will be as well a source of what Rowe calls "the 'news' that Roth Edmonds, surviving representative of the sins of slavery, is responsible for the fates of African-Americans who are as doomed by their migrations north . . . as their ancestors were by their captivity in the slave-holding South."[14] Recrimination, however, is not the signal point here.

More importantly, the return of the collective body, the communal body is articulated as a public speech act defiant in its claiming of rights and denouncing of guilt. It rejects privatization of racial pain and suffering, and it encompasses Tomasina and Eunice, Terrel and Tennie, and their children, Fonsiba, James, and Lucas, and all of their descendants, the unnamed woman and Butch, and their racial kin, Rider no less than Sam Fathers, just as much as it involves Hamp Worshamp and his wife, a soprano who carries the refrain from the spiritual in "a true constant," voiced announcement "without words beneath the strophe and antistrophe" of an insistent black social identity into the public sphere (363). The claims of this enlarged black family also move across race lines to constitute a coming together of the raped or ravished flesh, of the mixed-race progeny, across the boundaries of plantations and separation by artificial ownership papers ("Was"), across the boundary between life and death ("Pantaloon in Black"), across the boundary of the "natural world" and its societies that nonetheless permit, if not encourage, dispersal and separation ("The Old People," "The Bear," and "Delta Autumn"). The reunification of the black body, the body that was property under slavery, takes place despite the dispersal efforts of whites and with their concession to a driving, inexplicable, and incomprehensible black will (that counters the white "fathers will" of the text). Thus, Mollie's refrain, along with the call and response picked up by her natural brother, Hamp, and her surrogate "sister," Miss Worsham, fill the narrative present with the urgency of "Go Down, Moses," the most plainspoken spiritual of an embodied people, and with their uncompromising demand for emancipation and justice.

Faulkner's construction of Tomey's Turl's descendants functions to insert him into the cultural conversations of the late 1930s and early 1940s and to limn a dynamic psychoanalytic dimension to the text. In the aftermath of the first large wave of the Great Migration of blacks to the cities of the North, specifically to Chicago for black Mississippians, Faulkner witnessed the refusal of rural, impoverished, disenfranchised, and oppressed blacks to remain hostage in the South. The lure of cities and the promise of the North destablized the fixity of black people in the South and the rigidity of caste and class position. This destabilization not only undermined the economic, social, and political life of an as yet premodern Mississippi, but it also undermined the production of texts based on a simplistically racially polarized and bifurcated land, culture, and heritage. It is no wonder Faulkner exploits Butch's failed migration as an opportunity to celebrate the traditional ties of blacks to the South and to create an elegy to the old paternalistic virtues. Faulkner's production of the narrative of Butch's life and, especially, his death and burial underscores a desire for a particular type of remembered past to force shape and articulate meaning into an otherwise unpredictable and chaotic present.

The Great Depression and the New Deal alike become targets of Faulkner's discourse in *Go Down, Moses*. The political, ideological, economic, and material circumstances of the late 1930s and early 1940s contribute to the kinds of competing narratives Faulkner produced in that text, and they may be the subtextual impetus for the meditation on the disappearing wilderness and, with it, a diminished possibility of freedom from government controls. An almost direct transference of ideas occurs. It is in "The Bear," during the final hunt, that the men talk of demagogues and tyrants, both in the United States and abroad, and of economic realities and obsessions. These specific temporal references also contribute to Faulkner's personal take on the economy: " 'Half the people without jobs and half the factories closed by strikes. Half the people on public dole that wont work and half that couldn't work even if they would' " (323). Roosevelt's New Deal does not fare well in this castigation of public welfare and its entitlements. The process of recovery from the Depression rearranged society and realigned the rights of property owners with notions of public interests and created new entitlements. Strictures introduced by the New Deal to create a modern regulatory state and to transform an economically depressed society brought government increasingly into arenas of private property previously protected by law. Through the efforts of Roosevelt, a social security system, a minimum wage, and collective bargaining all began the process of reconfiguring power in the United States. These measures, combined with regulations of child labor and protections of women in the workplace, raised concerns about the interference of government in the rights to property and to privacy, particularly after Roosevelt's effort in 1937 to move the Supreme Court away from assisting big business by applying the concept of property in increasingly abstract ways. Such measures produced comparisons of Roosevelt with demagogues and dictators abroad.

Ironically, it was the Fourteenth Amendment to the Constitution, adopted to protect the civil rights of blacks, that facilitated the expansion of property rights protected under law. Passed by Congress in 1866 and ratified in 1868, the Fourteenth Amendment took the protection language of the Fifth Amendment, "no person shall be deprived of life, liberty, or property, without due process of law, nor shall private property be taken for public use, without just compensation." By the 1860s, however, the definition of property was based on an array of understandings in common and statutory law, but the legal meaning was shifting from "tangible things to intangibles," and the "contests over the right of all citizens to equal treatment reached the Supreme Court as property issues."[15] The shift was from contract to due process to protect property and to interpret constitutional property protection. Framed in language specific to persons, the Fourteenth Amendment within fifteen years of its adoption was used to protect new forms of property and to extend property concepts into economic areas in which a corporation was rendered a "person."[16] By 1937, the transformed meanings of property and its Fourteenth Amendment protection were at the center of Roosevelt's quarrel with the Supreme Court.

For Faulkner the situation was personal. The market forces, which rejected "Was" (circulated as "Almost"), were dictated by an economy recovering from the Great Depression but still close to the despair of deprivation that would not "buy" the comedic antics of happy slaves and benevolent masters. To make "Was" palatable and marketable, Faulkner situated it in a larger discourse interrogating the political economy itself, enslavement of humans who are also brothers, tyranny over people and land, and oppression in myriad forms, including ownership and property.

Simultaneously on the larger world stage, the rise of Hitler in Germany, aggression against people marked as "different," and war over land in Europe, all raised questions about Faulkner's own Mississippi. These he addressed in the discourses on property and the right of ownership in "The Bear" and in the narratives of the woods and hunting dispersed throughout *Go Down, Moses*. As he put it, "One nice thing about the woods: off there hunting, I dont fret and stew so much about Europe. But I'm only 43, I'm afraid I'm going to the damn thing yet."[17] In "Delta Autumn" Ike and his fellow hunters discuss how the United States will defeat tyrants like Hitler, no matter what they call themselves (" 'Smith or Jones or Roosevelt or Wilkie or whatever he will call himself in this country?' 'We'll stop him in this country . . . Even if he calls himself George Washington,' " [322]), and as men, they worry over going to war: " 'I reckon, when the time comes and some of you have done got tired of hollering we are whipped if we dont go to war and some more are hollering we are whipped if we do, it will cope with one Austrian paper-hanger, no matter what he will be calling himself' " (322–323). These cultural conversations are not necessarily one and the same, though they may well be interconnected and interpolated in similar veins.

How much of *Go Down, Moses*, then, is a self-reflexive move on Faulkner's part may be difficult to gauge, but the possibility of its being his game of arbitrary (self)compensation in which Tomey's Turl is both the object of the wager and the subject of the deal opens up the text, its complexities, and its significance in the Faulkner canon. Tomey's Turl's legacy reverberates in one of Faulkner's important compositions of the 1940s, the "Appendix / The Compsons / 1699–1945," written following the publication of *Go Down, Moses*.[18] The later text bears the marks of Turl's descendant, Butch Beauchamp, who is the spectral figure lurking inside the appendix to *The Sound and the Fury* as an initial aspect of Faulkner's construction of the racialized, flawed male attracted by the lure of the urban, of the easy life, and of the city vices. In the 1945 appendix Faulkner revises the black male Gibsons as reconstituted Butch Beauchamps. He thus signifies a fear of the movement of southern black men out of their traditional places in the rural South, which he explored in the last chapter of *Go Down, Moses* by means of Butch. In the appendix, TP's brief representation is an extension of Butch. From his specific clothing ("the fine bright cheap intransigent clothes") to his implicit behavior (prowling Memphis's Beale Street), TP, and by extension the black males of his generation, are purged from the traditional economic landscape of Faulkner's representative South, punished for their deviance, and left to the fluctuations of fate.

Without knowledge of the narrative, ideology, and style of *Go Down, Moses*, the appendix may seem an odd compilation, even for a writer who habitually reused his materials and revisited his characters. The appendix's elevation of an aggressively white masculine heraldry with a concomitant erasure of all traces of female lineage has the overtures of high, yet failed romance. But as a construction of masculinity following *Go Down, Moses* and its elevation of the white male saga from the 1840s to the 1940s, the appendix makes ideological sense. Its debasing of Caddy Compson into an icon of evil and its lauding of Jason Compson as a rational philosopher appear contradictory to their representation in *The Sound and the Fury* (1929). Its tortured inclusion of Ikkemotubbe as a "dispossessed American king," its extended referencing of Andrew Jackson as "Great White Father" embroiled in defending his hapless wife against bigamous charges, and its brief deprecation of black males seem gratuitous. The included references to black, urban, and female dissipation, the deleted negative references to Jews, and the suggested references to the male Compsons' right to aspiration through property and ownership all reside in historical and cultural ideologies that contributed to my discomfort with the text. Few of the critical discourses on the appendix have made it more palatable. The exoticizing of race, lineage, and gender taken together makes it unsettling reading for me as a woman of color.

Without dismissing my instinctive reactions, I read the Compson Appendix as Faulkner's project of self-reflexive history, which embeds and embodies the informing ideology of *Go Down, Moses*. The ideology underpinning the appendix finds its fullest articulation not in *The Sound and the Fury*, which it overtly references and extends, but rather in *Go Down, Moses*, which it suppresses and disguises. These interactive ideologies intersect in the narrative of patriarchy, property, power, race, and sexuality.

The appendix to *The Sound and the Fury* is a well-known document completed in October 1945, three years after *Go Down, Moses* and written specifically for Malcolm Cowley's collection for Viking Press, *The Portable Faulkner* (1946), a thematic anthology that revitalized Faulkner's career. Subsequently, however, the renamed "Appendix / Compson" appeared with new editions of the novel. Produced ostensibly to concretize the history of the Compson family dispersed throughout the novel, it follows a chronological structure, but the internal organization is more impressionistic than logical. The historicizing process blurs the distinction between fiction and biography by accommodating the period between 1929, the publication of *The Sound and the Fury*, and 1945, the production of the appendix. Spanning centuries, the site of narrative reality is the social and cultural contexts for the reinvented, reconceptualized subject. Its most obsessive subject is ownership, property, and masculine enterprises of competitive exchange.[19] At once an act of memory (the recollection of the novel) and an act of invention (the extension of the novel proper), the appendix interacts with the past project, *The Sound and the Fury*, and with the author's present historical moment, which he had more fully mediated not in his youth in the 1920s when he wrote *The South and the Fury*, but in his maturity in the 1940s when he produced *Go Down, Moses*. In the appendix, Faulkner owns his racial identity and clarifies the genealogy of his white southern familial double.

As a white masculinist construction of history, the appendix enacts a repositioning of the author himself from the margins to the center. The encoding of ownership and the concomitant creation of law as a protection of property is one residue of Faulkner's writing of *Go Down, Moses*. Concomitantly, the death of Caroline Barr in 1940, referenced in the dedication to *Go Down, Moses*, may also signal Faulkner's oppressive awareness of himself as no longer young, no longer the Billy in the care of "Mammy Callie." In recognizing the marginalization of himself as a white southern author, Faulkner revised *Go Down, Moses* alongside *The Sound and the Fury*. As a result, he rewrote not simply the conclusion of his 1929 novel but the implications of the lives of his characters and their positions in or out of history.

Though today white males are seldom considered marginal, in the period of the 1920s, when the novel was written, and again in the period of the 1940s, when the appendix was written, a white southern male, despite his position of power and authority within his cultural matrix of a caste- and class-bound southern society, was a marginalized figure, relative to the majority culture of the larger nation. While it would be a mistake to overemphasize the importance of H. L. Mencken's essay "The Sahara of the Bozart" (1917; 1922), it is no mistake to extrapolate from that essay one negative published attitude toward white southern writers living within the South.

Faulkner's youthful masquerades (Royal Air Force hero, for instance) and his disguises (hard-drinking creative genius in New Orleans of the

1920s, for example) may be read as attempts on his part to disassociate himself from the actuality of being who he was, a working-class white Mississippian on the downward curve of social significance. The romantic implications of his masking his identity, sometimes even as "the little black man," or assuming false identities are numerous, but the practical implications are specifically that he distanced himself from the relatively powerless position that the larger world, in particular the literary world, perceived a white male southerner, a Mississippian in particular, to occupy.[20] Faulkner recognized as much in 1942 when he wrote of his consignment to Mississippi: "I have been buried here for three years not for lack of money and I am stale. Even a military job will dig me up and out for a while."[21]

Following the publication of Go Down, Moses, Faulkner's own life and career was in as much of a shambles as Europe with Hitler changing its surface. He concluded in August 1945, when he was feeling "bad, depressed, dreadful sense of wasting time . . . of some kind of blow-up or collapse": "My books have never sold, are out of print; the labor (the creation of my apocryphal county) of my life, even if I have a few things yet to add to it, will never make a living for me."[22] The economic motive in his complaint is apparent. Money, sales, making a living at writing ("the labor" of his life) are unveiled in his laments. Unable to participate in World War II and deprived of service in World War I, Faulkner constructed a means of getting even in the appendix. As he wrote to Harold Ober in 1944, "I am 47 . . . I am like an aging mare."[23] His self-deceptive attempts to receive an air force or naval commission occupy a series of his letters from 1942 to the mid-1940s, though beginning in 1940, he was already contemplating participation in the war and trying on his old uniform:[24] "I can button it, even after twenty-two years; the wings look as brave as they ever did. I swore then when I took it off in '19, that I would never wear another. . . . But now I dont know. . . . But my feeling now is . . . what will be left after this one will certainly not be worth living for."[25]

The patriarchal symbolic order of the Compson clan signifies Faulkner's patriotic desire to participate in war as an enactment of masculinity. "This world is bitched proper this time," he complained of the war in 1942, "I'd like to be a dictator now. I'd take all these congressmen who refused to make military appropriations and I'd send them to the Philippines."[26] Beyond inclusion in a masculine enactment of patriotism, the patriarchal order of the Compson men is connected to Faulkner's personal desire to escape the influence of women: "But if I can get some money, I can get away for a while—either in service, or out of it. Incidentally, I believe I have discovered the reason inherent in human nature why warfare will never be abolished: it's the only condition under which a man who is not a scoundrel can escape for a while from his female kin."[27]

The creation of second stories for women and for blacks and the invention of an uninterrupted history for men in the appendix represent not only a continuation of the narrative fiction of *The Sound and the Fury* and an invention of a new fiction for the author, but also an interpolation of the ideological and thematic clusters in *Go Down, Moses*. In his exchange of letters with Malcolm Cowley, Faulkner identified himself as the "Garter King-at-Arms," meaning that he had the power of final arbiter and controlled his creation.[28] Cowley, however, understood the term to mean that "the Garter King-of-Arms presides over the Heralds' College, or College of Arms, which rules on questions having to do with armorial bearings and pedigrees."[29] While Cowley read the identification as Faulkner's artistic and aesthetic license allowing for the lack of agreement between "Appendix / The Compsons" and *The Sound and the Fury*, he did not perceive that the label also renegotiated Faulkner's own place as creator and inventor. The result of his renegotiation is perhaps projected onto *A Fable* (1950) which, though already in process while Faulkner was writing the appendix, proceeds from the implied concerns with warring over lands, morality, and recognition, all complicated by the various crosses the individual bears. He implied as much in 1944: "It's too bad I lived now though. Still too young to be unmoved by the old insidious succubae of trumpets, too old either to make one among them or to be impervious, and therefore too old to write, to have the remaining time to spend waiting for the trumpets and the lightning strokes of glory to have done. I have a considerable talent, perhaps as good as any coeval. But I am 46 now. So what I will mean soon by 'have' is 'had.'"[30]

Faulkner's erasure from significance in the historical moment during which he recreated the Compsons is inscribed in his positioning himself differently in the discourse. Masking his fears in the 1940s is similar to his masking his identity in the 1920s, only in his middle age, the game of masking is more revelatory. The appendix reflects an awareness of multiple historical moments, but what Faulkner did not quite succeed in conveying to Cowley is that the empirical materials from *The Sound and the Fury*, to which Cowley kept returning, were largely secondary to his project in the appendix. That project is not simply discursive. Faulkner's power over issues of progeny, gender, race, and history in the appendix renders his knowledge of the specific characters and events of the novel less important. The sexism and racism (and even the anti-Semitism that Cowley persuaded him to omit) stem from the material conditions and the social/cultural practices of the 1940s, which allowed Faulkner to practice a self-consciousness as male, as white, as southerner, as well as in relational roles as son, husband, father.[31]

Cowley's literalistic reading fastened on contradictions within the text, the discrepancies between the two texts; as he said, "The more I admired his Appendix, the more I found that some of the changes raised perplexing questions."[32] Cowley's more literal imagination did not allow him to read the main correspondence functioning in the space between the two texts—that is, Faulkner himself. The divergences between the novel and the appendix are marks of Faulkner's defining his own privileged condition at a point when his condition was more accurately marked by relative obscurity and lack of privilege. In the shaping of the appendix, he both legitimates and valorizes himself as creator, as author. In situating himself in relationship to what Fredric Jameson calls "the political unconscious" of dominant cultural discourses and their underlying "master narratives," Faulkner asserted his place in a literary continuum that had flowed on without him, or perhaps bypassed him in Mississippi. In retextualizing *The Sound and the Fury* as a hallmark of high modernism and in reinscribing the cultural narratives specific to the South and to Mississippi but already embedded within *The Sound and the Fury*, he arched his control over a new text, over the capacity to create that text, and over his own paradigmatic place within the literary history of American modernism. It is an exercise of power over progeny similar to Carothers McCaslin's attempted exercise of absolute will over his black and white offspring.

His pleasure in the completed appendix is unmistakable: "When you reprint THE SOUND AND THE FURY," he wrote to Robert Linscott in 1946, "I have a new section to go with it. I should have written this new section when I wrote the book itself. . . . When you read it, you will see how it is the key to the whole book, and after reading it, the 4 sections as they stand now fall into clarity and place."[33] As he wrote to Cowley: "The job is splendid. Damn you to hell anyway. But even if I had beat you to the idea, mine wouldn't have been this good. . . . By God, I didn't know myself what I had tried to do, and how much I had succeeded."[34]

To read the appendix is to read a history that is a mythologizing of a fantasy, a constructed past, that somehow bears the insignia of fact, not fiction. It is history designed to reinterpret characters in the context of a present moment, which by Faulkner's own account, was fraught with the debilitations of war and despotism. Cinematic in its sweep, the appendix is a visualization of *The Sound and the Fury* and a retextualization of the cultural narrative already always present in the novel. A highly idiosyncratic perspective, it is a self-enclosed, self-referential inscription of the author as inventor, filmmaker, screenwriter, and cinematographer: a conscious manipulation of Faulkner's exposure to the technologies of Hollywood.

The visual sweep intensifies the dominance of the Compson men. The appendix privileges the fathers in action storyboards and erases the mothers. It names the males and frees them from domesticity. They participate as cross-cultural forces little differentiated from one another by name or deed. From Scotland to Georgia to Kentucky to Mississippi, the different cultures and historical moments are melded into a similar patriarchal code with scant variation in social forms but with consistent attention to ocular spectating.

Yet it is Jason IV who is constructed as both quietly desperate and successful. With his bourgeois existence of minimal material consumption (he lives in an apartment above his business) and his not quite domesticated weekends spent with a woman ("big, plain, friendly, brazen-haired pleasant faced . . . no longer very young" [*The Portable Faulkner*, 718]), imported by bus from Memphis on weekends only, Jason lives an ideal life, if ideal can be ascribed to a man's being undomesticated by women and controlling his own fortune and devoid of familial responsibilities. "He was emancipated now. He was free" (718). Faulkner implicates his own otherwise inexpressible desires in his signification of Jason's freedom. Jason's economic motive and entrapment seem commensurate not only with Faulkner's own but also with Ike McCaslin's in *Go Down, Moses*.

If Quentin is the flawed hero of the novel, then Jason is the differently flawed hero of the appendix. Although Faulkner insisted that he had not rewritten Jason's character, even a novice reader and clearly a discerning one such as Cowley can decode the veiled celebratory attention paid to the entrepreneur, the sane bachelor who satisfies his sexual appetites on weekends and attends to his major expression of masculinity, his business enterprise, undisturbed and unencumbered on weekdays. Faulkner identified Jason of the appendix as "the new South . . . the one Compson and Sartoris who met Snopes on his own ground and . . . held his own."[35] The identification and the trope of freedom are the subtexts of an experiential core that is fantasized in application to Faulkner's own material reality. In eschewing property as land for property as money, Jason is the lone Compson to redefine the balance between property, acquisition, and ownership. His business is himself and he owns the business free and clear, without any interference from women and blacks: " 'In 1865,' he would say, 'Abe Lincoln freed the niggers from the Compsons. In 1933, Jason Compson freed the Compsons from the niggers' " (718). The references to freedom with the inference of enslavement speak back to the issues of property, ownership, economics, and inheritance as they intersect with race and responsibility.

Both women and blacks, however, bear the weight of the changed and destructive material world of the 1940s. Writing and creating from an alternative ideological and cultural base in the 1940s, Faulkner replaced his biases of the 1920s with a different set of biases, in which both females and blacks could be dismissed from history. Thus, the discursive act of invention in and of itself is value laden. The text strains toward the production of a completeness, a self-containment, that is not technically the Compson family genealogy.[36] Faulkner later objected to the title, suggesting instead "Compson / 1699–1945," because he said, "it's really an obituary, not a segregation."[37] Yet while the appendix extends the available historical information about the Compsons and suggests an obituary because of its measured funereal cadence, it destabilizes its referential text *The Sound and the Fury* by proceeding at several angles of difference in which females and blacks become the oppositional Other to the white, southern, male subjects.

Caddy Compson remains the central, othered presence. Her continuing story is the longest of the chronicles, though length is not the only marker of her centrality. She is the first woman included, and her daughter, Quentin, is the only other female given a place in the family history. Faulkner's gaze is on Caddy and on her relationship to a history which would have been unimaginable in the 1920s. Still transgressing boundaries culturally mandated for females, Caddy is imagined now in Europe, now with a German officer, now with another car, this time foreign-made, all of which project her transgressions onto a wide cultural space and re-embody her as a different southern female.[38] Caddy's precarious position in the 1940s, as an Eva Braun–like figure prostituting herself with evil, speaks to Faulkner's latent sense of the moral corruption of southern white women, such as Ike McCaslin's wife in *Go Down, Moses*, whom Faulkner later spoke of as "ethically a prostitute."[39] Unable to deal openly with his hostilities toward women (especially the women in his family who, he complained, were dependent on him for everything including Kotex and toilet paper), Faulkner deflected his rage and justified his hostility by reincarnating Caddy as spectacle — the face of corruption and evil, "ageless and beautiful, cold, serene and damned" (713).[40] The gap between the social and the cultural domain, between the textuality of the novel's discourse and the sexuality of the female's body, figures the absence of purpose for a woman such as Caddy in any ideology construed as southern by the 1940s.

Caddy is only real within sexual relations with men, but her actuality is always a function of Faulkner's desire for her. Her body is envisioned as a sexual commodity for the pleasure of a man, and yet as a fiction, a textualization, she is always denied Faulkner. Contained within a libidinal economy, as Minrose Gwin points out, Caddy is excluded from participation in any female-based relational activities, and thus she cannot be granted self-consciousness.[41] She must be externally positioned as object to satisfy the male, but only potentially so. That the specific male is a "German staffgeneral" (713) speaks to her lack of morals but more significantly to her lack of historical consciousness. Ultimately, Caddy remains icon, a visual symbol of masculine desire and longing, of male need and loss. In part, the iconography resonates with the author's sense of his own perceived, diminished ability to participate in contemporary history. In standing beside a machine, "an open powerful expensive chromium-trimmed sports car" (712–13), and a German officer, Caddy is appended to both the mechanistic world of power and the militaristic world of power seeking race and class dominance. Her stance is a re-iteration of the disruptiveness marking her presence and absence from the novel proper. In the appendix, however, she is no longer the disruptive feminine voice that Gwin identifies in the novel proper.[42] Although Melissa Meek, "the mouse-sized mouse-colored spinster" (713) who is described in direct relation to her lack of value in a sexual marketplace, would want to ascribe to Caddy a voice crying for help, for salvation, she cannot restore Caddy's language or recover her physicality. Caddy is rendered static and voiceless in the very reproduction of the photograph Melissa Meek covets and protects in her symbolic function as librarian, a preserver of texts, history, and ideology. Caddy exists as a commodity of exchange between Faulkner and the German staff general; in a symbolic sense, she serves as Faulkner's own entrance into the war.

The photograph, unseen by a reader of the text and unseen by the aged Dilsey, is the visualization of the would-be-possible, a concretizing of damnation and doom, which begins the appendix in the representation of Ikkemotubbe, whose name Faulkner insisted was Doom. Ikkemotubbe is the slave-owning chief of the Chickasaw who sold his quadroon concubine and their son, Sam Fathers, in *Go Down, Moses*.

Quentin, the last Compson treated in the appendix, is positioned in relation to doom and biological determinism: "QUENTIN. The last. Candace's daughter. Fatherless nine months before her birth, nameless at birth and already doomed to be unwed from the instant the dividing egg determined its sex" (719). Despite the reference to procreation, Faulkner dooms Quentin not only "to be unwed" but to be barren: "The last." Significantly, if she cannot fulfill the procreative function of the female and cannot inspire the creative function of the male—Faulkner the author—then Quentin's femaleness is threatening and unpredictable, and more dangerous than her mother's. In implicating the mother ("Candace's daughter"), rather than the father ("Fatherless nine months before her birth"), in the formation of Quentin's subjectivity, Faulkner indicts the maternal influence as biological not social. The negative maternal imprint survives the separation and rupture that is the history of Quentin's and Caddy's interaction, and ascribes to Caddy as mother and shaper of her daughter the power of the female as witch.

Quentin cannot recuperate Caddy and, thus, is exiled from both attachment and herself. Theft from her uncle, Jason, of the money sent for her support cannot overcome the physical loss of her mother, and she is represented without access to her desires or to speech. She can only grasp the symbolic materiality of the money, because Faulkner can only represent her in separation from sex and language.[43]

Cowley concludes that "nothing in [Quentin's] subsequent career . . . touched Faulkner's imagination"; however, there is another way to read Faulkner's dismissal of Quentin.[44] The product of his infatuation with Caddy is textual production. Quentin, on the other hand, is biological reproduction, and as such she syphons away the sexual energy that Faulkner explodes into first the novel and then the appendix. Her very existence is a threat to male domination. Faulkner represents Quentin's threat to Jason as economic and legal, to his ownership and his freedom. However, her existence is also a threat to Faulkner's own domination not simply of Caddy but of the text and potential texts she might engender. Writing Quentin out of history dismisses all but the textual progeny of Caddy and of Faulkner's diverted sexual desire. Dismissed from the discourse of desire enveloping and creating her mother, Quentin is not lost, like Caddy, but exiled from the text and the language of future possibility.

With the vanishing of Quentin from the appendix, after a prediction of her unglamorous maturity ("And so vanished; whatever occupation overtook her would have arrived in no chromium Mercedes; whatever snapshot would have contained no general of staff" [721]), the chronicle might well have ended. But it continues: "And that was all. These others were not Compsons. They were black" (721). The "all" already over, finalized or erased, the text begins anew. The project announced as a negative, "not Compsons," can only proceed from the negation of the "others." The othering of the those who "were black" is thus achieved in a few lines of text enclosing the Compson chronicle with its marginal opposite—the four black members of the Gibson family: TP, Frony, Luster, and Dilsey. Racial subjects, like female subjects, result from both representations and discursive practices, but the configuration of power and inequity is more striking in the representation of the blacks because, less antagonistic than that of the two white women, it patronizingly asserts a hierarchy from which the unequal Other is already excluded.

Without a stated history, the four race-defined characters are reduced to their relational status to a present delimited by various subjugations. TP, commodified and clothed by "the owners of Chicago and New York sweatshops," exists as a brightly colored figure attracted to the cheap surface glitter of a market economy. Luster, "a man, aged 14," is locked into both a childhood and a servitude to "an idiot twice his age," though by 1945 Benjamin has been in the State Asylum for twelve years. Frony, "married to a pullman porter," is nonetheless denied either agency or autonomy because her life can only be envisioned in terms of her mother's refusal "to go further" than Memphis, and in her subjugation to the family matriarch who is also always the Compsons', and

Faulkner's, mammy. For, as Lee Jenkins concludes about Faulkner's creation of Dilsey in the novel, "One sees the arrogant self-indulgence of
Faulkner's application of the dicta of his private obsessions, as revealed in
his creation of Dilsey, in honorable commendation of the life of Mammy
Caroline and as the pronouncement of a suitable benediction upon it."[45]

The slippage in the appendix is Faulkner's overdetermination to em-
power Dilsey within the black family though he disempowers her within
the ideological position of a white southern society; that is, she cannot affect either the world at war, Caddy in Europe, or Melissa Meek
in Jefferson. Unimaginable beyond her former place within the white
Compson household, Dilsey does not receive a textual marker. Her name
stands alone, creating an image and icon of the maternal, the caretaker-
caregiver, the undifferentiated Other, whose name melds into a "they":
"They endured." As an oblique reference to Dilsey, "They endured" may
be read as a refusal to re-engage with her character at all. "They endured" signals a pluralistic dismissal of her individual subjectivity and
the collapsing of all of her into all of her primarily male progeny. Her
function already always served within the novel, her positioning in the
Appendix is coda and denouement, not an extension or a clarification or
a reflection. She is situated as emblematically as is Caroline Barr in the
dedication to *Go Down, Moses*, in which "Mammy" and Caroline Barr
and Mississippi coalesce into a single symbolic unit. Yet, ironically, it
is Dilsey who, individuated in the novel, saw the first and the last, and
she who, in the appendix, refuses to see any remnants of the Compsons
at all. She does not gaze on Caddy, does not turn her gaze toward the
clipping of the reproduced photograph that Melissa Meek brings to her.
Whether the image is one of Caddy or not, Dilsey's eyes will not see, will
not speculate. Perhaps, it is out of this sightlessness, this myopic vision
turned now elsewhere to a space that Faulkner cannot occupy or invade,
that Dilsey, in the constructed collectivity of a black race, endured.

Read as a racial epitaph, the words, "They endured," function discursively to ascribe to a subsequent generation the traits and the proclivities
of *a* Dilsey, but not necessarily *the* Dilsey of *The Sound and the Fury*. In
fact, "They endured" may also be connected to Tomey's Turl's descendants in "Delta Autumn" and to the black Beauchamps/McCaslins seemingly erased from *Go Down, Moses*. The words "They will endure" appear
in "The Bear" when Ike McCaslin and his cousin McCaslin Edmonds
debate the meaning of property and ownership in the economic con-

text of southern plantation society, chattel slavery, sharecropping, tenant farming, and commissary ledgers. Ike believes that because of the exploitive economic system, blacks remain tied to the land and the old way of life. He sees it clearly in the records of the commissary ledgers: that portray economic peonage and bondage a quarter century after Emancipation (*Go Down, Moses,* 280–81).

Ike also envisions endurance, which becomes the repeated trope for black life in his explanation to McCaslin and in the descriptor for Dilsey in the appendix. The segment in "The Bear" is explicit: " 'Yes. Binding them for a while yet, a little while yet. . . . But not always, because *they will endure.* They will outlast us because they are—' " (281; emphasis added). While Ike cannot immediately complete his rationale, he does return to it: " 'Because *they will endure.* They are better than we are. Stronger than we are. Their vices are vices aped from white men or that white men and bondage have taught them: improvidence and intemperance and evasion—not laziness: evasion: of what white men had set them to, not for their aggrandizement or even comfort but his own—' " (281; emphasis added). He repeats his sentiment, "they will endure," yet a third time (286). His repetition suggests a truth hard won from the abuses of power and privilege in the plantation world of old Carothers and in the modern world of McCaslin and Ike himself.

The ideologies of right and power and control and tradition explicated in *Go Down, Moses* inform the appendix. Theoretically, the constructions of race and gender function together as a mask for the construction of a writerly self and of autonomy and authority. The subterfuge is conscious. The result is not, as Cowley would have us believe, that Faulkner regarded his creation with "a mixture of horror and unwilling affection," but rather that by means of his creation he reflected on his own position in a material world over which he exercised little control, which is implicit in a letter written to Malcolm Franklin in 1942: "Perhaps the time of the older men will come, the ones like me who are articulate in the national voice, who are too old to be soldiers, but are old enough and have been vocal enough to be listened to, yet not so old that we too have become another batch of decrepit old men looking stubbornly backward at a point 25 or 50 years in the past."[46] His obsessions figure what was to come: the ridiculing of women in texts of the 1950s, the complicated immersions in historical narratives of war, the dismissal of blacks from all but the most benign texts (*Intruder in the Dust* and *The Reivers*).

In constructing his Compsons and Gibsons in the appendix, Faulkner assumes both their different relation to one another (racial and gendered) and to the text already written. But more, he positions them differently in relation to the private and public spheres that the new text seeks to collapse. Faulkner's complicity with hierarchies and divisions he abhorred in foreign ideologues is apparent in his creation of historical objects and subjects governed and predicated on actual social events and economic relationships. The interconnected sets of personal relationships all are contingent on the signature of a specific middle-aged, frustrated Faulkner making a calculated attempt at fixity, at a removal of chaos from his own writerly and personal life, at an assertion of significance and stability of his own place in history. "Appendix / The Compsons / 1699–1945" is an emblem of artistic and social redirection marking *Go Down, Moses* as central to Faulkner's literary production thereafter.

Compensating Property

I wanted to be a nature poet and write hauntingly of southern landscapes lush with brilliant birds, animals green-framed in hanging moss, musky magnolia floral curtains, under spiraling hot, blue white moon spaces, wisteria and lemon-scented verbena, luminous sunscapes of bayous, riggolettes, rivers. I forgot "Poplar Trees Bear a Strange Fruit" and Billie Holiday's real blues, deep roots, blood red leaves, strong limbs, flexing, spreading North and South, charred black bodies, burnt fruit on the bitter vines. And coming of age in the 1960s, I did not forget that within the boundary of Mississippi a symbolic condition exists as signification of the threat to black rights and freedom within the state: Mississippi had not ratified the Thirteenth Amendment to the Constitution, and would not until 16 March 1995, in the last decade of the twentieth century. In 1865 that amendment had outlawed slavery, but Mississippi alone of the states refused to endorse the amendment. While that technicality basically had no impact on the end of slavery either within the United States or within the State of Mississippi, it is a legal legacy that speaks to the notorious recalcitrance of the state and its legal system in the treatment of blacks. In part, the material conditions for blacks in the state and the consensus white perception of the subservience of blacks can be read as giving rise to the cultural logic and ideologies infusing Faulkner's *Go Down, Moses*. Not to know this misses an opportunity to understand how the past informs the present, how race matters for whites—even under absurdly futile circumstances.

And so I could not be a nature poet. Instead, I turned the remnants of my poetic eye to the multiple worlds of the many-layered South, to Faulkner and his images, his discourses, his people, his Tomey's Turls, but also to black agency, black self-interest, and black achievement, as well as the indelible impact of slavery and slave law on the present. I am sometimes comforted, sometimes not, by the intellectual property I claim in these discordant discourses.

In my reflections here, I am asserting the importance of the three "I's" Derrick Bell proposed regarding the history of slavery and slave law: Information, Interpretation, and Inspiration. As Bell has maintained, "the stigma associated with slavery refuses to fade, along with the deeply embedded personal attitudes and public policy assumptions that supported it for so long. Indeed, the racism that made slavery feasible is far from dead . . . and the civil rights gains, so hard won, are being steadily eroded."[47] In pointing to the need for informative and accurate accounts of enslavement, for more interpretations of slavery in American law along with the inspiration of the spirituals that survival in full humanity is possible, Bell has also reminded all Americans that "the real scope and significance of slavery in the nation's past remains repressed," so much so that "most Americans cannot imagine, much less, concede, that black people are now, as were their forebears when they were brought to the New World, objects of barter for those who, while profiting from our existence, deny our humanity. . . . We simply cannot prepare realistically for our future without assessing honestly our past" (31). It is this message of current necessity that has animated my work on this project.

I reassert, too, that Tomey's Terrel and his descendants should not be "unrighted," in order to secure rights and identities for whites, because the exclusion from rights is symptomatic of a lack of power. The power associated with and engendered by rights is not lost on black southerners, like myself, who can recall being voiceless and invisible by the negation and erasure of rights, yet who can also remember being rendered citizen and subject by the affirming presence of rights. Inclusion in and access to the full rights of citizenship, with voting rights, can and did, in fact, change our concept of ourselves and our relation to one another. At the same time, we recognized how ordinary, rather than exceptional, racism is in American society, not simply in southern society. While we tried not to be rendered powerless or voiceless, we foresaw no possible remediation in law. Not that a change in civil-rights law went without being part of an enormous transformation in southern society, as Frederick Wirth has argued in *"We Ain't What We Was"* as part of his view that law creates new realities.[48] The sad reality for most black southerners of my generation is that the tension has persisted between what legal remedies can accomplish and what rights blacks seek to exercise.

In rethinking issues of race, gender, and enslavement at the center of this project, I also acknowledge how profoundly Toni Morrison has rearticulated the project that I claimed when during the political turmoil of the 1960s I could not become a nature poet, and when in 1963, the centenary of the Emancipation Proclamation, freedom for blacks in America was still relative and compromised. Morrison has termed "the fabrication of an Africanist persona [by white American authors] reflexive; an extraordinary meditation on the self; a powerful exploration of the fears and desires that reside in the writerly conscious. It is an astonishing revelation of longing, of terror, of perplexity, of shame, of magnanimity."[49] A "revelation" of shame, it is also a trope enabling the multiple interventions and subversions that energized and expanded late-twentieth-century American literary studies and that promise to continue to do so in the twenty-first.

Until the publication of *Playing in the Dark*, few readers of Morrison's fiction had access to her abiding concern with constructs of racialization in American literary studies, though some readers did know that her master's thesis included a treatment of William Faulkner. For Morrison herself, in her "serious" study of literature as a graduate student at Cornell, it was Faulkner who provided entrée into the concerns that would result decades later in her discourse on race and literary imagination. Her master's thesis, "Virginia Woolf's and William Faulkner's Treatment of the Alienated" (Cornell University, 1955), lends itself to and may be a transference of race issues.

For too long contained within critical readings of Faulkner was not only the assumption that the readers are white, but also the assumption that "white" readers will neither examine the racial Other in the texts nor meditate on the social consequences of the power hierarchy upheld in and by whiteness in the texts—nor tolerate or *read* "black" readers who attempt to do so. In the exercise of authority over the definitions and parameters of the reading field is an assertion of constrictive power. It is akin to Hubert Beauchamp's setting the stakes for the games of draw and stud poker. Power, we know from Foucault's meditations, functions as a form of exclusion, as an assertion of law and will, as a prohibition against freedom, and as a repressive norm.

Because Morrison so well understands both the power of whiteness in American literature and also the necessity for empowering blackness, she has enabled us all to reflect more freely and openly on William Faulkner's achievement as one major white twentieth-century writer who follows Melville in a serious confrontation of race in American life. With more insight, clarity, and artistry than any other white writer of his generation, specifically Hemingway and Fitzgerald, Faulkner represented issues of race, racialization, racial construction, and racial division. Most impressive about his achievement is not that he created black characters and positioned them within his fictional Yoknapatawpha, but rather that he envisioned what Melville represented as "the whiteness of whiteness." Faulkner constructed characters who are consciously white, racialized as white, and depicted the construction of whiteness within southern and American society. As a result, he allowed outsiders to know in ways not otherwise available to them one ongoing narrative of white people in psychological nudity. His treatment of white people, within the normalizing, universalizing elision of racial identity, but with the complexity of the burden of racial subjectivity is an extraordinary achievement, unequaled in the first half of the century and unparalleled in the second. I think here of *As I Lay Dying, The Hamlet, The Town,* and *The Mansion* as the most racialized of Faulkner's work—those with no visible black presence at all.

In his speech, "American Segregation and the World Crisis," delivered at the Twenty-first Annual Meeting of the Southern Historical Association on 10 November 1955, Faulkner stated, "It is our white man's shame that in our present southern economy, the Negro must not have economic equality; our double shame that we fear that giving him more social equality will jeopardize his present economic status; our triple shame that even then, to justify ourselves, we must becloud the issue with the purity of white blood; what a commentary that one remaining place on earth where the white man can flee and have his blood protected and defended by law, is Africa—Africa: the source and origin of the people whose presence in America will have driven the white man to flee from defilement."[50] In a remarkable analogy for one who also urged a "go slow now" response to desegregation, Faulkner links white-skin privilege and shame to the treatment of blacks in the aftermath of *Brown v Board of Education*, the 1954 U. S. Supreme Court decision in response to a suit challenging "separate but equal" public schools in Topeka, Kansas.[51] Faulkner ends that speech with references to slavery in the context of freedom.

> Soon now all of us—not just Southerners nor even just Americans, but all people who are still free and want to remain so—are going to have to make a choice . . . not between color nor race nor religion nor between East and West either, but simply between being slave and being free. And we will have to choose completely and for good. . . . We can choose a state of slavedom; and if we are powerful enough to be among the top two or three or ten, we can have a certain amount of license,—until someone more powerful rises and has us machine-gunned against a cellar wall. But we cannot choose freedom established on a hierarchy of degrees of freedom, on a caste system of equality like military rank. We must be free not because we claim freedom, but because we practice it; our freedom must be buttressed by a homogeny equality and unchallengeably free, no matter what color they are, so that all the other inimical forces . . .—systems political or religious or racist or national—will not just respect us because we practice freedom, they will fear us because we do.[52]

Infusing Cold War rhetoric and ideology into issues of race and desegregation in the United States, he envisions freedom for all in the context of a new freedom, expanding equal rights for blacks.

To own one's color and one's race (racial designation) in a time of pretended obliviousness to *white* as a racial designation is, on reflection, a quite remarkable way of comprehending the unmarked power of race and racial hierarchies. From the teens through the twenties and thirties, more often than not, race for white writers was assumed, naturalized, unmarked if they attended at all to race. The irony is, as Morrison suggests, "Whiteness, alone, is mute, meaningless, unfathomable, pointless, frozen, veiled, contained, dreaded, senseless, implacable. Or so our writers seem to say."[53] Yet the empirical surfaces of their texts reveal something quite different. Although the material consequences of specific movements forward and the act of imagining a future for Butch

Beauchamp within the South may have been too difficult and upsetting for Faulkner to imagine, he nonetheless posed the issue of racial dichotomy and racial definition in the last section of Go Down, Moses in such a way that social identity for Butch is not simply figured as a focus on blackness, as otherness, as displacement, as lack, or as absence.

Throughout the darkest days of legal segregation and racial antagonism, Faulkner's texts engaged a coterie of American critics, both black and white, in discourses on race, even though these critics may have been accused of labeling Faulkner "racist" rather than performing the "racial" criticism they undertook as cultural work. Ralph Ellison, James Baldwin, Irving Howe, and Leslie Fiedler are but a few of the names that come immediately to mind. And throughout my own education in the 1960s and 1970s, I understood that Faulkner's novels, like Thomas Jefferson's Notes on the State of Virginia (1785), manifested the contorted racial ideology and the hierarchical racial thinking that bifurcates so much of American literary, cultural, and social life — and this before the DNA confirmation of Jefferson's having fathered one child (and most probably six children) with Sally Hemings, a woman he kept as slave and concubine beginning in 1787 when she was fourteen and he forty-four.[54] Reading Faulkner meant engaging not merely an aesthetic discourse but a racial discourse as well.

Yet despite all the possibilities of subversion implicit in this strategy, until the late-twentieth-century moment when articulated discourses on race became audible, the utilization of southern literature for race-specific political or aesthetic projects was problematic. Ultimately, the interrogation of race in literature cannot be contained within a dominant ideology that by its very nature subordinates and dismisses or elides any concern with its other. And, as a potential structure for empowering black racial discourse, conventional southern literary discourse is a dead end, because its primary project, across time and space, class and gender, has been a naturalizing of whiteness and a consolidation of a racial hegemony, often under the guise of an alternative American culture or as a different ethnic (but very much white) group.

Every culture, racial hierarchies not withstanding, constructs its social reality out of self-interest. This is not to say that white colleagues in the enterprise of studying the literatures of the South were all of a piece in either their acceptance or rejection of the cultural analysis implicit or explicit in readings by blacks or about race; neither is it to say that the proffered models of analysis and critique were adequate or inadequate. It is to assert that, ultimately, southern literature as it was conventionally defined, as an all-white aesthetic enterprise, as a primarily white cultural project could not adequately contain or accommodate racial difference when that difference was not erased in the creative product or silenced in the critical methodology of a person maintaining a racially marked identity as intricately informing the project. It is perhaps too easy to forget this very simple point when at the end of the twentieth century and the beginning of the twenty-first, southern literature as a field has been reinvigorated by the study of race and by race as a category of analysis on a par with gender.[55] It is a reminder that ownership is as slippery an issue as ever and that intellectual property is a subject with myriad manifestations. Whose story and whose inquiry are questions that remain crucial to the work of a field of study as much as to Faulkner's fiction or Morrison's criticism, for instance. Despite Faulkner's naturalization of whiteness and his objectification of blacks, his texts did accommodate self-conscious and self-reflexive treatments of race, usually in the form of racial difference or of interracial relations.

Faulkner's writing also allowed something else evident in the late George Kent's 1972 *Blackness and the Adventure of Western Culture*. Kent, a tenured professor at the University of Chicago, produced his book within the developing nationalist movement in Chicago. His table of contents lists chapters on Claude McKay, Langston Hughes, Richard Wright, Gwendolyn Brooks, James Baldwin, and—bringing up the rear—William Faulkner.

In Kent's nationalistic critical project, the inclusion of Faulkner is not a gesture toward interracial intertexuality; it is a move toward positioning whites as Other, as the minority, as the object. Kent entitles the chapter "Faulkner and the Heritage of White Racial Consciousness: Notes on White Nationalism in Literature" and proceeds to interrogate Faulkner's iconic presence in the modern American literary landscape. Kent's key terms, "white nationalism" and "white racial consciousness," have much more currency now than they did in the early 1970s. Beginning with the observation that "when confronting Blackness, white writers are free to take a variety of attitudes toward . . . cultural drives, but they cannot escape from the fact that, as much as skin color, the cultural drives are transmitted by cultural instruments as the definition of whiteness," he moves on to the conclusion that for white writers such as Faulkner,

"Blackness" becomes both "a proliferation of racial myth and ritual" and a "validation of whiteness."[56] Kent argues that blacks within the imagination of white authors are "fantasies of symbolic and psychic need" and, thus, manifestations of "sickness." His project engages the larger American cultural landscape, though he is acutely aware of the specificity of region. "If Faulkner overcame aspects of Southern white consciousness, he was still a part of the general American white consciousness and its symbolic needs. The South simply exemplified more concretely the economic and psychological rituals that arise in the confrontation of the white consciousness with Blackness."[57]

Kent's own lapses into essentialism aside, his discourse on white racialism in American literature situates modern southern literature as its originary and positions William Faulkner as the "official text" (or, even, as the "*master* text") with which to decode racial discourse. Kent is noteworthy here for another reason, as Coco Fusco puts it in "Fantasies of Oppositionality": "To ignore white ethnicity is to redouble its hegemony by naturalizing it. Without specifically addressing white ethnicity, there can be no critical evolution of the construction of the other."[58]

Twenty years separate Morrison's and Kent's texts. The intellectual climate for Morrison in the 1990s was quite a different one from that which Kent experienced in the 1970s. In fact, and interestingly so, in 1997 the University Press of Mississippi published *Unflinching Gaze: Morrison and Faulkner Re-Envisioned*, in which critics "respond to the energy that emanates so powerfully from the interplay of Faulkner's and Morrison's literary discourses."[59] Racial discourse has become a given; Cornel West's *Race Matters* or Michael Eric Dyson's *Making Malcolm* or bell hooks's *Black Looks*, all participate in larger conversations about race that command readerly attention, market sales, as well as media play and public discourse. To speak of race, whether to forward theories of the construction of race in literature or to observe relationships of power across race lines, was neither acceptable or expected in the 1970s, when racial discourse was not considered a proper aspect of humanistic studies—of sociological studies perhaps (and only as "race relations"), but not of literary studies. But Kent found, as critics had before and after him, that there did exist a proverbial "back door" through which to enter into the interrogation of race in American literature of the twentieth century: William Faulkner. And William Faulkner wrote the kinds of explorations of white racial consciousness that would allow for serious attention to the black Others also in his books.

Kwame Anthony Appiah has moved against accepting the concept of race: "The truth is that there are no races, there is nothing in the world that can do all the work we ask race to do for us. . . . [including] the evil that is done by the concept [of race], and by easy—yet impossible—assumptions as to its application."[60] Perhaps this is the reasoning that led much of twentieth-century American literature that was not regional (or southern) to erase race from its pages and to naturalize whiteness. Perhaps Appiah is correct. Race has increasingly become metaphorical, as Toni Morrison has observed: "a way of referring to and disguising forces, events, classes, and expressions of social decay and economic division far more threatening to the body politic than biological 'race' ever was. . . . It has a utility far beyond economy, beyond the sequestering of classes from one another, and has assumed a metaphorical life so completely embedded in daily discourse that it is perhaps more necessary . . . than ever before." This elastic conception makes imperative race-conscious studies "as a means of meditation—both safe and risky—on one's own humanity."[61]

The notion of race as a "meditation . . . on one's own humanity" speaks directly to my concern with how property in persons haunts the present. Not surprisingly, it has spoken to many others at the turn of the twenty-first century, including creative writers. Out of just such a meditation, Albert Murray and Michael Harper have, for example, written poems on the subject of Faulkner and race. Murray's "William Faulkner Noun, Place and Verb" remembers a race-encumbered Mississippi and Faulkner's fiction, *Light in August*, *Absalom, Absalom!*, and *Go Down, Moses:*

> believes remembers
> recollects, records in commissary ledgers
> pharaoh-tale-accounts compounded in confounding
> convolutions of all-too-human-impacted
> good intentions which . . .
> reveal (or partly unconceal) himself:
> william faulkner.[62]

In Murray's "mulatto metaphors" and "ever in-creeping miscegenated thickets" lurks the fear of racial illusiveness.

Harper's elegiac poem, "Faulkner's Centennial Poem: September 25, 1997," memorializes Caroline Barr on the occasion of Faulkner's one hundredth birthday. Astutely yoking Faulkner's birth with Mammy Callie and cross-racial suckling, he uses the dedication "To Mammy" from *Go Down, Moses* as the starting point of his contemplation of the convergences of past and present on Caroline Barr's tombstone in a segregated cemetery, on "the edge of the black section / buffer-zone to white Confederates / on campus and off: / Ole Miss," and ultimately on "the spirit of place / in our idioms." His attention to Mammy Callie speaks directly to knotty issues of ownership, property in persons, slavery, and their psychological legacies, all evoked in his lines:

> we are at odds
> in the canebrake; this means
> who is human and who is not;
> the word *suckle* is in "The Bear."[63]

In the concluding stanza, Harper turns his idiom, which functions as "crossroad keys and amulets," to speak directly to Faulkner, with all of the energy, insight, and pain of the blues:

> You were a good postmaster;
> we would like Mammy Callie on a stamp;
> recompense is retribution:
> "My house fell down and I can't live there no mo"
> is what Bessie Smith sang
> about that flood;
> the graves of Ole Miss cannot be empty.

Memory for Harper, as for Murray, is an inescapable part of racial awareness, lingering within and resonating throughout his poem, in which recompense and retribution rest side by side in the material grave and on the figurative stamp, both linked now with the call for reparations for enslavement.

In the final analysis memory, that process of thinking back and reading reflexively, is regenerative. In situating *Go Down, Moses* in terms of political action, of the assertion of civil rights, and of resistance to ideological domination, I am reminded that unpacking social or literary scripts and constructing meaning contributes to the power of narrative in lives. Contemplation of Tomasina's son Terrel enables a meditative engagement with property and rights, with games as narratives of intervention but also produces discourses of hope. The act of resituating this text and its multiple engagements becomes compensation for the material reality that has made fairness and justice difficult to obtain, and apologies and reparations for slavery impossible to effect. Despite my personal optimism or the persuasive arguments of activists for social justice, such as Randall Robinson's on reparations, I am convinced that recent claims for reparation will gain no widespread support within the United States, not even within the most progressive of groups.[64] The reason is, I would speculate, that there is little understanding of enslavement, nor of its horrific toll on human beings and its lasting impact on private and public law in the United States. Yet, I find encouragement in two significant facts: first, in the last quarter of the twentieth century some of America's greatest literature has revisited enslavement and its profound impact on cultural and civic life in the United States, with Toni Morrison's *Beloved* being the high-water mark; and second, in the first year of the new millennium, the California State Assembly passed a resolution urging the United States Congress to study the issue of reparations for slavery.[65]

In the ongoing struggle for justice by descendants of slaves is the seldom forgotten resistance to subjugation and desire for empowerment animating their ancestors. The historical engagements with ownership, property in people in *Go Down, Moses* can foreground the social and legal contests for fairness and power that occur today. These struggles within contemporary strategies of resistance motivate my positioning Tomey's Turl as a "righted" challenge to domination, a "willful" site of resistance to oppression, and an empowered trump, especially for me—someone without the cards to play draw or stud poker, but who, like Turl, takes great pleasure in how the deal goes down.

NOTES

Introduction: The Game of Genre

1 *U.S. v Army*, 24 Fed. Cas. 792 (1859), in *Judicial Cases Concerning American Slavery and the Negro*, ed. Helen Tunnicliff Catterall (1926; reprint, New York: Octagon Books, 1968), 1:248.

2 *Dred Scott v Sandford*, 60 U.S. (19 How.) 393, 403 (1857).

3 Id., 407.

4 *U.S. v Army*, 1:248.

5 *Dred Scott v Sandford*, Id., 407.

6 Helen Merrell Lynd, *On Shame and the Search for Identity* (New York: Harcourt, Brace, 1958), 49. Lynd's pioneering book recognized Faulkner's preoccupation with shame, especially in *Light in August* (see Lynd, *On Shame*, 41–42).

7 William Faulkner, *Go Down, Moses* (1942; reprint, New York: Vintage International Books, 1990), 179; subsequent references appear parenthetically.

8 See my initial reading of Old Ben as a manifestation of the abstract construction, "The Negro" (in *Faulkner's "Negro": Art and the Southern Context* [Baton Rouge: Louisiana State University Press, 1983], 244–46). In a more recent reading of *Go Down, Moses*, Judith Lockyer reached a similar conclusion: "Abstract words like *freedom* and *humility* and *pride* provide the connection between Old Ben and black people" (*Ordered by Words: Language and Narration in the Novels of William Faulkner* [Carbondale: Southern Illinois University Press, 1991], 110).

9 Sontag contrasts time and space in terms of determinism and chance, because she understands time as "thrust[ing] us forward from behind, blow[ing] us through the narrow funnel of the present into the future" (*Under the Sign of Saturn* [New York: Vintage, 1981] 117).

10 Michel Foucault, *Discipline and Punish: The Birth of the Prison*, trans. Alan Sheridan (New York: Pantheon Books, 1977) 194.

11 See my beginning formulation of that reading in "The Game of Courts: *Go Down,*

Moses, Arbitrary Legalities, and Compensatory Boundaries," in *New Essays on Go Down, Moses,* ed. Linda Wagner Martin (New York: Cambridge University Press, 1996), 129–54. See also Thadious M. Davis, "Race Cards: Trumping and Troping in Constructing Whiteness," in *Faulkner at 100: Retrospect and Prospect,* ed. Donald M. Kartiganer and Ann J. Abadie (Jackson: University Press of Mississippi, 2000), 165–79.

12 Kimberlè Crenshaw, Neil Gotana, Gary Peller, and Kendall Thomas, introduction to *Critical Race Theory: The Key Writings that Formed the Movement,* ed. Kimberle Crenshaw, Neil Gotana, Gary Peller, and Kendall Thomas (New York: New Press, 1995), xiii.

13 Patricia J. Williams, *The Alchemy of Race and Rights: Diary of a Law Professor* (Cambridge: Harvard University Press, 1991), 219. Williams's writings on race and law helped to bring a wider audience to critical race theory.

14 Tzvetan Todorov, *Genres in Discourse,* trans. Catherine Porter (Cambridge: Cambridge University Press, 1990), 39.

15 Don Kyle, "Directions in Ancient Sport History," *Journal of Sport History* 10, no. 1 (1983: 7–34). Kyle emphasizes sport as competitive. See also Waldo E. Sweet, *Sport and Recreation in Ancient Greece: A Sourcebook with Translations* (New York: Oxford University Press, 1987), ix. Sweet observes the competitiveness of sport and its absence in recreation.

16 Change and instability, in fact, seem readily observable constants in *Go Down, Moses.* If, as Norbert Elias argues in *The Civilizing Process* (trans. Edmund Jephcott [New York: Urizen Books, 1978]), change is the normal condition of social life, then the representation of society in Faulkner's text adheres to the process of change as normality.

17 The title of the first edition was *Go Down, Moses and Other Stories.* Faulkner insisted that the reference to stories be dropped from all subsequent editions; however, his own announced plan for the book was for it to be "collected short stories, general theme being relation between white and negro races here" (*Selected Letters of William Faulkner,* ed. Joseph Blotner [New York: Vintage, 1978]; 139–40).

18 For historiographies of the text and its composition, see James Early, *The Making of Go Down, Moses"* (Dallas: Southern Methodist University Press, 1972); Joanne V. Creighton, *William Faulkner's Craft of Revision: The Snopes Trilogy, "The Unvanquished," and "Go Down, Moses"* (Detroit: Wayne State University Press, 1977), 85–148; Joseph Blotner, *Faulkner: A Biography,* 2 vol. (New York: Random House, 1974), 2:1064–80; and Michael Grimwood, *Heart in Conflict: Faulkner's Struggle with Vocation* (Athens: University of Georgia Press, 1987), 223–98.

19 Dirk Kuyk Jr., *Threads Cable-strong: William Faulkner's Go Down, Moses* (Lewisburg, Penn.: Bucknell University Press, 1983), 14. Kuyk comments further that the text "refuses to allow us a clear focus or simple juxtapositions and yet compels us by a multitude of devices to try to unify the text, both while we read it and afterwards when we contemplate our experience of reading it" (15).

20 Ibid., 15. Kuyk identifies what critics commonly hold as the unifying features, namely patterns of action and thematic parallels, but while rejecting these as being too re-

ductively simple, he manages to conclude similarly in the final paragraph of his book: "The fundamental pattern of *Go Down, Moses* is thus the paradox. The narrative affirms the static and dynamic patterns of juxtaposition and condensation.... Through these processes, according to *Go Down, Moses,* both myth and history are working toward the freeing of mankind; and both God and man are saying with one voice, 'Let my people go.' These paradoxical patterns are the threads cable-strong that bind *Go Down, Moses* together" (190).

21 Eric J. Sundquist, *Faulkner: The House Divided* (Baltimore, Md.: Johns Hopkins University Press, 1983), 132. Sundquist admits that his reading is speculative, but he points out that his attempt to reconstruct Faulkner's possible thinking about *Go Down, Moses* seems quite plausible given the novel's structure and its complex crises of blood and form (133).

22 Faulkner, *Go Down, Moses,* 257. The information about Tomey's Turl's birth is revealed in the McCaslin commissary ledgers in "The Bear," 255–59. For further information regarding the "night the stars fell," 12–14 November 1833, and its usage as both a marker of time in African American culture and a sign of the future, see Gladys-Marie Fry, *Stitched from the Soul: Slave Quilts from the Ante-bellum South* (New York: Dutton Studio Books, in association with the Museum of American Folk Art, 1990), 90.

23 Todorov, *Genres in Discourse,* 35.

24 Minrose Gwin, "Her Shape, His Hand: The Spaces of African American Women in *Go Down, Moses,*" in *New Essays on* Go Down, Moses, ed. Linda Wagner-Martin (New York: Cambridge University Press, 1996), 98. Gwin views the ledgers from the perspective provided by Toni Morrison's theory of Africanist narrative informing American literature set out in her *Playing in the Dark: Whiteness and the Literary Imagination* (Cambridge, Mass.: Harvard University Press, 1990).

25 Mary Frances Berry, *The Pig Farmer's Daughter and Other Tales of American Justice* (New York: Alfred A. Knopf, 1999), 4. In an earlier essay, Berry uses the phrase "legal elites" to refer to those who count, those who make the ultimate decisions in law ("Judging Morality: Sexual Behavior and Legal Consequences in the Late Nineteenth-Century South," *Journal of American History* 78, no. 3 (December 1991): 835–56; see 836.

26 A. Leon Higginbotham Jr., *In the Matter of Color: Race and the American Legal Process: The Colonial Period* (1978; reprint, Oxford: Oxford University Press, 1980), 391.

27 A. Leon Higginbotham Jr. and Anne F. Jacobs, "The 'Law Only as an Enemy': The Legitimization of Racial Powerlessness through the Colonial and Antebellum Criminal Laws of Virginia," *North Carolina Law Review* 70 (1992): 975. According to Higginbotham and Jacobs, inferiority as a precept functions to protect the ideal of the superiority of whites and the inferiority of blacks. The precept of property works not only to define the enslaved as the master's property and as without humanity but also to deny slaves the fruits of their own labor. Powerlessness, the third of the precepts, operates to ensure the submissiveness and dependency of blacks, whether enslaved or free, and to maintain for subjected blacks "a secondary system of justice with lesser rights and protections and greater punishments than for whites" (975).

28 Peter Bardaglio, *Reconstructing the Household: Families, Sex, and the Law in the Nine-teenth-Century South* (Chapel Hill: University of North Carolina Press, 1995), 29.

29 A. Leon Higginbotham Jr. and Barbara K. Kopytoff, "Property First, Humanity Second: The Recognition of the Slave's Human Nature in Virginia's Civil Law," *Ohio State Law Journal* 50 (1989): 540. In their lengthy essay Higginbotham and Kopy-toff argue from a variety of court cases that those in power in the past, particularly judges, not only ignored the claims of humanity of slaves by recognizing a broad basis of rights in the owner (512), but also "increased the harshness of racial oppression under slavery" (540).

30 Robin West, *Narrative, Authority and Law* (Ann Arbor: University of Michigan Press, 1993), 181.

31 Margaret A. Burnham, "An Impossible Marriage: Slave Law and Family Law," *Law and Inequality* 5, no. 2 (July 1987), 188. Burnham suggests ways in which law can be employed to flesh out the historian's understanding of social conditions existing under slavery (187–225).

32 Patricia J. Williams, *Alchemy of Race*, 233. Williams takes her title, "On Being the Object of Property," from Orlando Patterson who contends that slaves cannot be the subjects of property, only the objects of property. See Patterson's *Slavery and Social Death: A Comparative Study* (Cambridge: Harvard University Press, 1982). Williams subtitles her chapter, "A Gift of Intelligent Rage."

33 Patricia J. Williams, *Alchemy of Race*, 234. On rights, also see James W. Ely Jr., *The Guardian of Every Other Right: A Constitutional History of Property Rights* (New York: Oxford University Press, 1998); Lawrence Becker, *Property Rights: Philosophic Foundations* (London: Routledge, 1977); and George P. Fletcher, *Basic Concepts of Legal Thought* (New York: Oxford University Press, 1996).

34 Charles R. Lawrence III, Mari J. Matsuda, Richard Delgado, and Kimberlè Williams Crenshaw, introduction to *Words that Wound: Critical Race Theory, Assaultive Speech, and the First Amendment* (Boulder: Westview Press, 1993), 5–6. In their explanation of the interdisciplinary methodology of critical race theory, Lawrence et al. refer to several traditions: "liberalism, law and society, feminism, Marxism, post-structuralism, critical legal theory, pragmatism, and nationalism," all of which contribute to the "eclecticism [that] allows critical race theory to examine and incorporate those aspects . . . that effectively enable our voice and advance the cause of racial justice even as we maintain a critical posture" (6).

35 See Lawrence et al., introduction to *Words that Wound*, xiii.

36 Mari J. Matsuda, "Public Response to Racist Speech: Considering the Victim's Story," in *Words that Wound*, ed. Lawrence et al., 19. Matsuda points to the work of outsider jurisprudence as outsiders searching "for what Anne Scales has called the rachet—legal tools that have progressive effect, defying the habit of neutral principles to entrench existing power" (19–20).

37 Ibid., 19.

38 Faulkner may have read "Go Down Death—A Funeral Sermon" and the other sermon poems in James Weldon Johnson's *God's Trombones: Seven Negro Sermons in Verse* (New York: Viking Press, 1927) during the period of its first publication, when Faulk-

ner still considered himself a poet. The elegiac sermon preached by the Reverend Shegog in *The Sound and the Fury* (1929) may well have been influenced by Johnson's sermons in verse. Faulkner's private library did not include any creative works by African Americans from the 1920s, but it seems both plausible and highly likely that he read and was familiar with Johnson's books. Faulkner's usage in his early stories and novels of a Negro folk sermon and preacher in the last part of *The Sound and the Fury* and of blues and jazz, the new music created by African Americans, may well signal his familiarity with the work of James Weldon Johnson. See also my essay, "From Jazz Syncopation to Blues Elegy: Faulkner's Development of Black Characterization," in *Faulkner and Race: Faulkner and Yoknapatawpha, 1986*, ed. Doreen Fowler and Ann Abadie (Jackson: University Press of Mississippi, 1987), 70–92.

39 Frederick Douglass, in *The Life and Writings of Frederick Douglass*, ed. Philip S. Foner, vol. 5 (New York: International Publishers, 1950), 437.

40 Richard Newman, *Go Down, Moses: Celebrating the African-American Spiritual* (New York: Clarkson Potter, 1998), 23. Newman observes that the story of Moses and the Israelites in bondage in Egypt "resonated most strongly with the slaves' bitter experiences, while at the same time promising hope for deliverance" (23). The long version of "Go Down, Moses" printed in Newman's book (68–71) differs from that in James Weldon Johnson and J. Rosamund Johnson, *The Book of American Negro Spirituals: Including The Book of American Negro Spirituals [1925] and The Second Book of American Negro Spirituals [1926]* (New York: Viking Press, 1940). Eddie S. Glaude Jr. compares the historical uses African Americans have made of the Exodus story in constructing both a national identity and a racial ideology in *Exodus!: Religion, Race, and Nation in Early-Nineteenth-Century Black America* (Chicago: University of Chicago Press, 2000).

41 Cornel West, foreword to *Go Down, Moses: Celebrating the African-American Spiritual*, by Richard Newman (New York: Clarkson Potter, 1998), 9. West reminds us that "African-American spirituals constitute the most sustained phenomenology of New World evil. In stark contrast to most artists and intellectuals of European descent, the illiterate, articulate slaves were obsessed with the problem of evil as it pertained to the most undeniable darkness of America—slavery" (10).

42 Ibid., 9–10.

43 Linda Wagner-Martin, introduction to *New Essays on Go Down, Moses*, 9–10. Wagner-Martin distinguishes between Faulkner's focus on pride in texts such as *Absalom, Absalom!* and *The Sound and the Fury* and the turn to shame in *Go Down, Moses*, which she terms a "new start" (7).

44 George P. Fletcher, *Basic Concepts of Legal Thought* (New York: Oxford University Press, 1996), 79. Fletcher uses the biblical account of the debate between God and Abraham over the fate of Sodom and Gomorrah to explain the concept of justice: Abraham pleads that the righteous should not be destroyed with the wicked, and God responds that if Abraham can find fifty just people, he will spare the cities. God eventually reduces the number to ten, at Abraham's urging. Fletcher concludes, "The entire debate proceeds on the assumption that even God is bound by the principle that it is unjust to punish the innocent" (80).

45 There are several written versions of the spiritual, but the most accessible during Faulkner's writing of *Go Down, Moses* was the version published in *The Book of American Negro Spirituals*, edited and introduced by James Weldon Johnson, with musical arrangements by J. Rosamond Johnson (New York: Viking Press, 1925), 51. "Go Down, Moses" is the first spiritual in the volume, appearing immediately after Johnson's lengthy explanatory preface. In 1940 "Go Down, Moses" was again the first of the inclusions in the volume that combined *The Book of American Negro Spirituals* (1925) and *The Second Book of Negro Spirituals* (1926).

46 William Faulkner to Robert K. Haas, Wednesday [22 May 1940], in *Selected Letters*, 124.

47 Although "assaultive speech," as defined by Lawrence, Matsuda, Delgado, and Crenshaw, may seem too harsh to apply to Faulkner's casual use of the term *nigger*, it seems to capture some conception of the damage done by the intentional interjection of a negative, pejorative, and degrading term into a context that does not expect, demand, or reward its usage (Lawrence et al., introduction to *Words that Wound*, 1).

48 Faulkner, *Selected Letters*, 139–40.

49 My initial discussion of the genesis of *Go Down, Moses* appears in Thadious M. Davis, "Crying in the Wilderness: Legal, Racial, and Moral Codes in *Go Down, Moses*," *Mississippi College of Law Review* 4, no. 2 (spring 1984): 299–318 reprinted; in *Critical Essays on William Faulkner: The McCaslin Family*, ed. Arthur F. Kinney (Boston: G. K. Hall, 1990), 137–54.

50 In *The Making of* Go Down, Moses, Early discusses the manuscript changes regarding Tomey's Turl, his transformation from just another black-skinned slave into a near-white brother of his owners (73).

51 Carol M. Rose, *Property and Persuasion: Essays on the History, Theory, and Rhetoric of Ownership* (Boulder: Westview Press, 1994), 27.

52 Cheryl L. Harris, "Whiteness as Property," *Harvard Law Review* 106, no. 8 (June 1993): 1716.

53 A student of Robert Park at the University of Chicago and a teacher at Fisk University in Nashville, Doyle followed Herbert Spencer's idea from *Principles of Sociology* (New York: Appleton, 1882) that "ceremonial government was the most persistent form of social control," and he therefore undertook a study of the external forms in which race relations are symbolized. He was concerned with the forms, behavior, and codes of social usage required by custom and tradition when blacks and whites come into contact (Bertram Wilbur Doyle, *The Etiquette of Race Relations in the South: A Study in Social Contact* [Chicago: University of Chicago Press, 1937], viii, 11).

54 Hortense Powdermaker, *After Freedom: A Cultural Study in the Deep South* (1939; reprint New York: Atheneum, 1968), 23, 369. Powdermaker, who studied with Edward Sapir at Yale University, conducted her research in Mississippi during 1932–1933, completed several months of additional field work in 1934, and finished writing her study in 1936, well before the publication of John Dollard's *Caste and Class in a Southern Town* (New Haven: Yale University Press for the Institute of Human Relations, 1937), the best known of the anthropological studies of Mississippi in the 1930s. Powdermaker assisted Dollard in starting his research in Indianola.

55 *Harry and Others v Decker and Hopkins*, 1 Miss. (1 Walker) 36, 42 (1818).

56 *State v Jones*, 1 Miss. (1 Walker) 83, 84 (1820).

57 Burnham, "An Impossible Marriage," 188.

58 *State v Jones*, 83–86.

59 James T. Currie, "From Slavery to Freedom in Mississippi's Legal System," *Journal of Negro History*, 65, no. 2 (spring 1980): 113, 114–15.

60 *Minor v Mississippi*, 36 Miss. 630 at 634–635 (1859).

61 *Dred Scott v Sandford*, 407.

62 See Miss. Rev. Code, ch. XI, art. 1 (1857), on marriage; ch. XXXIII, art. 51, on contract with free blacks; ch. XXXIII, art. 62, on testimony against whites; ch. XXXIII, art. 51, on literacy; ch. XXXIII, art. 45, on passes.

63 Miss. Rev. Code, ch. XXXIII, art. 9 (1857).

64 There is no Black Code per se, but the statutes of 1865 dealing with the recently freed blacks are known as such.

65 See Miss. Laws, ch. IV, sec. 1 (1865), on suits; ch. IV, sec. 4, on testimony; ch. IV, sec. 3 on marriage; and ch. IV, sec. 1, on personal property.

66 Miss. Laws, ch. V, sec. 1 (1865).

67 See Miss. Laws, ch. XXIII, sec. 1 (1865), on firearms; ch. IV, sec. 1, on farm rentals; and ch. IV, sec. 5, on licensing.

68 Miss. Laws, ch. X, sec. 2 (1870).

69 Miss. Laws, chs. CCXICIV–CCXCV (1870).

70 *United States v Stanley*, 199 U.S. 3 (1883).

71 Miss. Const., art. III, sec. 5 (1890).

72 See Miss. Const., art. XII, sec. 241 (1890, amended 1972).

73 Miss. Const., art. XII, sec. 244 (1890, repealed 1975).

74 Miss. Const., art. XII, sec. 245 (1890).

75 *Sproule v Fredericks*, 69 Miss. 898; 11 So. 472 (1892); *Williams v Mississippi*, 170 U.S. 213 (1898); *Plessy v Ferguson*, 163 U.S. 537 (1896). The *Forest Register* newspaper is referenced in studies of Reconstruction in Mississippi; see for example, Wharton, *The Negro in Mississippi, 1865–1890*, 108, 183, 237.

76 *Plessy v Ferguson*, at 559, 562 (Harlan, J., dissenting). The 1896 Supreme Court ruling in this case has resonated into the contemporary period. For example, twenty years before his appointment to the Supreme Court in 1972, the current Chief Justice, William H. Rehnquist, wrote in a memo to then Supreme Court Justice Robert H. Jackson: "I think *Plessy v Ferguson* was right and should be reaffirmed" (quoted in "The Racial View of the Chief Justice of the United States," *Journal of Blacks in Higher Education* 23 (spring 1999): 72.

77 Neil R. McMillen, *Dark Journey: Black Mississippians in the Age of Jim Crow* (Urbana: University of Illinois Press, 1990), 202. Sidney Fant Davis was a judge in Sunflower County during the 1920s and indicated that "negro law" meant that black-on-black crime was not considered an offense and that blacks accused of petty crimes most often never made a court appearance because they were routinely beaten and flogged as punishment. McMillen concludes, "Under 'negro law' the gravity of any crime was determined in large part by its impact on white interests" (203).

78 Berry states that her formulation in 1971 "were a bit strong for some people," but she had intended to convey "that in any society law reflects the will of the powerful" ("Judging Morality," 835).

79 See Charles J. Kappler, comp. and ed., *Indian Affairs: Laws and Treaties*, 2d. ed. (Washington: Government Printing Office, 1904), 2:356; Mary Elizabeth Young, *Redskins, Ruffleshirts, and Rednecks: Indian Allotments in Alabama and Mississippi, 1830–1860* (Norman: University of Oklahoma Press, 1961), 41–42; Arrell M. Gibson, *The Chickasaws* (Norman: University of Oklahoma Press, 1971), 156; and C. John Sobotka Jr., *A History of Lafayette County, Mississippi* (Oxford, Miss.: Rebel Press, 1976), 20–21.

80 Not surprisingly, women are largely absent from the novel in part because they rarely own property in the world represented in the text, although from a series of legislative acts white women in Mississippi did have their right to property protected by law. The Mississippi Property Act of 1839, for instance, protected white married women's property from their husbands' creditors. See Elizabeth G. Brown, "Husband and Wife: Memorandum on the Mississippi Woman's Law of 1839," *Michigan Law Review* 42 (April 1944): 1110–21; and Sandra Moncrief, "Mississippi Married Women's Property Act of 1839," *Journal of Mississippi History* 47 (May 1980): 110–23.

81 On property, see Mary Jane Radin, *Reinterpreting Property* (Chicago: University of Chicago Press, 1993); Stephen R. Munzer, *A Theory of Property* (Cambridge: Cambridge University Press, 1990); Lawrence C. Becker and Kenneth Kipnis, eds., *Property: Cases, Concepts, Critiques* (Englewood Cliffs, N.J.: Prentice Hall, 1984); and David A. Schultz, *Property, Power, and American Democracy* (New Brunswick, N.J.: Transaction Publishers, 1992).

82 Stephen M. Ross, *Fiction's Inexhaustible Voice: Speech and Writing in Faulkner* (Athens: University of Georgia Press, 1989), 154–55. Ross labels *Go Down, Moses* a psychic text because it is dominated by what one character, Ike McCaslin, knows.

83 Ibid., 155.

84 Rose, *Property and Persuasion*, 5–6. She refers specifically to the work of David Carr, *Time, Narrative, and History* (Bloomington: Indiana University Press, 1986).

85 Todorov, *Genres in Discourse*, 28.

1 · The Game of Challenge

1 Martin J. Osborne and Ariel Rubinstein, *A Course in Game Theory* (Cambridge: MIT Press, 1994), 2.

2 William Faulkner, *Go Down, Moses* (1942; reprint, New York: Vintage International Edition), 3. See Meredith Smith, "A Chronology of *Go Down, Moses*," in *Critical Essays on William Faulkner: The McCaslin Family*, ed. Arthur F. Kinney (Boston: G. K. Hall, 1990), 269–77.

3 Tomey's Turl's parentage becomes the pivotal point in "The Bear," a subsequent chapter of *Go Down, Moses*, in which Ike McCaslin uncovers through reading old commissary ledgers a crucial piece of his family's history: that Carothers McCaslin is both Turl's father and his grandfather, because Turl's mother Tomasina is also

Carothers McCaslin's offspring. The opaque narrative method, veiled in humor and layered in time, thus depends both on storytelling and on reading texts.

4   Philip E. Lewis, "Le Rochefoucauld: The Rationality of Play," in *Game, Play, Literature*, ed. Jacques Ehrmann (Boston: Beacon Press, 1968), 138.

5   Martha Albertson Fineman, introduction to *At the Boundaries of Law: Feminism and Legal Theory*, ed. Martha Albertson Fineman and Nancy Sweet Thomadsen (New York: Routledge, 1991), xiv.

6   Mark V. Tushnet, *The American Law of Slavery, 1810–1960: Considerations of Humanity and Interest* (Princeton, N.J.: Princeton University Press, 1981), 157–59. See also David Brion Davis, *The Problem of Slavery in Western Culture* (Ithaca, N.Y.: Cornell University Press, 1966), 10, 165–66. Davis revisits the historical, moral, and intellectual issues related to the study of slavery and its legacy in *In the Image of God: Religion, Moral Values, and Our Heritage of Slavery* (New Haven, Conn.: Yale University Press, 2001).

7   Ira Berlin, *Many Thousands Gone: The First Two Centuries of Slavery in North America* (Cambridge, Mass.: Belknap Press of Harvard University, 1998), 4.

8   Christian Messenger, *Sport and the Spirit of Play in American Fiction* (New York: Columbia University Press, 1981), 263.

9   Tomey's Turl's game of running is similar to catching games described by Iona and Peter Opie as having the chief object of "reach[ing] a designated place, or accomplish[ing] a particular mission" (*Children's Games in Street and Playground* [Oxford: Clarendon Press, 1969], 124).

10 Leslie Howard Owens, *This Species of Property: Slave Life and Culture in the Old South* (New York: Oxford University Press, 1976).

11 Michael Oriard, *Sporting with the Gods: The Rhetoric of Play and Games in American Culture* (Cambridge: Cambridge University Press, 1991), 263–64. Oriard observes that the "triumphant spirit of the sporting myth" is not entirely displaced even in "The Bear" with its "tragic implications of race and violence" because "Faulkner's genius lay in holding both the myth and its counter-reality in suspension, in undercutting without destroying it all together" (263–64).

12 Johan Huizinga, *Homo Ludens: A Study of the Play Element in Culture* (New York: Harper and Row, 1970), 32.

13 Ibid., 26, 28.

14 Patricia J. Williams, *The Alchemy of Race and Rights: Diary of a Law Professor* (Cambridge, Mass.: Harvard University Press, 1991), 220.

15 In connecting the origin of games to ancient sports, Lewis Spence has speculated that "Athletic energy . . . was in primitive ages regarded as an outpouring of human vigour, the intention of which was to support and fortify the spirits of the dead in their task of producing growth and fertility in the grain crops, in vegetation and in the multiplication of flocks and herbs" (*Myth and Ritual in Dance, Game, and Rhyme* [London: Watts and Company, 1947], vi).

16 Daniel Hoffman, *Faulkner's Country Matters: Folklore and Fable in Yoknapatawpha* (Baton Rouge: Louisiana State University Press, 1989), 115.

17 James A. Snead, *Figures of Division: William Faulkner's Major Novels* (New York:

Methuen, 1986), 191. Snead uses the term in relation to the whole of *Go Down, Moses*, but it seems applicable to the self-conscious distancing of the McCaslin twins from slavery, even though Snead misidentifies the kinship relation between Buck, Buddy, and Turl, whom he calls "their own first cousin" (204).

18 Owens reports the 1845 example from a Maryland plantation and a diary entry (*This Species of Property*, 91).

19 Karen Sanchez-Eppler, "Bodily Bonds: The Intersecting Rhetorics of Feminism and Abolition," *Representations* 24 (fall 1988): 46. The problem with the "presumed alliance between abolitionist goals and domestic values," according to Sanchez-Eppler, is that for feminists it coheres women's power and incarceration in the domestic sphere, while for abolitionists "the domestic values that ostensibly offer a positive alternative to the mores of plantation society simultaneously serve to mask slavery's exploitations behind domesticity's gentler features." For the full argument, see pages 28–59. See also Karen Sanchez-Eppler, *Touching Liberty: Abolition, Feminism, and the Politics of the Body* (Berkeley: University of California Press, 1993).

20 Eric Dunning and Chris Rojek, "Introduction: Sociological Approaches to the Study of Sport and Leisure," in *Sport and Leisure in the Civilizing Process: Critique and Counter-Critique*, ed. Eric Dunning and Chris Rojek (Toronto: University of Toronto Press, 1992), xi.

21 Used to explain such phenomena as cooperation, revenge, pressure, or threats, the theory of repeated games also "examine[s] the logic of long-term interaction. It captures the idea that a player will take into account the effect of his current behavior on the other players' future behavior" (Osborne and Rubinstein, *A Course in Game Theory*, 133).

22 In their decoding of the language of personal adornment, Mary Ellen Roach and Joanne Bubolz Eicher state that personal adornment functions as a facilitator in social rituals and as a sexual symbol ("The Language of Personal Adornment," in *The Fabrics of Culture: The Anthropology of Clothing and Adornment*, ed. Justine M. Cordell and Ronald A. Schwarz [New York: Mouton, 1979], 7–21). See also Helen Bradley Foster's introduction to *"New Raiments of Self": African American Clothing in the Antebellum South* (Oxford: Berg, 1997), 1–17.

23 I first noticed Faulkner's deployment of games in *Light in August*; in that text, he specifically uses the language of moves and players in a game of chess in the narration of Joe Christmas's death. During the same period of composing the stories that would form *Go Down, Moses*, Faulkner also completed the detective stories that became *Knight's Gambit* (1948) and that also incorporate the strategies of chess. Mary Montgomery Dunlap cites numerous allusions to chess in "William Faulkner's 'Knight's Gambit' and Gavin Stevens," *Mississippi Quarterly* 23 (1970): 223–39.

24 Reuben Fine, *The Psychology of the Chess Player* (New York: Dover, 1967), 10. Fine reviews Ernest Jones's "The Problem of Paul Morphy" (read to the British Psychoanalytical Society in 1930 and published in 1931) and concludes from Jones that in chess the "unconscious motive actuating the players is not the mere love of pugnacity characteristic of all competitive games, but the grimmer father-murder. The mathematical quality of the game gives chess a peculiar anal-sadistic quality. The sense

of overwhelming mastery on the one side matches that of inescapable helplessness on the other. It is this anal-sadistic feature that makes the game so well adapted to gratify at the same time both the homosexual and antagonistic aspects of the father-son contest" (1). See also Fine's "General Remarks on Chess," 11–26.

25 Elliott Hearst and Michael Wierzbicki, "Battle Royal: Psychology and the Chessplayer," in *Sports, Games, and Play: Social and Psychological Viewpoints*, ed. Jeffrey H. Goldstein (Hillsdale, N.J.: Lawrence Erlbaum Associates, 1979), 30–32, 55.

26 "Was" is a comic prefiguration of the denied obsessions of the narrator Ike and, as Nancy B. Sederberg outlines, of the more serious hunts presented throughout the narrative ("'A Momentary Anesthesia of the Heart': A Study of the Comic Elements in Faulkner's *Go Down, Moses*," in *Faulkner and Humor: Faulkner and Yoknapatawpha, 1986*, ed. Doreen Fowler and Ann J. Abadie [Jackson: University Press of Mississippi, 1986], 79–96). She bases her reading on Henri Bergson's *Laughter: An Essay in the Meaning of the Comic* (New York: Macmillan, 1911).

27 A. James Casner and W. Barton Leach, *Cases and Text on Property*, 3d ed. (Boston: Little, Brown, 1984), 10.

28 *Pierson v Post*, 3 Caines 175, 2 Am. Dec. 264 (New York Supreme Court 1805). For the complete judgment, see John Proffatt, comp., *The American Decisions: Cases of General Value and Authority Decided in the Courts of the Several States from the Earliest Issue of the State Reports to the Year 1869* (San Francisco: Lawyers Co-op. Publishing, 1910), 264–67.

29 Joseph William Singer, "Property," in *The Politics of Law: A Progressive Critique*, ed. David Kairys (New York: Basic Books, 1998), 241–42. Singer points out, "Individual labor and first possession appear legitimate interests that others should respect," and that while "*Pierson v. Post* is often used to make this point" (241), this view is not accurate because, historically speaking, property rights in the United States have not followed the rule of first possession or of labor.

30 Faulkner visited Stone at Yale in April 1918 because he needed to escape Oxford before his sweetheart married someone else. His romance with Estelle Oldham had ended disastrously, and on 18 April 1918 she was to marry Cornell Franklin, a lawyer who coincidentally studied law at the University of Mississippi. Faulkner roomed with Stone who was to complete his L.L.B. in the summer. See Joseph Blotner, *Faulkner: A Biography*, 2 vol. (New York: Random House, 1974), I:203–4.

31 See Susan Snell, "Phil Stone and William Faulkner: The Lawyer and the Poet," *Mississippi College of Law Review* 4, no. 2 (1984): 169–92, and her biography, *Phil Stone of Oxford: A Vicarious Life* (Athens: University of Georgia Press, 1991).

32 See Jay Watson's enumeration of the attorneys in Faulkner's personal history and social circle in *Forensic Fictions: The Lawyer Figure in Faulkner* (Athens: University of Georgia Press, 1993), 6–10. Watson also observes that in November 1924 Phil Stone published an endorsement for Faulkner's first book, *The Marble Faun*, in the *Yale Alumni Weekly*: "this poet is my personal property. . . . I urge all my friends and class-mates to buy his book" (quoted in Jay Watson, *Forensic Fictions*, 10). I find the use of *property* striking not only for its statement of possession and occupancy but also for its connection to sale and purchase and thus by extension to slavery.

33 Morris Wolff, for instance, appraises Faulkner as "an excellent [amateur] 'curbstone lawyer'" ("Faulkner's Knowledge of the Law," *Mississippi College of Law Review* 5 [spring 1984]: 245). See also Michael Millgate, *Faulkner's Place* (Athens: University of Georgia Press, 1997), 96–109. In a chapter entitled "Undue Process: Faulkner and the Law," Millgate takes up both Faulkner's knowledge of law and his representation of "the persistent failure and even perversion of the legal system" as a "symbol of the profound malaise within society at large" (97).

34 Carol M. Rose, *Property and Persuasion: Essays on the History, Theory, and Rhetoric of Ownership* (Boulder, Colo.: Westview Press, 1994), 9. See also her consideration of *Pierson v Post*, 12–14.

35 Ibid., 13.

36 Ibid.

37 C. B. Macpherson, "The Meaning of Property," in *Property: Mainstream and Critical Positions*, ed. C. B. Macpherson (Toronto: University of Toronto Press, 1978), 3.

38 See Patricia J. Williams, *Alchemy of Race and Rights*, 156–57 for a discussion of *Pierson v Post*.

39 Oriard contends in his chapter "Play, Sport, and Southern Honor" that sport, the duel, and hospitality were the social rituals in which honor in the South found expression (*Sporting with the Gods*, 83).

40 Huizinga, *Homo Ludens*, 27.

41 William Faulkner, interview by Jean Stein, in *Lion in the Garden: Interviews with William Faulkner, 1926–1962*, ed. James B. Meriwether and Michael Millgate (New York: Random House, 1968), 255. Faulkner clearly intended to stress the symbolic, referential complexity of the title because he changed the name of the story from "Almost" (narrated by young Bayard Sartoris of *The Unvanquished* and in reference to the almost-entrapment in marriage) to "Was" (narrated by the boy Isaac McCaslin and in reference to a temporal space).

42 *Allen v Freeland*, in Tushnet, *American Law of Slavery*, 160.

43 Quoted in Margaret A. Burnham, "An Impossible Marriage: Slave Law and Family Law," *Law and Inequality* 5, no. 2 (July 1987): 200.

44 Like *Go Down, Moses, Sanctuary* contains an extended description of a poker game, the wager, the question ("'Who dealth these cards, Eustace?'"), and the outcome (a pass leading to Graham's win). The second poker game in *Go Down, Moses* echoes and expands the account of the poker game in the livery stable in *Sanctuary*, with Eustace Graham occupying the places of both Tomey's Turl (the dealer) and Buddy McCaslin (the phenomenal card player and winner). See William Faulkner, *Sanctuary* (1931; reprint, New York: Vintage Books, 1987), 275–76.

45 Tushnet, *American Law of Slavery*, 157, 158–59.

46 Ibid., 157–58.

47 For explanations of the card games in "Was," see Robert L. Yarup, "The Poker Game in 'Was,'" *Explicator* 41 (summer 1983): 43–45, reprinted in *Critical Essays on William Faulkner: The McCaslin Family*, ed. Arthur F. Kinney (Boston: G. K. Hall, 1990): 278–79; Carl Anderson, "Faulkner's 'Was': 'A Deadlier Purpose than Simple Pleasure,'" *American Literature* 61, no. 3 (October 1989): 414–28; and Nancy Dew Tay-

lor, *Annotations to William Faulkner's* Go Down, Moses (New York: Garland, 1994), 25–29.

48 Snead, *Figures of Division*, 192.

49 See E. N. Elliot's 1860 proslavery writings quoted in Thomas D. Morris, *Southern Slavery and the Law, 1619–1860* (Chapel Hill: University of North Carolina Press, 1996), 62.

50 Charles A. Reich, "The New Property," in *Property: Mainstream and Critical Positions*, ed. C. B. Macpherson (Toronto: University of Toronto Press, 1978), 180. Reich concludes, "It is as if property shifted the burden of proof; outside, the individual has the burden; inside, the burden is on government to demonstrate that something the owner wishes to do should not be done" (180).

51 Cornel West, epilogue to *Race Matters* (New York: Vintage, 1994), 156–57.

52 Quoted in Jeffrey H. Goldstein, "Outcomes in Professional Team Sports: Chance, Skill, and Situational Factors," in *Sports, Games, and Play: Social and Psychological Viewpoints*, ed. Jeffrey H. Goldstein (Hillsdale, N.J.: Lawrence Erlbaum Associates, 1979), 406. Goldstein's observation that "outcome may be based on chance and situational variables" (407) is useful to consider in relation to Tomey's Turl role in the poker game. See also E. J. Langer, "The Illusion of Control," *Journal of Personality and Social Psychology* 32 (1975): 311–28.

53 Michael Omi and Howard Winant, *Racial Formation in the U.S.: From the 1960s to the 1990s* (New York: Routledge, 1994), 61.

54 Henry Louis Gates Jr., "Writing 'Race' and the Difference It Makes, in *"Race," Writing, and Difference*, ed. Henry Louis Gates Jr. (Chicago: University of Chicago Press, 1985), 5.

55 Berlin, *Many Thousands Gone*, 13.

56 Faulkner's representation of Tomey's Turl is largely comic and mainly arises out of the tradition of minstrelsy. Turl moves slowly, speaks in humorous riddles, and plays the fool; his appearance and its incongruities (particularly his near-white skin) become the object of ridicule.

57 Walter Johnson, *Soul by Soul: Life Inside the Antebellum Slave Market* (Cambridge, Mass.: Harvard University Press, 1999), 13.

58 See Mary Frances Berry, *Black Resistance/White Law: A History of Constitutional Racism in America*, rev. ed. (New York: Penguin, 1995), xi.

59 Berlin, *Many Thousands Gone*, 2. On the basis of exhaustive research, Berlin insists that slavery was a negotiated relationship, however asymmetrical and despite the power of the masters and their maintenance of the institution by brute and violent force. He states that "although racial domination took many forms, at critical moments some white and black people met as equals and stood shoulder-to-shoulder against those they deemed a common enemy. And on some rare occasions, slaves enjoyed the upper hand. Although much of slave life took shape beyond the masters' eyes from sundown to sunup, slaves also created their own world under the owners' noses from sunup to sundown" (5).

60 See Osborne and Rubinstein, *A Course in Game Theory*, 255. "A coalitional model is distinguished from a noncooperative model primarily by its focus on what groups

of players can achieve rather than on what individual players can do and by the fact that it is does not consider the details of two groups of players function internally" (255–56).

61 See William Goodell, *The American Slave Code in Theory and in Practice: Distinctive Features Shown by Its Statutes, Judicial Decisions, and Illustrative Facts* (1853; reprint, New York: Negro Universities Press, 1968), 309. *The American Slave Code*, a compilation, was originally published by the American and Foreign Anti-Slavery Society to disseminate information about the evils of slavery.

62 According to Vernon Bartlett, "Most games of dice are played in order to win something from somebody else, but many of them really come in the category of games that are designed to avoid boredom" (*The Past of Pastimes* [Hamden, Conn.: Archon Books, 1969], 18).

63 Joseph C. Mihalich, *Sports and Athletics: Philosophy in Action* (Totowa, N.J.: Littlefield, Adams, 1982), 80.

64 Throughout the nineteenth century and well into the twentieth, men of science and learning believed that blacks were insensitive to pain and suffering because, like Indians, they were closer to a "savage" rather than civilized state. See S. Weir Mitchell, "Civilization and Pain," *Journal of the American Medical Association* 18 (1892); and A. P. Merrill, "An Essay on Some Distinctive Peculiarities of the Negro Race," *Memphis Medical Recorder* 4 (1855).

65 Alan Hyde, *Bodies of Law* (Princeton, N.J.: Princeton University Press, 1997), 48. Hyde believes a "chief function of law in advanced societies is to provide a totalizing vocabulary, under which people will become incapable of articulating any modalities of human interaction except as the relations between buyers and sellers in markets, and between bearers of abstract rights" (48).

2 · The Object of Property

1 Faulkner's text creates some confusion about Turl's appearance by using three different shades to refer to his skin color. See *Go Down, Moses*, 6, 26, 28.

2 Orlando Patterson takes the view of common law that in neither sociological nor economic terms can relations exist between a person and a thing and that slavery is condition of power and not merely the treatment of human beings as property (*Slavery and Social Death: A Comparative Study* [Cambridge, Mass.: Harvard University Press, 1982], 20, 21–22).

3 Thomas D. Morris, *Southern Slavery and the Law, 1619–1860* (Chapel Hill: University of North Carolina Press, 1996), 2, 57. See also Morris's chapter "Slaves as Property—Chattels Personal or Realty, and Did It Matter?" (61–80). Morris concludes that the statutory definition of slaves as "chattel personal, or as realty, or as an immovable did next to nothing to benefit the slave. These were not moral categories, they were legal categories" (77).

4 C.B. Macpherson, "The Meaning of Property," in *Property: Mainstream and Critical Positions*, ed. C. B. Macpherson (Toronto: University of Toronto Press, 1978).

5 John Locke, *Two Treatises of Government*, ed. Peter Laslett (New York: Mentor, 1965),

305–6. Locke maintains that the origin of property lies in labor and comes into existence when a person applies labor to objects that belong to no one: "Whatsoever, then, he removes out of the State that Nature hath provided, and left it in, he hath mixed his *Labour* with, and joyned to it something that is his own, and thereby make it his *Property*. . . . For this *Labour* being the unquestionable Property of the Labourer, no Man but he can have a right to what that is once joyned to, at least where there is enough, and as good left in common for others" (306). Locke's underlying conception is that individuals "own" themselves, have property in themselves.

6 John Stuart Mill, *Principles of Political Economy with Some of Their Application to Social Philosophy*, 2 vol. (New York: D. Appleton, 1899), I: 298–99. Mill's commentary on the subjects of property is in book 2 ("Distribution") chapter 2 ("Property"), part 7; however, his discussion of slavery is in chapter 5 ("Of Slavery"), 314–20.

7 Thomas D. Morris, *Southern Slavery*, 1; emphasis added. Morris develops the connection between race and enslavement, and between color and slavery in his chapter "Race in Southern Slave Law," 17–36.

8 In a discourse on law and property Jeremy Bentham states, "That which in the natural state was an almost invisible thread, in the social state becomes a cable. Property and law are born together. Before laws were made there was no property; take away laws and property ceases" (*Principles of the Civil Code* (1802), in *The Works of Jeremy Bentham*, ed. John Bowring [Edinburg: William Tait, 1843], 2:297–358).

9 Jean-Jacques Rousseau, *Discourse on the Origins of Inequality* (1755, trans. Franklin Philip, ed. Patrick Coleman (Oxford: Oxford University Press, 1994); however, that same year in his *Discourse on Political Economy*, he presented the right to property as the most sacred of rights and the foundation of civil society.

10 See Miss. Laws, ch. 46, p. 72 (1839). In five sections, "An Act for the protection and preservation of the rights of Married Women" provided that "any married woman may become seized or possessed of any property, real or personal, by direct bequest, demise, gift, purchase, or distribution, in her own name, and as of her own property: *Provided*, the same does not come from her husband after coverture" (ch. 46, sec. 1). The remaining four sections all pertained to a woman's possession of property in slaves and their increase.

11 Elizabeth G. Brown, "Husband and Wife: Memorandum on the Mississippi Woman's Law of 1839," *Michigan Law Review* 42 (April 1944): 1114–15. Brown's groundbreaking, detailed article presents the possible origins of the Married Woman's Law of 1839, the historical debate and public responses to the statute, and a comparison between the Mississippi law and subsequent married women's property laws in Michigan (1844), Maine (1844), and New York (1848), and a Texas state constitution provision (1845), as well as the earlier Territory of Orleans civil law (1807) of the Louisiana Territory (Brown 1110–21). One aspect of Brown's important research on the history of the law is *Fisher v Allen*, 2 Howard (Miss) 611 (1837), a case she uncovered that involves a Chickasaw woman's right to prevent her property (one of the slaves left to her by her father) from being confiscated by her husband's creditor. Betsy Love Allen was able to prevent Fisher from confiscating the slave she had deeded to her daughter, Susan, because her marriage to John Allen was a valid

Chickasaw union under which the husband acquired no right to the wife's property. *Fisher v Allen* may have been one of the precursors of the Married Woman's Law of 1839 (Brown 1117-18). See also Sandra Moncrief, "The Mississippi Married Women's Property Act of 1839," *Journal of Mississippi History* 47 (May 1980): 110-25, which is based on Brown's pioneering work.

12 Jay Watson, *Forensic Fictions: The Lawyer Figure in Faulkner* (Athens: University of Georgia Press, 1993), 3.

13 Martha Albertson Fineman, "Introduction" to *At the Boundaries of Law: Feminism and Legal Theory*, ed. Martha Albertson Fineman and Nancy Sweet Thomadsen (New York: Routledge, 1991), xiii.

14 *Harry and Others v Decker and Hopkins*, 1 Miss. (1 Walker) 36, 42 (1818). In the case of a petition for freedom for three individuals who had been in the Northwest Territory, the decision was "in favor of liberty" when its ordinance and sixth article declared against the existence of slavery and involuntary servitude, and when the state of Indiana adopted its constitution, including the sixth article of the Northwest ordinance. The ruling was that "if the petitioners were not freed by the 6th article of the ordinance, they became so by the adoption of the constitution of Indiana." Moreover, since the people of Indiana were declared free, "Slavery is condemned by reason and the laws of nature. It exists and can only exist through municipal regulations, and in matters of doubt, . . . the courts must lean '*in favorem vitae et libertatis.*'" This condemnation of slavery and support of liberty would not be repeated in Mississippi's subsequent legal history.

15 *State v Jones*, 1 Miss. (1 Walker) 83, 84 (1820).

16 *State v Jones*, 1 Miss. (1 Walker) 84-85 (1820).

17 Zillah R. Eisenstein, *The Female Body and the Law* (Berkeley: University of California Press, 1988), 46. Eisenstein emphasizes that "law as a discourse occupies a space between the 'real' and 'idea.' . . . Law operates as a political language because it establishes and curtails choices and action" (46). In the first half of the nineteenth century, laws regulating slavery became increasingly restrictive in defining the rights of the enslaved.

18 *State v Mann*, 13 N.C. 168 (1829).

19 *State v Mann*, 13 N.C. (2 Dev.) 263 (1829), in Mark V. Tushnet, *The American Law of Slavery, 1810-1960: Considerations of Humanity and Interest* (Princeton, N.J.: Princeton University Press, 1981), 55-58. See Harriet Beecher Stowe, *A Key to Uncle Tom's Cabin: Presenting the Original Facts and Documents upon which the Story Was Founded. Together with Corroborative Statements Verifying the Truth of the Work* (Boston: John P. Jewell, 1854), 147-48.

20 *Minor v Mississippi*, 36 Miss. 630 at 634-635 (1859).

21 William Blackstone, *Commentaries on the Laws of England*, 4 vol. (1769; reprint, Chicago: University of Chicago Press, 1979). Although Blackstone objected to slavery as "repugnant to reason," his definition of property was extended to slave property in the colonial period.

22 Among the important documentary texts are John W. Blassingame, ed., *Slave Testimony: Two Centuries of Letters, Speeches, Interviews, and Autobiographies* (Baton Rouge:

Louisiana State University Press, 1977); James Mellon, ed., *Bullwhip Days: The Slaves Remember, An Oral History* (New York: Avon Books, 1988); John Langston Gwaltney, *Drylongso: A Self Portrait of Black America* (1980; reprint, New York: New Press, 1993); Ira Berlin, Barbara J. Fields, Steven F. Miller, Joseph P. Reidy, and Leslie S. Rowland, eds., *Free at Last: A Documentary History of Slavery, Freedom, and the Civil War* (Edison, N.J.: Blue and Grey Press, 1997).

23 See, for example, Frances Smith Foster, *Written by Herself: Literary Production by African American Women, 1746–1892* (Bloomington: Indiana University Press, 1993); Jennifer Fleischner, *Mastering Slavery: Memory, Family, and Identity in Women's Slave Narratives* (New York: New York University Press, 1996). Fleischner answers Nell Irvin Painter's call in "Soul Murder and Slavery: Toward a Fully Loaded Cost Accounting" for analysis of the psychological costs of slavery (in *Black on White: Black Writers on What It Means to Be White*, ed. David R. Roediger (1995; reprint, New York: Schocken Books, 1998). See also Painter's *Southern History across the Color Line* (Chapel Hill: University of North Carolina Press, 2002), 15–39; John W. Blassingame, *The Slave Community: Plantation Life in the Antebellum South* (1972; reprint, New York: Oxford University Press, 1979); and Herbert Gutman, *The Black Family in Slavery and Freedom, 1750–1925* (New York: Vintage Books, 1977).

24 Henry Bibb to William Gatewood, 23 March 1844, in Blassingame, *Slave Testimony*, 48–49. Bibb states that his only regret is that he did not run away earlier in his life.

25 Henry Bibb to Albert G. Sibley, 23 March 1852 in Blassingame, *Slave Testimony*, 49–50.

26 Henry Bibb to Albert G. Sibley, 7 October 1852, in Blassingame, *Slave Testimony*, 53.

27 Miss. Rev. Code, ch. xi, art. 1 (1857); ch. xxxiii, art. 51, 62, 45, 9.

28 Davidson Burns McKibben, "Negro Slave Insurrections in Mississippi, 1800–1865," *Journal of Negro History* 34, no. 2 (January 1949): 73–94; on the insurrection of 1835, see 76–79. See also Christopher Morris, "An Event in Community Organization: The Mississippi Slave Insurrection Scare of 1835," *Journal of Social History* 22, no. 1 (1988): 92–111.

29 E. N. Elliott quoted in Thomas D. Morris, *Southern Slavery*, 62.

30 George M. Stroud, *A Sketch of the Laws Relating to American Slavery in the Several States of the United States of America* (1827; reprint, New York: Negro Universities Press, 1968), 11.

31 Karl Kroeber, *Retelling/Rereading: The Fate of Storytelling in Modern Times* (New Brunswick, N.J.: Rutgers University Press, 1992), 71.

32 Importantly, however, though he does not speak at length and remains largely inarticulate within the text, Tomey's Turl does express himself and his expressive gestures signal his inner dynamic, his needs, his desires, his wants, all of which circulate within his relational stance to running away and to courting Tennie on a neighboring plantation, despite his masters' disapproval.

33 Peter Kolchin, *American Slavery, 1619–1877* (New York: Hill and Wang, 1993), 111; emphasis added.

34 Williams explains that defenses in contract law play up the powerlessness of victims who plead duress, undue influence, or fraud: "most successful defenses feature

women, particularly if they are old and widowed; illiterates; blacks; and other minorities; the abjectly poor; and the old and infirm. A white male student of mine once remarked that he couldn't imagine 'reconfiguring his manhood' to live up to the 'publicly craven defenselessness' of defenses like duress and undue influence" (*The Alchemy of Race and Rights: Diary of a Law Professor* (Cambridge, Mass.: Harvard University Press, 1991), 155–56.

35 Ibid., 160.

36 See Catherine Clinton, *The Plantation Mistress: Woman's World in the Old South* (New York: Pantheon Books, 1982), 6. Clinton argues that "Patriarchy was the bedrock upon which the slave society was founded, and slavery exaggerated the pattern of subjugation that patriarchy had established."

37 William Waller Hening, *The Statutes at Large: Being a Collection of All the Laws in Virginia, from the First Session of the Legislature in the Year 1619*, 13 vol. (Richmond, Va.: W. Gray Printers, 1819–1823), 2:170. See also A. Leon Higginbotham Jr., *In the Matter of Color: Race and the American Legal Process: The Colonial Period* (1978; reprint, Oxford: Oxford University Press, 1980), 43. Higginbotham reads the built-in bias of the drafters of the statute in their alarm not at fornication but at interracial fornication as "more immoral and deviant" (43–45). Thomas D. Morris cites two earlier cases that suggest confusion in the law before the 1662 law. In a 1652 Virginia case a planter sold a black girl who was only ten years old "with her Issue and produce during her (or either of them) for their Life tyme" and "their Successors forever"; and in a 1655–1656 case, Elizabeth Key, the daughter of a slave woman by a white man, won her freedom on the basis of her father's status: "by the Common Law the Child of a Woman slave begott by a freeman ought to bee free" (*Southern Slavery*, 44).

38 Although initially under Common Law a child born to an unmarried woman belonged to no one, by the eighteenth century the child of unmarried parents followed the condition of the mother. The Virginia slave law from the seventeenth century (1662) predates the codification in English Common Law.

39 Higginbotham, *In the Matter of Color*, 44.

40 Angela Y. Davis, *Women, Culture, and Politics* (New York: Vintage Books, 1990), 47. Though class considerations may seem inapplicable to women in slavery, they must be taken into account in order to encompass the multifaceted aspects of enslaved women's identities. In this instance, caste may be a viable substitute.

41 *State v Mann*, 13 N.C. 266 (1829).

42 Higginbotham, *In the Matter of Color*, 9.

43 Melton A. McLaurin, *Celia, a Slave* (1991; reprint, New York: Avon Books, 1993), 21. McLaurin recounts the story of Celia's purchase, rape, and sexual violation at the hands of Newsom, and the narrative of her trial for his murder when, after five years of sexual abuse and having borne two children by Newsom, she killed him. On the night before her execution in December 1855, the then nineteen-year-old Celia admitted that in attempting to protect herself, she had killed Newsom: "as soon as I struck him the Devil got into me, and I struck him with the stick until he was dead, and then rolled him into the fire and burnt him up" (quoted in McLaurin, *Celia*, 135).

44 Ibid., 138.

45   *State v Mann*, 13 N.C. 266 (1829). See also John Spencer Bassett, *Slavery in the State of North Carolina* (Baltimore: Johns Hopkins University Press, 1899), 23–24.

46   Constance Hill Hall's *Incest in Faulkner: A Metaphor for the Fall* (Ann Arbor, Mich.: UMI Research Press, 1986) does not include the incest so central to *Go Down, Moses*. More recently, Gwendolyn Chabrier, in *Faulkner's Families: A Southern Saga* (Staten Island, N.Y.: Gordian Press, 1993), does make mention of Carothers's incestuous relations with his mulatto daughter as "the only example in Faulkner's work of consummated incest, at least where immediate family members were involved" (129). Karl F. Zender also addresses "L. Q. C. McCaslin's incestuous coupling with his daughter Tomasina as an act of sexual tyranny parallel in meaning with the curse of possession" and domination of the earth in *Go Down, Moses* ("Faulkner and the Politics of Incest," *American Literature* 70, no. 4 [December 1998], 755).

47   Thomas R. R. Cobb, *Inquiry into the Law of Negro Slavery* (Philadelphia: T. S. J. W. Johnson, 1858), 2:99. In assembling his compendium, Cobb allowed that the slave was both person and property, but he placed the slave largely outside the formulations and protections of common law.

48   Ibid., 90.

49   Peter Bardaglio, *Reconstructing the Household: Families, Sex, and the Law in the Nineteenth-Century South* (Chapel Hill: University of North Carolina Press, 1995), 39.

50   *Ward v Dulaney*, 23 Miss. 410, at 426 (1852).

51   Reinhold Niebuhr, *Moral Man and Immoral Society: A Study in Ethics and Politics* (1932; reprint, New York: Charles Scribner's Sons, 1960), xx.

52   Ibid., xxii–xxiii.

53   Joel Williamson, *New People: Miscegenation and Mulattoes in the United States* (1980; reprint, New York: New York University Press, 1984), 54.

54   Sigmund Freud, *Three Essays on the Theory of Sexuality*, trans. James Strachey (New York: Basic Books, 1962), 91.

55   David Cole, "Strategies of Difference: Litigating for Women's Rights in a Man's World." *Law and Inequality* 2 (February 1984): 45. Cole's argument has been used by feminist legal theorists to engage the way law exists inside privilege that is gendered male and hierarchical.

56   Eisenstein's chapter "The Engendered Discourse(s) of Liberal Law(s)" takes up the issue of the classification of women within law, but it does not take up the difference of race or of enslavement. See especially Eisenstein, *Female Body and the Law*, 55. Eisenstein also quotes Catherine MacKinnon's similar view on women within law. MacKinnon states that in law women can be the same as men, "the male standard" and "gender neutrality"; or women can be different from men, that is "the female standard" or "special protection": "You can be the same as men, and *then* you will be equal, or you can be different from men, and then you will be *women*" ("Feminist Discourse, Moral Values, and the Law: A Conversation," *Buffalo Law Review* 34 (winter 1985): 20, 21.

57   White women were, as Nancy Isenberg has pointed out, "subject to paternal considerations because they were, in theory, political subjects in the miniature government of the family. They were not only seen to be lacking a will of their own but

were treated as though they were suffering from the same disability as resident aliens; that is they were classified as having partial or dual allegiance" (*Sex and Citizenship in Antebellum America* [Chapel Hill: University of North Carolina Press, 1998], 34). In an 1849 Massachusetts suit brought by a black female to oppose separate schools for blacks, Chief Justice Lemuel Shaw applied common law in his decision that women, as much as children, were entitled to paternal protections and considerations, but they were not entitled to the same civil and political powers as men (*Roberts v City of Boston*, 59 Mass. [5 Cush.] 206 [1849]).

58 Saidiya V. Hartman, *Scenes of Subjection: Terror, Slavery, and Self-Making in Nineteenth-Century America* (New York: Oxford University Press, 1997), 97. Harriet Jacobs's *Incidents in the Life of a Slave Girl: Written by Herself* (ed. Jean Fagan Yellin [1861; reprint, Cambridge, Mass.: Harvard University Press, 1987]) is a specific example of the different production of female gender to which Hartman refers.

59 Clinton, *Plantation Mistress*, 221–22.

60 Mary Frances Berry, *Pig Farmer's Daughter and Other Tales of American Justice* (New York: Alfred A. Knopf, 1999), 242, 183. Berry devotes a chapter, "Suffer the Children: Incest and Rape," to the court's treatment of rape and incest cases.

61 Eugene D. Genovese, *Roll, Jordan, Roll: The World the Slaves Made* (New York: Pantheon, 1974), 417; emphasis added. Genovese's lapse in failing to observe the dynamic of power in describing sexual relations between slave owners and slaves as love is not typical of his study.

62 Patricia J. Williams, *Alchemy of Race*, 17.

63 Ibid., 19.

64 Ibid.

65 Angela Y. Davis, *Women, Race, and Class* (New York: Vintage Books, 1983), 23–24.

66 Ibid., 24.

67 Nell Irvin Painter, "Soul Murder and Slavery," 327.

68 Quoted in Williamson, *New People*, 55–56. Williamson does not cite the name of the family or the repository for the letter; he states, "A copy of this letter is in my possession. This material was supplied to me through the courtesy of an archive in which the papers of this family are deposited" (202). The testator, however, is clearly the prominent politician James Henry Hammond of South Carolina. See also Drew Gilpin Faust, *James Henry Hammond and the Old South: A Design for Mastery* (Baton Rouge: Louisiana State University Press, 1982), 87. Hammond bought Sally and her year-old daughter, Louisa, in 1839. He fathered children by Sally, made Louisa his concubine as soon as she turned twelve, and produced more children with her.

69 Carol Bleser, *Secret and Sacred: The Diaries of James Henry Hammond, a Southern Slaveholder* (New York: Oxford University Press, 1988), 17–21, 212–13.

70 Margaret A. Burnham, "An Impossible Marriage: Slave and Family Law, *Law and Inequality* 5, no. 2 (July 1987): 194. Burnham distinguishes between the ideology which under "civil law of marriage and child legitimation did not apply to the slave," and the concept of "nature's laws grouping men, women, and children in family formation . . . because the slave *had* a family of owners" (195).

71 Ibid., 189.

72 Ibid.

73 Mary Boykin Miller Chesnut, *A Diary from Dixie*, ed. Ben Ames Williams (Cambridge, Mass.: Harvard University Press, 1961), 162. See also C. Vann Woodward, *Mary Chestnut's Civil War* (New Haven, Conn.: Yale University Press, 1981), 26; and Elisabeth Muhlenfeld, *Mary Boykin Chesnut: A Biography* (Baton Rouge: Louisiana State University Press, 1981).

74 Clinton observes, "Each huge southern household conferred proportionate authority on the 'father' of the vast plantation family. These dependents . . . formed a solid base of power that extended into the apparatus of the state. The more dependents, the more power, and the more power, the larger the share of influence within the state apparatus. Thus, slavery, while it did not alone create women's oppression, did accentuate sex roles and perpetuated women's subordinate status" (Clinton, *Plantation Mistress*, 6).

75 Harris apparently put up Emeline and their two daughters as collateral for his loans, and repeatedly pawned his shadow family as a way of paying his debts. The cycle stopped in 1858 with Harris's acceptance of an advance for Emeline, Delia, and Hellen from Col. Falkner, who took the three into his yard to live. Joel Williamson, *William Faulkner and Southern History* (New York: Oxford University Press, 1993), 64–73.

76 Ibid., 64.

77 Thomas D. Morris, *Southern Slavery*, 102.

78 *Bryan v Walton*, 14 Georgia 200 (1853).

79 Williamson, *William Faulkner and Southern History*, 64.

80 See James Early's explanation of Faulkner's attempts to achieve aesthetic unity for the disparate stories by means of the fourth part of "The Bear" (*The Making of* Go Down, Moses [Dallas: Southern Methodist University Press, 1972], 4).

81 Jacobs, *Incidents*, 51. See the chapter entitled "Sketches of Neighboring Slaveholders," in which Jacobs compiles a veritable litany of the abuses in slavery. She suggests, "If you want to be fully convinced of the abominations of slavery, go on a southern plantation, and call yourself a negro trader. Then there will be no concealment; and you will see and hear things that will seem to you impossible among human beings with immortal souls" (52).

82 Ibid., 52.

83 See Robin West, "Economic Man and Literary Woman: One Contrast," in *Law and Literature: Text and Theory*, ed. Lenora Ledwon (New York: Garland, 1996), 127–38.

84 Oliver Wendell Holmes Jr., quoted in Thomas D. Morris, *Southern Slavery*, 61.

85 Sojourner Truth, "When Woman Gets Her Rights Man Will Be Right" (1867), in *An Anthology of African-American Feminist Thought*, ed. Beverly Guy-Sheftall (New York: Free Press, 1995), 37. See also Nell Irvin Painter's chapter, "Woman Suffrage," in *Sojourner Truth: A Life, A Symbol* (New York: W. W. Norton, 1996), 220–33.

86 Williams, *Alchemy of Race*, 159.

87 Ibid., 164–65.

88 Patterson, *Slavery and Social Death*, 5.

89 Anna Julia Cooper, quoted in Bert James Loewenberg and Ruth Bogin, eds., *Black*

Women in Nineteenth-Century American Life (University Park: Pennsylvania State University Press, 1976), 319. See also Wilma King, " 'Suffer with Them till Death': Slave Women and Their Children in Nineteenth-Century America," in *More than Chattel: Black Women and Slavery in the Americas*, ed. David Barry Gaspar and Darlene Clark Hine (Bloomington: Indiana University Press, 1996): 147–68. King points out, "Slave women, unable to control their fertility or to make necessary decisions about their own bodies, had little to say about feminity, values, or what would eventually happen to their children" (148).

90 Dorothy Roberts, *Killing the Black Body: Race, Reproduction, and the Meaning of Liberty* (New York: Pantheon Books, 1997), 23. Roberts states, "The social order established by powerful white men was founded on two inseparable ingredients: the dehumanization of Africans on the basis of race, and the control of women's sexuality and reproduction. The American legal system is rooted in this monstrous combination of racial and gender domination" (23).

91 Eisenstein, *Female Body and the Law*, 79–80.

92 Ibid., 93.

93 Thomas D. Morris, *Southern Slavery*, 90.

94 King, " 'Suffer with Them till Death,' " 147.

95 Edward Said, *Culture and Imperialism* (New York: Alfred A. Knopf, 1993), 56.

96 See Noel Polk, " 'How the negros [*sic*] became McCaslins too . . . ': A New Faulkner Letter," *Southern Cultures* (fall 1999): 103–8. Polk suggests that the newly uncovered letter now authorizes the reading of miscegenation and incest, though he also adds that the letter "does not change the problematic nature of Isaac's reading or misreading . . . since of course the letter is external to the novel. It may well, however, force readers to question why Faulkner did not put the information more directly into the ledgers" (107).

97 For example, Leon F. Litwack reasons, "Every slave had the capacity for outrage and resistance. And no slaveholding family, especially one which thought it commanded the affection and loyalty of its blacks, could know for certain when any one of them might choose to give expression to his or her outrage and what form that expression would take" (" 'Blues Falling Down like Hail': The Ordeal of Black Freedom," in *New Perspectives on Race and Slavery in America: Essays in Honor of Kenneth M. Stampp*, ed. Robert H. Abzug and Stephen E. Maizlish (Lexington: University of Kentucky Press, 1986), 110.

98 Adrian Howe, "The Problem of Privatized Injuries: Feminist Strategies for Litigation," in *At the Boundaries of Law: Feminism and Legal Theory*, ed. Martha Albertson Fineman and Nancy Sweet Thomadsen (New York: Routledge, 1991), 149.

99 Entry in the Rowland Chambers Diary, 11 June 1860, quoted in Leslie Howard Owens, *This Species of Property: Slave Life and Culture in the Old South* (Oxford: Oxford University Press, 1976), 94; see also 93, 95–96. Owens bases his conclusions regarding "fatalistic suicide" on Emile Durkheim, *Suicide: A Study in Sociology* (New York: Free Press, 1951), 276.

100 Traci C. West, *Wounds of the Spirit: Black Women, Violence, and Resistance Ethics* (New York: New York University Press, 1999), 63.

101 The description of Eunice's trancelike walk into the creek is suggestive of the accounts of slaves who drowned themselves in a ritualistic attempt to return home. Owens states, "slaves who had recently arrived from Africa sang songs in the evening and then some walked in a trance to the ocean and drowned while trying to swim home" (*This Species of Property*, 94).

102 See also Monique Guillory, "Under One Roof: The Sins and Sanctity of the New Orleans Quadroon Balls," in *Race Consciousness: African-American Studies for the New Century*, ed. Judith Jackson Fossett and Jeffery A. Tucker (New York: New York University Press, 1997), 67–92. Guillory traces the commercialization of the mixed-race and near-white women in the New Orleans quadroon balls.

103 Hortense J. Spillers, "Interstices: A Small Drama of Words," in *Pleasure and Danger: Exploring Female Sexuality*, ed. Carole Vance (Boston: Routledge, 1984), 78. Spillers reiterates her reservations about applying the term *sexuality* in the context of enslavement in "Mama's Baby, Papa's Maybe: An American Grammar Book," *Diacritics* 17, no. 2 (summer 1987): 64–81.

104 Patricia Hill Collins, *Black Feminist Thought: Knowledge, Consciousness, and the Politics of Empowerment* (New York: Routledge, 1990), 123–24.

105 bell hooks, *Killing Rage: Ending Racism* (New York: Henry Holt, 1995), 16, 12. hooks surmises that blacks were taught to repress their rage as part of the colonizing process, and the lessons continue to resonate today. She quotes Toni Morrison on how expressing rage might have saved Pecola, the little black girl who is brutalized and dehumanized in *The Bluest Eye:* "anger is better, there is a presence in anger" (12).

106 Robin West, "The Difference in Women's Hedonic Lives: A Phenomenological Critique of Feminist Legal Theory," *Wisconsin Women's Law Journal* 3 (1987): 81–145.

107 Traci C. West, *Wounds of the Spirit*, 55.

108 While I take Mulenfeld's point that Eunice's suicide shames "the race who wronged and dehumanized her" (and in particular I would reference Ike McCaslin as a representative of that race and also of the family), I am less certain that Eunice's suicide "empowers her descendants." Elisabeth Muhlenfeld, "The Distaff Side: The Women of *Go Down, Moses*," in *Critical Essays on William Faulkner: The McCaslin Family*, ed. Arthur F. Kinney (Boston: G. K. Hall, 1995), 205. Spillers sees enslaved women as psychically as well as physically wounded by the sexual use of their bodies for breeding slaves ("Mama's Baby, Papa's Maybe," 64–81).

109 *George, a Slave v State*, 37 Miss. 316, 318, 320 (1859).

110 *George, a Slave v State*, id. at 317. A Mississippi statute passed after *George v State* made the rape of a black female under the age of twelve by a slave or black freeman a crime punishable by death or whipping (1859 Miss. Laws 102).

111 Thomas D. Morris, *Southern Slavery*, 306.

112 Traci West further states that although shame is "precipitated and initiated by acts . . . it can seep into our consciousness and become rooted in who we are. Thus it functions as more than simply a response to acts that we have done or endured, in the way that guilt does. Because shame has a psychic identity, it can readily merge with the social stigmas based on race and gender that are usually already at work on black women's psyches" (*Wounds of the Spirit*, 67).

113   Paul Finkelman, introduction to *Race and Law before Emancipation*, vol. 2, *Race, Law, and American History: The African American Experience*, ed. Paul Finkelman (New York: Garland, 1992), vii.

114   Henry Bibb to William Gatewood, 23 March 1844, in Blassingame, *Slave Testimony*, 49.

115   See Faulkner's sketch, "New Orleans," published in the *Double Dealer* (January–February 1925), and his representation of New Orleans in *Absalom, Absalom!*; see also Violet Harrington Bryan, *The Myth of New Orleans in Literature: Dialogues of Race and Gender* (Knoxville: University of Tennessee Press, 1993), 79–94.

116   Taylor, *Annotations*, 153. Taylor speculates that the repetition of the words "*Fathers will*" in connection with both Thucydus and Tomey's Turl and of the words "*bought by*" in connection with their mothers link the two in being sons of slave owners— Tomey's Turl in Carothers McCaslin's case and Thucydus in the case of Carothers McCaslin's father.

117   Deborah Gray White, *Ar'n't I a Woman?: Female Slaves in the Plantation South* (New York: W. W. Norton, 1985), 68. White cites the narratives of Henry Bibb, William Wells Brown, and Josiah Henson, among others, as examples of the mirroring of the black man's powerlessness in the abuse of the women in his family.

118   Lillian Feder, *Crowell's Handbook of Classical Literature* (New York: Harper Colophon, 1964), 421.

119   Thucydides, *The Peloponnesian War*, bk. 1, ch. 22, quoted in Charles Joyner, "Texts, Texture, and Context: Toward an Ethnographic History of Slave Resistance," in *Varieties of Southern History: New Essays on a Region and Its People*, ed. Bruce Clayton and John Salmond (Westport, Conn.: Greenwood Press, 1996), 21–40. In what I take to be a fortuitous link to my connecting his epigraph for an essay on slave resistance to a black and enslaved character in Faulkner, Joyner begins his essay, "The day dawned bleak and chill that Friday in the Virginia Tidewater, and a gray light out of the northeast seemed to envelop everything." The sentence echoes the opening of the fourth section (the Dilsey, Easter Sunday section) of Faulkner's *The Sound and the Fury:* "The day dawned bleak and chill."

120   Thomas D. Morris cites the *Revised Statutes of the State of North Carolina*, 1:590; see his discussion of the dissatisfaction with marriage prohibitions as an embarrassing aspect of slave law (*Southern Slavery*, 29).

121   *State v Samuel*, 19 N.C. (2 Dev. and Bat.) 179 (1836). Ruffin held that the very concept of legal marriage could not pertain to slaves because it contradicted "the law of nature and of reason": "How can that be deeded to any purpose a legal marriage, which does not, in any respect, conform to the only legal regulations upon the subject of marriage?" (180, 181–82). He presumed both the immorality of slaves and the right to control their slave property.

122   Burnham, "Impossible Marriage," 211.

123   See ibid. for examples of owner impediments or encouragement to slave marriages. In Mississippi during 1870 Republican Governor James L. Alcorn revealed that 3,427 blacks in thirty-one counties purchased marriage licenses, as compared to 2,204 whites (Gutman, *Black Family*, 429). See also Amy Dru Stanley, *From Bondage to Con-*

tract: *Wage Labor, Marriage, and the Market in the Age of Slave Emancipation* (Cambridge: Cambridge University Press, 1998). Stanley argues that in emancipation, contract of marriage and wage labor signaled freedom and self-ownership, and that contract served to distinguish between the commodity relations of freedom and bondage.

124 White, *Ar'n't I a Woman?*, 86. White presents several cases in which slave women clearly controlled their ability to reproduce. One suggestive example is a South Carolina case (1869) in which a woman sold as barren and "unsound" in 1857 produced three children after emancipation (85).

125 *Frazier v Spear* 5 Ky. (2 Bibb) 385, 386 (1811).

126 Burnham, "Impossible Marriage," 216.

127 Patterson, *Slavery and Social Death*, 50.

128 *Alfred, a Slave v State*, 37 Miss. 296 (1859).

3 · The Game of Boundaries

1 Ken Binmore, *Essays on the Foundation of Game Theory* (Cambridge: Basil Blackwell, 1990), 3. In defining a game, Binmore states, "A game is being played by a group of individuals whenever the fate of an individual in the group depends not only on his own actions but also on the actions of the rest of the individuals in the group" (1). He includes activities for which the designation "game" is unfamiliar but in which the welfare of individuals depends as much on the actions of others as on their own (e.g., "war, the arms race, competition for survival among animals or for status among humans, international treaty negotiations, wage bargaining, elections, or the operation of market economies, 1).

2 Peter Brooks, *Reading for the Plot: Design and Intention in Narrative* (New York: Alfred A. Knopf, 1984), xiv.

3 Ibid., xi.

4 Jennifer Nedelsky, "Law, Boundaries, and the Bounded Self," *Representations* 30 (spring 1990): 162. Nedelsky argued in an earlier study that in the development of the American Constitution, the concept of property served to define the notion of rights as limit, and "that this notion is an attempt to address the inevitable tension between the individual and the collective" (*Private Property and the Limits of American Constitutionalism* [Chicago: University of Chicago Press, 1991], 164).

5 Patricia J. Williams, *The Alchemy of Rights and Reason: Diary of a Law Professor* (Cambridge, Mass.: Harvard University Press, 1991), 164.

6 Peter Kolchin, *American Slavery, 1619–1877* (New York: Hill and Wang, 1993), 111.

7 See Susan Willis, "Aesthetics of the Rural Slum: Contradictions and Dependency in 'The Bear,' " *Social Text* 2 (summer 1979): 82–103; Francis Lee Utley, Lynn Z. Bloom, and Arthur F. Kinney, eds. *Man, Bear, and God: Seven Approaches to William Faulkner's "The Bear"* (New York: Random House, 1964); Albert J. Devlin, "History, Sexuality, and the Wilderness in the McCaslin Family Chronicle," in *Critical Essays on William Faulkner: The McCaslin Family*, ed. Arthur F. Kinney (Boston: G. K. Hall, 1990), 189–98; and Lawrence Buell, "Faulkner and the Claims of the Natural World,"

in *Faulkner and the Natural World: Faulkner and Yoknapatawpha, 1996*, ed. Donald M. Kartiganer and Ann J. Abadie (Jackson: University Press of Mississippi, 1999), 1–18.

8 John T. Matthews's chapter, "The Ritual Mourning in *Go Down, Moses,*" is a reading that emphasizes the articulation of grief, mourning, and loss (*The Play of Faulkner's Language* [Ithaca, N.Y.: Cornell University Press, 1982], 213–73).

9 Orlando Patterson, *Freedom*, vol. 1, *Freedom in the Making of Western Culture* (New York: Basic Books, 1991), xiii. Patterson also calls attention to the work of David Brion Davis, particularly *The Problem of Slavery in Western Culture*, in which Davis undertakes to explain why slavery was redefined as evil, both morally and socioeconomically, in the late eighteenth century and to demonstrate that "the promotion of personal liberty" rather than emancipation of enslaved blacks was "the latent ideological significance of the antislavery movement" in the United States (Patterson, *Freedom*, xiii).

10 Doreen Fowler, *Faulkner: The Return of the Repressed* (Charlottesville: University Press of Virginia, 1997), 149.

11 Ibid.

12 See William Blackstone, *Commentaries on the Laws of England*, 4 vol. (1769; reprint, Chicago: University of Chicago Press, 1979), 4:374.

13 I use the term metaphorically here to suggest the way in which after their marriage Rider and Mannie were bound in a utopian idealization, a unity that collapsed their separate identities into one. Marylynn Salmon explains that unity of person in American law was merely an ideal, not an actuality, but it was never completely abandoned as a legal principle. The concept of unity of person under common law was that after marriage men and women no longer acted as individuals but together constituted a legal entity with specific rights, responsibilities, and restrictions (mainly against women) in which their interests were bound together under law (*Women and the Law of Property in Early America* [Chapel Hill: University of North Carolina Press, 1986], 14–15).

14 The game of *apodidraskinda*, which Pollux describes, may be the equivalent of hide-and-seek, according to the *Britannica Micropaedia Ready Reference*, 15th ed., vol. 5 (Chicago: Britannica, 1992): 913.

15 J. Bowyer Bell, *To Play the Game: An Analysis of Sports* (New Brunswick, N.J.: Transaction Books, 1987), 61. Bell points out that, in effect, games "play much the same role as does the individual superego, monitoring and reflecting the raw demands that the id makes on the ego. The more effective the superego, the less strain and disturbance, the more perfect the adjustment" (61). Moreover, he points out that whether deployed on a conscious or unconscious level, "To use one game in opposition to another, to devise an optional game, to build or raze a game for nongame purposes— all the conscious or unconscious uses of *a* game are on the microgametic strategic level" (143).

16 See the entry "Children's Games" in *Colliers' Encyclopedia*, vol. 6 (New York: Macmillan, 1995): 226J–226L.

17 *Colliers' Encyclopedia* (ibid.) places a social, developmental spin on children's games and in particular older games such as hide-and-seek.

18 Binmore, *Essays on the Foundation of Game Theory*, 1. Binmore cautions that parlor games and real-life games should not be taken as absolutely similar, but that the analogy holds for their strategic aspects.

19 Roth Edmonds as the representative of that system runs the business of the plantation and controls the commissary, both of which have contractual authority over the lives of black sharecroppers like Lucas.

20 This point is developed by Mary Frances Berry, *The Pig Farmer's Daughter and Other Tales of American Justice* (New York: Alfred A. Knopf, 1999), 4.

21 Antebellum southern white ideology accounts in part for the inconsistencies and instability in the laws of slavery because whites were both divided and ambivalent about the justice of enslavement as well as the nature of slave personality. See William W. Fisher III, "Ideology and Imagery in the Law of Slavery," *Chicago-Kent Law Review* 68, no. 3 (1993), 1051–83; see especially 1080–81.

22 J. Bowyer Bell, *To Play the Game*, 1.

23 John T. Matthews, "Touching Race in *Go Down, Moses*," in *New Essays on Go Down, Moses*, ed. Linda Wagner-Martin (Cambridge: Cambridge University Press, 1996), 34.

24 Mark V. Tushnet, *The American Law of Slavery, 1810–1960: Considerations of Humanity and Interest* (Princeton, N.J.: Princeton University Press, 1981), 148.

25 *George v State*, 37 Miss. 316 (1859); see Tushnet, *American Law of Slavery*, 85.

26 *Dred Scott v Sanford*, 60 U.S. (19 How.) 393, 407 (1856).

27 Patterson, *Freedom*, 4.

28 Nedelsky, "Law, Boundaries, and the Bounded Self," 183.

29 Nedelsky emphasizes that the fear of having spatial and psychological boundaries invaded by those in need is accompanied by an assertion of rights, of entitlement to protection from contact with or awareness of the needy (ibid.).

30 See Carol Shammas, Marylynn Salmon, and Michael Dahlin, *Inheritance in America: From Colonial Times to the Present* (New Brunswick, N.J.: Rutgers University Press, 1987), 37. This line of inheritance under common law is explained in Blackstone, *Commentaries*, 2:208–38.

31 Herbert G. Gutman provided extensive tables on black marriages after freedom, drawn from records of the republican administrations, particularly in North Carolina and Mississippi (*The Black Family in Slavery and Freedom, 1750–1925* (New York: Vintage Books, 1977), 429, 425–31.

32 John W. Blassingame, *The Slave Community Plantation Life in the Antebellum South* (1972; reprint, New York: Oxford University Press, 1979), 164–65. Blassingame found that enslaved men often vowed never to marry rather than to face the consequences of vulnerability to the sale, separation, and mistreatment of their loved ones.

33 Implicit in Turl's determination to marry and to have that marriage acknowledged publically is the conception of marriage as an institution intended "to create a public structure of rights and duties, not alterable by the wills, goals, or desires of husbands and wives," or in the case of slaves, the owners (Hendrik Hartog, "Marital Exits and Marital Expectations in Nineteenth-Century America," *Georgetown Law Journal* 80 [1991]: 95).

34 Gregory S. Alexander, *Commodity and Propriety: Competing Visions of Property in American Legal Thought, 1776–1970* (Chicago: University of Chicago Press, 1997), 162. Although Alexander has a chapter on slavery, "Commodifying Humans: Property in the Antebellum Legal Discourse of Slavery," which is an analysis of the impact of commodification on proslavery legal discourse, he does not examine blacks or slaves in his analysis of marriage as a contract and legal institution (211–40). For an analysis of marriage and its significance for blacks after emancipation, see Amy Dru Stanley, *From Bondage to Contract: Wage Labor, Marriage, and the Market in the Age of Slave Emancipation* (Cambridge: Cambridge University Press, 1988).

35 One of Faulkner's starting points for the book that was to become *Go Down, Moses* was the short story "A Point of Law," which together with "Gold Is Not Always" became "The Fire and the Hearth" (the second chapter of the book). For historiographies of the text and its composition, see Joanne V. Creighton, *William Faulkner's Craft of Revision: The Snopes Trilogy, "The Unvanquished," and "Go Down, Moses"* (Detroit: Wayne State University Press, 1977), 85–148; James Early, *The Making of Go Down, Moses* (Dallas: Southern Methodist University Press, 1972); and Michael Grimwood, *Heart in Conflict: Faulkner's Struggles with Vocation* (Athens: University of Georgia Press), 223–98.

36 See Lee Jenkins's relevant treatment of Ash's racialization and its representation in his inadequacy and inability to become a hunter, and on the brotherhood of hunters. *Faulkner and Black-White Relations: A Psychoanalytic Approach* (New York: Columbia University Press, 1981), 243.

37 Elisabeth Muhlenfeld, "The Distaff Side: The Women of *Go Down, Moses*," in *Critical Essays on William Faulkner: The McCaslin Family*, ed. Arthur F. Kinney (Boston: G. K. Hall, 1995), 198.

38 Recent studies attempt to explore more fully the gender issues related to both men and women within the text. See, for example, Minrose C. Gwin, *The Feminine and Faulkner: Reading (Beyond) Sexual Difference* (Knoxville: University of Tennessee Press, 1990); and Diane Roberts, *Faulkner and Southern Womanhood* (Athens: University of Georgia Press, 1994). See also Jay Martin, "Faulkner's 'Male Commedia': The Triumph of Manly Grief," and Anne Goodwyn Jones, "Male Fantasies? Faulkner's War Stories and the Construction of Gender," both in *Faulkner and Psychology: Faulkner and Yoknapatawpha, 1991*, ed. Donald M. Kartiganer and Ann J. Abadie (Jackson: University Press of Mississippi, 1994).

39 Blackstone, *Commentaries*, 1:430.

40 Salmon points out that although married women continued to be femes coverts in the 1830s, they were increasingly able to control their own property and to maintain separate estates. She identifies the improvement in property laws as evolutionary, a part of the process of social and political change, which included "increasing economic diversification and stability, legal professionalism, improvement in women's education, shifting attitudes toward marriage that arose with liberal divorce laws, and the enhanced social roles of women that came with republican motherhood" (*Women and the Law*, xvi–xvii).

41 J. Bowyer Bell, *To Play the Game*, 6.

42 Johan Huizinga, *Homo Ludens: A Study of the Play Element in Culture* (New York: Harper and Row, 1970), 31.

43 Huizinga posits that in "its earliest phases culture has the play-character. In the twin union of play and culture, play is primary. It is an objectively recognizable, a concretely definable thing, whereas culture is only the term which our historical judgment attaches to a particular instance" (*Homo Ludens*, 66).

44 Iona and Peter Opie, *Children's Games in Street and Playground* (Oxford: Clarendon Press, 1969), 178.

45 Leo Frobenius, quoted in Huizinga, *Homo Ludens*, 34–35.

46 Reuben Fine, *The Ideas Behind the Chess Openings* (New York: David McKay, 1949), 4. Faulkner seems to return to the idea of the gambit not only in *Go Down, Moses* and *Knight's Gambit* but also in the major narratives throughout the remainder of his career. His now famous Nobel Prize speech (1950) is a primary example.

47 J. Bowyer Bell, *To Play the Game*, 129.

48 See A. H. Maslow's pyramid diagram of human needs in his assessment of human psychology in *Motivation and Personality* (New York: Harper and Row, 1970).

49 Judith Sensibar reads the world of the hunt as "homosocial and homoerotic" and Sam Fathers as mothering Ike ("Who Wears the Mask? Memory, Desire, and Race in *Go Down, Moses*," in *New Essays on* Go Down, Moses, ed. Linda Wagner-Martin (Cambridge: Cambridge University Press, 1996), 110.

50 Thomas Atkinson, *Handbook of the Law of Wills and Other Principles of Succession Including Intestacy and Administration of Decedents' Estates*, 2d ed. (St. Paul, Minn.: West Publishing, 1953), 1.

51 Henry Campbell Black, *Black's Law Dictionary: Definitions of the Terms and Phrases of American and English Jurisprudence, Ancient and Modern* 6th ed. (St. Paul, Minn.: West Publishing, 1990), 1598. See 1598 also for the multiple definitions of *will* cited from *Black's Law Dictionary*.

52 Thomas L. Smith, *Elements of the Laws: or, Outlines of the System of Civil and Criminal Laws in Force in the United States and in Several States of the Union* (Philadelphia: J. B. Lippincott, 1882), 59. These natural rights are absolute rights under common law. In addition to the right to property, they include the right of personal security and the right of personal liberty which is considered the most important (Smith, 56).

53 William Bowe and Douglas Parker, *Revised Treatise Page on the Law of Wills Including Probate, Will Contests, Evidence, Taxation, Conflicts, Estate Planning, Forms, and Statutes Relating to Wills* (1901; reprint, Cincinnati: W. H. Anderson, 1960), 1:59.

54 Ibid., 60.

55 See James A. Ballentine, ed., *Ballentine's Law Dictionary with Pronunciations*, 3d ed., ed. William S. Anderson (San Francisco: Bancroft-Whitney, 1969), 936.

56 Brooks, *Reading for the Plot*, 61.

57 Orlando Patterson maintains that the constituent elements of slavery were the master's power to inflict violence on a slave, the slave's natal alienation, and the slave's dishonored condition (*Slavery and Social Death: A Comparative Study* [Cambridge, Mass.: Harvard University Press, 1982], 1–5, 17–34).

58 For an analysis of the eighteenth- and nineteenth-century inheritance system and its

relation to the evolution of American capitalism and family, see Shammas, Salmon, and Dahlin, *Inheritance in America*, 3–20.

59 Robin West, *Narrative, Authority, and Law* (Ann Arbor: University of Michigan Press, 1993), 31. West theorizes that a relentless desire and need for authority ultimately causes Kafka's characters to seek out authority. Her point seems particularly applicable to Ike McCaslin and his relation to his grandfather.

60 Shammas, Salmon, and Dahlin, *Inheritance in America*, 39.

61 Blackstone, *Commentaries*, vol. 2, section 2. He maintained that the protection of the right of property is the "principle aim of society" (1:120).

62 Ibid., 1:16, 124. Blackstone argued that ownership of property and the regulations governing use and transfer are determined by society, but he also saw property as one of three absolute rights, the other two being security and liberty (see 1:124–36).

63 Morris Cohen, "Property and Sovereignty," in *Property: Mainstream and Critical Positions*, ed. C. B. Macpherson (Toronto: University of Toronto Press, 1978), 155–56.

64 Thomas L. Smith, *Elements of the Laws*, 96.

65 Kuyk, *Threads Cable-strong: William Faulkner's* Go Down, Moses (Lewisburg, Penn.: Bucknell University Press, 1983), 123; see also Kuyk's discussion of sharing and relinquishing (118–28).

66 Alan Watson, *Slave Law in the Americas* (Athens: University of Georgia Press, 1989), 131. Watson sets out a series of propositions regarding slavery and slave laws that suggest that in societies where slavery is based on race, the manumission of slaves, the training and education of slaves and their descendants, and the incorporation of freed people into the society, all present greater problems and obstacles because of the public dimension of enslavement (131–33).

67 Adrienne D. Davis, "The Private Law of Race and Sex: An Antebellum Perspective," *Stanford Law Review* 51, no. 2 (January 1999): 225. In examining the interaction between race, sex, and estate law in cases of intestate succession and testamentary transfers, Davis reveals how private law functioned to maintain racial hierarchy and property rights. Davis also presents a number of cases in which white men attempted testamentary transfers to the children they fathered with enslaved women.

68 Shammas, Salmon, and Dahlin, *Inheritance in America*, 35.

69 Berry, *Pig Farmer's Daughter*, 85.

70 Kent Anderson Leslie, *Woman of Color, Daughter of Privilege: Amanda America Dickson, 1848–1893* (Athens: University of Georgia Press, 1995), 37–39. Leslie treats the case as an example of how racial barriers were transgressed at the will of the white male elite. Similar examples have emerged both from the pre-war and postwar South. In *Freedom's Child: The Life of a Confederate General's Black Daughter* (Chapel Hill, N.C.: Algonquin Books, 1998), for example, Carrie Allen McCray presents the story of Malinda Rice, born in slavery in 1856, who in 1873 at the age of sixteen went to work for the prominent white general John Robert Jones in Harrisburg, Virginia, and shortly thereafter gave birth to his daughter Mary Magdalene Rice on 2 March 1875. Rice acknowledged his daughter and accepted her into his household, where Malinda continued to serve as his housekeeper. Some of the details of the liaison came to light in 1883 when, after only two years of marriage, the second wife of General Jones sued him for divorce on the grounds of adultery with Malinda Rice (54–55).

71 Leslie, *Woman of Color*, 80.

72 Ibid., 95.

73 Adrienne D. Davis, "Private Law," 226–27.

74 Leslie, *Woman of Color*, 101–2.

75 Leslie quotes Justice Hall from the *Georgia Supreme Court Reports*, 78 Georgia, 442, 414. The Dickson case was also followed in the black and white press in 1887, including the *Atlanta Constitution*, the *Milledgeville Union Recorder*, the *Sparta Ishmaelite*, the *Savannah Tribune*, and the *Cleveland Gazette*. See also Jonathan M. Bryant, "Race, Class, and Law in Bourbon, Georgia: The Case of the David Dickson's Will," *Georgia Historical Quarterly* 71 (summer 1987): 226–42.

76 *Mitchell v Wells*, 35 Miss. 235 (1859). Mitchell, the executor, prevented Nancy Wells from inheriting her father's bequest because he argued that she was a slave who had lived as a slave in Mississippi.

77 John Codman Hurd, *The Law of Freedom and Bondage in the United States*. 2 vol. (Boston: Little, Brown, 1858), 2:148. The 1842 legislation also made it unlawful "for any person, by last will or testament, to make any devise or bequest of any slave or slaves for the purpose of emancipation" (2:149). Article 9 of the Code of 1857 would further extend this provision.

78 *Shaw v Brown*, 35 Miss. 246 (1858). Id. at 307–8, 315–21. See also Paul Finkelman, *An Imperfect Union* (Chapel Hill: University of North Carolina Press, 1981), 232–33.

79 Lawrence M. Friedman, *A History of American Law* (1973; 2nd ed., New York: Simon & Schuster, 1985), 195. By 1860 "all manumission by will or deed" was outlawed throughout the South and Maryland (195).

80 Vernon Lane Wharton, *The Negro in Mississippi, 1865–1890* (1947; reprint, New York: Harper and Row, 1965), 12.

81 *Talbott v Norager*, 7 Miss. (1 Cush.) 572 (1851).

82 Miss. Rev. Code, ch. xxxiii and ch. xii, art 80 (1857). See also Currie, "From Slavery to Freedom in Mississippi's Legal System," 112–125.

83 Charles S. Sydnor, "The Free Negro in Mississippi before the Civil War," in *Articles in American Slavery*, vol. 17 of *Free Blacks in a Slave Society*, ed. Paul Finkelman (New York: Garland, 1994), 775. Sydnor points out, "The basic provision concerning the emancipation of slaves occurred in a law that was passed June 18, 1822. According to this act, slaves might be manumitted by will or by a properly witnessed and recorded document, if it could be proved to the satisfaction of the state legislature that some meritorious act had been done by the slave for the owner or the state" (773). See also Charles S. Sydnor, *Slavery in Mississippi* (1933; reprint, Baton Rouge: Louisiana State University, 1966).

84 *Hinds et al. v Brazealle et al.*, 3 Miss. 837 (1838). See Sydnor, "The Free Negro," 449. See also Christine McDonald, "Judging Jurisdictions: Geography and Race in Slave Law and Literature of the 1830s," *American Literature* 71 (December 1999): 625–55.

85 *The Slave, Grace*, 2 Haggard Admiralty (Great Britain) 94 (1827). Grace sued for freedom in Antigua on the basis that her free status in England prevented her re-enslavement. Justice William Scott, Lord Stowell, ruled that "once a freeman ever a freeman" (the decision by Lord Mansfield in *Somerset v Stewart* [1772]) applied only to England, and that "temporary freedom," even though gained in England, was

"superseded upon the return of the slave" (id. at 127, 124). Lord Stowell's decision hinged on Grace's voluntary return to Antigua and on his reading of *Somerset* as a forced return of an enslaved person to a master in the West Indies.

86 Michel Foucault, *The History of Sexuality*, vol. 1, *An Introduction* (New York: Vintage Books, 1990), 156.

87 Ibid. Foucault seems in this instance to link sex and love because he also says that bestowing a high value on love in the West has made death acceptable.

88 The long scene (297–301) is located in the fourth section of "The Bear," the same section as the revelation of Carothers McCaslin's sexual and moral violations. Faulkner positions the scene at the end of the section, so that its very location emphasizes not only the erotic content but also the contest of wills, which figures throughout the section.

89 Muhlenfeld, "The Distaff Side," 204. Muhlenfeld links Ike's wife to his mother Sophonsiba's "dogged determination to take her appropriate place in society" (203). See also Fowler, *Faulkner*, 152. Fowler notices the connection between the land and the body of Ike's wife; she reads the scene and the wife's desire in Lacanian terms of the phallus and of lack (152–53).

90 Born in 1772, Carothers is after all approximately sixty years old when he impregnates his daughter; his son, Ike's own reluctant father, Buck, also fathers Ike when he is at least sixty. The exact ages are clouded by Faulkner's inattention to details and sloppy revisions as he moved from stories to a story cycle to a novel and as he incorporated pieces previously written into the new whole. On the discrepancies and contradictions in ages, see Devlin, "History, Sexuality, and the Wilderness," 191–92.

91 Brooks, *Reading for the Plot*, 260.

92 In an oddly hopeful reading, Zender considers Roth Edmond's affair with his black cousin "an attenuated form of sibling incest, in which taboos of race, region, and class are defied (at least temporarily) in the service of *egalitarian love*" ("Faulkner and the Politics of Incest," *American Literature* 70, no. 4 [December 1998]: 755; emphasis added). Lee Jenkins, on the other hand, has no doubt that the woman loves Roth, but he wonders "*why*" she would. Jenkins explains "her protestations of love, as a black, for a white who dishonorably uses and abuses her and cannot bring himself to allow himself to respect her, as simply one more, though immeasurably more complex, instance of the white need for black forgiveness" (*Faulkner and Black-White Relations: A Psychoanalytic Approach* [New York: Columbia University Press, 1981], 242.

4 · The Subject of Property

1 Lawrence Friedman, *A History of American Law* 2nd ed. (New York: Simon and Schuster, 1985), 197.

2 *Black Code* (1806), sec. 10, 154; the *Digest of 1808*, chap. 2, art. 19. Immovables such as land and buildings were defined by their nature; others including livestock, sawmills, sugar refineries, and farm implements could be designated immovables by destination, by their attachment to a building. The Louisiana Civil Code of 1825 continued the designation of slaves as immovables under the law, but as Judith Kelleher Schafer

observes, the confusions in the legal definitions of slaves as persons and as property and especially in determining how to classify slaves as a type of property persisted through the 1850s. She cites, for example, *Stephens v Graves* (1854), which ruled that any slave arriving in Louisiana "ceased to be personal property" and became "real estate," and *Boatner v Wade* (1859), which regarded slaves as "a kind of property which may be removed from place to place, with the utmost facility" (*Slavery, the Civil Law, and the Supreme Court of Louisiana* (Baton Rouge: Louisiana State University Press, 1994), 25–27.

3 Friedman, *History of American Law*, 197–98.

4 Robin West, *Narrative, Authority, and Law* (Ann Arbor: University of Michigan Press, 1993), 360. West suggests that natural law is dominated by a romantic quest in which law itself is the romantic hero, "morally virtuous and historically triumphant." "The natural lawyer defines law in such a way as to ensure the moral worth of legal supremacy" (360). Read as a natural lawyer, Ike and his inability to change his own conception of property and ownership, of race and racial ideology—even after he recognizes the wrongs of both a property system and a race system in his society—become clearer.

5 See Joseph William Singer, "The Continuing Conquest: American Indian Nations, Property Law, and 'Gunsmoke,'" *Reconstruction* 1, no. 3 (1991): 97, 102.

6 Judith Lockyer, *Ordered by Words: Language and Narration in the Novels of William Faulkner* (Carbondale: Southern Illinois University Press, 1991), 100. Lockyer concludes, "The narrative effort of *Go Down, Moses* is to detach from the culture and thus the horrors of slavery and capitalism while implicitly presenting them as excesses of an essentially good and true order. The effort mirrors Ike's faith in the absolute truths of God and nature, faith both ennobles and threatens Ike's struggle" (100–101).

7 See Jean-Jacques Rousseau, *Discourse on the Origins of Inequality*, Second Discourse (1755), trans. Franklin Philip, ed. Patrick Coleman (Oxford: Oxford University Press, 1994).

8 Thomas L. Smith, *Elements of the Laws: or, Outlines of the System of Civil and Criminal Laws in Force in the United States and in the Several States of the Union* (Philadelphia: J. B. Lippincott, 1882), 61–62.

9 Frances L. Ansley cites the history of discovery and conquest of American Indian lands as illustrative of the role of race in property law. ("Race and the Core Curriculum in Legal Education," *California Law Review* 79 [1991]: 1511, 1532.

10 Jeremy Bentham, *Principles of the Civil Code* (1802), in *The Works of Jeremy Bentham*, ed. John Bowring (Edinburgh: William Tait, 1843), 2:297.

11 *Dred Scott v Sandford*, 60 U.S. (19 How.) 393 (1856); id. at 407.

12 Carl Schurz recorded in Senate Executive Documents, no. 2, 39th Congress, 1st session, 21. Quoted in Vernon Lane Wharton, *The Negro in Mississippi, 1865–1890* (1947; reprint, New York: Harper and Row, 1965), 82.

13 A. Leon Higginbotham, *Shades of Freedom: Racial Politics and Presumptions of the American Legal Process* (New York: Oxford University Press, 1996), 61. Higginbotham calls the decision "nothing more than a southern manifest on the institution of slavery." See his review of the case, the trials, and the decisions (61–67).

14 *Dred Scott v Sandford*, 407.

15 Melvin Miller Rader, *Ethics and Society: An Appraisal of Social Ideals* (New York: Henry Holt, 1950), 224–25.

16 Karl F. Zender points out "Faulkner's career between *The Sound and the Fury* and *Go Down, Moses* consists in large measure of a deepening understanding of what the word 'love' means and the rage of inequalities its adherents must struggle to overcome. How the meaning of the word has altered and expanded in the fifty years since *Go Down, Moses*, how it can be expected to alter still further, whether 'love' is any longer alone sufficient to heal the divisions that rive our nation—these are issues for writers other than Faulkner to explore" ("Faulkner and the Politics of Incest," *American Literature* 70, no. 4 [December 1998]: 760). One of the more significant points, however, about Ike McCaslin's encounter with the unnamed woman, the mother of Roth Edmond's son, who is rejected because of her race and positioned subserviently because of her gender, is that in the 1940s, love was not enough to ferment individual let alone societal change.

17 Karl F. Zender, *The Crossing of the Ways: William Faulkner, the South, and the Modern World* (New Brunswick, N.J.: Rutgers University Press, 1989), 69, 70; emphasis added. Zender follows Joseph Blotner in pointing to the decrease in Faulkner's creative drive in the early 1940s as the cause of his creating familial and financial obligations that would disrupt his attention to writing: "They created a kind of busywork that could simultaneously fill the void caused by his failure to write and be used as an excuse for it" (73).

18 Ibid., 67.

19 John Carlos Rowe, "The African-American Voice in Faulkner's *Go Down, Moses*," in *Modern American Short Story Sequences*, ed. Gerald Kennedy (Cambridge: Cambridge University Press, 1995), 91–92.

20 G. W. F. Hegel expounds a theory of property and personality: " 'To claim that external world as its own' personality requires the institution of property. Property enables an individual to put his will into a 'thing' " (*Elements of the Philosophy of Right*, part I, trans. H. B. Nisbet [Cambridge: Cambridge University Press, 1991], 73–103). On Hegel's philosophy of property freedom, see J. W. Harris, *Property and Justice* (Oxford: Clarendon Press, 1996), 232–37. John Brigham's conclusion that "Hegel's notion of property is that property is a realisation of freedom" seems appropos of Faulkner in his acquisition of land and most especially of his character Lucas Beauchamp (*Property and the Politics of Entitlement* [Philadelphia: Temple University Press, 1990], 138).

21 William James, *The Principles of Psychology*, 2 vol. (New York: Henry Holt, 1890) 1:291, 293.

22 See Joseph Blotner, *Faulkner: A Biography* (New York: Random House, 1974) 2:984–91, for a description of Faulkner's purchases of property during the 1930s and his attempts to finance and maintain his real estate. On Faulkner's purchase of a 320-acre farm seventeen miles northeast of Oxford, see also Joel Williamson, *Faulkner and Southern History* (New York: Oxford University Press, 1993), 260.

23 See Linda Wagner-Martin, introduction to *New Essays on* Go Down, Moses, ed. Linda Wagner-Martin (Cambridge: Cambridge University Press, 1996).

24 Michael Grimwood expertly called attention to the significance of Faulkner's near-death experience in *Heart in Conflict: Faulkner's Struggle with Vocation* (Athens: University of Georgia Press, 1987), 224, 298. The incident is also described briefly in Frederick R. Karl, *William Faulkner: American Writer* (Chapel Hill: University of North Carolina Press, 1989), 649.

25 Daniel J. Singal, *William Faulkner: The Making of a Modernist* (Chapel Hill: University of North Carolina Press, 1997), 261–62. See also his detailed explanation of the physical implications and medical results of Faulkner's collapse (258–61).

26 Faulkner's father, Murry, was an alcoholic who was treated at the same clinic in Byhalia where Faulkner would also be confined after his more serious bouts with alcohol. In addition to Grimwood, Karl, and Singal on Faulkner's health and alcohol, see both Blotner, *Faulkner, A Biography* and Williamson, *William Faulkner and Southern History* for biographical accounts.

27 The period from 1940 to the mid-1950s was marked by a noticeable decrease in Faulkner's literary production. After *Go Down, Moses*, he would not produce another manuscript for six years, though during this period he was writing for Warner Brothers Studios, and his heavy drinking would lead to neurological problems and to what Saxe Commins would term "a complete disintegration of a man" (Saxe Commins to Robert K. Haas and Bennett Cerf, 8 October 1952, in Louis Daniel Brodsky and Robert W. Hamblin, *Faulkner: A Comprehensive Guide to the Brodsky Collection*, 2 vol. (Jackson: University Press of Mississippi, 1982), 2:89–91.

28 The full dedication reads: "To Mammy / Carolina Barr / Mississippi [1840–1940] / Who was born in slavery and who gave to my family a fidelity without stint or calculation of recompense and to my childhood an immeasurable devotion and love."

29 Rowe, "African-American Voice," 84. Rowe argues that "Faulkner seems caught by the contradiction of his own aesthetic and political logics: On the one hand, he emulates the white Southern patriarch in the responsibility he assumes for his extended family; on the other hand, he knows that the sins of such families can be redeemed only by publicizing the scandal of slavery *and* by encouraging its victims to revolt against the social psychological habits that are as much the insidious 'legacy' of slavery as the legal and economic bonds of postbellum racism" (77).

30 Minrose C. Gwin, "Her Shape, His Hand: The Spaces of African American Women in *Go Down, Moses*," in *New Essays on* Go Down, Moses, ed. Linda Wagner-Martin (Cambridge: Cambridge University Press, 1996), 80.

31 Judith Sensibar, "Who Wears the Mask? Memory, Desire, and Race in *Go Down, Moses*," in *New Essays on* Go Down, Moses, ed. Linda Wagner-Martin (Cambridge: Cambridge University Press, 1996), 114.

32 Ibid., 106–7.

33 Ibid., 109.

34 Given the available information, Caroline Barr was probably born between 1845 and 1849. For a summary of sources on her age, see Don H. Doyle, *Faulkner's County: The Historical Roots of Yoknapatawpha* (Chapel Hill: University of North Carolina Press, 2001), 123, 402.

35 See William Faulkner, "Mississippi," *Holiday* (April 1954), reprinted in *Essays,*

Speeches, and Public Letters of William Faulkner, ed. James B. Meriwether (New York: Random House, 1965), 16–17, 19–20, 39–43.

36 William Faulkner, "A Letter to Bishop Robert E. Jones, 15 March 1940," in the *Georgia Review* (fall 2001): 530–34. In the same issue, the *Georgia Review* published a typescript that Faulkner supplied Bishop Jones of his eulogy for Caroline Barr and that Faulkner entitled "Spoken by William Faulkner at Mammy's service, fourth February, 1940" (535). In an accompanying article, Bert Welling follows Judith Sensibar's argument in "Who Wears the Mask? Memory, Desire, and Race in *Go Down, Moses*" ("In Praise of the Black Mother: An Unpublished Faulkner Letter on 'Mammy' Caroline Barr," *Georgia Review* [fall 2001]: 536–42).

37 William Faulkner, *The Wild Palms* (New York: Random House, 1939); retitled *If I Forget Thee, Jerusalem* (New York: Vintage International, 1995), 273.

38 Faulkner to Robert K. Haas, Saturday [5 October 1940], and Faulkner to Bennett Cerf et al., 15 December 1940, in *Selected Letters of William Faulkner,* ed. Joseph Blotner (1977; reprint, New York: Vintage: 1978), 136.

39 Cheryl Harris, "Whiteness as Property," *Harvard Law Review* 106, no. 8 (June 1993): 1709–91. Harris elucidates how whiteness itself came to be considered as property owned by its possessors. Harris's extensive and important essay is excerpted in *Black on White: Black Writers on What It Means to Be White,* ed. David R. Roediger (New York: Random House, 1998), 103–18. I refer to both the longer version and to the more accessible excerpted version in this chapter.

40 Harris, "Whiteness as Property" in *Black on White,* 104.

41 Brief for Plaintiff in Error, at 8, 9, *Plessy v Ferguson,* 163 U.S. 537 (1896). Homer A. Plessy was identified as having "seven eighths Caucasion and one eighth African blood" (id. at 541), and it was argued that he was being deprived, without due process of law, of property rights in whiteness enjoyed by white citizens. In his dissent, Justice John Marshall Harlan stated that "in view of the Constitution, in the eye of the law, there is in this country no superior, dominant, ruling class of citizens. There is no caste here. Our constitution is color-blind, and neither knows nor tolerates classes among citizens. In respect of civil rights, all citizens are equal before the law" (id. at 557). However, Justice Harlan also conceded, "The white race deems itself to be the dominant race in this country. And so it is, in prestige, in achievements, in education, in wealth and in power. So, I doubt not, it will continue to be for all time, if it remains true to its great heritage and holds fast to the principles of constitutional liberty" (id. at 559). He recognizes that white people have achieved a certain racial dominance that carried prestige but cannot name it as a property value of whiteness.

42 George Washington Cable, *The Grandissimes: A Story of Creole Life* (1879; reprint, New York: Hill and Wang, 1957), 59. Cable's blunt Creole character, Agricola Fusilier, attempts to educate an uncomprehending German American in the naturalness of whiteness and inevitability of white privilege.

43 Ian F. Haney-Lopez, *White by Law: The Legal Construction of Race* (New York: New York University Press, 1996), xiv. Haney-Lopez writes convincingly of the legal measures and interpretation that formulated both race and racial hierarchy in the United States. David R. Roediger also argues that "race" achieves "meaning through the agency of human beings in concrete historical and social contexts, and is not a bio-

logical or natural category" (*Toward the Abolition of Whiteness: Essays on Race, Politics, and Working Class History* [London: Verso, 1994], 2).

44 Patricia J. Williams, *Seeing a Colour-Blind Future: The Paradox of Race* (London: Virago, 1997), 50–51. In a chapter entitled "The War Between the Worlds," Williams examines the fluctuations of racial categorization and the contortions of logic necessary to maintain supposedly distinct racial categories (54–57). See also Theodore W. Allen, *The Invention of the White Race* (London: Verso, 1994).

45 Toni Morrison, *Playing in the Dark: Whiteness and the Literary Imagination* (Cambridge, Mass.: Harvard University Press, 1992).

46 Wagner-Martin, introduction, 10, 7.

47 Michael Omi and Howard Winant, *Racial Formation in the U.S.: From the 1960s to the 1990s* (New York: Routledge, 1994), 178. See also Grace Elizabeth Hale, *Making Whiteness: The Culture of Segregation in the South, 1890–1940* (New York: Pantheon Books, 1998).

48 Cheryl Harris, "Whiteness as Property," 1714.

49 Heinz Kohut's work in *The Search for Self* (1978) is the basis for Joseph Adamson's and Hilary Clark's summary of the grandiose and the "idealized selfobject" in "Introduction: Shame, Affect, Writing," in *Scenes of Shame: Psychoanalysis, Shame, and Writing*, ed. Joseph Adamson and Hilary Clark (Albany: State University of New York Press, 1999), 20–21.

50 Omi and Winant, *Racial Formation*, 178.

51 See Winthrop Jordan, *White over Black: American Attitudes toward the Negro, 1550–1812* (Baltimore: Johns Hopkins University Press, 1969), 93–95.

52 Ch. IV, 3 Laws of VA 252 (Hening 1823), enacted 1705. The 1705 definition of mulatto was for the purpose of eligibility for holding office. See A. Leon Higginbotham Jr. and Barbara K. Kopytoff, "Racial Purity and Interracial Sex in the Law of Colonial and Antebellum Virginia," *Georgetown Law Journal* 77 (1989): 1977.

53 Higginbotham and Kopytoff maintain that the 1785 law "was the only time Virginia law was changed to allow persons with a greater proportion of Negro ancestry to be deemed white" (1978). See Ch. LXXVIII, 12 laws of VA 184 (Hening 1823), enacted 1785.

54 Alan Watson, *Slave Law in the Americas* (Athens: University of Georgia Press, 1989), 1. Watson cautions that in history and throughout the field of law, rulers are often "indifferent to the nature of the legal rules in operation," and that point, frequently overlooked or denied, "is the greatest cause of misunderstanding the nature of law, the relationship of law and society, and the course of legal development" (1).

55 Cheryl Harris, "Whiteness as Property," 1715.

56 Rowe, "African-American Voice," 80. In fact, Theresa M. Towner opens a discourse on race in the novels after *Go Down, Moses*, but her paradigm remains largely tied to a conceptualization of race within a black-white binary and without sufficient pressure on whiteness in Faulkner's texts (*Faulkner on the Color Line: The Later Novels* (Jackson: University Press of Mississippi, 2000), especially "Flesh and the Pencil: Racial Identity and the Search for Form" (3–28) and " 'How Can A Black Man Ask?': Orality, Race, and Identity" (29–47).

57 Haney-Lopez, *White by Law*, 185.

58   Lee Jenkins, *Faulkner and Black-White Relations: A Psychoanalytic Approach* (New York: Columbia University Press, 1981), 21.

59   Donald Nathanson, *Shame and Pride: Affect, Sex, and the Birth of the Self* (New York: Norton, 1992), 138. Nathanson bases his conclusion on the work of Silvan Tomkins, *Affect, Imagery, Consciousness*, 2 vol. (New York: Springer, 1962, 1963).

60   Lillian Smith links shame to the maturing white child's awareness of the racial etiquette demanded by southern custom (*Killers of the Dream* [New York: Norton, 1949]). Fred Hobson has more recently explored the ideology in narratives written by white southerners whose racial apotheosis is similar to New England religious conversion narratives (*But Now I See: The White Southern Racial Conversion Narrative* [Baton Rouge: Louisiana State University Press, 1999]).

61   Terry Eagleton, *Criticism and Ideology: A Study of Marxist Literary Theory* (London: Verso, 1975), 58. Without assuming a one-for-one corollary, I am pointing out that the race and caste structure of Faulkner's experiential reality in the South reinforced white privilege and consolidated class values, which he in turn mined in his representation of the McCaslin-Edmonds family.

62   Haney-Lopez, *White by Law*, 185.

63   Mab Segrest, *Memoir of a Race Traitor* (Boston: South End Press, 1994), 4. Segrest writes eloquently about her Alabama upbringing and her family's beliefs and racial prejudices.

64   Ibid., 195.

65   See Ellen Barry's informative article, "White Like Me," *Providence Phoenix*, 11 July 1997, 8-12. Haney-Lopez has suggested not only that "*Race Traitor* represents the potential for deconstructing Whiteness" but also that "more importantly, the advice proffered in *Race Traitor* also highlights the power of Whites to exercise choice with respect to their racial identity" (*White by Law*, 190).

66   The aim to racialize whiteness and deconstruct the term and its function in power relations is evident currently in numerous books and special issues of periodicals: Vron Ware's *Beyond the Pale: White Women, Racism, and History* (London: Verso, 1992); Ruth Frankenberg's *White Women, Race Matters: The Social Construction of Whiteness* (Minneapolis: University of Minnesota Press, 1993); Theodore W. Allen's *The Invention of the White Race* (London: Verso, 1994); and Matt Wray's *White Trash: Race and Class in America* (New York: Routledge, 1997). All share in formulating the current discourses on whiteness. Being in part white responses to theoretical analyses of race at the end of the 1980s, these recent discourses on white raciality also take their impetus from Cornel West's popular *Race Matters* (Boston: Beacon Press, 1993) and Morrison's *Playing in the Dark* (1992).

67   Cornel West, *Race Matters*, 8.

68   My working title for a segment of this chapter presented as a paper for Faulkner's centenary at the "Faulkner and Yoknapatawpha" conference in Oxford, Mississippi, was "Thirteen Black Birds and One Hundred White Doves: A Birthday Gift." That title acknowledges both Faulkner's one hundredth birthday and the fact that texts, of course, are multiply interpretable. Texts occupy political, social, moral, philosophical, aesthetic, and cultural spaces, and perform multiple forms of work, and are

endlessly elastic. The title forecasts, too, that the matter of race is like a gift—given and accepted or rejected, but not inherent in a natal advent.

69 James Baldwin, "On Being White and Other Lies," *Essence* (April 1984): 90–92.

70 Gwin ("Her Shape, His Hand," 83–84) takes her concept of safe spaces from Patricia Hill Collins (*Black Feminist Thought: Knowledge, Consciousness, and the Politics of Empowerment* [New York: Routledge, 1990], 95), and her notion of locations from which black women feel empowered to resist objectification as the Other.

71 Jacques Lacan, *The Four Fundamental Concepts of Psycho-Analysis*, ed. Jacques-Alain Miller, trans. Alan Sheridan (New York: Norton, 1978), 84.

72 Helen Block Lewis, "Shame and the Narcissistic Personality," in *The Many Faces of Shame*, ed. Donald Nathanson (New York: Guilford, 1987), 107–8.

73 Kohut's term *selfobject* refers to the way the child perceives significant others (Kohut, *Search for Self*).

74 Mississippi law defined a person of one-fourth or more Negro blood as a mulatto. See the numbers for the mulatto slave and free population, Census of 1860 (Recapitulation), and Charles S. Sydnor, "The Free Negro in Mississippi before the Civil War," in *Articles in American Slavery*, vol. 17 of *Free Blacks in a Slave Society*, ed. Paul Finkelman (New York: Garland, 1989), 443, 461. Sydnor cites at least seven court cases in which slave owners admitted paternity of slaves in the process of either willing them property or emancipating them.

75 Patricia J. Williams, *The Alchemy of Race and Rights: Diary of a Law Professor* (Cambridge, Mass.: Harvard University Press, 1991), 21.

76 Margaret A. Burnham, "An Impossible Marriage: Slave Law and Family Law," *Law and Inequality* 5, no. 2 (July 1987): 225.

77 For an analysis of limited work options and living conditions available to black women after the Emancipation, see Tera W. Hunter, *To 'Joy My Freedom: Southern Black Women's Lives and Labors after the Civil War* (Cambridge, Mass.: Harvard University Press, 1997).

78 See Sigmund Freud, "Introductory Lectures on Psychoanalysis," *The Standard Edition of the Complete Psychological Works of Sigmund Freud*, 24 vols., translated under the general editorship of James Strachey, in collaboration with Anna Freud, assisted by A. Strachey and A. Tyson. 15:200–202.

79 Albert J. Devlin, "History, Sexuality, and the Wilderness in the McCaslin Family Chronicle," in *Critical Essays on William Faulkner: The McCaslin Family*, ed. Arthur F. Kinney (Boston: G. K. Hall, 1990), 193. Devlin also argues for Ike's identification with his mother and that Sophonsiba has a severe and negative impact on Ike's defining adult experiences—his passivity, his acceptance of a sexless marriage, his pervasive guilt (193).

80 Ira Berlin, *Many Thousands Gone: The First Two Centuries of Slavery in North America* (Cambridge, Mass.: Belknap Press of Harvard University, 1998), 1.

81 Haney-Lopez, *White by Law*, 191.

82 Theodor W. Adorno, *Minima Moralia: Reflections from Damaged Life*, trans. E. F. N. Jephcott (London: New Left Books, 1974), 166.

83 Faulkner's own maternal grandfather, Charles E. Butler, disappeared from Oxford

in 1887 with money he held as the town's marshall and, by several reliable accounts, with an octoroon woman. This biographical incident, along with that of his paternal great-grandfather's shadow family with an enslaved woman, may well have surfaced as memory and emotional nexus in the representation of interracial liaisons in *Go Down, Moses*. See the accounts of Charles Butler and Col. William C. Falkner in Blotner, *Faulkner: A Biography* (1:57) and Williamson, *William Faulkner and Southern History* (64–73).

84 Gilles Deleuze and Felix Guattari, *A Thousand Plateaus: Capitalism and Schizophrenia*, trans. Brian Massumi (Minneapolis: University of Minnesota, 1987), 2:178. See also Robert J. C. Young, *Colonial Desire: Hybridity in Theory, Culture, and Race* (London: Routledge, 1995), 60.

85 Deleuze and Guattari, *Thousand Plateaus*, 180.

86 Texts of scientific racism include Lothrop Stoddard's *The Rising Tide of Color against White World-Supremacy* (New York: C. Scribner's Sons, 1920) and *The Revolt against Civilization: The Menace of the Under Man* (New York: C. Scribner's Sons, 1922); and Charles Conant Josey's *Race and National Solidarity* (New York: C. Scribner's Sons, 1923). See Elazar Barkan, *Retreat of Scientific Racism: Changing Concepts of Race in Britain and the United States between the World Wars* (Cambridge: Cambridge University Press, 1992); Reginal Horsman, *Race and Manifest Destiny: The Origins of American Racial Anglo-Saxonism* (Cambridge, Mass.: Harvard University Press, 1981); and George M. Frederickson, *The Black Image in the White Mind: The Debate on Afro-American Character and Destiny, 1817–1914* (New York: Harper and Row, 1971).

87 See Darwin T. Turner's treatment of Percival Brownlee as Faulkner's "conscious ideology of free slaves being worse off than slaves with masters" ("Faulkner and Slavery," in *The South and Faulkner's Yoknapatawpha: The Actual and the Apocryphal*, ed. Evans Harrington and Ann Abadie (Jackson: University Press of Mississippi, 1977), 76–77.

88 In *Fictions of Labor: William Faulkner and the South's Long Revolution*, Richard Godden considers *Go Down, Moses* only briefly in the "Afterword" and in terms of Sam's blood and his positioning as Ike's surrogate father, as a "genealogical revision" that "leads away from the issue of bound labor and toward a utopian space." Godden's focus, however, on Faulkner's fiction during the New Deal, a period of radical labor transformation, and on patterns of social exchange within free labor rather than bound labor would suggest not only that *Go Down, Moses* is more integral to issues of labor than he claims, but also that both blood and paternity are more complicated than he allows in a cursory attention to Sam Fathers. See Godden's afterword (233–34).

89 Reinhold Niebuhr, *Moral Man and Immoral Society: A Study in Ethics and Politics* (1932; reprint, New York: Charles Scribner's Sons, 1960), 266. Niebuhr contends, "Where rights and interests are closely interwoven, it is impossible to engage in a shrewd and prudent calculation of comparative rights. Where lives are closely intertwined, happiness is destroyed if it is not shared. Justice by assertion and counter-assertion therefore becomes impossible. . . . Love must strive for something purer than justice if it would attain justice. Egoistic impulses are so much more powerful than altruistic ones that if the latter are not given stronger than ordinary support, the justice which even good men design is partial to those who design it" (266).

5 · Conclusion: The Game of Compensation

1   Lee Jenkins, *Faulkner and Black-White Relations: A Psychoanalytic Approach* (New York: Columbia University Press, 1981), 242.

2   *Hudgins v Wrights*, 11 Va. (1806). See Tucker, id. at 139, in William Waller Hening, *The Statutes at Large: Being a Collection of All the Laws of Virginia, from the First Session of the Legislature in the Year 1619*. 13 vol. (Richmond, Va.: W. Gray Printers, 1819–1823). Tucker, however, disagreed with the trial judge's reasoning that the Virginia Declaration of Rights of 1776, which declared all men free and equal, applied to Africans and those of African descent, and he stated instead that the Bill of Rights "was meant to embrace the case of free citizens, or aliens only; and not by a side wind to overturn *the rights of property,* and give freedom to those very people whom *we have been compelled from imperious circumstances to retain,* generally, in the same bondage that they were in at the revolution, in which they had no concern, agency or interest" (emphasis added). For excerpts from the decision, see Paul Finkelman, ed. *The Law of Freedom and Bondage: A Casebook* (New York: Oceana, 1986) 22–24. For a discussion of *Hudgins v Wrights* and the legal determination of race according to the hair and physical appearance of the individual, see A. Leon Higginbotham and Barbara K. Kopytoff, "Racial Purity and Interracial Sex in the Law of Colonial and Antebellum Virginia," *Georgetown Law Journal* 77 (1989): 1967–2029.

3   *Hudgins v Wrights*, id. at 141; emphasis added.

4   See Pierre Nora, *Lieux de memoire: Rethinking the French Past*, ed. Lawrence D. Kritzman, trans. Arthur Goldhammer, 3 vol. (New York: Columbia University Press, 1996–1998).

5   Molly Beauchamp, "Mollie" in this final chapter, refers to the legal system as "the Law," and says to Stevens, "you the Law" (354), in requesting that he find Butch.

6   This is not the subject taken up by Faulkner; it becomes the concern of another major novelist from Mississippi, Richard Wright. See, in particular, his *Uncle Tom's Children, Black Boy, American Hunger,* and *Native Son,* all of which point to the inevitable (forced) migration of blacks from Mississippi. Historical scholarship has detailed extensively the conditions blacks faced in the South after Emancipation and into the twentieth century. See, for example, Jay R. Mandle, *The Roots of Black Poverty: The Southern Plantation Economy after the Civil War* (Durham, N.C.: Duke University Press, 1978); Leon F. Litwack, *Been in the Storm So Long: The Aftermath of Slavery* (New York: Random House, 1979); and Joel Williamson, *The Crucible of Race: Black-White Relations in the American South since Emancipation* (New York: Oxford University Press, 1984).

7   In a Lacanian reading of "Go Down, Moses," Doreen Fowler regards the commissary not merely as "a storehouse of the plantation owner's wealth" but, significantly, as a symbol of "the completeness of being identified with the Name-of-the-Father," and concludes: "By breaking into the store, Butch is attempting to raid the father's plenty—to find the missing phallus. Roth punishes the son's desire to be the symbolic Father or Other by expelling him; and this dooms Butch to a lifelong search to fill the gap that is the self. Accordingly, all of Butch's subsequent crimes are crimes

against the Law of the Father that ordains lack. In Jefferson, he strikes at a police officer with a piece of iron pipe—a phallic symbol; and in Chicago he is executed for the murder of another officer of the law (the Law)" (*Faulkner: The Return of the Repressed* [Charlottesville: University Press of Virginia, 1997], 162).

8 Jay R. Mandle points out that after Emancipation, the slave-owning classes managed to preserve their economic and class dominance with a functional, legal crushing of a free market for wage labor ("Black Economic Entrapment after Emancipation in the United States," in *The Meaning of Freedom: Economics, Politics, and Culture after Slavery,* ed. Frank McGlynn and Seymour Drescher [Pittsburgh, Penn.: University of Pittsburgh Press, 1992], 69, 71). Mandle uses the economist Gerald David Jaynes's analysis of the state's punishing control of agricultural labor after the Civil War (*Branches without Roots: Genesis of the Black Working Class in the American South, 1862–1882* (New York: Oxford University Press, 1986).

9 Sundquist, *Faulkner: The House Divided* (Baltimore, Md.: Johns Hopkins University Press, 1983), 132.

10 See Carole Marks, *Farewell—We're Good and Gone: The Great Black Migration* (Bloomington: Indiana University Press, 1989); Nicholas Lemann, *The Promised Land: The Great Black Migration and How It Changed America* (New York: Random House, 1991); and Milton C. Sernett, *Bound for the Promised Land: African American Religion and the Great Migration* (Durham, N.C.: Duke University Press, 1997) for extensive treatments of black migration from the South to the urban North and in particular to Chicago, which Sernett refers to as Canaan. Marks focuses the migration in terms of black workers, employment, labor, and economics; her concern is with "labor migrations," modern population movements in which the search for employment causes workers "to move from less developed peripheries to more developed cores" (4). Both Sernett and Lemann use the biblical Exodus story in the context of twentieth-century black life.

11 In comparison to Wright's Bigger, Faulkner's Butch fails to articulate his own meaning, his sense of the injustice he has suffered as a black youth in the South. Thus, Faulkner's representation of Butch seems badly dated, even though it encompasses some aspects of the contemporary late 1930s and early 1940s scene.

12 Vernon Bartlett, *The Past of Pastimes* (Hamden, Conn.: Archon Books, 1969), 152. Bartlett depends upon Huizinga's *Homo Ludens* for much of his argument about the great value of play.

13 John Carlos Rowe calls *Go Down, Moses* "a sustained elegy for the disappearance of the Old South and the failure of the New South to overcome the moral ruin of a system built on slavery," as well as Faulkner's attempt to redeem "his own work from hopeless elegy, desperate nostalgia" ("The African-American Voice in Faulkner's *Go Down, Moses,*" in *Modern American Short Story Sequences,* ed. Gerald Kennedy [Cambridge: Cambridge University Press, 1995], 80). John T. Matthews views the text in terms of the crisis of loss, rites of mourning, the articulation of grief, and erasure (*The Play of Faulkner's Language* [Ithaca, N.Y.: Cornell University Press, 1982], 212–13, 242, 271).

14 Rowe, "African-American Voice," 81.

15 Brigham, *Property and the Politics of Entitlement* (Philadelphia: Temple University

Press, 1990), 6, 30. Brigham argues that although "marginalized in debates about the Constitution since 1937," when Roosevelt interrupted the court's expansion into due process protection, property "has remained important in decisions by the Supreme Court on the meaning of clauses in the Constitution, and property has for a long time been at the heart of political theory in the West" (5).

16 Harry Elmer Barnes, *Social Institutions: In An Era of World Upheaval* (New York: Prentice-Hall, 1942), 183–85. Writing in the same cultural moment and milieu as *Go Down, Moses*, that is, after the New Deal and during World War II, Barnes was particularly troubled by what he saw as the misinterpretation and misapplication of the Fourteen Amendment. "The Supreme Court of the United States admitted to legal protection under the concept of property and property rights such matters as monopoly and the restraint of free trade the ability to charge such railroad rates as the railroads saw fit, the right to manufacture shoddy material and to use short weights in making sales, the right to escape the taxation of income, inheritances, and stock dividends, the right to maintain any working conditions that businessmen saw fit to impose upon their employees, the right to outlaw union labor, and the right of business practices to evade government control" (184). He also saw the Supreme Court as attempting for the sake of propertied interests to circumvent the New Deal, because, early on, "the Court upheld, as property rights, freedom from the restrictions of the National Recovery Act and the Agricultural Act. It upheld the immunity of the soft coal industry from adequate government control and set aside the New York State minimum wage act" (185).

17 William Faulkner, *Selected Letters of William Faulkner*, ed. Joseph Blotner (1977; reprint, New York: Vintage, 1978), 138.

18 See Thadious M. Davis, "Reading Faulkner's Compson Appendix: Writing History from the Margins," in *Faulkner and Ideology: Faulkner and Yoknapatawpha, 1992*, ed. Donald M. Kartiganer and Ann F. Abadie (Jackson: University Press of Mississippi, 1995), 238–52.

19 In "This Sex Which Is Not One," Luce Irigaray deploys these terms in her description of texts with male signatures. (in *Feminisms: An Anthology of Literary Theory and Criticism*, ed. Robyn R. Warhol and Diane Price Herndl [New Brunswick, N.J.: Rutgers University Press, 1991], 350–56).

20 See Carvel Collins, ed., *William Faulkner New Orleans Sketches* (1958; reprint, New York: Random House, 1968), and Carvel Collins, comp., *William Faulkner: Early Poetry and Prose* (Boston: Little, Brown, 1962), and for a discussion of his early poetry in the context of his disguises, see Judith Sensibar, *The Origins of Faulkner's Art* (Austin: University of Texas Press, 1984).

21 Faulkner to Harold Ober [received 22 June 1942], in Faulkner, *Selected Letters*, 153.

22 Faulkner to Harold Ober, Monday [20 August 1945], in ibid., 199.

23 Faulkner to Harold Ober, 20 December 1944, in ibid., 187.

24 See, for example, Faulkner to Robert K. Haas [received 27 March 1942]: "I am going before a Navy board and Medical for a commission, N.R. I will go to the Bureau of Aeronautics, Washington, for a job. I am to get full Lieut. and 3200.00 per year, and I hope a pilot's rating to wear the wings. I dont like this desk job particularly, but I think better to get the commission first and then try to get a little nearer the gunfire,

which I intend to do. . . . This is in confidence" (ibid., 149–50). See also, Faulkner to Harold Ober, March 1942; and Faulkner to Bennett Cerf, June 1942 (ibid., 150, 152).

25   Faulkner to Robert K. Haas, Monday [27 May 1940], in ibid., 125.

26   Faulkner to Robert K. Haas, 21 January 1942, in ibid., 148.

27   Faulkner to Harold Ober, [received 22 June 1942], in ibid., 153.

28   Faulkner to Malcolm Cowley, Saturday [27 October 1945], in ibid., 206.

29   Malcolm Cowley, *Faulkner-Cowley File: Letters and Memories, 1944–1962* (New York: Viking Press, 1966), 45.

30   Faulkner to Harold Ober, Saturday [22 April 1944], in Faulkner, *Selected Letters*, 181.

31   See Cowley on Faulkner's use of "Jew owners of New York and Chicago sweatshops": "In these present days, I'd drop out the word 'Jew.' . . . With all that's going on I'd rather not see a false argument over anti-Semitism interjected into the reviews" (*Faulkner-Cowley File*, 60).

32   Cowley, *Faulkner-Cowley File*, 41.

33   Faulkner to Robert N. Linscott, 4 February 1946, in Faulkner, *Selected Letters*, 220–21.

34   Cowley, *Faulkner-Cowley File*, 90–91. Faulkner admired the finished version of the appendix published in *The Portable Faulkner*, ed. Malcolm Cowley (1946; revised ed., New York: Viking Press, 1967), 7.

35   *Faulkner-Cowley File*, 25.

36   See, for example, the inclusions of Andrew Jackson and the Gibson family.

37   Faulkner to Robert N. Linscott [late May or early June 1946], in Faulkner, *Selected Letters*, 237.

38   The contrast in the appendix is specifically with Melissa Meek, the librarian whose life is bounded by Jefferson and whose work is protecting the morals of the young from the corrupting influence of textuality.

39   See *Faulkner in the University: Class Conferences at the University of Virginia, 1975–1978*, ed. Frederick L. Gwynn and Joseph Blotner (Charlottesville: University Press of Virginia, 1958), 275.

40   See Faulkner to Robert K. Haas, Friday [3 May 1940] (Faulkner, *Selected Letters*, 122). See also Anne Goodwyn Jones, "'The Kotex Age': Women, Popular Culture, and *The Wild Palms*," in *Faulkner and Popular Culture: Faulkner and Yoknapatawpha, 1988*, ed. Doreen Fowler and Ann J. Abadie (Jackson: University Press of Mississippi, 1988), 142–147.

41   Minrose C. Gwin, *The Feminine and Faulkner: Reading (Beyond) Sexual Difference* (Knoxville: University of Tennessee Press, 1990), 47.

42   Ibid., 61.

43   This representation would appear to be the case, despite Faulkner's portrayal of Quentin's promiscuity in the novel proper. I am indebted here to Luce Irigaray's response as to whether in a relationship with a man a woman discovers her mother ("Women's Exile," trans. Couze Venn, in *The Feminist Critique of Language*, ed. Deborah Cameron [London: Routledge, 1990], 80–91).

44   Cowley, *Faulkner-Cowley File*, 41.

45   Jenkins, *Faulkner and Black-White Relations*, 165. On Dilsey's representation, see Thadious M. Davis, *Faulkner's "Negro": Art and the Southern Context* (Baton Rouge:

Louisiana State University Press, 1983), 102–18. On the irony of Dilsey's position within the Compson household, see Jenkins, *Faulkner and Black-White Relations*, 171–76.

46 Cowley, *Faulkner-Cowley File*, 41. Faulkner to Malcolm A. Franklin, Saturday [5 December 1942], in Faulkner, *Selected Letters*, 166.

47 Derrick Bell, "Learning the Thee 'I's' of America's Slave Heritage," in *Slavery and the Law*, ed. Paul Finkelman (Madison, Wis.: Madison House Publishers, 1997), 31.

48 Frederick M. Wirth, *"We Ain't What We Was": Civil Rights in the New South* (Durham, N.C.: Duke University Press, 1997), 193. Wirth conducted his research in Panola County, Mississippi, and was concerned especially with the possibility of social change taking place through law.

49 Toni Morrison, *Playing in the Dark: Whiteness and the American Literary Imagination* (Cambridge, Mass.: Harvard University Press, 1992), 17.

50 William Faulkner, "American Segregation and the World Crisis," in *Three Views of the Segregation Decisions* (Atlanta: Southern Regional Council, 1956), 12.

51 *Brown v Board of Education*, 347 U.S. 483 (1954).

52 Faulkner, "American Segregation," 12.

53 Morrison, *Playing in the Dark*, 59.

54 Historian Fawn Brodie's *Thomas Jefferson: An Intimate History* (New York: Norton, 1974) was the first contemporary historical text to assert the relationship between Jefferson and Hemings, who was the half-sister of his deceased wife, Martha Wayles Jefferson. More recently, Annette Gordon-Reed in *Thomas Jefferson and Sally Hemings: An American Controversy* (Charlottesville: University Press of Virginia, 1997) pointed out that the oral histories from the Hemings descendants and from blacks identifying Jefferson as the father of Sally Hemings's children seem to have more validity than the dismissive denials of trained Jefferson scholars such as Joseph J. Ellis, whose *The American Sphinx: The Character of Thomas Jefferson* (New York: Vintage, 1998) rejected any claims of Jefferson's paternity of Hemings's children. Gordon-Reed cites, however, the memoir of Madison Hemings, published in 1873, that presented a convincing account of Thomas Jefferson's being his father. More recent and "scientific" proof has supported the oral tradition surrounding Jefferson and Hemings. DNA of descendants of Hemings's youngest son, Eston, matched Thomas Jefferson's DNA; geneticists were unable to test the descendants of Hemings's additional sons, so their claims could not be validated with DNA evidence. See Eugene A. Foster et al., "Jefferson Fathered Slave's Last Child," *Nature*, no. 396 (5 November 1998): 27–28. Reactions to the discovery have included both denial and acceptance on the parts of Jefferson scholars and white relatives. Julia Jefferson Westerinen, a white descendant of Eston Hemings (the son of Jefferson and Hemings who later became the white E. H. Jefferson), announced that she intended to declare herself "black" on the 2000 census to support affirmative action, but mainly, as she put it, "to show people that I am not afraid to be black." Julia Jefferson Westerinen quoted in Brent Staples, "A Hemings Family Turns from Black to White, to Black," *New York Times*, 17 December 2001, A20.

55 See, for example, recent studies by Fred Hobson, *But Now I See: The White Southern Racial Conversion Narrative* (Baton Rouge: Louisiana State University Press, 1999);

Barbara Ladd, *Nationalism and the Color Line in George W. Cable, Mark Twain, and William Faulkner* (Baton Rouge: Louisiana State University Press, 1996); Patricia McKee, *Producing American Races: Henry James, William Faulkner, Toni Morrison* (Durham, N.C.: Duke University Press, 1999); Patricia Yaeger, *Dirt and Desire: Reconstructing Southern Women's Writings 1930–1990* (Chicago: University of Chicago Press, 2000).

56 George Kent, *Blackness and the Adventure of Western Culture* (Chicago: Third World Press, 1972), 166.

57 Ibid., 167.

58 Coco Fusco, "Fantasies of Oppositionality," *Screen*, "The Last Special Issue on Race?" 29, no. 4 (autumn 1988); reprinted in *Art, Activism, and Oppositionality*, ed. Grant H. Kester (Durham, N.C.: Duke University Press, 1998), 60–75.

59 Carol A. Kolmerten, Stephen M. Ross, and Judith Bryant Wittenberg, eds. *Unflinching Gaze: Morrison and Faulkner Re-Envisioned* (Jackson: University Press of Mississippi, 1997), xi. A year earlier, Philip M. Weinstein's *What Else but Love? The Ordeal of Race in Faulkner and Morrison* (New York: Columbia University Press, 1996) had appeared and prepared the way for further comparative studies of the two authors.

60 Kwame Anthony Appiah, *In My Father's House: Africa in the Philosophy of Culture* (New York: Oxford University Press, 1992).

61 Morrison, *Playing in the Dark*, 52–53, 63.

62 Albert Murray, "William Faulkner Noun, Place and Verb," *New Republic* (11 December 2000): 35. Murray's poem also appears in his essay, "Me and Old Uncle Billy and the American Mythosphere," as simply "William Faulkner," in *Faulkner at 100: Retrospect and Prospect*, ed. Donald M. Kartiganer and Ann J. Abadie (Jackson: University Press of Mississippi, 2000), 238–49.

63 Michael S. Harper, "Faulkner's Centennial Poem: September 25, 1997," *Crazy Horse*, 1997; collected in Michael S. Harper, *Songlines in Michaeltree: New and Collected Poems* (Urbana: University of Illinois Press, 2000), 282–283.

64 See Randall Robinson, *The Debt: What America Owes to Blacks* (New York: Dutton, 2000). Robinson answered questions about the reparations movement in Ronald Roach, "Fighting the Good Fight," *Black Issues in Higher Education* 18 (8 November 2001): 28–31. See also Charles J. Ogletree Jr., "Litigating the Legacy of Slavery," *New York Times*, 31 March 2002, sec. 4, p. 9. David Brion Davis, director of Yale University's Gilder Lehrman Center for the Study of Slavery, Resistance, and Abolition, maintains that the reparations debate is also about the role of slavery in American history. "Free at Last: The Enduring Legacy of the South's Civil War Victory," *New York Times*, 20 August 2001, sec. 4, p. 1.

65 California is thus far the only state to join with city governments, such as Chicago, Cleveland, Dallas, and Detroit, in calling for federal action regarding reparations for slavery. In addition to congressional hearings, the California Assembly also called for Congress to apologize to African Americans for the "fundamental injustice, cruelty, brutality and inhumanity of slavery," for a national monument as a memorial to those who suffered under slavery and as a reminder of the human toll during the centuries-long institution of slavery.

BIBLIOGRAPHY

Adamson, Joseph, and Hilary Clark, eds. *Scenes of Shame: Psychoanalysis, Shame, and Writing.* Albany: State University of New York Press, 1999.

Adorno, Theodor W. *Minima Moralia: Reflections from Damaged Life.* Translated by E. F. N. Jephcott. London: New Left Books, 1974.

Alexander, Gregory S. *Commodity and Propriety: Competing Visions of Property in American Legal Thought, 1776–1970.* Chicago: University of Chicago Press, 1997.

Allen, Theodore W. *The Invention of the White Race.* London: Verso, 1994.

Anderson, Carl. "Faulkner's 'Was': 'A Deadlier Purpose than Simple Pleasure.'" *American Literature* 61, no. 3 (October 1989): 414–28.

Ansley, Frances L. "Race and the Core Curriculum of Legal Education." *California Law Review* 79 (1991): 1511–32.

Appiah, Kwame Anthony. *In My Father's House: Africa in the Philosophy of Culture.* New York: Oxford University Press, 1992.

Atkinson, Thomas. *Handbook of the Law of Wills and Other Principles of Succession Including Intestacy and Administration of Decedents' Estates.* 2d ed. St. Paul, Minn.: West Publishing, 1953.

Azbug, Robert H., and Stephen E. Maizlish, eds. *New Perspectives on Race and Slavery in America: Essays in Honor of Kenneth M. Stampp.* Lexington: University of Kentucky Press, 1986.

Baldwin, James. "On Being White and Other Lies." *Essence* (April 1984): 90–91.

Ballentine, James A., ed. *Ballentine's Law Dictionary with Pronunciations.* 3d ed., edited by William S. Anderson. San Francisco: Bancroft-Whitney Co., 1969.

Bardaglio, Peter. *Reconstructing the Household: Families, Sex, and the Law in the Nineteenth-Century South.* Chapel Hill: University of North Carolina Press, 1995.

Bardolph, Richard, ed. *The Civil Rights Record: Black Americans and the Law, 1849–1976.* New York: Thomas Y. Crowell, 1970.

Barkan, Elazar. *Retreat of Scientific Racism: Changing Concepts of Race in Britain and the United States between the World Wars.* Cambridge: Cambridge University Press, 1992.

Barnes, Harry Elmer. *Social Institutions: In an Era of World Upheaval.* New York: Prentice-Hall, 1942.

Barry, Ellen. "White Like Me." *Providence Phoenix,* 11 July 1997, 8–12.

Bartlett, Vernon. *The Past of Pastimes.* Hamden, Conn.: Archon Books, 1969.

Bassett, John Spencer. *Slavery in the State of North Carolina.* Baltimore: Johns Hopkins University Press, 1899.

Becker, Lawrence. *Property Rights: Philosophic Foundations.* London: Routledge, 1977.

Becker, Lawrence, and Kenneth Kipnis, eds. *Property: Cases, Concepts, Critiques.* Englewood Cliffs, N.J.: Prentice Hall, 1984.

Bell, Derrick. "Learning the Three 'I's' of America's Slave Heritage." In *Slavery and the Law,* edited by Paul Finkelman. Madison, Wis.: Madison House Publishers, 1997.

Bell, J. Bowyer. *To Play the Game: An Analysis of Sports.* New Brunswick, N.J.: Transaction Books, 1987.

Bentham, Jeremy. *Principles of the Civil Code* (1802). In *The Works of Jeremy Bentham.* Edited by John Bowring. 2:297–358. Edinburgh: William Tait, 1843.

Bergson, Henri. *Laughter: An Essay in the Meaning of the Comic.* New York: Macmillan, 1911.

Berlin, Ira. *Many Thousands Gone: The First Two Centuries of Slavery in North America.* Cambridge, Mass.: Belknap Press of Harvard University, 1998.

Berlin, Ira, Barbara J. Fields, Steven F. Miller, Joseph P. Reidy, and Leslie S. Rowland, eds. *Free at Last: A Documentary History of Slavery, Freedom, and the Civil War.* Edison, N.J.: Blue and Grey Press, 1997.

Berry, Mary Frances. *Black Resistance/White Law: A History of Constitutional Racism in America.* Rev. ed. New York: Penguin Books, 1995.

——. "Judging Morality: Sexual Behavior and Legal Consequences in the Late Nineteenth-Century South." *The Journal of American History* 78, no. 3 (December 1991): 835–56.

——. *The Pig Farmer's Daughter and Other Tales of American Justice.* New York: Alfred A. Knopf, 1999.

Binmore, Ken. *Essays on the Foundation of Game Theory.* Cambridge: Basil Blackwell, 1990.

Biographical and Historical Memoirs of Mississippi. Chicago: Goodspeed, 1891.

Black, Henry Campbell. *Black's Law Dictionary: Definitions of the Terms and Phrases of American and English Jurisprudence, Ancient and Modern.* 6th ed. St. Paul, Minn.: West Publishing, 1990.

Blackstone, William. *Commentaries on the Laws of England.* 4 vol. 1769. Reprint, Chicago: University of Chicago Press, 1979.

Blassingame, John W. *The Slave Community: Plantation Life in the Antebellum South.* 1972. Reprint, New York: Oxford University Press, 1979.

——, ed. *Slave Testimony: Two Centuries of Letters, Speeches, Interviews, and Autobiographies.* Baton Rouge: Louisiana State University Press, 1977.

Bleser, Carol. *Secret and Sacred: The Diaries of James Henry Hammond, a Southern Slaveholder.* New York: Oxford University Press, 1988.

Blotner, Joseph. *Faulkner: A Biography.* 2 vol. New York: Random House, 1974.

——. *Faulkner: A Biography.* Rev. ed. New York: Random House, 1984.

Booker, M. Keith. *Literature and Domination: Sex, Knowledge, and Power in Modern Fiction.* Gainesville: University Press of Florida, 1993.

Bowe, William, and Douglas Parker. *Revised Treatise Page on the Law of Wills Including Probate, Will Contests, Evidence, Taxation, Conflicts, Estate Planning, Forms, and Statutes Relating to Wills.* 1901. Reprint, Cincinnati: W. H. Anderson, 1960.

Brigham, John. *Property and the Politics of Entitlement.* Philadelphia: Temple University Press, 1990.

Britannica Micropaedia Ready Reference. "Hide and Seek." 15th edition. Vol. 2. Chicago: Britannica, 1992.

Brodie, Fawn. *Thomas Jefferson: An Intimate History.* New York: Norton, 1974.

Brodsky, Louis Daniel, and Robert W. Hamblin. *Faulkner: A Comprehensive Guide to the Brodsky Collection.* 2 vol. Jackson: University Press of Mississippi, 1982.

Brooks, Peter. *Reading for the Plot: Design and Intention in Narrative.* New York: Alfred A. Knopf, 1984.

Brown, Elizabeth Gaspar. "Husband and Wife: Memorandum on the Mississippi Woman's Law of 1839." *Michigan Law Review* 42 (April 1944): 1110–21.

Bryan, Violet Harrington. *The Myth of New Orleans in Literature: Dialogues of Race and Gender.* Knoxville: University of Tennessee Press, 1993.

Bryant, Jonathan M. "Race, Class, and Law in Bourbon, Georgia: The Case of David Dickson's Will." *Georgia Historical Quarterly* 71 (summer 1987): 226–42.

Buell, Lawrence. "Faulkner and the Claims of the Natural World." In *Faulkner and the Natural World: Faulkner and Yoknapatawpha, 1996,* edited by Donald M. Kartiganer and Ann J. Abadie, 1–18. Jackson: University Press of Mississippi, 1999.

Burnham, Margaret A. "An Impossible Marriage: Slave Law and Family Law." *Law and Inequality* 5, no. 2 (July 1987): 187–225.

Cable, George Washington. *The Grandissimes: A Story of Creole Life.* 1879. Reprint, New York: Hill and Wang, 1957.

Cameron, Deborah, ed. *The Feminist Critique of Language.* London: Routledge, 1990.

Carr, David. *Time, Narrative, and History.* Bloomington: Indiana University Press, 1986.

Casner, A. James, and W. Barton Leach. *Cases and Texts on Property.* 3d ed. Boston: Little Brown, 1984.

Catterall, Helen Tunnicliff, ed. *Judicial Cases Concerning American Slavery and the Negro.* Vol. 1. 1926. Reprint, New York: Octagon Books, 1968.

Chabrier, Gwendolyn. *Faulkner's Families: A Southern Saga.* Staten Island, N.Y.: Gordian Press, 1993.

Chapman, John W., ed. *Compensatory Justice.* New York: New York University Press, 1991.

Chesnut, Mary Boykin Miller. *A Diary from Dixie.* Edited by Ben Ames Williams. Cambridge, Mass.: Harvard University Press, 1961.

Claiborne, J. F. H. *Mississippi as a Province, Territory, and State.* Vol. 1. Jackson, Miss.: Power and Barksdale, 1880.

Clayton, Bruce, and John Salmond, eds. *Varieties of Southern History: New Essays on a Region and Its People.* Westport, Conn.: Greenwood Press, 1996.

Clinton, Catherine. *The Plantation Mistress: Woman's World in the Old South.* New York: Pantheon Books, 1982.

Clinton, Catherine, and Nina Silber, eds. *Divided Houses: Gender and the Civil War.* New York: Oxford University Press, 1992.

Cobb, Thomas R. R. *Inquiry in to the Law of Negro Slavery.* Philadelphia: T. S. J. W. Johnson, 1858.

Cohen, Felix S. *Ethical Systems and Legal Ideals: An Essay on the Foundation of Legal Criticism.* Ithaca, N.Y.: Cornell University Great Seal Books, 1933.

Cohen, Morris. "Property and Sovereignty." In *Property: Mainstream and Critical Positions,* edited by C. B. Macpherson, 153–75. Toronto: University of Toronto Press, 1978.

Cole, David. "Strategies of Difference: Litigating for Women's Rights in a Man's World." *Law and Inequality* 2 (February 1984): 33–96.

Collier's Encyclopedia. "Childhood/Children's Games." Vol. 6. 226J–226L. New York: Macmillan, 1995.

Collins, Carvel, comp. *William Faulkner: Early Poetry and Prose.* Boston: Little, Brown, 1962.

——, ed. *William Faulkner: New Orleans Sketches.* 1958. Rev. ed. New York: Random House, 1968.

Collins, Patricia Hill. *Black Feminist Thought: Knowledge, Consciousness, and the Politics of Empowerment.* New York: Routledge, 1990.

Cordell, Justine M., and Ronald A. Schwarz, eds. *The Fabrics of Culture: The Anthropology of Clothing and Adornment.* New York: Mouton, 1979.

Cowley, Malcolm, ed. *The Faulkner-Cowley File: Letters and Memories, 1944–1962.* New York: Viking Press, 1966.

——, ed. *The Portable Faulkner.* 1946. Rev. ed. New York: Viking Press, 1967.

Creighton, Joanne V. *William Faulkner's Craft of Revision: The Snopes Trilogy, "The Unvanquished," and "Go Down, Moses".* Detroit: Wayne State University Press, 1977.

Crenshaw, Kimberlè, Neil Gotana, Gary Peller, and Kendall Thomas, eds. *Critical Race Theory: The Key Writings that Formed the Movement.* New York: New Press, 1995.

Currie, James T. "From Slavery to Freedom in Mississippi's Legal System." *Journal of Negro History* 65, no. 2 (spring 1980): 112–25.

Davis, Adrienne D. "The Private Law of Race and Sex: An Antebellum Perspective." *Stanford Law Review* 51, no. 2 (January 1999): 221–88.

Davis, Angela Y. *Women, Culture, and Politics.* New York: Vintage Books, 1990.

——. *Women, Race, and Class.* New York: Vintage Books, 1983.

Davis, David Brion. *In the Image of God: Religion, Moral Value, and Our Heritage of Slavery.* New Haven, Conn.: Yale University Press, 2001.

——. *The Problem of Slavery in Western Culture.* Ithaca, N.Y.: Cornell University Press, 1966.

Davis, Thadious M. "Crying in the Wilderness: Legal, Racial, and Moral Codes in *Go Down, Moses.*" *Mississippi College Law Review* 4, no. 2 (spring 1984): 299–318; reprinted in *Critical Essays on William Faulkner: The McCaslin Family,* edited by Arthur R. Kinney, 137–54. Boston: G. K. Hall, 1990.

——. *Faulkner's "Negro": Art and the Southern Context.* Baton Rouge: Louisiana State University Press, 1983.

——. "From Jazz Syncopation to Blues Elegy: Faulkner's Development of Black Characterization." In *Faulkner and Race: Faulkner and Yoknapatawpha, 1986*, edited by Doreen Fowler and Ann Abadie, 70–92. Jackson: University Press of Mississippi, 1987.

———. "The Game of Courts: Go Down, Moses, Arbitrary Legalities, and Compensatory Boundaries." In *New Essays on* Go Down, Moses, edited by Linda Wagner-Martin, 129–54. New York: Cambridge University Press, 1996.

———. "Race Cards: Trumping and Troping in Constructing Whiteness." In *Faulkner at 100: Retrospect and Prospect*, edited by Donald M. Kartiganer and Ann J. Abadie, 165–79. Jackson: University Press of Mississippi, 2000.

———. "Reading Faulkner's Compson Appendix: Writing History from the Margins." In *Faulkner and Ideology: Faulkner and Yoknapatawpha, 1992*, edited by Donald Kartiganer and Ann Abadie, 238–52. Jackson: University Press of Mississippi, 1995.

Deleuze, Giles and Felix Guattari. *A Thousand Plateaus: Capitalism and Schizophrenia*. 2 vols. Translated by Brian Massumi. Minneapolis: University of Minnesota Press, 1987.

Devlin, Albert J. "History, Sexuality, and the Wilderness in the McCaslin Family Chronicle." In *Critical Essays on William Faulkner: The McCaslin Family*, edited by Arthur F. Kinney, 189–98. Boston: G. K. Hall, 1990.

Dollard, John. *Caste and Class in a Southern Town*. New Haven: Yale University Press for the Institute of Human Relations, 1937.

Doyle, Bertram Wilbur. *The Etiquette of Race Relations in the South: A Study in Social Control*. Chicago: The University of Chicago Press, 1937.

Doyle, Don H. *Faulkner's County: The Historical Roots of Yoknapatawpha*. Chapel Hill: University of North Carolina Press, 2001.

Du Bois, W. E. B. *Black Reconstruction in America: An Essay toward a History of the Part Which Black Folk Played in the Attempt to Reconstruct Democracy in America, 1860–1880*. New York: Harcourt, Brace, 1935.

Dunlap, Mary Montgomery. "William Faulkner's 'Knight's Gambit' and Gavin Stevens." *Mississippi Quarterly* 23 (1970): 223–39.

Dunning, Eric, and Chris Rojek, eds. *Sport and Leisure in the Civilizing Process: Critique and Counter-Critique*. Toronto: University of Toronto Press, 1992.

Durkheim, Emile. *Suicide: A Study in Sociology*. New York: Free Press, 1951.

Duval, Mary V. *History of Mississippi and Civil Government with Appendix containing the Constitution of Mississippi adopted November 1, 1890*. Louisville, Ky.: Courier-Journal Job, 1892.

Eagleton, Terry. *Criticism and Ideology: A Study of Marxist Literary Theory*. London: Verso, 1975.

Early, James. *The Making of* Go Down, Moses. Dallas: Southern Methodist University Press, 1972.

Ehrmann, Jacques, ed. *Game, Play, Literature*. Boston: Beacon Press, 1968.

Eisenstein, Zillah R. *The Female Body and the Law*. Berkeley: University of California Press, 1988.

Elias, Norbert. *The Civilizing Process*. Translated by Edmund Jephcott. New York: Urizen Books, 1978.

Ellis, Joseph J. *The American Sphinx: The Character of Thomas Jefferson*. New York: Vintage, 1998.

Ely, James W., Jr. *The Guardian of Every Other Right: A Constitutional History of Property Rights*. New York: Oxford University Press, 1998.

Faulkner, William. *Absalom, Absalom!* The corrected text, edited by Noel Polk. 1936. Reprint, New York: Vintage International, 1986.

——. "American Segregation and the World Crisis." In *Three Views of the Segregation Decisions*. Atlanta: The Southern Regional Council, 1956.

——. "Appendix/Compson/1699–1945." In *The Portable Faulkner*, edited by Malcolm Cowley, 704–21. 1946. Rev. ed. New York: Viking Press, 1967.

——. *Go Down, Moses*. 1942. Reprint, New York: Vintage International Edition, 1990.

——. *If I Forget Thee, Jerusalem [The Wild Palms]*. 1939. Reprint, New York: Vintage International, 1995.

——. *Knight's Gambit*. New York: Random House, 1948.

——. "A Letter to Bishop Robert E. Jones, 15 March 1940." *Georgia Review* (fall 2001): 530–34.

——. *Light in August*. The corrected text, edited by Noel Polk. 1932. Reprint, New York: Vintage International, 1985.

——. *The Marble Faun*. Boston: Four Seas, 1924.

——. "Mississippi." *Holiday* (April 1954); reprinted in *Essays, Speeches, and Public Letters of William Faulkner*. Ed. James B. Meriwether. New York: Random House, 1965.

——. "New Orleans." *Double Dealer* (January–February 1925). Reprint in *William Faulkner: New Orleans Sketches*. Edited by Carvel Collins. 1958. Rev. ed., New York: Random House, 1968.

——. *Sanctuary*. The corrected text, edited by Noel Polk. 1932. Reprint, New York: Vintage Books, 1987.

——. *Selected Letters of William Faulkner*. Edited by Joseph Blotner. 1977. Reprint, New York: Vintage, 1978.

——. *The Sound and the Fury*. 1929. Reprint, New York: W. W. Norton, 1987.

——. "Spoken by William Faulkner at Mammy's service, fourth February, 1940." *The Georgia Review* (Fall 2001): 534.

——. *The Wild Palms*. New York: Random House, 1939.

——. *William Faulkner: Early Poetry and Prose*. Compiled by Carvel Collins. Boston: Little, Brown, 1962.

Faust, Drew Gilpin. *James Henry Hammond and the Old South: A Design for Mastery*. Baton Rouge: Louisiana State University Press, 1982.

Feder, Lillian. *Crowell's Handbook of Classical Literature*. New York: Harper Colophon, 1964.

Fine, Reuben. *The Ideas Behind Chess Openings*. New York: David McKay, 1949.

——. *The Psychology of the Chess Player*. New York: Dover, 1967.

Fineman, Martha Albertson, and Nancy Sweet Thomadsen, eds. *At the Boundaries of Law: Feminism and Legal Theory*. New York: Routledge, 1991.

Fineman, Martha Albertson. Introduction to *At the Boundaries of Law: Feminism and Legal Theory*, edited by Martha Albertson Fineman and Nancy Sweet Thomadsen, xi–xvi. New York: Routledge, 1991.

Finkelman, Paul. *An Imperfect Union: Slavery, Federalism, and Comity*. Chapel Hill: University of North Carolina Press, 1981.

——. Introduction to *Race and Law Before Emancipation*. Vol. 2, *Race, Law, and American History: The African American Experience*, edited by Paul Finkelman. New York: Garland, 1992.

——, ed. *Free Blacks in a Slave Society*. Vol. 17, *Articles in American Slavery*. New York: Garland, 1989.

——, ed. *The Law of Freedom and Bondage: A Casebook*. New York: Oceana, 1986.

——, ed. *Slavery and the Law*. Madison, Wis.: Madison House Publishers, 1997.

Fisher, William W., III. "Ideology and Imagery in the Law of Slavery." *Chicago-Kent Law Review* 68, no. 3 (1993): 1051–83.

Fleischner, Jennifer. *Mastering Slavery: Memory, Family, and Identity in Women's Slave Narratives*. New York: New York University Press, 1996.

Fletcher, George P. *Basic Concepts of Legal Thought*. New York: Oxford University Press, 1996.

Foner, Philip S., ed. *The Life and Writings of Frederick Douglass*. 5 vol. New York: International Publishers, 1950–1978.

Fossett, Judith Jackson, and Jeffrey A. Tucker, eds. *Race Consciousness: African-American Studies for the New Century*. New York: New York University Press, 1997.

Foster, Eugene A., et al. "Jefferson Fathered Slave's Last Child." *Nature* 396 (November 1998): 27–28.

Foster, Frances Smith. *Written by Herself: Literary Production by African American Women, 1746–1892*. Bloomington: Indiana University Press, 1993.

Foster, Helen Bradley. *"New Raiments of Self": African American Clothing in the Antebellum South*. Oxford: Berg, 1997.

Foucault, Michel. *Discipline and Punish: The Birth of the Prison*. Translated by Alan Sheridan. New York: Pantheon Books, 1977.

——. *The History of Sexuality*. Vol. 1, *An Introduction*. New York: Vintage Books, 1990.

Fowler, Doreen. *Faulkner: The Return of the Repressed*. Charlottesville: University Press of Virginia, 1997.

Fowler, Doreen, and Ann J. Abadie, eds. *Faulkner and Humor: Faulkner and Yoknapatawpha, 1984*. Jackson: University Press of Mississippi, 1986.

——. *Faulkner and Popular Culture: Faulkner and Yoknapatawpha, 1988*. Jackson: University Press of Mississippi, 1990.

——. *Faulkner and Race: Faulkner and Yoknapatawpha, 1986*. Jackson: University Press of Mississippi, 1987.

Frankenberg, Ruth. *White Women, Race Matters: The Social Construction of Whiteness*. Minneapolis: University of Minnesota Press, 1993.

Franklin, John Hope, and Loren Schweninger, ed. *Runaway Slaves: Rebels on the Plantation*. New York: Oxford University Press, 1999.

Frederickson, George M. *The Arrogance of Race: Historical Perspectives on Slavery, Racism, and Social Inequality*. Middletown, Ct.: Wesleyan University Press, 1988.

——. *The Black Image in the White Mind: The Debate on Afro-American Character and Destiny, 1817–1914*. New York: Harper and Row, 1971.

Freud, Sigmund. "Introductory Lectures on Psycho-analysis." In vol. 15 of *The Standard Edition of the Complete Psychological Works of Sigmund Freud*, 3–239. Translated under the general editorship of James Strachey, in collaboration with Anna Freud, assisted by A. Strachey and A. Tyson. 24 vol. London: Hogarth Press, 1953–1974.

——. *Three Essays on the Theory of Sexuality.* Translated by James Strachey. New York: Basic Books, 1962.

Friedman, Lawrence. *A History of American Law.* 2nd ed. New York: Simon and Schuster, 1985.

Fry, Gladys-Marie. *Stitched from the Soul: Slave Quilts from the Ante-bellum South.* New York: Dutton Studio Books, in association with the Museum of American Folk Art, 1990.

Fusco, Coco. "Fantasies of Oppositionality." *Screen,* "The Last Special Issue on Race?" 29, no. 4 (autumn 1988); reprinted in *Art, Activism, and Oppositionality,* edited by Grant H. Kester, 60–65. Durham, N.C.: Duke University Press, 1998.

Gaspar, David Barry and Darlene Clark Hine, eds. *More than Chattel: Black Women and Slavery in the Americas.* Bloomington: Indiana University Press, 1996.

Gates, Henry Louis, Jr. "Writing 'Race' and the Difference It Makes." In *"Race," Writing, and Difference,* edited by Henry Louis Gates Jr., 1–20. Chicago: University of Chicago Press, 1985.

Genovese, Eugene D. *Roll, Jordan, Roll: The World the Slaves Made.* New York: Pantheon, 1974.

Gibson, Arrell M. *The Chickasaws.* Norman: University of Oklahoma Press, 1971.

Glaude, Eddie S., Jr. *Exodus!: Religion, Race, and Nation in Early-Nineteenth-Century Black America.* Chicago: University of Chicago Press, 2000.

Godden, Richard. *Fictions of Labor: William Faulkner and the South's Long Revolution.* Cambridge: Cambridge University Press, 1997.

Goldstein, Jeffrey H. "Outcomes in Professional Team Sports: Chance, Skill, and Situational Factors." In *Sports, Games, and Play: Social and Psychological Viewpoints,* edited by Jeffrey H. Goldstein. Hillsdale, N.J.: Lawrence Erlbaum Associates, 1979.

Goodell, William. *The American Slave Code in Theory and in Practice: Distinctive Features Shown by Its Statues, Judicial Decisions, and Illustrative Facts.* 1853. Reprint, New York: Negro Universities Press, 1968.

Gordon-Reed, Annette. *Thomas Jefferson and Sally Hemings: An American Controversy.* Charlottesville: University Press of Virginia, 1997.

Grimwood, Michael. *Heart in Conflict: Faulkner's Struggles with Vocation.* Athens: University of Georgia Press, 1987.

Guillory, Monique. "Under One Roof: The Sins and Sanctity of New Orleans Quadroon Balls." In *Race Consciousness: African-American Studies for the New Century,* edited by Judith Jackson Fossett and Jeffrey A. Tucker, 67–92. New York: New York University Press, 1997.

Gutman, Herbert G. *The Black Family in Slavery and Freedom, 1750–1925.* New York: Vintage Books, 1977.

Guy-Sheftall, ed. *Words of Fire: An Anthology of African-American Feminist Thought.* New York: New Press, 1995.

Gwaltney, John Langston. *Drylongso: A Self-Portrait of Black America.* 1980. Reprint, New York: New Press, 1993.

Gwin, Minrose C. *The Feminine and Faulkner: Reading (Beyond) Sexual Difference.* Knoxville: University of Tennessee Press, 1990.

——. "Her Shape, His Hand: The Spaces of African American Women in Go Down, Moses." In *New Essays on* Go Down, Moses, edited by Linda Wagner-Martin, 73–100. Cambridge: Cambridge University Press, 1996.

Gwynn, Frederick L., and Joseph Blotner, eds. *Faulkner in the University: Class Conferences at the University of Virginia, 1957–1958.* Charlottesville: University Press of Virginia, 1959.

Hale, Grace Elizabeth. *Making Whiteness: The Culture of Segregation in the South, 1890–1940.* New York: Pantheon Books, 1998.

Hall, Constance Hill. *Incest in Faulkner: A Metaphor for the Fall.* Ann Arbor, Mich.: UMI Research, 1986.

Haney-Lopez, Ian F. *White by Law: The Legal Construction of Race.* New York: New York University Press, 1996.

Harper, Michael S. "Faulkner's Centennial Poem: September 25, 1997." *Crazyhorse,* 1997; reprinted in *Songlines in Michaeltree: New and Collected Poems,* by Michael S. Harper, 282–83. Urbana: University of Illinois Press, 2000.

Harrington, Evans, and Ann J. Abadie, eds. *The South and Faulkner's Yoknapatawpha: The Actual and the Apocryphal.* Jackson: University Press of Mississippi, 1977.

Harris, Cheryl. "Whiteness as Property." *Harvard Law Review* 106, no. 8 (June 1993): 1709–1791; reprinted in *Black on White: Black Writers on What It Means To Be White,* edited by David R. Roediger, 103–18. New York: Random House, 1998.

Harris, J. W. *Property and Justice.* Oxford: Clarendon Press, 1996.

Hartman, Saidiya V. *Scenes of Subjection: Terror, Slavery, and Self-Making in Nineteenth-Century America.* New York: Oxford University Press, 1997.

Hartog, Hendrik. *Man and Wife in America: A History.* Cambridge, Mass.: Harvard University Press, 2000.

——. "Marital Exits and Marital Expectations in Nineteenth-Century America." *Georgetown Law Journal* 80, no. 1 (Oct. 1991): 95–129.

Hearst, Elliott, and Michael Wierzbicki. "Battle Royal: Psychology and the Chessplayer." In *Sports, Games, and Play: Social and Psychological Viewpoints,* edited by Jeffrey H. Goldstein. Hillsdale, N.J.: Lawrence Erlbaum Associates, 1979.

Hegel, G. W. F. *Elements of the Philosophy of Right,* part 1. Translated by H. B. Nisbet. Cambridge: Cambridge University Press, 1991.

Hening, William Waller. *The Statutes at Large: Being a Collection of All the Laws of Virginia from the First Session of the Legislature in the Year 1619.* 13 vol. Richmond, Va.: W. Gray Printers, 1819–1823.

Higginbotham, A. Leon, Jr. *In the Matter of Color: Race and the American Legal Process: The Colonial Period.* 1978. Reprint, Oxford: Oxford University Press, 1980.

——. *Shades of Freedom: Radical Politics and the Presumptions of the American Legal Process.* New York: Oxford University Press, 1996.

Higginbotham, A. Leon, Jr., and Anne F. Jacobs. "The 'Law Only as an Enemy': The Legitimization of Racial Powerlessness through the Colonial and Antebellum Criminal Laws of Virginia." *North Carolina Law Review* 70 (1992): 969–1070.

Higginbotham, A. Leon, Jr., and Barbara K. Kopytoff. "Property First, Humanity Second: The Recognition of the Slave's Human Nature in Virginia's Civil Law." *Ohio State Law Journal* 50 (1989): 511–40.

——. "Racial Purity and Interracial Sex in the Law of Colonial and Antebellum Virginia." *Georgetown Law Journal* 77 (1989): 1967–2029.

Hobson, Fred. *But Now I See: The White Southern Racial Conversion Narrative.* Baton Rouge: Louisiana State University Press, 1999.

Hoff, Joan. *Law, Gender, and Injustice: A Legal History of U.S. Women.* New York: New York University Press, 1991.

Hoffman, Daniel. *Faulkner's Country Matters: Folklore and Fable in Yoknapatawpha.* Baton Rouge: Louisiana State University Press, 1989.

Hogan, Patrick Colm. *On Interpretation: Meaning and Inference in Law, Psychoanalysis, and Literature.* Athens: University of Georgia Press, 1996.

hooks, bell. *Killing Rage: Ending Racism.* New York: Henry Holt, 1995.

Horsman, Reginal. *Race and Manifest Destiny: The Origins of American Racial Anglo-Saxonism.* Cambridge, Mass.: Harvard University Press, 1981.

Howe, Adrian. "The Problem of Privatized Injuries: Feminist Strategies for Litigation." In *At the Boundaries of Law: Feminism and Legal Theory,* edited by Martha Albertson Fineman and Nancy Sweet Thomadsen, 148–67. New York: Routledge, 1991.

Huizinga, Johan. *Homo Ludens: A Study of the Play Element in Culture.* New York: Harper and Row, 1970.

Hunter, Tera W. *To 'Joy My Freedom: Southern Black Women's Lives and Labors after the Civil War.* Cambridge, Mass.: Harvard University Press, 1997.

Hurd, John Codman. *The Law of Freedom and Bondage in the United States.* 2 vol. Boston: Little, Brown, 1858.

Hutchinson, Anderson. *Code of Mississippi.* Jackson: Price and Fall, 1848.

Hutchinson, Peter. *Games Authors Play.* London: Methuen, 1983.

Hyde, Alan. *Bodies of Law.* Princeton, N.J.: Princeton University Press, 1997.

Ignatiev, Noel. *How the Irish Became White.* New York: Routledge, 1995.

Irigaray, Luce. "This Sex Which Is Not One." In *Feminisms: An Anthology of Literary Theory and Criticism,* edited by Robyn R. Warhol and Diane Price Herndl, 350–56. New Brunswick, N.J.: Rutgers University Press, 1991.

——. "Women's Exile." Translated by Couze Venn. In *The Feminist Critique of Language,* edited by Deborah Cameron, 80–91. London: Routledge, 1990.

Isenberg, Nancy. *Sex and Citizenship in Antebellum America.* Chapel Hill, N.C.: University of North Carolina Press, 1998.

Jacobs, Harriet. *Incidents in the Life of a Slave Girl: Written by Herself.* Edited by Jean Fagan Yellin. 1861. Reprint, Cambridge, Mass.: Harvard University Press, 1987.

James, William. *The Principles of Psychology.* 2 vol. New York: Henry Holt, 1890.

Jaynes, Gerald David. *Branches without Roots: Genesis of the Black Working Class in the American South, 1862–1882.* New York: Oxford University Press, 1986.

Jenkins, Lee. *Faulkner and Black-White Relations: A Psychoanalytic Approach.* New York: Columbia University Press, 1981.

Johnson, James Weldon. *God's Trombones: Seven Negro Sermons in Verse.* New York: Viking Press, 1927.

Johnson, James Weldon, and J. Rosamund Johnson. *The Book of American Negro Spirituals: Including The Book of American Negro Spirituals [1925] and The Second Book of American Negro Spirituals [1926]*. New York: Viking Press, 1940.

Johnson, Walter. *Soul by Soul: Life Inside the Antebellum Slave Market*. Cambridge, Mass.: Harvard University Press, 1999.

Jones, Anne Goodwyn. "'The Kotex Age': Women, Popular Culture, and *The Wild Palms*." In *Faulkner and Popular Culture: Faulkner and Yoknapatawpha, 1988*, edited by Doreen Fowler and Ann J. Abadie, 142–62. Jackson: University Press of Mississippi, 1990.

———. "Male Fantasies? Faulkner's War Stories and the Construction of Gender. In *Faulkner and Psychology: Faulkner and Yoknapatawpha, 1991*, edited by Donald M. Kartiganer and Ann J. Abadie, 21–55. Jackson: University Press of Mississippi, 1994.

Jones, Anne Goodwyn, and Susan V. Donaldson, eds. *Haunted Bodies: Gender and Southern Texts*. Charlottesville: University Press of Virginia, 1997.

Jordan, Winthrop. *White over Black: American Attitudes toward the Negro, 1550–1812*. Baltimore: Johns Hopkins University Press, 1969.

Josey, Charles Conant. *Race and National Solidarity*. New York: C. Scribner's Sons, 1923.

Joyner, Charles. "Texts, Texture, and Context: Toward an Ethnographic History of Slave Resistance." In *Varieties of Southern History: New Essays on a Region and Its People*, edited by Bruce Clayton and John Salmond, 12–40. Westport, Conn.: Greenwood Press, 1996.

Kairys, David, ed. *The Politics of Law: A Progressive Critique*. New York: Basic Books, 1998.

Kappler, Charles J., comp. and ed. *Indian Affairs: Laws and Treaties*. 2 vol. 2d ed. Washington, D.C.: Government Printing Office, 1904.

Karl, Frederick R. *William Faulkner: American Writer*. Chapel Hill: University of North Carolina Press, 1989.

Karst, Kenneth L. *Law's Promise, Law's Expression: Vision of Power in the Politics of Race, Gender, and Religion*. New Haven, Conn.: Yale University, 1993.

Kartiganer, Donald M., and Ann J. Abadie, eds. *Faulkner and Ideology: Faulkner and Yoknapatawpha, 1992*. Jackson: University Press of Mississippi, 1995.

———. *Faulkner and Psychology: Faulkner and Yoknapatawpha, 1991*. Jackson: University Press of Mississippi, 1994.

———. *Faulkner and the Natural World: Faulkner and Yoknapatawpha, 1996*. Jackson: University Press of Mississippi, 1999.

———. *Faulkner at 100: Retrospect and Prospect*. Jackson: University Press of Mississippi, 2000.

Kennedy, Gerald, ed. *Modern American Short Story Sequences*. Cambridge: Cambridge University Press, 1995.

Kent, George. *Blackness and the Adventure of Western Culture*. Chicago: Third World Press, 1972.

Kester, Grant H., ed. *Art, Activism, and Oppositionality*. Durham, N.C.: Duke University Press, 1998.

Kimbrough, Edward. *Night Fire*. New York: Rinehart, 1946.

King, Wilma. "'Suffer with Them till Death': Slave Women and Their Children in Nineteenth-Century America." In *More than Chattel: Black Women and Slavery in the Ameri-*

cas, edited by David Barry Gaspar and Darlene Clark Hine, 147–68. Bloomington: Indiana University Press, 1996.

Kinney, Arthur F., ed. *Critical Essays on William Faulkner: The McCaslin Family.* Boston: G. K. Hall, 1990.

——. *Go Down, Moses: The Miscegenation of Time.* New York: Twayne Publishers, 1996.

Kohut, Heinz. *The Search for Self: Selected Writings of Heinz Kohut.* Edited by Paul Ornstein. New York: International Universities Press, 1978–1991.

Kolchin, Peter. *American Slavery, 1619–1877.* New York: Hill and Wang, 1993.

Kolmerten, Carol A., Stephen M. Ross, and Judith Bryant Wittenberg, eds. *Unflinching Gaze: Morrison and Faulkner Re-Envisioned.* Jackson: University Press of Mississippi, 1997.

Krass, Josif A., and Shawkat M. Hammoudeh. *The Theory of Positional Games with Applications in Economics.* New York: Academic Press of Harcourt Brace Jovanovich, 1981.

Kroeber, Karl. *Retelling/Rereading: The Fate of Storytelling in Modern Times.* New Brunswick, N.J.: Rutgers University Press, 1992.

Kuyk, Dirk, Jr., *Threads Cable-strong: William Faulkner's* Go Down, Moses. Lewisburg, Penn.: Bucknell University Press, 1983.

Kyle, Don. "Directions in Ancient Sport History." *Journal of Sport History* 10, no. 1 (1983): 7–34.

Lacan, Jacques. *The Four Fundamental Concepts of Psycho-Analysis.* Edited by Jacques-Alain Miller. Translated by Alan Sheridan. New York: Norton, 1978.

Ladd, Barbara. *Nationalism and the Color Line in George W. Cable, Mark Twain, and William Faulkner.* Baton Rouge: Louisiana State University Press, 1996.

Langer, E. J. "The Illusion of Control." *Journal of Personality and Social Psychology* 32 (1975): 311–28.

Lawrence, Charles, III, Mari Matsuda, Richard Dalgado, and Kimberlè Williams Crenshaw. *Words that Wound: Critical Race Theory, Assaultive Speech, and the First Amendment.* Boulder: Westview Press, 1993.

Lemann, Nicholas. *The Promised Land: The Great Black Migration and How It Changed America.* New York: Random House, 1991.

Leslie, Kent Anderson. *Woman of Color, Daughter of Privilege: Amanda America Dickson, 1848–1893.* Athens: University of Georgia Press, 1995.

Lewis, Helen Block. "Shame and the Narcissistic Personality." In *The Many Faces of Shame,* edited by Donald Nathanson. New York: Guilford, 1987.

Lewis, Philip E. "Le Rochefoucauld: The Rationality of Play." In *Game, Play, Literature,* edited by Jacques Ehrmann. Boston: Beacon Press, 1968.

Litwack, Leon F. *Been in the Storm So Long: The Aftermath of Slavery.* New York: Random House, 1979.

——. "'Blues Falling Down Like Hail': The Ordeal of Black Freedom." In *New Perspectives on Race and Slavery in America: Essays in Honor of Kenneth M. Stampp,* edited by Robert H. Abzug and Stephen E. Maizlish, 109–27. Lexington: University of Kentucky Press, 1986.

Locke, John. *Two Treatises of Government, 1679–1680,* edited by Peter Laslett. New York: Mentor Books, New American Library, 1965.

Lockyer, Judith. *Ordered by Words: Language and Narration in the Novels of William Faulkner.* Carbondale: Southern Illinois University Press, 1991.

Loewen, James W. and Charles Sallis, eds. *Mississippi: Conflict and Change.* New York: Pantheon, 1974.

Loewenberg, Bert James, and Ruth Bogin, eds. *Black Women in Nineteenth-Century American Life.* University Park: Pennsylvania State University Press, 1976.

Lofgren, Charles A. *The Plessy Case: A Legal-Historical Interpretation.* New York: Oxford, 1987.

Lynd, Helen Merrell. *On Shame and the Search for Identity.* New York: Harcourt, Brace, 1958.

MacCormick, Neil. *Legal Right and Social Democracy: Essays in Legal and Political Philosophy.* Oxford: Clarendon Press, 1982.

MacKinnon, Catherine. "Feminist Discourse, Moral Values, and the Law: A Conversation." *Buffalo Law Review* 34 (winter 1985): 11–85.

Macpherson, C. B. "The Meaning of Property." In *Property: Mainstream and Critical Positions,* edited by C. B. Macpherson, 1–13. Toronto: University of Toronto Press, 1978.

Mandle, Jay R. "Black Economic Entrapment after Emancipation in the United States." In *The Meaning of Freedom: Economics, Politics, and Culture after Slavery,* edited by Frank McGlynn and Seymour Drescher, 69–84. Pittsburgh, Penn.: University of Pittsburgh Press, 1992.

——. *The Roots of Black Poverty: The Southern Plantation Economy after the Civil War.* Durham, N.C.: Duke University Press, 1978.

Marks, Carole. *Farewell—We're Good and Gone: The Great Black Migration.* Bloomington: Indiana University Press, 1989.

Martin, Jay. "Faulkner's 'Male Commedia': The Triumph of Manly Grief." In *Faulkner and Psychology: Faulkner and Yoknapatawpha, 1991,* edited by Donald M. Kartiganer and Ann J. Abadie, 123–64. Jackson: University Press of Mississippi, 1994.

Maslow, A. H. *Motivation and Personality.* New York: Harper and Row, 1970.

Matsuda, Mari J. "Public Response to Racist Speech: Considering the Victim's Story." In *Words that Wound: Critical Race Theory, Assaultive Speech, and the First Amendment,* edited by Charles R. Lawrence III et al. Boulder, Colo.: Westview Press, 1993.

Matthews, John T. *The Play of Faulkner's Language.* Ithaca, N.Y.: Cornell University Press, 1982.

——. "Touching Race in *Go Down, Moses.*" In *New Essays on Go Down, Moses,* edited by Linda Wagner-Martin, 21–47. Cambridge: Cambridge University Press, 1996.

McCray, Carrie Allen. *Freedom's Child: The Life of a Confederate General's Black Daughter.* Chapel Hill, N.C.: Algonquin Books, 1998.

McDonald, Christine. "Judging Jurisdictions: Geography and Race in Slave Law and Literature of the 1830s." *American Literature* 71 (December 1999): 625–55.

McGlynn, Frank, and Seymour Drescher, eds. *The Meaning of Freedom: Economics, Politics, and Culture after Slavery.* Pittsburgh, Penn.: University of Pittsburgh Press, 1992.

McKee, Patricia. *Producing American Races: Henry James, William Faulkner, Toni Morrison.* Durham, N.C.: Duke University Press, 1999.

McKibben, Davidson Burns. "Negro Slave Insurrections in Mississippi, 1800–1865." *Journal of Negro History* 34, no. 2 (January 1949): 73–94.

McLaurin, Melton A. *Celia, A Slave.* 1991. Reprint, New York: Avon Books, 1993.

McMillen, Neil R. *Dark Journey: Black Mississippians in the Age of Jim Crow.* Urbana: University of Illinois Press, 1990.

Mellon, James, ed. *Bullwhip Days: The Slaves Remember, An Oral History.* New York: Avon Books, 1988.

Meriwether, James B., and Michael Millgate, eds. *Lion in the Garden; Interviews with William Faulkner, 1926–1962.* New York: Random House, 1968.

Merrill, A. P. "An Essay on Some Distinctive Peculiarities of the Negro Race." *Memphis Medical Recorder* 4 (1855): 1–17.

Messenger, Christian. *Sport and the Spirit of Play in American Fiction.* New York: Columbia University Press, 1981.

Mihalich, Joseph C. *Sports and Athletics: Philosophy in Action.* Totowa, N.J.: Littlefield, Adams, 1982.

Mill, John Stuart. *Principles of Political Economy with Some of Their Application to Social Philosophy.* 2 vol. New York: D. Appleton, 1899.

Millgate, Michael. *Faulkner's Place.* Athens: University of Georgia Press, 1997.

Mitchell S. Weir. "Civilization and Pain." *Journal of the American Medical Association* 18 (1892): 108.

Moncrief, Sandra. "Mississippi Married Women's Property Act of 1839." *Journal of Mississippi History* 47 (May 1980): 110–23.

Morris, Christopher. "An Event in Community Organization: The Mississippi Slave Insurrection Scare of 1835." *Journal of Social History* 22, no. 1 (1988): 92–111.

Morris, Thomas D. *Southern Slavery and the Law, 1619–1860.* Chapel Hill: University of North Carolina Press, 1996.

Morrison, Toni. *Playing in the Dark: Whiteness and the Literary Imagination.* Cambridge, Mass.: Harvard University Press, 1992.

Morton, Patricia, ed. *Discovering the Women in Slavery: Emancipating Perspectives on the American Past.* Athens: University of Georgia Press, 1996.

Mott, Stephen Charles. *Biblical Ethics and Social Change.* New York: Oxford University, 1982.

Muhlenfeld, Elisabeth. "The Distaff Side: The Women of *Go Down, Moses.*" In *Critical Essays on William Faulkner: The McCaslin Family,* edited by Arthur F. Kinney, 198–212. Boston: G. K. Hall, 1995.

——. *Mary Boykin Chesnut: A Biography.* Baton Rouge: Louisiana State University Press, 1981.

Munzer, Stephen R. *A Theory of Property.* Cambridge: Cambridge University Press, 1990.

Murray, Albert. "William Faulkner Noun, Place and Verb." *New Republic* (11 December 2000): 35; reprinted in "Me and Old Uncle Billy and the American Mythosphere," in *Faulkner at 100: Retrospect and Prospect,* edited by Donald M. Kartiganer and Ann J. Abadie, 238–49. Jackson: University Press of Mississippi, 2000.

Nathanson, Donald. *Shame and Pride: Affect, Sex, and the Birth of the Self.* New York: Norton, 1992.

——, ed. *The Many Faces of Shame.* New York: Guilford, 1987.

Nedelsky, Jennifer. "Law, Boundaries, and the Bounded Self." *Representations* 30 (spring, 1990): 162–89.

———. *Private Property and the Limits of American Constitutionalism*. Chicago: University of Chicago Press, 1990.

Newman, Richard. *Go Down, Moses: Celebrating the African-American Spiritual*. New York: Clarkson Potter, 1998.

Niebuhr, Reinhold. *Moral Man and Immoral Society: A Study in Ethics and Politics*. 1932. Reprint, New York: Charles Scribner's Sons, 1960.

Nora, Pierre. *Lieux de memoire: Rethinking the French Past*, Edited by Lawrence D. Kritzman. Translated by Arthur Goldhammer. 3 vol. New York: Columbia University Press, 1996–1998.

Northrup, F. S. C. *The Complexity of Legal and Ethical Experience*. 1959. Reprint, Westport, Conn.: Greenwood, 1978.

Olson, Charles. *Call Me Ishmael*. San Francisco: City Lights Books, 1947. Reprint with afterword by Merton M. Sealts Jr. Baltimore, Md.: Johns Hopkins University Press, 1997.

Omi, Michael, and Howard Winant. *Racial Formation in the U.S.: From the 1960s to the 1990s*. New York: Routledge, 1994.

Opie, Iona, and Peter Opie. *Children's Games in Street and Playground*. Oxford: Clarendon Press, 1969.

Oriard, Michael. *Sporting with the Gods: The Rhetoric of Play and Games in American Culture*. Cambridge: Cambridge University Press, 1991.

Osborne, Martin J., and Ariel Rubinstein. *A Course in Game Theory*. Cambridge, Mass.: MIT Press, 1994.

Owens, Leslie Howard. *This Species of Property: Slave Life and Culture in the Old South*. Oxford: Oxford University Press, 1976.

Painter, Nell Irvin. "Soul Murder and Slavery: Toward a Fully Loaded Cost Accounting." In *Black on White: Black Writers on What It Means to Be White*, edited by David R. Roediger, 326–31. 1995. Reprint, New York: Schocken Books, 1998.

———. *Sojourner Truth: A Life, A Symbol*. New York: W. W. Norton, 1996.

———. *Southern History across the Color Line*. Chapel Hill: University of North Carolina Press, 2002.

Patterson, Orlando. *Slavery and Social Death: A Comparative Study*. Cambridge, Mass.: Harvard University Press, 1982.

———. *Freedom*. Vol. 1, *Freedom in the Making of Western Culture*. New York: Basic Books, 1991.

Pettit, Philip. *Judging Justice: An Introduction to Contemporary Political Philosophy*. London: Routledge and Kegan Paul, 1980.

Poindexter, George. *The Revised Code of the Laws of Mississippi*. Natchez: Francis Baker, 1824.

Polk, Noel. " 'How the negros [*sic*] became McCaslins too. . . .': A New Faulkner Letter." *Southern Cultures* (fall 1999): 103–8.

Powdermaker, Hortense. *After Freedom: A Cultural Study in the Deep South*. 1939. Reprint, New York: Antheneum, 1968.

Proffatt, John, comp. *The American Decisions: Cases of General Value and Authority Decided in the Courts of the Several States from the Earliest Issue of the State Reports to the Year 1869*. San Francisco: Lawyers Co-op. Publishing, 1910.

"The Racial View of the Chief Justice of the United States." *Journal of Blacks in Higher Education* 23 (spring 1999): 72.

Rader, Melvin Miller. *Ethics and Society: An Appraisal of Social Ideals.* New York: Henry Holt, 1950.

Radin, Mary Jane. *Reinterpreting Property.* Chicago: University of Chicago Press, 1993.

Railey, Kevin. *Natural Aristocracy: History, Ideology, and the Production of William Faulkner.* Tuscaloosa: University of Alabama Press, 1999.

Reich, Charles A. "The New Property." In *Property: Mainstream and Critical Positions,* edited by C. B. Macpherson, 177–98. Toronto: University of Toronto Press, 1978.

Riley, Franklin L. *School History of Mississippi.* Richmond, Va.: B. F. Johnson, 1900.

Ripley, C. Peter, Roy E. Finkenbine, Michael F. Hembree, and Donald Yacovone, eds. *Witness for Freedom: African American Voices on Race, Slavery, and Emancipation.* Chapel Hill, N.C.: University of North Carolina Press, 1993.

Roach, Mary Ellen, and Joanne Bubolz Eicher. "The Language of Personal Adornment." In *The Fabrics of Culture: The Anthropology of Adornment,* edited by Justine M. Cordell and Ronald A. Schwarz, 7–21. New York: Mouton, 1979.

Roach, Ronald. "Fighting the Good Fight." *Black Issues in Higher Education* 18 (8 November 2001): 28–31.

Roberts, Diane. *Faulkner and Southern Womanhood.* Athens: University of Georgia Press, 1994.

Roberts, Dorothy. *Killing the Black Body: Race, Reproduction, and the Meaning of Liberty.* New York: Pantheon Books, 1997.

Robinson, Randall. *The Debt: What America Owes to Blacks.* New York: Dutton, 2000.

Roediger, David R. *Toward the Abolition of Whiteness: Essays on Race, Politics, and Working Class History.* London: Verso, 1994.

———. *The Wages of Whiteness: Race and the Making of the American Working Class.* London: Verso, 1991.

———, ed. *Black on White: Black Writers on What It Means to Be White.* New York: Random House, 1998.

Rose, Carol M. *Property and Persuasion: Essays on the History, Theory, and Rhetoric of Ownership.* Boulder, Colo.: Westview Press, 1994.

Ross, Stephen David. *The Nature of Moral Responsibility.* Detroit: Wayne State, 1973.

Ross, Stephen M. *Fiction's Inexhaustible Voice: Speech and Writing in Faulkner.* Athens: University of Georgia Press, 1989.

Roth, Alvin E., ed. *The Shapley Value: Essays in Honor of Lloyd S. Shapley.* Cambridge: Cambridge University Press, 1988.

Rousseau, Jean-Jacques. *Discourse on the Origins of Inequality.* Second Discourse (1755). Translated by Franklin Philip. Edited by Patrick Coleman. Oxford: Oxford University Press, 1994.

Rowe, John Carlos. "The African-American Voice in Faulkner's *Go Down, Moses.*" In *Modern American Short Story Sequences,* edited by Gerald Kennedy, 76–97. Cambridge: Cambridge University Press, 1995.

Said, Edward. *Culture and Imperialism.* New York: Alfred A. Knopf, 1993.

Salmon, Marylynn. *Women and the Law of Property in Early America.* Chapel Hill: University of North Carolina Press, 1986.

Sanchez-Eppler, Karen. "Bodily Bonds: The Intersecting Rhetorics of Feminism and Abolition." *Representations* 24 (fall 1988), 28–59.

——. *Touching Liberty: Abolition, Feminism, and the Politics of the Body.* Berkeley: University of California Press, 1993.

Schafer, Judith Kelleher. *Slavery, the Civil Law, and the Supreme Court of Louisiana.* Baton Rouge: Louisiana State University Press, 1994.

Schultz, David A. *Property, Power, and American Democracy.* New Brunswick, N.J.: Transaction Publishers, 1992.

Sederberg, Nancy B. "'A Momentary Anesthesia of the Heart': A Study of the Comic Elements in Faulkner's *Go Down, Moses.*" In *Faulkner and Humor: Faulkner and Yoknapatawpha, 1984*, edited by Doreen Fowler and Ann J. Abadie, 79–96. Jackson: University Press of Mississippi, 1986.

Segrest, Mab. *Memoir of a Race Traitor.* Boston: South End Press, 1994.

Sensibar, Judith. *The Origins of Faulkner's Art.* Austin: University of Texas Press, 1984.

——. "Who Wears the Mask? Memory, Desire, and Race in *Go Down, Moses.*" In *New Essays on* Go Down, Moses, edited by Linda Wagner-Martin, 101–27. Cambridge: Cambridge University Press, 1996.

Sernett, Milton C. *Bound for the Promised Land: African American Religion and the Great Migration.* Durham, N.C.: Duke University Press, 1997.

Shammas, Carol, Marylynn Salmon, and Michael Dahlin. *Inheritance in America: From Colonial Times to the Present.* New Brunswick, N.J.: Rutgers University Press, 1987.

Singal, Daniel J. *William Faulkner: The Making of a Modernist.* Chapel Hill: University of North Carolina Press, 1997.

Singer, Joseph William. "The Continuing Conquest: American Indian Nations, Property Law, and 'Gunsmoke.'" *Reconstruction* 1, no. 3 (1991): 97–103.

Singer, Joseph William. "Property." In *The Politics of Law: A Progressive Critique*, edited by David Kairys, 240–58. New York: Basic Books, 1998.

Smith, Lillian. *Killers of the Dream.* New York: Norton, 1949.

Smith, Mark M. *Mastered by the Clock: Time, Slavery, and Freedom in the American South.* Chapel Hill: The University of North Carolina Press, 1997.

Smith, Meredith. "A Chronology of *Go Down, Moses.*" In *Critical Essays on William Faulkner: The McCaslin Family*, edited by Arthur F. Kinney, 269–77. Boston: G. K. Hall, 1990.

Smith, Thomas L. *Elements of the Laws: or, Outlines of the System of Civil and Criminal Laws in Force in the United States and in Several States of the Union.* Philadelphia: J. B. Lippincott, 1882.

Snead, James A. *Figures of Division: William Faulkner's Major Novels.* New York: Methuen, 1986.

Snell, Susan. "Phil Stone and William Faulkner: The Lawyer and the Poet." *Mississippi College of Law Review* 4, no. 2 (1984): 169–92.

——. *Phil Stone of Oxford: A Vicarious Life.* Athens: University of Georgia Press, 1991.

Sobotka, C. John, Jr. *A History of Lafayette County, Mississippi.* Oxford, Miss.: Rebel Press, 1976.

Sontag, Susan. *Under the Sign of Saturn.* New York: Vintage, 1981.

Spence, Lewis. *Myth and Ritual in Dance, Game, and Rhyme*. London: Watts and Company, 1947.

Spencer, Elizabeth. *The Voice at the Back Door*. 1956. Reprint, New York: Time Incorporated, 1965.

Spencer, Herbert. *Principles of Sociology*. New York: D. Appleton, 1882.

Spillers, Hortense J. "Interstices: A Small Drama of Words." In *Pleasure and Danger: Exploring Female Sexuality*, edited by Carole Vance, 73–100. Boston: Routledge, 1984.

———. "Mama's Baby, Papa's Maybe: An American Grammar Book." *Diacritics* 17, no. 2 (summer 1987): 64–81.

Stanley, Amy Dru. *From Bondage to Contract: Wage Labor, Marriage, and the Market in the Age of Slave Emancipation*. Cambridge: Cambridge University Press, 1998.

Stoddard, Lothrop. *The Revolt against Civilization: The Menace of the Under Man*. New York: C. Scribner's Sons, 1922.

———. *The Rising Tide of Color against White World-Supremacy*. New York: C. Scribner's Sons, 1920.

Stoljar, Samuel. *Moral and Legal Reasoning*. London: Macmillan, 1980.

Stone, Alfred H. "Early Slave Laws in Mississippi." *Publications of the Mississippi Historical Society* 2 (1899): 133–45.

Stone, Julius. *Human Law and Human Justice*. Stanford, Calif.: Stanford University, 1965.

Stone, Phil. "Endorsement for Faulkner's First Book, *The Marble Faun*." *Yale Alumni Weekly* (November 1924): 10.

Stowe, Harriet Beecher. *A Key to Uncle Tom's Cabin: Presenting the Original Facts and Documents upon which the Story Was Founded. Together with Corroborative Statements Verifying the Truth of the Work*. Boston: John P. Jewell, 1854.

Stowe, Steven M. *Intimacy and Power in the Old South: Ritual in the Lives of the Planters*. Baltimore, Md.: Johns Hopkins University Press, 1987.

Stroud, George M. *A Sketch of the Laws Relating to Slavery in the Several States of the United States of America*. 1827. Reprint, New York: Negro Universities Press, 1968.

Sugarman, David, ed. *Legality, Ideology and the State*. London: Academic Press, 1983.

Sundquist, Eric J. *Faulkner: The House Divided*. Baltimore, Md.: Johns Hopkins University Press, 1983.

Sweet, Waldo E. *Sport and Recreation in Ancient Greece: A Sourcebook with Translations*. New York and Oxford: Oxford University Press, 1987.

Sydnor, Charles S. "The Free Negro in Mississippi before the Civil War." In *Articles in American Slavery*. Vol. 17 of *Free Blacks in a Slave Society*, edited by Paul Finkelman. New York: Garland, 1989.

———. *Slavery in Mississippi*. 1933. Reprint, Baton Rouge: Louisiana State University, 1966.

Taylor, Nancy Dew. *Annotations to William Faulkner's Go Down, Moses*. New York: Garland, 1994.

Thomas, Brook. *American Literary Realism and the Failed Promise of Contract*: Berkeley: University of California Press, 1997.

Thompson, Lawrence. *William Faulkner: An Introduction and Interpretation*. 1963. Reprint, New York: Barnes and Noble, 1967: 81–98.

Todorov, Tzvetan. *Genres in Discourse*. Translated by Catherine Porter. Cambridge: Cambridge University Press, 1990.

Tomkins, Silvan. *Affect, Imagery, Consciousness.* 2 vol. New York: Springer, 1962, 1963.

Towner, Theresa M. *Faulkner on the Color Line: The Later Novels.* Jackson: University Press of Mississippi, 2000.

Truth, Sojourner. "When Woman Gets Her Rights Man Will Be Right" (1867). In *Words of Fire: An Anthology of African-American Feminist Thought,* edited by Beverly Guy-Sheftall, 37–38. New York: New Press, 1995.

Turner, Darwin T. "Faulkner and Slavery." In *The South and Faulkner's Yoknapatawpha: The Actual and the Apocryphal,* edited by Evans Harrington and Ann J. Abadie. Jackson: University Press of Mississippi, 1977.

Tushnet, Mark V. *The American Law of Slavery, 1810–1960: Considerations of Humanity and Interest.* Princeton, N.J.: Princeton University Press, 1981.

Utley, Francis Lee, Lynn Z. Bloom, and Arthur F. Kinney, eds. *Man, Bear, and God: Seven Approaches to William Faulkner's "The Bear".* New York: Random House, 1964.

Vance, Carole, ed. *Pleasure and Danger: Exploring Female Sexuality.* Boston: Routledge, 1984.

Vickery, Olga. *The Novels of William Faulkner: A Critical Interpretation.* 1959. Reprint, Baton Rouge: Louisiana State University, 1964: 124–44.

Wagner-Martin, Linda. Introduction to *New Essays on Go Down, Moses,* edited by Linda Wagner-Martin, 1–20. Cambridge: Cambridge University Press, 1996.

——, ed. *New Essays on* Go Down, Moses. New York: Cambridge University Press, 1996.

Ware, Vron. *Beyond the Pale: White Women, Racism, and History.* London: Verso, 1992.

Warhol, Robyn R., and Diane Price Herndl, eds. *Feminisms: An Anthology of Literary Theory and Criticism.* New Brunswick, N.J.: Rutgers University Press, 1991.

Watson, Alan. *Slave Law in the Americas.* Athens: University of Georgia Press, 1989.

Watson, Jay. *Forensic Fictions: The Lawyer Figure in Faulkner.* Athens: University of Georgia Press, 1993.

Weinstein, Philip M. *What Else but Love? The Ordeal of Race in Faulkner and Morrison.* New York: Columbia University Press, 1996.

Welling, Bert. "In Praise of the Black Mother: An Unpublished Faulkner Letter on 'Mammy' Caroline Barr." *Georgia Review* (fall 2001): 536–42.

West, Cornel. Epilogue to *Race Matters.* New York: Vintage Books, 1994.

——. Foreword to *Go Down, Moses: Celebrating the African-American Spiritual,* by Richard Newman. New York: Clarkson Potter, 1998.

——. *Race Matters.* Boston: Beacon Press, 1993.

West, Robin. "The Difference in Women's Hedonic Lives: A Phenomenological Critique of Feminist Legal Theory." *Wisconsin's Women Law Journal* 3 (1987): 81–145.

——. "Economic Man and Literary Women: One Contrast." In *Law and Literature: Text and Theory,* edited by Lenora Ledwon, 127–38. New York: Garland, 1996.

——. *Narrative, Authority, and Law.* Ann Arbor: University of Michigan Press, 1993.

West, Traci C. *Wounds of the Spirit: Black Women, Violence, and Resistance Ethics.* New York: New York University Press, 1999.

Weston, Michael. *Morality and the Self.* Oxford: Basil Blackwell, 1975.

Wharton, Vernon Lane. *The Negro in Mississippi, 1865–1890.* 1947. Reprint, New York: Harper and Row, 1965.

White, Deborah Gray. *Ar'n't I a Woman?: Female Slaves in the Plantation South*. New York: W. W. Norton, 1985.

Wiegman, Robyn. *American Anatomies: Theorizing Race and Gender*. Durham, N.C.: Duke University Press, 1995.

Williams, Gregory Howard. *Life on the Color Line: The True Story of a White Boy Who Discovered He Was Black*. New York: Dutton, 1995.

Williams, Patricia J. *The Alchemy of Race and Rights: Diary of a Law Professor*. Cambridge, Mass.: Harvard University Press, 1991.

———. *Seeing a Colour-Blind Future: The Paradox of Race*. London: Virago, 1997.

Williamson, Joel. *The Crucible of Race: Black-White Relations in the American South since Emancipation*. New York: Oxford University Press, 1984.

———. *New People: Miscegenation and Mulattoes in the United States*. 1980. Reprint, New York: New York University Press, 1984.

———. *William Faulkner and Southern History*. New York: Oxford University Press, 1993.

Willis, Susan. "Aesthetics of the Rural Slum: Contradictions and Dependency in 'The Bear.'" *Social Text* 2 (summer 1979): 82–103.

Willoughby, Westel W. *Social Justice: A Critical Essay*. New York: Macmillan, 1900.

Wirth, Frederick M. *"We Ain't What We Was": Civil Rights in the New South*. Durham, N.C.: Duke University Press, 1997.

Wolff, Morris. "Faulkner's Knowledge of the Law." *Mississippi College of Law Review* 5 (spring 1984).

Woodward, C. Vann. *Mary Chesnut's Civil War*. New Haven, Conn.: Yale University Press, 1981.

Wray, Matt. *White Trash: Race and Class in America*. New York: Routledge, 1997.

Wyatt-Brown, Bertram. *Honor and Violence in the Old South*. New York: Oxford University Press, 1986.

———. "The Mask of Obedience: Male Slave Psychology in the Old South." In *Haunted Bodies: Gender and Southern Texts*, edited by Anne Goodwyn Jones and Susan V. Donaldson. Charlottesville: University Press of Virginia, 1997.

Yaeger, Patricia. *Dirt and Desire: Reconstructing Southern Women's Writings, 1930–1990*. Chicago: University of Chicago Press, 2000.

Yarup, Robert L. "The Poker Game in 'Was.'" *Explicator* 41 (summer 1983): 43–45. Reprinted in *Critical Essays on William Faulkner: The McCaslin Family*, edited by Arthur Kinney, 278–79. Boston: G. K. Hall, 1990.

Young, Mary Elizabeth. *Redskins, Ruffleshirts, and Rednecks: Indian Allotments in Alabama and Mississippi, 1830–1860*. Norman: University of Oklahoma Press, 1961.

Young, Robert J. C. *Colonial Desire: Hybridity in Theory, Culture, and Race*. London: Routledge, 1995.

Zender, Karl F. *The Crossing of the Ways: William Faulkner, the South, and the Modern World*. New Brunswick, N.J.: Rutgers University Press, 1989.

———. "Faulkner and the Politics of Incest." *American Literature* 70, no. 4 (December 1998): 739–65.

Court Cases

Alfred, a Slave v State, 37 Miss. (1859).

Allen v Freeland, 3 Rand-Virginia (1825).

Boatner v Wade, 14 Louisiana Ann. 695 Monroe (1859).

Brown v Board of Education, Topeka, Kansas, 347 U.S. 483 (1954).

Bryan v Walton, 14 Georgia 200 (1853).

Dred Scott v Sandford, 19 Howard (60 U.S.) 393 (1857).

Fisher v Allen, 2 Howard (Miss.) (1837).

Frazier v Spear, 5 Kentucky (2 Bibb) (1811).

George, a Slave v State, 37 Miss. (1859).

Harry and Others v Decker and Hopkins, 1 Miss. (1 Walker) (1818).

Hinds et al. v Brazealle et al., 3 Miss. (1938).

Hudgins v Wrights, 11 Virginia (1860).

Minor v Mississippi, 36 Miss. (1859).

Mitchell v Wells, 35 Miss. (1859).

Pierson v Post, 3 Caines 175, 2 Am. Dec. 264 (New York Supreme Court 1805).

Plessy v Ferguson, 163 U.S. 537 (1896).

Roberts v City of Boston, 59 Mass. (5 Cush.) 206 (1849).

Shaw v Brown, 35 Miss. (1858).

The Slave, Grace, 2 Haggard Admiralty (Great Britain) 94 (1827).

Somerset v Stewart, Left 1 (Great Britain), (1772).

Sproule v Fredericks, 69 Miss. (1892).

State v Jones, 1 Miss. (1 Walker) (1820).

State v Mann, 13 North Carolina (1829).

State v Samuel, 19 North Carolina (2 Dev. & Bat.) 179 (1836).

Stevens v Graves, 9 Louisiana Ann. 239 New Orleans (1854).

Talbott v Norager, 7 Miss. (1851).

United States v Army, 24 Fed. Case 792 (1859).

United States v Stanley, 199 U.S. 3 (1883).

Ward v Dulaney, 23 Miss. (1852).

Williams v Mississippi, 170 U.S. 213 (1898).

Faulkner's characters are listed by first name.

Absalom, Absalom!, 4, 12, 54, 110, 153–54, 202–3
Adamson, Joseph, 299 n.49
Adorno, Theodor, 130, 215–16
African Americans: endurance of, 249–50; Fourteenth Amendment (U.S. Constitution) and, 237, 304 n.16; "Go Down, Moses" (spiritual) and, 20–25; law and racial oppression, games of, 130–31; manumission of, 114–15, 161–64, 212–13, 293 nn.77, 79, 83; music of, 266 n.34; Negroes, history of term, 202; northern migrations of, 232, 235–36, 238, 304 n.10; rage repression by, 111, 285 n.105; sermons of, 266 n.34. *See also* Legal system; Property; Race; Slaves/slavery
Alexander, Gregory, 289 n.34
Allen, Theodore W., 298 n.44, 300 n.66
Amodeus "Buddy" McCaslin, 45–51, 55, 61–62, 127, 182, 217–18
Ansley, Frances L., 180, 295 n.9
Appiah, Kwame Anthony, 259

Baldwin, James, 209, 256
Bardaglio, Peter, 16, 93

Barkan, Elazar, 302 n.86
Barnes, Harry Elmer, 304 n.16
Barr, Caroline: death of, 190–94, 297 nn.28, 34, 36; maternal role of, 148, 190–94, 230; ownership of, 190–94; racial boundaries and, 205, 261–62, 299 n.60; shame and, 5, 205, 299 n.60
Barry, Ellen, 300 n.65
Bartlett, Vernon, 276 n.62, 304 n.12
"The Bear": ownership rights of, 175–83, 238; slave ledgers in, 14–15, 50–51, 102, 217, 265 n.22, 270 n.3; whiteness in, 197–98, 217, 220
Becker, Lawrence, 266 n.33, 270 n.81
Bell, Derrick, 252, 307 n.47
Bell, J. Bowyer, 288 n.15
Bentham, Jeremy, 10, 80, 181, 277 n.8
Bergson, Henry, 273 n.26
Berlin, Ira, 69, 70, 215, 275 n.59
Berry, Mary Frances, 15, 35, 69, 96–97, 159, 265 n.25, 282 n.60
Bibb, Henry, 85–86, 113
Binmore, Ken, 287 n.1, 288 n.18
Black Code of 1806 (Louisiana), 175, 294 n.2
Blackstone, William, 16, 59, 126, 142, 153, 278 n.21, 288 n.30, 291 nn.61, 62
Blassingame, John, 139, 289 n.32

Blotner, Joseph, 4, 264 n.18, 296 n.22
Brigham, John, 296 n.20, 304 n.15
Brodie, Fawn, 307 n.54
Brooks, Cleanth, 4, 22
Brooks, Peter, 121, 123, 172
Brown, Elizabeth G., 270 n.80, 277 n.11
Burnham, Margaret, 28, 213, 266 n.31

Cable, George Washington, 198–99,
    298 n.42
Carothers McCaslin: Eunice and, 14,
    106–7, 108–11, 284 n.101; incest of, 14–
    15, 48, 50, 51, 92–95, 97–98, 280 n.46;
    Isaac "Ike" McCaslin, relations with,
    79, 97, 118, 159, 180, 182; shame of, 203–
    5; Thucydus and, 113–17; Tomasina and,
    50, 92–94, 97, 104–5, 112; Tomey's Turl
    and, 14, 15, 50, 162, 164, 270 n.3; white-
    ness of, 200–201, 203–6, 299 n.60, 300
    n.61; will of, 150, 152, 153, 162, 164
Catterall, Helen Tunnicliff, 263 n.1
Chabrier, Gwendolyn, 280 n.46
Chesnut, Mary Boykin, 100
Civil Code (Louisiana, 1825), 294
Clark, Hilary, 299 n.49
Clark, Joshua G., 30
Clinton, Catherine, 96, 280 n.36
Cobb, Thomas R. R., 93, 281 n.47
Cohen, Morris, 154
Cole, David, 281 n.55
Collins, Carvel, 305 n.20
Collins, Patricia Hill, 300 n.70
Commins, Saxe, 297 n.27
Compson Appendix, 238–40, 242–51,
    305 n.18
Constitution, U.S., 161, 237, 298 n.41,
    304 n.16
Cooper, Anna Julia, 106, 283 n.89
Court cases: Alfred, a Slave v State, 118;
    Boatner v Wade, 294 n.2; Brown v Board
    of Education, 255; Bryan v Walton, 102;
    Dred Scott v Sandford, 1–2, 132, 163, 183;
    Fisher v Allen, 277 n.11; Frazier v Spear,
    117; George, a Slave v State, 112, 132;
    Harry and Others v Decker and Hopkins,

28, 83, 278 n.14; Hinds et al. v Brazealle,
    et al., 162, 163–64; Hudgins v Wrights,
    224–25, 302 n.2; Mitchell v Wells, 161–62,
    163, 293 n.76; Nelson v Nelson, 107; Pier-
    son v Post, 56–60, 132, 273 n.29; Plessy v
    Ferguson, 34, 82, 198, 269 n.76, 298 n.41;
    Shaw v Brown, 162, 293 n.78; The Slave,
    Grace (1826), 163–64, 293 n.85; Sproule
    v Fredericks, 34; State v Boon (North
    Carolina), 30; State v Celia, a slave,
    91–92, 280 n.43; State v Jones (Missis-
    sippi), 30, 83; State v Mann, 91; State v
    Mann (North Carolina), 83–84; State
    v Samuel, 116; Stephens v Graves, 294
    n.2; Talbott v Norager, 163; United States
    v Stanley, 33; U.S. v Army, 1, 2; Ward v
    Dulaney, 93; Williams v Mississippi, 34
Coverture, 142–43, 165
Cowley, Malcolm, 242–44, 247, 250,
    306 n.31
Craft, Ellen, 70
Creighton, Joanne V., 264 n.18
Crenshaw, Kimberlè Williams, 264 n.12,
    266 n.34, 268 n.47

Dahlin, Michael, 289 n.30, 291 n.58
Delgado, Richard, 266 n.34, 268 n.47
Davis, Adrienne D., 159, 292 n.67
Davis, Angela Y., 98, 281 n.40
Davis, David Brion, 271 n.6, 287 n.9,
    308 n.64
Davis, Sidney Fant, 34, 269 n.77
Davis, Thadious M., 239, 305 n.18
Deleuze, Gilles, 216, 217
"Delta Autumn," 143, 170–72, 202–3, 216,
    223–26, 233, 238
Devlin, Albert J., 214, 301 n.79
Dickson, Amanda America, 160–61, 292
    nn.70, 75
Douglass, Frederick, 1, 21
Doyle, Bertram Wilbur, 28, 268 n.53
Doyle, Don H., 297 n.34
Du Bois, W. E. B., 207
Dunlap, Mary Montgomery, 272 n.23
Dunning, Eric, 272 n.20

Durkheim, Emile, 109
Dyson, Michael Eric, 258

Eagleton, Terry, 205, 300 n.61
Early, James, 264 n.18, 268 n.50, 283 n.80
Eicher, Joanne Bubolz, 272 n.22
Eisenstein, Zillah R., 96, 106-7, 278 n.17,
    281 n.56
Elias, Norbert, 264 n.16
Elliott, E. N., 86
Ellis, Joseph J., 307 n.54
Ellison, Ralph, 256
Ely, James W., 266 n.33
Entail, 159
Eunice: identity of, 106-7; suicide of, 14,
    108-11, 284 n.101, 285 n.108; Thucy-
    dus, marriage with, 113-14, 116-17, 286
    nn.120, 121, 123

Falkner, William C., 101, 102
Family: Caroline Barr as, 5, 25, 148, 190-
    95, 230, 297 nn.28, 34, 36; inheritance
    and, 136, 159-61, 292 nn.70, 75; kin-
    ship in, 233-34; legal status of, 45, 70;
    names in, 225-26; race and, 200-201,
    203-4, 209; slavery and, 61-64, 98-
    100, 106-7, 116-18; surrogate fathers
    as, 144-45; Tomey's Turl, descendents
    of, 38, 43-45, 170-71. See also Marriage;
    Ownership; Women
Faulkner, William: Caroline Barr and,
    5, 25, 148, 190-95, 205, 230, 297 nn.28,
    34, 36; chess and, 54-55, 147-48, 272
    nn.23-25; Compson Appendix and, 238-
    40, 242-51, 305 n.18; creative decline
    of, 190, 195-96, 241-42, 297 nn.26, 27;
    criticism of, 256, 257; family life of,
    188-89, 195, 301 n.83; games, use of,
    127-28; on incest, 94, 101, 102, 104, 280
    n.46; law themes of, 82; lawyers and,
    58, 273 nn.30-32, 274 n.33; on love, 184,
    295 n.16; Malcolm Cowley and, 242-43,
    247, 250, 306 n.31; property and, 35, 133,
    155-56, 185-88, 296 nn.20, 22; racism
    of, 19, 24-25, 195-96, 200, 242-43, 268

nn.45, 47, 306 n.31; shame and, 190, 196,
    200; *The Sound and the Fury*, 238-40,
    242-51, 305 n.18; Toni Morrison and,
    253, 258; whiteness and, 194-95, 200-
    203, 208, 240, 253-55, 257-58; women,
    relations with, 245-47, 306 n.38
Feder, Lillian, 115
Feme covert, 165
Fiedler, Leslie, 256
Fine, Reuben, 55, 148, 272 n.24
Fineman, Martha Albertson, 271 n.5
Finkelman, Paul, 302 n.2
"The Fire and the Hearth," 129-30, 141,
    171-72, 200-202
Fisher, William W., III, 288 n.21
Fletcher, George, 23, 266 n.33, 267 n.44
Fonsiba Beauchamp, 165-66, 184
Foster, Helen Bradley, 272 n.22
Foucault, Michel, 8, 167, 168, 254, 263 n.10
Fowler, Doreen, 125, 303 n.7
Frankenberg, Ruth, 300 n.66
Frederickson, George M., 302 n.86
Freud, Sigmund, 74, 94, 214
Friedman, Lawrence, 174, 293 n.79
Frobenius, Leo, 147
Fry, Gladys-Marie, 265 n.22
Fusco, Coco, 258, 308 n.58

Games: chess, 54-55, 147-48, 272 nn.23-
    25; courtship of, 52-54, 62, 141; ele-
    ments of play in, 233, 304 n.12; fox
    chases, 56-58, 61, 273 n.29; of gender,
    47-48; hide-and-seek, 127-28, 288 n.15;
    hunting as, 55-56, 60-62, 70, 141-48,
    156, 274 n.39; laws as, 9, 45, 129-31, 134-
    35, 140, 141; poker, 64-71, 274 n.44; of
    race, 69-70, 129-31; repetition in, 53,
    272 n.21; sexual conquest as, 93-94; of
    slavery, 49-50, 64-76, 120, 275 n.59;
    sport as social ritual, 60-62, 143-44,
    274 n.39; storytelling as, 26, 40-41, 43-
    44; Tomey's Turl's run as, 44-47, 53,
    58, 145, 271 n.9
Gates, Henry Louis, Jr. 68-69
Gavin Stevens, 227-28, 233, 303 n.5

Genovese, Eugene D., 97, 282 n.61
George Wilkins, 135–36, 141
Gibson, Arrell, 270 n.79
Glaude, Eddie S., 267 n.40
Godden, Richard, 302 n.88
Go Down, Moses: biblical references in, 14, 81; Compson Appendix and, 238–40, 242–44, 305 n.18; games in, 44–45, 47, 120–21; genre of, 10–11, 264 n.17; "Go Down, Moses" (spiritual) and, 20–25, 268 n.45; hunting in, 60–62, 141–44, 274 n.39; masculinity in, 142–43; moral codes in, 38; slaves as property in, 27–28, 79–80; "Was," 43, 53–54, 61, 87, 140–41, 180, 220, 274 n.41; whiteness in, 200, 208–9; wilderness in, 125, 287 n.7. *See also* Amodeus "Buddy" McCaslin; "The Bear"; Carothers McCaslin; Isaac "Ike" McCaslin; Ownership; Property; Race; Sophonsiba Beauchamp McCaslin; Slaves/slavery; Theosophilus "Buck" McCaslin; Tomey's Turl
Goodell, William, 276 n.61
Gordon-Reed, Annette, 307 n.54
Gotana, Neil, 264 n.12
The Grandissimes, 198–99
Grimwood, Michael, 189, 264 n.18, 296 n.24
Guattari, Felix, 216, 217
Guillory, Monique, 284 n.102
Gutman, Herbert, 289 n.31
Gwin, Minrose, 15, 191–92, 246, 265 n.24, 290 n.38, 297 n.30, 300 n.70

Haas, Robert, 25
Hale, Grace Elizabeth, 299 n.47
Hall, Constance Hill, 280 n.46
Hall, John, 30
Hammond, James Henry, 99–100
Haney-Lopez, Ian F., 199, 203, 215, 298 n.43, 300 n.65
Harlan, John Marshall, 34, 298 n.40
Harper, Michael, 259–60, 308 n.63
Harris, Cheryl L., 27, 197–98, 298 n.39
Harris, J. W., 296 n.20

Hartman, Saidiya, 96, 282 n.58
Hearst, Elliott, 273 n.25
Hegel, G. W. F., 186, 296 n.20
Hemings, Sally, 256, 307 n.54
Higginbotham, A. Leon: on children of slaves, 90; on racial identity, 299 n.53, 302 n.2; on slaves as property, 15–16, 17–18, 265 nn.26, 27, 266 n.29
Hitchcock, Jeff, 207–8
Hobson, Fred, 299 n.60, 307 n.55
Hoffman, Daniel, 47, 61
hooks, bell, 111, 258, 285 n.105
Horsman, Reginal, 302 n.86
Howe, Adrian, 108, 111
Howe, Irving, 256
Hubert Beauchamp, 44, 65–66, 155, 210, 213–124, 216
Huizinga, Johan, 144, 290 n.43, 304 n.12
Hunting, 55–56, 60–62, 70, 143–48, 156, 274 n.39
Hurd, John Codman, 293 n.77
Hyde, Alan, 76, 276 n.65

Ignatiev, Noel, 207
Inheritance, 153, 155, 157, 159, 175
Irigaray, Luce, 305 n.19, 306 n.43
Isaac "Ike" McCaslin: Carothers McCaslin and, 97, 105, 118, 164–65, 181–82; civil death of, 122, 126; on Eunice's suicide, 108–11, 284 n.101, 285 n.108; family and, 155, 167, 176–79; ledgers and, 14–15, 103–4, 152–53, 181–82; on love, 184, 221, 295 n.16, 302 n.89; marriage of, 169–70, 301 n.79; memory and, 214–15, 220; on property rights, 79–81, 164–65, 175–79, 181–85, 214, 216, 295 n.6; race and, 134, 145–46, 206, 216, 222; Rider ("Pantaloon in Black") and, 71–75, 124, 126, 288 n.13; Roth Edmonds and, 129–31, 134, 288 n.19; Sam Fathers and, 148, 167, 182, 220; on sexual aggression, 97, 105–10, 118, 214; sexuality of, 126, 167–71, 212, 214, 294 n.90; shame of, 126, 151–52, 165–66, 168, 177, 182, 212; on slavery, 79–80, 164–66, 220; Tomey's

Isaac "Ike" McCaslin (*cont'd*)
Turl and, 14–15, 38, 43–45, 105, 107–8, 122–24, 179, 182–84; whiteness of, 167–68, 204–6, 216–17, 220–22; wilderness and, 125–26, 148, 182; and young woman from "Delta Autumn," 224, 225–26, 233
Isenberg, Nancy, 281 n.57

Jacobs, Anne F., 265 n.27
Jacobs, Harriet, 103, 282 n.58, 283 n.81
James, William, 186–87
James Beauchamp (Tennie's Jim), 171, 184
Jameson, Fredric, 243
Jefferson, Thomas, 256, 307 n.54
Jehlen, Myra, 4
Jenkins, Lee, 142, 205, 224, 290 n.36, 294 n.92, 306 n.45
Johnson, J. Rosamund, 267 n.40, 268 n.45
Johnson, James Weldon, 20–21, 266 n.38, 267 n.40, 268 n.45
Johnson, Walter, 69
Jones, Anne Goodwyn, 290 n.38, 306 n.40
Jones, Ernest, 55
Jordan, Winthrop, 299 n.51
Josey, Charles Conant, 302 n.86
Joyner, Charles, 115, 286 n.119

Kafka, Franz, 152, 291 n.59
Kappler, Charles J., 270 n.79
Kent, George, 257–58
Kimbrough, Edward, 25
King, Wilma, 107, 283 n.89
Kipnis, Kenneth, 270 n.81
Kohut, Heinz, 201, 212, 299 n.49, 301 n.73
Kolchin, Peter, 124
Kopytoff, Barbara, 17–18, 266 n.29, 299 n.53, 302 n.2
Kuyk, Dirk, 11, 154–55, 264 nn.19, 20, 292 n.65
Kyle, Don, 264 n.15

Lacan, Jacques, 211, 301 n.71, 303 n.7
Ladd, Barbara, 307 n.55
Lamar, Lucius Quintus Cincinnatus, 39
Langer, Ellen, 68

Lawrence, Charles R., 266 n.34, 268 n.47
Ledgers, 152–53, 181
Legal system: black criminality and, 228, 232, 269 n.77, 303 n.6; Constitution, U. S., 237, 298 n.41, 304 n.16; coverture in, 142–43, 165, 290 n.40; family kinship in, 233–34; games and, 9, 45, 129–31, 134–35, 140, 141; gender privilege in, 94–96, 111–13, 281 nn.55–57; inheritance in, 50–51, 105–6, 136, 154–55, 159–62, 170, 292 nn.67, 70, 75, 293 nn.76, 77; manumission in, 114–15, 161–64, 212–13, 293 nn.77, 79, 83; marriage of slaves in, 116–17, 139–43, 286 n.123, 289 nn.31–34; moral codes and, 22–23, 93–94; reparations for slavery, 108–9, 260–61, 308 nn.64, 65; Supreme Court, 237, 304 nn.15, 16; Virginia statute (1705), 159; whiteness in, 159–61, 198, 202, 292 nn.70, 75, 298 n.41, 299 n.53; women slaves in, 90–92, 96–97, 106–7, 111, 280 n.40, 283 n.90, 293 n.85. *See also* Court cases; Mississippi; Property; Race; Slaves/slavery
Lemann, Nicholas, 304 n.10
Leslie, Kent Anderson, 292 nn.70, 75
Lewis, Helen Block, 211, 301 n.72
Linscott, Robert, 243
Litwack, Leon F., 284 n.97, 303 n.6
Locke, John, 10, 79, 177, 276 n.5
Lockyer, Judith, 178, 263 n.8, 295 n.6
Lucas Beauchamp, 39; ancestry of, 136–37, 156, 158; Carothers McCaslin and, 135–36, 201; as games player, 129–36; manhood of, 137, 157–58; marriage and, 139–43; Molly Beauchamp and, 137–40, 158; money and, 39, 137, 157–58; on race and power, 136–38; whiteness and, 131–32, 136, 140, 209
Lynd, Helen Merrell, 5, 263 n.5

MacKinnon, Catherine, 281 n.56
Macpherson, C. B., 79
Mandle, Jay, 303 nn.6, 8
Marks, Carole, 304 n.10

Marriage: courtship and, 52–54, 62, 141; coverture and, 142–43, 165, 290 n.40; of Isaac "Ike" McCaslin, 169–70, 301 n.79; love in, 97, 139, 170, 282 n.61, 289 n.32; of slaves, 52, 62–64, 112–17, 139–43, 286 nn.120, 121, 123, 289 nn.31–34; as union, 126–27, 288 n.13

Martin, Jay, 290 n.38

Marx, Karl, 10

Masculinity: clothing and, 53–54; hunting and, 55–56, 60–62, 70, 141–48, 156, 274 n.39; money and, 137, 157–58; patriotism and, 240–42; poker and, 64–71, 274 n.44; property and, 82, 128–29, 166–67; race and, 44, 47, 114, 137–39, 201–2, 219–20; sports and, 9–10, 60–62, 143–44, 274 n.39; whiteness and, 82, 222, 240–41, 305 n.24; wilderness and, 125–26, 147, 167, 287 n.7. See also Games; Sex and sexuality; Women

Maslow, A. H., 291 n.48

Matsuda, Mari, 19–20, 266 nn.34, 36, 268 n.47

Matthews, John, 130, 304 n.13

McCaslin "Cass" Edmonds, 5, 43, 44, 123, 175

McCray, Carrie Allen, 292 n.70

McKee, Patricia, 307 n.55

McLaurin, Melton A., 280 n.43

McMillen, Neil, 34, 269 n.77

Melville, Herman, 254

Mencken, H. L., 240

Merrill, A. P., 276 n.64

Messenger, Christian, 46

Mihalich, Joseph, 72

Mill, John Stuart, 79–80, 277 n.6

Millgate, Michael, 4

Mississippi: Constitution of (1890), 34–35, 163; Caroline Barr and, 193–94; Chickasaws in, 35; court cases in, 30, 83, 112, 132, 161–63, 293 nn.76, 78; manumission in, 163–64, 293 nn.77, 79, 83; mulattoes in, 212, 301 n.74; post-Emancipation, 231, 303 n.6; race relations in, 28–34, 86, 301 n.74; slave legislation in, 31–33, 80,

82, 83, 277 n.10; Women's Law (1839), 82, 270 n.80, 277 n.10

Mississippi Code, 163, 165–66

"Mississippi Plan," 34–35

Mitchell, S. Weir, 276 n.64

Molly Beauchamp: Carothers McCaslin and, 201; Lucas Beauchamp and, 137–39, 158, 209–10; as property, 142–43, 209; Samuel Worsham Beauchamp (Butch) and, 223, 227–29, 231–33, 234–35

Moncrief, Sandra, 270 n.80

Morgenstern, Oskar, 128

Morris, Thomas D., 78, 109, 276 n.3, 277 n.7, 286 n.120

Morrison, Toni: on Africanist narrative, 199, 265 n.24; on black women and slave law, 18; Faulkner and, 253, 258; on race, 259; on rage, 285 n.105; on whiteness, 199, 254–55, 300 n.66

Muhlenfeld, Elisabeth, 170, 285 n.108, 294 n.89

Munzer, Stephen, 270 n.81

Murray, Albert, 259, 308 n.62

Nathanson, Donald, 299 n.59

Natural lawyer, 174, 175, 176, 181

Nedelsky, Jennifer, 123–24, 133, 134, 287 n.4, 289 n.29

Newman, Richard, 21–22, 267 n.40

Niebuhr, Reinhold, 93–94, 221, 302 n.89

Nora, Pierre, 226, 303 n.4

"The Old People," 5, 142, 147, 190

Omi, Michael, 68, 200, 299 n.47

Opie, Iona, 271 n.9

Opie, Peter, 271 n.9

Oriard, Michael, 46, 59, 274 n.39

Osborne, Martin, 272 n.21, 275 n.60

Osceola, 206–7

Owens, Leslie Howard, 109, 284 n.99

Ownership: of black women's bodies, 53, 89–93, 98, 106–7, 193, 280 n.46; egoism and, 93–94; labor and, 45, 48–50, 79–80, 86–87, 177, 276 n.5; ledgers and, 14–15, 50–51, 99, 114–15, 152, 265

Ownership (*cont'd*)
n.22, 270 n.3; manhood and, 133, 289
n.29; names and, 12, 225–26; *Pierson v
Post*, 56–60, 273 n.29; of reproductive
females, 89–96, 106–7, 111–13, 171, 193,
283 nn.89, 90, 285 n.108; sexual exploitation as, 52–53, 90–96, 110–11, 117–18,
137–38, 284 n.102; *State v Celia, a slave*,
91–92, 280 n.43; *State v Mann*, 91; wills
and, 149–53, 159–61, 292 nn.67, 70, 75,
293 nn.76, 77. *See also* Property; Race;
Slaves/slavery; Whiteness

Painter, Nell Irvin, 99
"Pantaloon in Black," 71–75, 124, 126–27
Patrimony, 162, 176. *See also* Isaac "Ike"
McCaslin
Patterson, Orlando: on freedom, 125, 132,
287 n.9; on slaves as property, 78, 151,
266 n.32, 276 n.2; on will in slavery, 151,
291 n.57
Peller, Gary, 264 n.12
Percival Brownlee, 218–19
Plessy, Homer A., 34, 82, 198, 269 n.76,
298 n.41
Polk, Noel, 108, 284 n.96
Powdermaker, Hortense, 28, 268 n.54
Property: black women's bodies as, 106–7,
193; celibacy and, 217; family kinship
and, 233–34; Fourteenth Amendment
(U.S. Constitution) on, 161, 237, 304
nn.15, 16; of indigenous peoples, 176–
77, 180, 295 n.9; inheritance and, 50–51,
105–6, 136, 154–55, 159–62, 170, 292
nn.67, 70, 75, 293 nn.76, 77; labor and,
45, 48–50, 79–80, 86–87, 177, 276 n.5;
Pierson v Post, 56–60, 132, 273 n.29;
shame of ownership, 151–52, 168, 177;
slaves as, 15–18, 59–60, 65–67, 73–74, 77–
80, 85–87, 174–75, 266 n.29, 294 n.2, 302
n.2; wills and, 149–53; women's ownership of, 82, 143, 277 nn.10, 11, 290 n.40

Race: alliances between, 229–31; in American literature, 256–58, 307 n.54; class

and, 68, 96, 202–5, 214–15, 221–22, 280
n.40; constructions in literature, 258–60,
308 nn.62, 63; critical race theory, 25,
266 n.34; estate law, 159–61, 292 nn.67,
70, 75, 293 nn.76, 77; Faulkner and, 19,
24–25, 195–96, 200, 242–43, 268 nn.45,
47, 306 n.31; games of, 67–70, 129–
31; gender and, 96, 201–2; masculinity
and, 44, 47, 114, 137–39, 201–2, 219–
20; mixed, 22, 110, 114, 145, 160, 212–16,
224–27, 284 n.102; mutability of, 212–
15, 224–25, 258–62, 301 n.74, 302 n.2;
racial identity of Tomey's Turl, 26, 45,
51–52, 54, 66–68, 77, 268 n.50, 276 n.1;
scientific racism, 217, 302 n.86; whiteness, 199–200, 202, 204–8, 298 n.44,
300 nn.61, 66. *See also* Sex and sexuality;
Shame; Slaves/slavery; Whiteness
Rader, Melvin, 184
Radin, Mary Jane, 270 n.81
Reich, Charles A., 67–68, 275 n.50
Rider ("Pantaloon in Black"), 71–75, 124,
126–27, 288 n.13
Roach, Mary Ellen, 272 n.22
Roberts, Diane, 290 n.38
Roberts, Dorothy, 106
Robinson, Randall, 261, 308 n.64
Roediger, David R., 207, 298 n.43
Rojek, Chris, 272 n.20
Roosevelt, Franklin, 236–37, 304 n.15
Rose, Carol M., 26, 40, 59, 274 n.34
Ross, Stephen, 38, 270 n.82
Roth Edmonds, 146, 185, 208–9, 216,
221–22, 288 n.19, 294 n.92
Rousseau, Jean-Jacques, 81–82, 178–79,
277 n.9
Rowe, John Carlos, 185, 191, 203, 255, 297
n.29, 299 n.56, 304 n.13
Rubinstein, Ariel, 272 n.21, 275 n.60

Said, Edward, 108
Salmon, Marylynn, 288 n.13, 289 n.30, 290
n.40, 291 n.58
Sam Fathers, 114, 125, 133, 142, 148, 167,
182

Samuel Worsham Beauchamp (Butch): the law and, 227–29, 303 n.7; manhood of, 231–35, 304 n.11; northern migrations of African Americans and, 232, 235–36, 238, 304 n.10; slavery and, 223–24, 228–29, 303 n.7

Sanchez-Eppler, Karen, 53, 272 n.19

Scales, Anne, 266 n.36

Schafter, Judith Kelleher, 294 n.2

Schultz, Davis, 270 n.81

Sederberg, Nancy, 273 n.26

Segrest, Mab, 206–7, 300 n.63

Sensibar, Judith, 193, 291 n.49, 297 nn.31, 36, 305 nn.20, 60

Sernett, Milton C., 304 n.10

Sex and sexuality: assault/rape, 90–94, 96–98, 103, 112–13, 280 n.43; chess and, 54–55, 272 n.24; clothing and, 53–54; incest, 14–15, 48, 50, 51, 92–95, 97–98, 280 n.46; Isaac "Ike" McCaslin and, 97, 105–10, 118, 126, 167–71, 212, 214, 294 n.90; love, 97, 139, 170, 282 n.61, 289 n.32; ownership and, 52–53, 90–96, 110–11, 117–18, 137–38, 284 n.102; reproduction, 89–94, 106, 111–13, 126, 283 nn.89, 90, 285 n.108; in *The Sound and the Fury*, 245–48; woman's value and, 246–47, 306 n.38

Shame: of property ownership, 68, 151–52, 168, 177, 179; slavery and, 5, 22–23, 165, 182, 211–12, 222, 234–35, 300 n.70; of whiteness, 126, 203–5, 254, 255, 299 n.60

Shammas, Carol, 289 n.30, 291 n.58

Singal, Daniel J., 190, 296 n.25

Singer, Joseph William, 176, 273 n.29

Slaves/slavery: black as designation of, 212; capitalism and, 35, 52, 101–2, 130–31, 174–75, 177; children of, 90, 101, 107, 111, 116–18; class and, 68, 96, 202–5, 214–15, 280 n.40; commodification of, 48, 101–2, 114, 289 n.34; family and, 61–64, 98–100, 106–7, 116–18, 144–45, 233–34; as game, 49–50, 64–76, 120, 275 n.59; "Go Down, Moses" (spiritual) and, 20–25, 268 n.45; Jim Crow laws and, 33, 213,

233; labor of, 45, 48–50, 79–80, 86–87, 177, 212–14, 276 n.5; ledgers and, 14–15, 50–51, 99, 114–15, 152, 265 n.22, 270 n.3; manumission of, 114–15, 161–64, 212–13, 293 nn.77, 79, 83; marriage and, 52, 62–64, 112–17, 139–43, 286 nn.120, 121, 123, 289 nn.31–34; Negro as designation of, 212; personhood of, 30–31, 33, 47, 65–66, 84, 86–87, 132; as property, 15–18, 59–60, 65–67, 73–74, 77–80, 85–87, 104–5, 174–75, 177, 213, 266 nn.29, 32, 294 n.2, 302 n.2; reparations, 108–9, 260–61, 308 nn.64, 65; resistance to, 86, 92, 103, 211, 218, 300 n.70; sexual reproduction of, 89–96, 106, 111–13, 283 nn.89, 90, 285 n.108; shame of, 5, 22–23, 165, 182, 211–12, 234–35, 300 n.70; suicide of, 108–11, 284 n.101, 285 n.108; Tomey's Turl as runaway, 44–47, 53, 58, 145, 271 n.9

Smith, Lillian, 299 n.60

Smith, Thomas, 179, 291 n.52

Snead, James, 48, 271 n.17

Sobotka, C. John, 270 n.79

Sontag, Susan, 7, 263 n.9

Sophonsiba Beauchamp McCaslin, 53, 54, 211, 213

The Sound and the Fury, 238–40, 242–51, 305 n.18

Spence, Lewis, 271 n.15

Spencer, Elizabeth, 25

Spillers, Hortense J., 110, 112, 285 nn.103, 108

Stanley, Amy Dru, 286 n.123, 289 n.34

Stoddard, Lothrop, 302 n.86

Stone, Phil, 58, 273 nn.30–32

Stowe, Harriet Beecher, 84

Suicide, 14, 106–17, 284 n.101, 285 n.108

Sundquist, Eric, 12, 229, 265 n.21

Sweet, Waldo, 264 n.15

Sydnor, Charles S., 293 n.83

Taney, Roger B., 1–2, 132, 163, 183

Taylor, Nancy Dew, 114, 284 n.116

Tennie, 44, 65, 69, 124, 127, 139–40, 211

Theosophilus "Buck" McCaslin:
Carothers McCaslin, relations with, 48,
50, 55; hide-and-seek and, 127; racialization of, 52, 182; sexuality of, 48, 51,
145; slaves, relations with, 48–50, 217–
18; Sophonsiba Beauchamp, courtship
with, 53; Tomey's Turl and, 45–47, 52,
61–62
Thomas, Kendall, 264 n.12
Thomas Sutpen, 54, 153–54
Thucydus, 113–17, 139, 154, 162, 164
Todorov, Tzvetan, 9, 40
Tomasina, 14, 50, 92–94, 97, 104–5, 112,
216, 270 n.3
Tomey's Turl: birth of, 13–14, 265 n.22,
270 n.3; centrality in Go Down, Moses,
8–13; as comic character, 25–26, 140–41,
275 n.56; Compson Appendix and, 238–
40, 305 n.18; empowerment of, 18–19,
88–89; games and, 44–45, 47, 53, 119–
22, 127, 272 n.21; hunting and, 55–56, 70,
145–46, 156; inheritance of, 105–6, 154–
55, 162, 164–65; Isaac "Ike" McCaslin
and, 38, 43–45, 105, 107–8, 122–23, 179,
182–84; racial identity of, 26, 45, 51–
52, 54, 66–68, 77, 268 n.50, 276 n.1;
running and, 46–47, 53, 58, 145, 271 n.9;
Samuel Worsham Beauchamp (Butch)
and, 223, 227–29, 231–33; silence of, 87–
89, 279 n.32; slavery and, 60–62, 87–89;
Tennie and, 44, 52, 65, 69, 124, 127,
139–40, 211; young woman from "Delta
Autumn" and, 223–24
Tomkins, Silvan, 299 n.59
Towner, Theresa M., 299 n.56
Truth, Sojourner, 104
Turner, Darwin T., 302 n.87
Turner, Nat, 22
Tushnet, Mark V., 64, 271 n.6

Von Neumann, John, 128

Wagner-Martin, Linda, 22, 200
"Was," 43, 53–56, 61, 87, 140–41, 180, 220,
274 n.41

Watson, Alan, 157, 202, 292 n.66, 299 n.54
Watson, Jay, 82, 273 n.32
Welling, Bert, 297 n.36
West, Cornel, 22, 68, 208, 258, 300 n.66
West, Robin, 18, 104, 111, 152, 176, 285
n.106, 291 n.59, 295 n.4
West, Traci, 113, 285 n.112
Westerinen, Julia Jefferson, 307 n.54
White, Deborah Gray, 114, 117, 285 n.117,
286 n.124
Whiteness: in "The Bear," 197–98, 217,
220; of Carothers McCaslin, 200–201,
203–6, 299 n.60, 300 n.61; class and,
68, 96, 202–5, 215, 280 n.40, 300 n.61;
dress and, 223–24; Faulkner and, 194–
95, 200–203, 208, 240, 253–55, 257–58;
games of, 69–70; of Lucas Beauchamp,
131–32, 136, 140, 209; masculinity and,
82, 201–4, 240–41, 305 n.24; Plessy v
Ferguson, 34, 82, 198, 269 n.76, 298 n.41;
as property, 34, 82, 198–202, 269 n.76,
298 n.41; racialization of, 199–200, 202,
204–8, 298 n.44, 300 nn.61, 66; shame
of, 126, 203–5, 299 n.60; Toni Morrison
on, 199, 254–55, 300 n.66; white, history
of term, 202
Wierzbicki, Michael, 273 n.25
Williams, Patricia J.: on racial categorization, 199, 298 n.44; on rights of African
Americans, 9, 89, 124, 264 n.13, 279
n.34; on sexual domination, 97–98; on
slaves as property, 18, 59–60, 104–5, 213,
266 n.32
Williamson, Joel, 101, 282 n.68, 303 n.6
Wills, 149–54, 157, 160, 164–65, 166–67,
170, 172–73
Winant, Howard, 68, 200, 299 n.47
Wirth, Frederick M., 253, 307 n.48
Wolff, Morris, 274 n.33
Women: alliances between, 229–31; assault
on, 90–94, 96–98, 103, 112–13; birth
control and, 117, 286 n.124; black masculinity and, 87, 137–39; children and,
90, 101, 107, 111, 116–18; coverture of,
142–43, 165, 290 n.40; in legal system,

82, 94–96, 111–12, 277 n.10, 281 nn.55–57; manumission of, 212–13; marriage and, 52, 62–64, 112–17, 139–43, 286 nn.120, 121, 123, 288 n.13, 289 nn.31–34; mixed-race, 22, 110, 114, 145, 212–16, 224–27, 284 n.102; as property owners, 82, 143, 270 n.80, 277 nn.10, 11, 290 n.40; race and, 96, 214–15, 229–31, 281 nn.56, 57; rage repression by, 111, 285 n.105; reproduction and, 89–96, 106, 111–13, 171, 247–48, 283 nn.89, 90, 285 n.108; sexual exploitation of, 52–53, 90–96, 110–11, 117–18, 280 n.43, 284 n.102;

in slave law, 18, 91–92, 96, 111, 280 n.43; in *The Sound and the Fury*, 245–46

Wray, Matt, 300 n.66

Wright, Richard, 232, 303 n.6, 304 n.11

Yaeger, Patricia, 307 n.55

"Year stars fell," 13–14

Yellin, Jean Fagan, 282 n.58

Young, Mary Elizabeth, 270 n.79

Zack Edmonds, 209

Zender, Karl F., 185, 294 n.92, 295 n.16

Thadious M. Davis is Gertrude Conaway Vanderbilt
Professor of English, Vanderbilt University. She is the
author of *Nella Larsen, Novelist of the Harlem Renaissance:
A Woman's Life Unveiled* (1994) and *Faulkner's "Negro":
Art and the Southern Context* (1982). She also coedited
(with James Leonard) *Satire or Evasion? Black Perspectives
on Huckleberry Finn* (Duke University Press 1992).

Library of Congress Cataloging-in-Publication Data
Davis, Thadious M.
Games of property : law, race, gender, and Faulkner's *Go Down,
Moses* / Thadious M. Davis.
Includes bibliographical references and index.
ISBN 0-8223-3103-9 (cloth : acid-free paper)
ISBN 0-8223-3139-x (pbk. : acid-free paper)
1. Faulkner, William, 1897–1962. Go down, Moses. 2. African
American women in literature. 3. Southern States—In literature.
4. Property in literature. 5. Sex role in literature. 6. Race in
literature. 7. Law in literature. I. Title.
PS3511.A86G6335 2003   813'.52—dc21   2002154969